A
Guide for
Achieving
Lasting Peace
in Israel

MAKE
PEACE.

Based on the Teachings of The Lubavitcher Rebbe
RABBI MENACHEM M. SCHNEERSON

Preliminary Edition

ELISHA PEARL

**YONAH
PRESS**

SICHOS IN ENGLISH

YONAH
PRESS

MAKE PEACE

Published and Copyrighted © 2024 by
SICHOS IN ENGLISH
788 Eastern Parkway | Brooklyn, New York 11213
718.778.5436 | Fax 718.735.4139
www.sie.org

All rights reserved. No part of this publication may be reproduced, stored in a retrieval system, or transmitted in any form or by any means, electronic, mechanical, photocopying, recording, or otherwise, without prior permission from the respective copyright holder.
The SIE logo is a trademark of Sichos In English.

Preliminary Edition - August 2024

5784 · 2024

ISBN 978-1-938163-40-1

Typography, template, and cover design by Spotlight Design

אַחֵינוּ כָּל בֵּית יִשְׂרָאֵל

הַנְּתוּנִים בַּצָּרָה וּבַשִּׁבְיָה

הָעוֹמְדִים בֵּין בַּיָם וּבֵין בַּיַבָּשָׁה

הַמָּקוֹם יְרַחֵם עֲלֵיהֶם

וְיוֹצִיאֵם מִצָּרָה לִרְוָחָה

וּמֵאֲפֵלָה לְאוֹרָה

וּמִשִּׁעְבּוּד לִגְאֻלָּה

הָשָׁתָא בַּעֲגָלָא וּבִזְמַן קָרִיב

וְנֹאמַר אָמֵן

DEDICATED TO

The Jewish People, whose strength and resilience are unparalleled;

The soldiers of the Israel Defense Forces, whose courage and sacrifice are unwavering;

The broader Jewish community in Israel, standing resolute and undeterred by their adversaries;

The Jewish families living in Judea and Samaria, determined and brave as ever;

Remembering forever the victims of the Simchas Torah atrocities on October 7th, 2023.

———

We pray that those currently held in captivity swiftly return safely to their loved ones.

*I will **make peace** in the land.*
When you lie down no one will make you afraid.
I will remove evil beasts from the land, and the sword will
not pass through your land.

LEVITICUS 26:6

*The laws of the Torah are not vengeance
in the world, but mercy, kindness,
and peace in the world.*

MAIMONIDES[1]

*The entire Torah was given only
to **make peace** in the world, as it is said,*[2]
"Its ways are pleasant and all of its paths are peace."

MAIMONIDES[3]

I cry out, because I am in pain.
And when it hurts, one screams!

THE REBBE[4]

Each one *of the fallen, G-d forbid,*
*is an **entire world** lost.*

THE REBBE[5]

*I **am peace,** but when I speak, they are for war.*

PSALMS 120:7

CONTENTS

PART 3
The Soul of the Struggle

PART 4
Pragmatic Policy and Domestic Governance

ENDORSEMENTS

מוסדות אור שמח מרכז טננבאום ע.ר. 58-00-21343-00
רח׳ שמעון הצדיק 22-28 ירושלים ת.ד. 18103
טל: 02-581-0315

Sivan 5784

Michtav Bracha

ב״ה

   The Lubavitcher Rebbe was one of the most influential Jewish leaders of the 20th century, and his teachings continue to inspire and guide countless individuals worldwide. In "Make Peace: A Strategic Guide for Achieving Lasting Peace in Israel," Rabbi Elisha Pearl has performed a great service by presenting the Rebbe's insights on the Land of Israel and the path to achieving genuine, sustainable peace.

   The Rebbe's love for Eretz Yisrael was boundless, rooted in his deep understanding of its spiritual significance and its central role in the Jewish people's destiny. At the same time, he approached the Arab-Israeli conflict with a clear-eyed, pragmatic perspective, informed by his vast Torah knowledge, keen understanding of human nature, and grasp of geopolitical realities.

   One of the Rebbe's most crucial insights was his rejection of the false dichotomy between the Land of Israel and the pursuit of peace. He argued forcefully that surrendering territory to implacable enemies would not lead to peace but would only embolden those who seek Israel's destruction. This position, though controversial at the time, has been tragically validated by the failures of the Oslo Accords and the Gaza disengagement.

   Yet the Rebbe was no warmonger. He consistently advocated for treating all people, including Arabs living in Israel, with respect and human dignity. He believed that true peace could only be achieved through a combination of strength, steadfastness, faith in G-d, and a commitment to Jewish values and identity.

   I recommend this book to anyone seeking to understand the Rebbe's perspective on Israel and the pursuit of peace. May its insights guide us towards a brighter, more secure, and peaceful future for the Jewish homeland and the entire Jewish people.

With blessing,

Rabbi Yitzchak Breitowitz,
18 Sivan 5784
Jerusalem

Rabbi Joseph Gutnick

IT IS WITH GREAT HONOR and privilege that I lend my support and endorsement to "Make Peace" which delves into the wisdom of the Lubavitcher Rebbe OBM, on addressing the serious security concerns facing both the Land of Israel and the Jewish diaspora.

On more than "one hundred and one occasions" (as the Rebbe put it to me once), the Rebbe passionately argued that concessions and compromises would only beget further concessions and compromises, ultimately jeopardizing the lives of the Jewish people in the Land of Israel and leading to increased violence and tragedy.

All the other options have been tried and exhausted. Adhering to the Rebbe's Torah based guidance offers the only promising path toward achieving a lasting and sustainable peace in the Holy Land.

I extend my heartfelt congratulations to the author, Rabbi Pearl, and the dedicated team at Yonah Press for their exceptional work in producing this thorough and thought-provoking volume that compellingly articulates the Rebbe's vision for lasting peace in the Land of Israel. "Make Peace" is a must-read for anyone interested in the future of the Land of Israel and the Jewish people.

Rabbi Joseph Gutnick
Emissary of the Lubavitcher Rebbe
for the Integrity of the Land of Israel

Preface

SIMCHAS TORAH. One of the most joyous days on the Jewish calendar celebrates the deep bond between the Jewish people, G-d, and His Torah. On October 7, 2023, the holiday took a devastating turn.

As morning broke in Israel, soldiers began receiving urgent messages to report to their units. Many went into combat that day. Jews around the world, in the midst of rejoicing, began to hear disturbing rumors about events in the Land of Israel. We didn't know what to think. As the holiday ended, we were shocked and sickened by the images we saw. We experienced indescribable pain when we heard what had happened to our brothers and sisters. We felt deeply uncertain about the long road ahead.

Jews around the world were grasping for insight; many did not know where to turn and a flood of competing voices began commenting on the massacres and how to respond to them. More broadly, the massacres thrust the entire question of the Jewish presence in Israel into the global spotlight yet again. Many began to question Israel's legitimacy and the right to Jewish self-defense. In the midst of this cacophony of opinions, we felt that one great Jewish leader — the Lubavitcher Rebbe, Rabbi Menachem Mendel Schneerson — had addressed nearly all of the many questions and issues burning today. His voice needed to enter the conversation.

In the days following the October 7 massacres, we set out on a mission with the help of numerous Chabad institutions and emissaries worldwide, along with many other friends of Israel and the Jewish people. As disciples of the Rebbe and expositors of his teachings, we began to mine the thousands of pages and hundreds of recorded hours of his wisdom on Israel's security.[1]

We aimed to distill the Rebbe's insights on Israel's security and destiny for modern readers. Israel's security was close to the Rebbe's heart. The Rebbe's approach, while passionate and deeply rooted in Jewish tradition, also reflected the facts on the ground.

We believe that the Rebbe's perspective is crucial for fostering an informed global dialogue that promotes lasting peace rather than ongoing conflict. This book aims to convey that perspective, highlighting how, sadly, many of the Rebbe's insights remain as relevant today as when they were first taught. We may have collectively failed to apply the Rebbe's approach in the past. However, history and recent events have shown how correct, even prophetic, his words were. The time to apply them is now. As the Rebbe put it when discussing a work on Israel's history:[2]

> Most crucially, emphasize that its relevance is not confined to the past, but rather [the historical insights] it offers [provide] unequivocal proof of the approach that must be adopted at present. Spare no effort in galvanizing public opinion around this vital message. May it be G-d's Will that these efforts ensure that the matter does not devolve into a politicized partisan affair.

The Rebbe, ever a man of faith, never ceased believing in the individual and collective ability to correct past wrongs. We need not confine ourselves to any previous failings or poorly made decisions. Together, we can create a bright future and actively **make peace**. We fervently pray that war quickly becomes a relic of the past. At that time, in the Messianic era, war will serve solely as a metaphor for the spiritual battles associated with personal and collective growth and dedication to serving G-d.[3] Until then, it is imperative to adopt and disseminate the Rebbe's perspective on the struggle for the Land of Israel, as it holds the key to lasting peace.

Yonah Press

3 Tammuz, 5784
[July 9, 2024]

INTRODUCTION

An Endless Cycle?

HAMAS' BRUTAL MASSACRE on October 7, 2023, shocked the world. Many condemned the Gazan terrorists for their unspeakable cruelty. Yet Israel's enemies worldwide immediately took to the streets, first celebrating the attacks[1] and then demanding that Israel halt its response.

Those with limited historical awareness might see October 7's carnage as a singularly disturbing event. However, a broader view shows that it is part of a longstanding cycle of conflict. Although the names and forms of the groups hostile to Israel have changed over time — from fedayeen to Fatah, the Palestine Liberation Organization (PLO), Hamas, Islamic Jihad, Hezbollah, and the Islamic Republic of Iran — the conflict's fundamental nature remains unchanged.

More broadly, the October 7 attacks represent another chapter in the long history of antisemitism and, even more generally, in that of global terrorism. Israel's plight exemplifies the battle between order and chaos the world over.[2]

Israel has gone to war to defend its people. The IDF's response, while portrayed as barbaric, has been measured and disciplined.[3] Once again, global media coverage focuses on Israel while bloodier conflicts rage unnoticed. From Myanmar[4] to Haiti,[5]

Syria[6] to Ukraine,[7] Yemen[8] to Azerbaijan,[9] and Sudan[10] to Somalia,[11] human rights violations, war, and famine abound.[12] These fights over territorial claims, ethnic hostilities, or even mundane gang violence, cause untold human suffering of far greater magnitude than that in Israel and Gaza. Yet, for some reason, Israel takes the spotlight.[13]

We have been here before. This is not the first time Israel has been targeted by terrorists, taken retaliatory measures, and faced international criticism. This raises the question: Is this just another phase in an endless cycle, or is there a principled approach to end the cycle and **make peace**?[14]

The teachings of the Lubavitcher Rebbe, Rabbi Menachem Mendel Schneerson, one of the 20th century's premier Jewish leaders, offer insight into resolving this challenge. From the outset of his leadership in 1950 the Rebbe engaged with Israeli leaders of all types. Numerous Israeli Prime Ministers, politicians, diplomats, and security personnel sought his counsel and blessing.[15] From his public platform and in private meetings and letters, the Rebbe offered a grand strategy: a comprehensive military and political analysis that clarifies the steps to achieve lasting peace.[16]

The Rebbe consistently highlighted the critical importance of religious conviction and psychological resilience alongside military action. He noted that history has demonstrated how psychological vulnerabilities have led to setbacks, even when Israeli military power was formidable. We must withstand pressure and remain resolute. This strength, he posited, is inextricably linked to *emunah* (faith) in G-d, adherence to Torah principles, and an unwavering belief in our right to the Land.

The Rebbe emphasized that viewing the Torah not only as a transcendent holy text, but as a practical guidebook, can give us determination and offer concrete solutions to real-world issues. This demands not only consummate familiarity with the Torah's texts and traditions, but also immersion in the concrete factors and disciplines relevant to any given situation.[17]

The Rebbe's nuanced approach does not neatly fit into any political party's platform, nor can it be defined by classic left-right dichotomies. While some mischaracterize the Rebbe as a radical,[18] in fact, he sought harmonious coexistence for all parties involved in the conflict. He did not dehumanize the Jewish people's opponents, instead emphasizing that all people are created in G-d's image.

The Rebbe's position is deeply humanitarian. His care for all humanity outstrips simplistic narratives that offer quick fixes for peace. This explains why the Rebbe demanded that we develop an informed and rigorous position on how to achieve lasting peace. His critiques of entities such as the U.N. and foreign governments stemmed not from cynicism, but from a realist perspective and a sense of disappointment in their failure to fulfill their potential redemptive roles in fostering peace.

This book explores the conflict through the lens of the Rebbe's wisdom, addressing its key questions and offering principled solutions for its resolution. What follows is a brief overview of the book's narrative.

PART 1
Simplistic Solutions for Peace

PART 1 critically assesses seemingly kinder options for resolving the conflict's military dimension, such as ceasefires (**Chapter 1**), international mediation (**Chapter 2**), and Land for Peace negotiations (**Chapter 3**). It explains why these are bound to fail, both from a theoretical standpoint and as demonstrated by historical evidence.

PART 2
Effective Military Solutions

PART 2 discusses the Rebbe's advocacy of decisive military action based on a fusion of Jewish legal principles with realpolitik. He argues that credible deterrence (**Chapter 4**) and proactive defense (**Chapter 5**) prevent war. If conflict erupts, swiftly and relentlessly subduing opponents will ultimately save lives on both sides (**Chapter 6**). While this assertive position may seem hawkish, it aims to minimize violence and restore stability.[19] Exercising military restraint might appear compelling at first, but if doing so eventually leads to more bloodshed, it is not the truly peaceful solution.

PART 3
The Soul of the Conflict

PART 3 delves into the ideological roots of the conflict. After exploring several competing narratives, it establishes the Jewish people's Torah-based claim to the Land of Israel, arguing that it is the only narrative that can firmly justify the Jewish presence there (**Chapter 7**). It then addresses arguments from those who claim to speak in the name of the Torah and argue against current Jewish sovereignty over the Land of Israel (**Chapter 8**). Finally, it emphasizes the critical importance of ideological strength, robust Torah education, and widespread *mitzvah* observance for Israel to truly prevail in the conflict, especially given the ideological fervor of Israel's opponents (**Chapter 9**).

PART 4
Pragmatic Policy and Governance

PART 4 tackles several practical policy questions. It argues that Israel should remain resolute in defending its security needs, even in the face of strong international pressure (**Chapter 10**). It then explores Israel's relationship with the United States, advocating for Israel to cultivate the relationship while still maintaining an independent stance aligned with the Torah's vision (**Chapter 11**). It discusses the importance of the Israeli government encouraging Jewish people to settle throughout the entire Land of Israel, including Judea, Samaria, and Gaza (**Chapter 12**), and the necessity of asserting Israeli governance over these territories (**Chapter 13**). It then offers guidance on pragmatic approaches to addressing domestic terrorism and prisoner exchanges (**Chapter 14**). Finally, it discusses Jewish unity as both a deterrent against attack and as an imperative for Jews worldwide to support Israel's cause (**Chapter 15**).

The Key Principles:
Pikuach Nefesh and Peace

The overriding halachic concern that will guide us in this work is ***pikuach nefesh***, the principle that saving lives is the highest priority.[20] Accordingly, we always need to ask: Which strategy will save the most lives? The meta-halachic[21] principle here is **peace**.[22]

We want something that will end the cycle and **make peace**.[23] All human beings, including those who are fighting against us, are created in G-d's image.[24] As such, every Jew has the responsibility to care for the life of every person among the world's nations.[25] As the Rebbe taught, though enemies threaten us, we should aim not to destroy them, but rather to end their enmity. This follows our Sages'[26] teaching to eliminate **sins**, not **sinners,** with the confidence that one-time enemies can become friends.[27]

PART 1

Simplistic Solutions For Peace

They say, "Peace! Peace!" But there is no peace.
JEREMIAH 8:11

They have misled my people saying, "Peace, peace,"
but there is no peace. They build a weak wall
and plaster it flimsily.
EZEKIEL 3:10

INTRODUCTION
TO PART I

IN ANY ARMED conflict, the most urgent dimension is the actual war. While ideology and politics are more fundamental, ending the war is most pressing to prevent further death and destruction. So, how do we end it? This section explores the problem, illustrating the dynamics of the cycle in which Israel is locked with its enemies.

Sketching the Cycle

Before our deep dive, let's sketch the cycle of conflict we seek to end in order to finally **make peace** once and for all. The 2023 Israel-Hamas War bears striking resemblance to most of Israel's major military engagements since 1982. If we examine the previous Gaza wars beginning soon after Israel's 2005 disengagement, as well as the two Lebanon wars, a familiar cycle emerges:

1) A terrorist group (PLO/ Hamas/ Hezbollah), embedded in a supportive civilian population, attacks Israel with a mix of killings, kidnappings, and missile fire.

2) Following attacks and losses, Israel hesitates to retaliate forcefully. Finally, a particularly severe incident provokes domestic and international outcry.[1]

3

3) Many countries, as well as the United Nations, rush to prevent Israel from attacking, citing the humanitarian damage that an Israeli military response will inflict on the civilian population in which the terrorists are entrenched.

4) Ignoring these protests, Israel attacks, grazing the terrorist organization, eliminating some of its operatives and leaders, and destroying some weapons. In the process, since these organizations are situated in densely populated urban areas, women, children, and noncombatants are unfortunately killed.

5) International media displays images of death, destruction, and crying children, provoking widespread outcry over Israel's military response.

6) Israel begins to cave to international pressure and shifts to waging a slow war. Restrained attacks are followed by temporary ceasefires, which are then violated by the other side. In response, Israel retaliates once again. Yet, by this point, its military efficacy has been blunted.

7) Finally, Israel relents to a full ceasefire.

8) The terrorist group declares victory, telling the population that its resistance caused Israel to capitulate.

9) The terrorist group fundraises for more advanced weapons, which it receives from anti-Israel entities. It recruits new militants to join its ranks.

10) The terrorist group begins firing rockets and initiating cross-border skirmishes.

11) Israel retaliates.

12) The cycle repeats.

If the current Israel-Hamas war ends in a manner similar to previous rounds of conflict, we can reasonably expect another Gaza or Lebanon war a few years down the line. We can also expect that Israel's enemies elsewhere will be emboldened. War is terrible. Some who have strong partisan feelings may not feel the pain of those dying on the other side. "They deserve it," they say. But for those who have human empathy, the tragic images on both sides evoke shock, compassion, and anger. Why can't it just stop? Let's begin by exploring some seemingly straightforward solutions to ending the cycle of violence.

Surely there must be some easy, peaceful solution to stop the bloodshed? Why do people have to be so cruel? This mindset leads well-intentioned people to propose solutions aimed at quickly resolving the conflict, restoring peace, and stopping the flood of horrific images.[2]

Some such suggestions include:

1) Immediate ceasefire (often under the slogan "Ceasefire Now") — which we will explore in **Chapter 1**.

2) Negotiations led by the international community, and perhaps even more active international involvement such as deploying peacekeeping forces — the topic of **Chapter 2**.

3) Land for Peace — a suggestion we will critically interrogate in **Chapter 3**.

Let's examine each of these proposals by exploring the past conduct of terrorist groups along with the Rebbe's perspective. This can offer some measure of clarity as to how these proposals might work if tried again in the future.

CHAPTER 1
Ceasefire! (Now!)

His pleasantries are smooth like butter, but his heart is at war. His compliments are soothing as oil, but they are drawn swords.

PSALMS 55:22

You have deceived this people and Jerusalem saying 'You will have peace' when the sword is at our throats.

JEREMIAH 4:10

AN IMMEDIATE CEASEFIRE appears to be the most straightforward solution to any armed conflict. The logic is simple: People are killing each other — so why not just **stop it**? Perhaps Hamas has committed violent acts against Jews, including massacring over one thousand and kidnapping hundreds. And they might have launched a few thousand rockets. Yet those events are in **the past**; stopping the violence now could prevent further suffering. Taking the high road might eventually lead to peace. Though this approach may sound appealing, there are several reasons why on deeper inspection, this apporach will be ineffective.:

A | A Net Victory for Terror

Ceasefires can be perceived as tolerance of violence, inviting more severe atrocities in the future.[1] Moreover, terror attacks are calculated to gain significant publicity, making a ceasefire without decisive action against them a tacit victory. Furthermore, such a move would directly jeopardize Israeli security, and also fails to address the critical issue of the hostages.

B | Ceasefire as a Tactical Pause

The underlying hope is that a ceasefire would pave the way to enduring peace. But can a ceasefire before completing military objectives truly lead to such peace? Let's consult the historical record. Ceasefires between Israel and Hamas are a fragile affair, with a short list including the ceasefires of June 2008, January 2009, November 2012, August 2014, June 2021, and May 2023. On each of these occasions, Hamas broke the ceasefire. Given this impressive list of ceasefires made and subsequently broken, it appears that ceasefires with Hamas, Hezbollah, and similar organizations do not achieve the intended outcome of fostering long-term peace.

Israel's interest in a ceasefire clearly stems from a desire to protect its citizens from further harm. But what might motivate Israel's enemies to clamor for a ceasefire? Rafael Eitan, an Israeli general who served in the 1982 Lebanon War, offered the following insight:[2]

> We again saw the well-known Middle Eastern tactic that has recurred in every battle and war. The moment an Arab country receives a heavy blow, the world wakes up and forces us to enter a ceasefire in order that we not achieve our objective.

In Eitan's view, such ceasefires are not sincere attempts at peace, but rather a tool used by the enemy from a position of weakness to stop Israeli advances. Eitan further suggests that such hostile groups weaponize the "international community" to pressure

Israel into agreeing to a ceasefire.

Let's imagine that terrorist groups propose ceasefires when they are at a disadvantage in order to ensure their survival. What follows next? Will the terrorists abandon their aspirations of Israel's destruction, lay down their arms, and begin to build the Gazan economy? Will Gaza turn into a peaceful oasis? Once again, the historical record provides glaring insight into the outcomes of ceasefires.

C | Time to Regroup: Terror Groups and Ceasefires

Israel's enemies utilize ceasefires as opportunities to regroup. So, ceasefires are not recipes for peace, but for wars of attrition. The weaker side, in this case Hamas or Hezbollah (but the same was true of Hamas' key terrorist predecessor, the PLO — Palestine[3] Liberation Organization — and all other skilled terrorist groups), uses ceasefires to prevent its destruction and to regroup.[4] Its aim is to emerge more powerful in the future and harm Israel.

At the very least, it seeks to slowly damage Israel, sow terror in its communities, and tarnish Israel's public image, weakening the country. Israel's enemies, in their various guises, have infinite patience.[5] As long as they survive, they maintain the hope that they can cripple Israel until they finally annihilate it: either by wearing down Israel's collective resolve or by holding on long enough for geopolitics to shift.[6]

D | The Insurgent's Playbook

One theme that we will return to in this book is that Hamas, Hezbollah and their ilk are best understood not as localized phenomenona, but as examplse in the wider global trend of terrorist organizations. While Western media tends to focus on Islamist terrorism, we have no shortage of other modern terrorist groups to consider. One crucial example of a hardened terrorist group that was ultimately defeated is the Tamil Tigers. For nearly thirty years, until their decisive defeat in 2009 by the Sri Lankan military, the Tamil Tigers perpetrated incessant acts of terrorism against the Sri Lankan people in a bid to create an independent Tamil ethnic state within Sri Lanka.

During the Sri Lankan Civil War (1983-2009), the Tigers requested ceasefires several times, often using the international community as leverage. The Tigers invariably[7] used the ceasefires as opportunities to rearm, consolidate their power, and weaken Sri Lanka. We should view Hamas' requests for ceasefires through this lens. Hamas may be cruel, but they are not stupid. Terrorism is a political strategy, and we should expect terrorist groups to implement the strategy to the fullest.[8] Ceasefires are an important weapon in any skilled terrorist's arsenal.[9]

E | Cultural Precedent: *Hudna*

To better understand how Hamas employs ceasefires, it's important to consider some cultural context.[10] When Hamas and similar groups declare a ceasefire, they use the term "*hudna*," roughly translated as a truce or a period of calm,[11] modeled on the medieval "Treaty of Hudaybiyyah."[12]

The Treaty of Hudaybiyyah, intended to last ten years, held for only two, ultimately leading to the surrender of the originally more powerful party. This treaty served as precedent for Anwar Sadat's 1979 peace treaty with Israel.[13] On several occasions, Yasser Arafat, leader of the PLO, also compared his participation in the Oslo accords[14] with Israel to the Treaty of Hudaybiyyah.[15] The implication of these comparisons is that, from the Islamist perspective, peace agreements are regarded as temporary measures. Ceasefires are no different; they serve as strategic pauses, allowing time for the weaker side to regroup and ultimately gain the upper hand.[16]

Hamas leaders have routinely offered *hudnas*. Notably, in 2004,

Hamas leader Abdel Aziz al-Rantissi offered Israel a ten-year *hudna* in return for:

1) A complete Israeli withdrawal from Judea and Samaria.

2) The right of return for all Palestinian refugees.

3) The establishment of a Palestinian state in the West Bank and Gaza.

However, he emphasized that this *hudna* would not indicate Hamas' recognition of Israel. Instead, he offered the *hudna* as it would be "difficult to liberate all our land at this stage."[17] The phrase "all of our land" refers to the entire territory of Israel.[18] Given this historical context, a *hudna* is a tool of war, used to pause the battle to regroup and eventually destroy one's enemies.[19]

Let's now explore the Rebbe's explicit commentary on actual cases of ceasefires:

Ceasefire:
A Prelude to the Yom Kippur War

In 1970, after a three-year war with Israel known as the War of Attrition, Egypt proposed a ceasefire with Israel. The Rebbe offered the following insight into Egypt's motivation for the ceasefire:[20]

> *[Egyptian President Nasser's] sudden request for a ceasefire is not motivated by a desire for peace, as any intelligent person would understand. A peace treaty can be discussed even during war, [so Egypt's insistence on a ceasefire raises suspicions about their true intentions]. [It is evident that] Egypt wants a ceasefire since they cannot rebuild their fortifications and rearm while Israel is bombing. Nasser's aim is to use the ceasefire as a means for future war, [not to engage in sincere peace negotiations].*

The moment a ceasefire is signed, [Egypt] will [immediately begin] rebuilding its fortifications along the Suez Canal. Furthermore, a ceasefire will render all of the money spent and soldiers' lives sacrificed in vain, since Egypt will [simply] regroup and launch another attack against Israel [in the future]. How can we justify the money we spent and the soldiers' lives we sacrificed? And how can we justify the future expenditures?

[Moreover,] during World War II, when the defeated side[21] requested a ceasefire before entering into peace negotiations, allied military experts unanimously rejected the proposal. They explained that a ceasefire would be exploited [by the defeated nations] for rearmament. [The experts] also argued that a ceasefire would lower the odds of [achieving a] lasting peace.

In fact, Nasser immediately violated the terms of the ceasefire, taking advantage of it to rearm Egypt, significantly bolstering its military position. This move played a crucial role when Egypt, under the leadership of Anwar Sadat, initiated the Yom Kippur War in 1973.[22]

In a 1970 letter to IDF's head of Southern Command and future prime minister Ariel Sharon, the Rebbe had more to say on the ceasefire with Egypt — comments that again seem relevant to Israel's contemporary enemies:[23]

With each passing day, our opponents become stronger and fortify [their positions further]. Despite the formal protests [from Israel and the United States,] the enemy uses each day to intensify their power and import the most advanced modern weaponry. It is clear that the United States will not go to war with the Soviet Union over [potential Egyptian aggression against Israel, especially considering Egypt's status as a Soviet client state at the time].

Regarding the outcry over Egypt's failure to honor its promises, no one [genuinely] believed they would refrain from exploiting the ceasefire. [This sentiment was shared by] members of the government in Israel, the United States, and the Soviet Union, given [Egypt's] history [of breaking promises] three years ago [during the Six-Day War] and fourteen years prior [during the 1956 Sinai War], as well as on several other occasions. Arguments will continue to accumulate, but ultimately, the decision will be made to maintain the current status quo.

Consequently, it is apparent that during the peace negotiations, after the opposing side has entrenched [and fortified their military positions], Israel will find itself at a disadvantage. The security situation will have completely changed between the day the ceasefire was implemented and the conclusion of the negotiations regarding the demands and terms [of the peace treaty].

I hope that the other side will make a foolish move, as they did at the start of the Six-Day War, which will necessitate the cancellation of the ceasefire. In such a scenario, G-d will once again work miracles, enabling the swift mobilization of all forces after the ceasefire ends. Defense will be renewed through an attack, the only effective means of doing so, and all forces will be fully mobilized, not in the half-hearted manner seen until now, but in a true defense. Only then is there hope for a lasting ceasefire and finally achieving peace. The current situation, however, leads directly to the renewal of war, G-d forbid, under far worse conditions than those present at the start of the ceasefire.

I have elaborated [on this matter] in response to your comment [suggesting] that my writings about the canal are no longer relevant. I fear that this issue will soon become pertinent once again. [While] I hope to be proven wrong in my assessment, based on the prevailing attitudes, it unfortunately seems unlikely.

A full three years before Egypt's fateful violation of the ceasefire which began the 1973 Yom Kippur War, the Rebbe saw the proverbial "writing on the wall." At the end of a 1970 talk addressing Israel's ill-advised ceasefire with Egypt, the Rebbe broke down crying, citing the verse,[24] "Why have I come, yet there is no one? I have called out, yet no one answers." This captures the Rebbe's sense of urgency over Israel's precarious security and his sadness over the fact that, despite his clear vision on the matter, no one seemed to listen. Now, more than fifty years later, we see retrospectively that failing to follow the Rebbe's prescription has created enduring sorrow.[25]

Ceasefire in Lebanon:
From Victory to War of Attrition

The Rebbe spoke at extensive length about how terrorists manipulate the international community into enforcing a ceasefire, thus halting their adversary's advance. The terrorists then have the opportunity to violate the ceasefire by attacking their opponents while still within enemy territory awaiting negotiations. When their opponents subsequently retaliate, the terrorists can appeal to the international community for yet another ceasefire. Later in the book, we will delve deeper into how the PLO used this very tactic against Israel during the First Lebanon War.[26]

Summary

We see, then, that there are at least five compelling reasons for skepticism about the effectiveness of unconditional ceasefires without completing military objectives:

1) Ceasefires demonstrate a tolerance for violence.

2) Ceasefires allow terrorist groups to survive, regroup, and rearm.

3) Ceasefires are a classic insurgent strategy used in modern warfare to weaken states, irrespective of cultural context.

4) In Hamas' and Hezbollah's cultural context, ceasefires have a clear precedent as an implement of war.

5) Ceasefires both dishonor the memory of the fallen and squander the funds spent on defense.

If this is the case, then:

1) Unconditional ceasefires with hostile militant groups are not in Israel's interest, until the hostile militant group ceases to pose a credible threat.

2) Those calling for a ceasefire are either unintentionally or intentionally seeking to strengthen Israel's enemies.

In light of the above, a ceasefire will only perpetuate the cycle of violence by allowing Hamas, or some more violent successor, to survive and fight another day. If we aim to end the cycle of violence and allow both Jews and Palestinians to lead prosperous, happy, terror-free lives, then a ceasefire, no matter how initially attractive it may seem, is not the answer. But what if we modified the ceasefire? What if, instead of an unconditional ceasefire, the international community and the U.N. would monitor and enforce the ceasefire?

CHAPTER 2

Outsourcing to the International Community

The sword shall not pass through your Land...
LEVITICUS 26:6

*You have been a staff of reeds for the House of Israel.
When they grasped you with their hands, you splintered and
shattered their shoulders; when they leaned on you, you
broke and caused them to collapse.*
EZEKIEL 29:6-7[1]

THE INTERNATIONAL COMMUNITY seems to have tremendous sympathy and concern for the Israeli-Palestinian conflict. International media discusses it endlessly, and leaders the world over opine freely on the conflict, offering to help resolve it in some way. Surely, the international community would like to see fewer deaths on both sides of the conflict, along with peace and prosperity in the region. Perhaps, instead of merely pushing for a ceasefire, the international community should mediate the ceasefire's implementation.

Ethical Double Standards

The Rebbe viewed this approach skeptically. He observed that those urging Israel to exercise restraint often do not apply the same standards to themselves. When Israel retaliates in response to attacks, these international voices criticize Israel's actions, urging Israel to seek legal recourse through organizations like the U.N. This, the Rebbe explains, is impractical and ineffective. Such organizations, which are usually biased against Israel to begin with, do not reach meaningful verdicts or enforce anything of consequence. The enemy, emboldened by this indecisive response, continues their aggression, expecting nothing more than symbolic condemnation. Consider the following talk by the Rebbe, delivered in 1969, that sounds very apropos to 2024:[2]

> *Somehow, there is the expectation amongst the nations that no direct action be taken against those who seek to harm us. Rather, they expect us to send [friendly] letters to those who rise to kill us and state: "Listen here, Mr. Cossack,[3] your intention to strike the Jews is against the U.N. Charter. You must first ask for permission from the U.N. General Assembly." Then, the U.N. will proceed to hold many meetings over many months to decide on the matter. Surely all parties recognize that this lengthy bureaucratic process will only encourage [the aggressors] to perpetuate their violent acts.*

> *Of course, they have already started attacking and will continue doing so, expecting nothing more than a mere censure: "Listen here, Mr. Cossack, your actions are in violation of the Charter." The inevitable result [of such a policy] is that the enemy will continue to attack the Jews with impunity and then shift their focus to targeting non-Jews worldwide.*

> *Israel's enemies have received millions of dollars in foreign aid from Western countries. However, when these countries criticize their violent behavior, Israel's enemies continue with their attacks and disregard the complaints. The complaints are*

directed to ineffective organizations such as the International Court of Justice at the Hague,[4] while the enemies continue their attacks, receive international funding, and mock international peacekeepers. When the international community complains about atrocities committed by terrorists against the non-Jewish world, they should consider — where were you when the terrorists targeted the Jews? When terrorists attacked the Jews, you said that the Jews needed to send a formal complaint through the foreign minister and adhere to the U.N.'s protocol with its endless meetings. Why, then, are you [the international community] surprised when the terrorists laugh at you and take your money?

Likewise, in recent times, Hamas remains undeterred by U.N. condemnations such as former Secretary-General Ban Ki-moon's solemn proclamation that their attacks were "shocking,"[5] or current Secretary-General António Guterres' belated expression of being "appalled" by Hamas' kidnappings.[6] Often, the U.N. and the international community either overlook such attacks[7] or respond with ineffective statements, devoid of concrete action.

Bring in the Troops! Examining the Success of International Peacekeeping Forces

Unfortunately, the comical ineptitude of the U.N. has been enduring. Its track record of biased and unenforced resolutions is too lengthy to enumerate. However, in the name of peace, many still advocate that international peacekeeping forces on the ground may be a helpful enforcement of a ceasefire agreement. Let's examine the historical record and ponder how well this suggestion has worked for Israel in the past:

A | The Suez Crisis and UNEF

In 1956, the Suez Crisis broke out.[8] Egypt, under the leadership of President Gamal Abdel Nasser, blocked the straits of Tiran, an important international shipping route. Recognizing this as an act of war, Israel, together with the United Kingdom and France, invaded the Sinai Peninsula (then occupied by Egypt) with the goal of reopening the route. While initially successful, under diplomatic pressure from the United States[9] and Russia, the invading forces withdrew. In the aftermath, the United Nations Emergency Force (UNEF) was deployed to the Sinai Peninsula to keep the peace between Israel and Egypt.[10]

UNEF remained in the Sinai Peninsula until 1967, when Egypt asked it to evacuate. It summarily did so, highlighting its (in)effectiveness in preventing conflict.[11] Egypt, left unchecked, then massed troops to invade Israel. Israel preemptively struck Egypt in what became known as the Six-Day War. After the Six-Day War, Israel and Egypt would go on to fight two more wars, until finally signing a peace treaty in 1979, followed by a tenuous, cold peace.[12] U.N. Peacekeeping Forces did not bring about this outcome: Israeli triumph on the battlefield did. This led Egypt to realize that further conflict with Israel was not in its interest.[13]

B | Terror From Lebanon and UNIFIL

While the United Nations Peacekeeping Forces were ineffective in Israel and Egypt's wars, they have been even more troublesome in Lebanon. Lebanon, Israel's northern neighbor, has been a failed state for decades, with a weak government rife with civil wars, foreign invasions, and general factional unrest.[14]

In 1971, Jordan evicted the PLO, the primary Palestinian group terrorizing Israel at the time. This came after the PLO threatened to assassinate the Jordanian King and fomented the Jordanian Civil War. The PLO moved to Southern Lebanon, exerting military control over the region. They subsequently used this area as a base for attacks on Northern Israel. They continued their dual policy: running a military operation clashing with their host state and simultaneously using their host state as an operations base from which to attack Israel.

In 1978, the PLO carried out the Coastal Road massacre. They hijacked a bus on the Israeli Coastal Highway, murdering 38 Israeli civilians, including 13 children, and injuring 76. In response, Israel launched Operation Litani[15] against PLO bases in Lebanon, but held back from totally eliminating the PLO. The U.N. solemnly called upon Israel to immediately withdraw its troops and established the United Nations Interim Force in Lebanon (UNIFIL).[16] UNIFIL's stated goal was to secure the southern Lebanese border and prevent additional terrorist infiltration into Israel.

Independently of UNIFIL's presence and of the Israel-PLO conflict, Lebanon was internally suffering from a fifteen-year civil war between Christian and Muslim factions, as well as from war with Syria who, depending on the period, supported different sides of the conflict. The PLO instigated this war and simultaneously continued to attack Israel, even with UNIFIL's presence. Moreover, UNIFIL impeded Israel's response to PLO terrorism so as not to endanger UNIFIL peacekeepers in the crossfire.[17]

In June 1982, Israel finally invaded Southern Lebanon with the intention of neutralizing the PLO. Three months into fighting a stop-and-go war, Israel finally struck the PLO hard enough that their leadership agreed to evacuate Lebanon.[18] Yet, in the fog of war, a new, more formidable militant group arose: Hezbollah. While Israel and its Lebanese-Christian allies initially contained Hezbollah, with Israel's withdrawal from Lebanon in 2000, Hezbollah's power greatly increased.

Hezbollah began to fire rockets into Northern Israel and conduct cross-border attacks, leading Israel to retaliate with the Second Lebanon War in 2006. The war aimed to decisively neutralize Hezbollah as a threat. The U.N. imposed a ceasefire,[19] solemnly calling for Hezbollah's disarmament, meant to be overseen by UNIFIL.[20] However, since 2006, instead of disarming, Hezbollah has become a far more formidable threat, with many more, better trained fighters and a large arsenal of missiles and rockets capable of reaching anywhere in Israel.[21]

Despite UNIFIL's presence in Lebanon for nearly half a century and countless ceasefires brokered by the U.S. and the U.N., Israel is in a far worse security position vis-à-vis Lebanon than ever before. This state of affairs leads most military experts to see a **third** full-scale Lebanon War as inevitable to neutralize Hezbollah's threat.[22]

Summing up the U.N.'s prodigious record of failure with respect to Israel, the Rebbe said:[23] "We do not want the false consolation of the U.N.'s 'sword of peace.' Heaven save us from the way they guarded us in Lebanon, and earlier, at the Suez Canal and in the Sinai desert."

C | Not Just Bad for the Jews: Syria's Genocide and UNIFIL's Silence

Israel did not primarily bear the brunt of the Lebanese Civil War — the Lebanese people did. Towards the beginning of the Lebanese Civil War,[24] in 1976, Syria invaded Lebanon. Syria ostensibly intervened to prevent the Lebanese government's collapse and to maintain a balance between the warring factions, including Christian militias, Palestinian groups, and Lebanese Muslim factions. However, Syria's true motives were not humanitarian, but strategic, aiming to exert influence over Lebanon and **prevent the rise of a Palestinian state** which could challenge Syrian authority in the region.

During this intervention, Syria slaughtered noncombatant men, women, and children on a daily basis. This was no secret. Although the U.N. and other nations vehemently protested Syria's actions, they did not do anything to end the violence. No one came to Lebanon's rescue. **Practically**, no one cared.[25]

These examples demonstrate that Israel cannot depend on U.N. peacekeeping missions to enforce ceasefires. To underscore this, let's examine one notable example of U.N. peacekeeping failure around the world, from among many examples.

D | Not Only a Middle Eastern Problem: UNAMIR and the Rwandan Genocide

For centuries, two primary ethnic groups have lived in Rwanda: the Hutu and Tutsi. In 1962, following a revolution, the Rwandan government switched from Tutsi to Hutu control. Exiled Tutsis formed a militarized political movement, the Rwandan Patriotic Front, with the goal of restoring Tutsi sovereignty. In 1990, the Tutsi militants invaded, sparking a civil war that lasted until 1993, when the hostilities temporarily ceased with the signing of the Treaty of Arusha. Subsequently, the U.N. dispatched the United Nations Assistance Mission for Rwanda (UNAMIR) to keep the peace in Rwanda. Then, in 1994, over a period of several months, armed Hutu militias slaughtered over 500,000 Tutsis while UNAMIR's forces looked on.

Summary

The Rebbe asks us to consider how seriously Israel should regard international assurances of aid if it were in crisis. Given the international community's bleak, unreliable track record to this day, the Rebbe counsels against relying on it.[26]

Israel's experiences with international peacekeeping forces indicate that they are unhelpful, and even detrimental, often facilitating terrorist groups.[27] Rwanda's experience further illustrates how relying on international peacekeeping is a risky gamble. So, clearly international mediation, particularly in the form of U.N. "peacekeeping," will **not make peace**.[28] As the Rebbe puts it, our goal is to manifest G-d's blessing of "I shall set peace upon the Land and the sword [armies] shall not pass through your land,"[29] not even "the sword of peace [armies that come in peace],"[30] such as U.N. peacekeepers.[31]

CHAPTER 3

Land
for Peace

The leech has two daughters [who cry] Give! Give!
PROVERBS 30:15[1]

I have devoured, and I will continue to devour.
MIDRASH, BEREISHIS RABBAH 19:12[2]

PERHAPS THE KEY to ending the cycle of violence and making lasting peace is not merely stopping the fighting, but resolving the underlying issues. Many cite Palestinian desire for statehood and self-determination as the core reason for the conflict. According to this view, if only these would be provided, then there would be peace.

At the start of the 2023 war, influential global leaders stated that after the war, lasting peace can only be achieved through a two-state solution which envisions the establishment of two separate, independent states — one for the Jewish people and one for the Palestinian people. Some of these world leaders include President of the United States Joe Biden,[3] Secretary of State Antony Blinken,[4] U.N. Secretary-General António Guterres,[5] Russian President Vladimir Putin,[6] and Chinese President Xi Jinping.[7]

To test this proposition, let's look at the positions of Israel's opponents and consider whether a two-state solution would **make peace** and save Jewish and Arab lives. What are the intentions of the violent "resistance" movements Israel has faced since its founding and before? Do they truly yearn for peaceful co-existence?

Subtle Imagery

If we examine the emblems of the major Palestinian groups, we find that they all contain a striking feature: an image of Israel's entire territory. This is true not only of the Islamist Hamas and Palestinian Islamic Jihad (PIJ), but also of the purportedly moderate PLO and its subsidiary Fatah.[8]

This striking fact indicates that these groups aspire to control **all** of Israel's land; Israeli withdrawals from Judea, Samaria, and even Jerusalem will not satisfy their demands. These groups hold all the political power in Palestinian autonomous regions, with Hamas ruling Gaza and tolerating PIJ presence, and the Palestinian Authority (PA) — under PLO auspices — governing cities with Palestinian majorities in Judea and Samaria, such as Bethlehem, Hebron, Shechem (Nablus), and Ramallah.

Micah Goodman, a contemporary Israeli scholar, notes that "ending the occupation" carries different meanings for different groups. For the Israeli left, ending the occupation means Israel's complete withdrawal from Judea and Samaria. However, for supporters of the Palestinian narrative, it implies the complete dissolution of Israel as a state and Arab reoccupation of cities like Safed, Tel Aviv, Ashkelon, and Haifa.[9]

Voices of Palestinian Leadership

Beyond merely examining flags, a closer look at the preamble to the Hamas Charter offers more insights. There, we read:[10]

Palestine is a land that was seized by a racist, anti-human, and colonial Zionist project that was founded on a false promise (the Balfour Declaration), on recognition of a usurping entity, and on imposing a fait accompli by force. Palestine[11] symbolizes the resistance that shall continue until liberation is accomplished, until the return is fulfilled, and until a fully sovereign state is established with Jerusalem as its capital.

It's difficult to imagine a group with such a mission statement making peace with Israel if given some land.

Another interesting fact to consider is that over the past 50 years, the Arab leaders in Hebron, a city with a massive Palestinian population, have either been directly involved in the murder of Jews or are closely related to those who were.[12] As the Rebbe exclaimed in 1970:[13]

The [current] mayor of Hebron[14] [or his close relative] (either his brother or father) participated in the 1929 pogrom against the Jewish residents of the city. Historical photographs from that period clearly demonstrate the mayor's connection to the massacre. Far from hiding this fact, the mayor actually takes pride in having expelled the Jews from Hebron. [Now,] the city is being handed over to the [very] same Arab leadership [whose predecessors were] responsible for murdering Jews in the 1929 [massacre].

And what do the government representatives answer me? [They claim that] there is a "status quo" in place, as Hebron has been under Arab control for thirty years already. But what kind of "status quo" is this? The situation here is [one of] "you have killed and also taken possession."[15] They killed the Jews and then inherited their property. Is this what one calls a "status quo"?

Not much has substantially changed since the Rebbe offered these observations in the 1970s. As of this writing, the current mayor of Hebron, Tayseer Abu Sneineh, who has been in office since 2017, was previously sentenced to life imprisonment for his role in an attack that resulted in the death of six Jewish civilians and injured 20 others. He was later released in a prisoner exchange. Despite Sneineh's murderous past and his continued lectures and tours on the attack, he does not seem to have been disqualified from leadership in Palestinian public opinion.[16]

Looking further at Palestinian leadership, Mahmoud Abbas, who is chairman of the PA and seen as a moderate by the West, is not a credible peace partner given his history of Holocaust denial[17] and approving support of the October 7 massacres.[18]

There are no other significant Palestinian political groups, and both Hamas and Fatah have a taste for one-party rule. New elections have not been held since 2006, shortly after Israel's unilateral withdrawal from Gaza. Hamas and Fatah fought a bloody civil war in 2007, culminating in the Battle of Gaza, where Hamas evicted Fatah from the Gaza Strip.[19] With these facts in mind, it is difficult to identify a viable counterpart with whom Israel could negotiate a two-state solution to **make peace**.[20]

A Broader Regional Challenge

If somehow, the formidable challenges toward making peace with the Palestinians were overcome, and miraculously, that population would lose its hostility, would surrendering land secure peace? What of Hezbollah or Iran? If Israel were to enter into Land for Peace negotiations, would Hezbollah or Iran cease their hostilities? Hezbollah-affiliated news outlets, such as Al-Ahed[21] and Al-Manar,[22] label the entire State of Israel as "the temporary entity." Al-Ahed describes the residents of Northern Israel, an area recognized as part of Israel in the 1948 United Nations Partition Plan, as "settlers," and refers to Israeli cities and towns in this region as "settlements."[23]

Similarly, Iranian news outlets refer to the entire Israel as the "oppressive and arrogant enemy" and a "child-killing Zionist" regime.[24] They praise Palestinian attacks on Israel and describe the "occupied territories" (including Sderot, Be'er Sheva, Ashkelon, and Tel Aviv – all within the original 1948 boundaries of the State of Israel) as having been turned into "hell for the Zionists."[25] This rhetoric demonstrates that they do not recognize the legitimacy of any part of Israel, suggesting that Hezbollah or Iran would likely continue fighting Israel even if it gave up land for peace.

What about Islamists across the world? Consider Osama Bin Laden's thoughts on the matter:[26]

> *If you want a real settlement that guarantees your security in your country and safeguards your economy... then you have to implement a roadmap that returns the **Palestine land** to us, all of it, from the sea to the river, it is an Islamic land not subject to being traded or granted to any party.*

Clearly, while many in the Western world distinguish between Judea and Samaria and the territory the U.N. granted to Israel in 1948, Israel's most concerning enemies do not make this distinction.

Historical Context

Let's examine the historical record. Arabs have perpetrated sporadic pogroms against Jews in the Land of Israel for over a thousand years.[27] Yet Arab political violence against Jews in the Land of Israel only began in earnest in the 1920s with the arrival of larger numbers of Jews from abroad, many fleeing violence and antisemitism in Europe. Fueled by resentment towards the swelling numbers of Jews the Arabs resorted to violence.[28]

Between 1920 and 1948, Arabs in Israel staged several riots and attacks against Jews. Perhaps most notable is the 1929 Hebron massacre,[29] when Arabs brutally attacked the Jewish community, massacring 67 Jews, mutilating and raping[30] many of them, and injuring 58.[31] We thus see how politically motivated violence against Jews perpetrated by Arabs predated the founding of the

State. Since 1948, when the newly-formed State of Israel repelled assaults from seven different Arab armies,[32] it has faced a steady stream of attacks by various terrorist groups. Fatah, formed in 1959, carried out its first attack against Israel in 1965, two years before Israel gained control of Judea and Samaria from Jordan and of Gaza from Egypt in the Six-Day War.[33]

Terrorism against Jews in the Land of Israel existed long before Judea and Samaria came under Jewish control, predating even the establishment of the State of Israel. Why, then, would giving up Judea and Samaria resolve the issue? It seems that this suggestion is either deliberately misleading or reflects ignorance on the part of Western powers seeking easy solutions to the conflict. Palestinian responses to the two-state solution typically fall either into the category of outright rejection (Hamas, PIJ, and Hezbollah) or lukewarm and fickle acceptance (PA), without committing to any proposals.

Withdrawal and Autonomy

It seems that there's no viable peace partner for a two-state solution. Moreover, Israel's opponents have voiced their aspiration for a single state called Palestine, encompassing all of Israeli territory. Given this backdrop, what steps could lead to peace short of the Jewish people leaving Israel altogether?

A common Western belief is that, in spite of Palestinian's actual voices, peace can be achieved by partial Israeli withdrawal. Some assume that Arabs are just blustering with more opposition to Israel than they actually have. Many argue that perhaps leaving Judea, Samaria, and Gaza **would** result in peace, giving the Arabs in the Land of Israel a sense of autonomy and self-determination. It would lead to a cessation of terror and the emergence of a flourishing economy alongside Israel. To assess this possibility, let's revisit the historical record and see if such an approach has worked in the past.

A | The Oslo Accords

In 1993, Israeli Prime Minister Yitzchak Rabin signed the Oslo Accords with Yasser Arafat, leader of the PLO. The Accords granted Palestinian autonomy in areas with Palestinian majorities, including Gaza, Jericho, Hebron, Shechem (Nablus), and Ramallah. However, the Oslo Accords did not lead to peace; instead, terrorist attacks escalated, culminating in the Second Intifada,[34] which lasted from 2000-2005.

The Second Intifada, marked by a surge in terrorist attacks (including widespread suicide bombings), saw various PLO groups[35] and Hamas as particularly violent contributors. History repeatedly demonstrates that concessions lead to more violence.[36] The Intifada did not end because of concessions, but as a result of decisive Israeli military action in Operation Defensive Shield.[37] In this operation, the Israel Defense Forces (IDF) raided autonomous Palestinian areas, arresting terrorists and seizing weapons.[38] Rather than fostering peace, the autonomy had allowed Palestinian areas to become bases for attacks against Israel. The Intifada only ended with intensive Israeli military action and the construction of security barriers in Judea, Samaria, and Gaza which effectively prevented terrorist infiltration.

This context also explains why the security barriers surrounding Gaza and parts of Judea and Samaria are not "apartheid walls." These barriers did not exist when Israel conquered the territory from Jordan in 1967, and although Israelis were suspicious of the Arab population who had either supported or actively participated in violence against Israelis, there was a general optimism among Israelis for peace and collaboration. Israel only constructed the security barriers in response to relentless terrorist attacks and suicide bombings.

B | The Gaza Disengagement

In 2003, Israeli Prime Minister Ariel Sharon[39] proposed a unilateral Israeli disengagement from Gaza, which would involve removing all Jewish settlements and handing full control of the area over to the Palestinians. Executed in 2005, this plan forcibly evicted 8,000 Jews from their homes and demolished their communities. The following year, Hamas won the Palestinian elections and violently ousted Fatah, turning Gaza into a base for ongoing attacks against Israel. The disengagement did not bring peace; instead, Gaza became a haven for groups like Hamas and PIJ, posing a significant threat to Israel.

C | Ceding Judea and Samaria

It seems, then, that Land for Peace is a failed policy. But what if Israel is just not giving up enough land? Maybe if it gave away all of Judea and Samaria, Israel's enemies would be mollified and everyone could live in peace.

Would Israel's withdrawal from these areas, held since 1967, satiate Palestinian ambitions, or will it simply be a steppingstone to incrementally achieve total Palestinian domination?

At the moment, the PLO controls the West Bank and, while corrupt,[40] it cooperates with Israel to some degree.[41] Nonetheless, even the "moderate" PLO has a "pay for slay" policy, offering stipends to families of suicide bombers and others who murder Jews.[42] Moreover, the PLO can only maintain power backed as it is by Israeli military presence in Judea and Samaria. Should Israel withdraw, a Palestinian civil war, the likes of the 2007 Palestinian civil war in Gaza, might occur, in which case Hamas, or one of the similarly virulent terrorist groups throughout Judea and Samaria could take control.

Even if Hamas were not to take control, many independent terrorist groups flourish in Judea and Samaria, including (but not limited to) the Tulkarm Brigade, Lion's Den, Jenin Brigades, and Tubas Brigade.[43] This places Israel in a precarious position. While withdrawing from Judea and Samaria might bring peace in some "ideal" world, that hypothetical world appears quite distant from the real world. If Judea and Samaria were to become terror bases similar to Gaza, Israel would be in serious trouble.

Rockets and cross-border attacks would be much more damaging and would undermine Israel's security, crippling its economy and transforming the entire state into a war zone.

Land for Terror: A Counterintuitive Phenomenon

In the long history of Land for Peace, the doctrine has only brought additional terrorism — not peace.[44] Instead of ending the cycle of conflict, Land for Peace has exacerbated it. Both Israelis and Palestinians are less safe since the Oslo Accords and the Gaza disengagement. And Palestinians are now more likely to be killed, either by Hamas[45] or by Israel retaliating against Hamas attacks.[46] As the Rebbe observed:[47]

> We once thought that if the Arabs learned of our plans to give away land, it would lead to [peace and] quiet. However, [the opposite occurred.] The moment Israel discussed the possibility of giving land, terrorist attacks began to proliferate. [In fact,] the number of terrorist attacks dramatically increased after the signing of the Camp David Accords, [when Israel first made significant territorial concessions.]

Land for Peace inspires further terrorist attacks, as the ultimate objective on the Islamist side is to completely undermine the Jewish state and replace it with an Islamist one.[48] If Israel stands strong, then the Palestinian population will relinquish its territorial ambitions and pursue productive endeavors instead of terror.[49] If, however, Israel shows weakness and readiness to compromise, then, as history has proven, it will only invite more terrorist attacks and incite further conflict.[50]

Outside of the Israeli-Palestinian conflict, the doctrine of "Land for Peace" is unheard of. Historically, when a country won territory in a defensive war, they retained the territory. Land for Peace seems to be a construct specially invented to territorially diminish Israel.[51]

Land for Peace is a failed experiment. The ideal premise of Land for Peace is: Israel granting the Palestinians greater autonomy, followed by increased cooperation from the Palestinians, which then prompts Israel to offer even further autonomy. In fact, Israel has repeatedly offered increased autonomy to the Palestinians. However, instead of leading to peace, this has often been exploited by Palestinian factions to perpetrate more violence, which in turn prompts Israeli retaliation to restore security. Consequently, Land for Peace and attempts at a two-state solution cannot be the elusive solution we need to **end the cycle** and **make peace**.

Conclusion

We have seen that despite their attractiveness, solutions like unconditional ceasefires without accomplishing military objectives, relying on the international community, and Land for Peace, all bring war and do not make peace.

What, then, is the solution? It would seem that the various Palestinian terror groups, along with Iran and Hezbollah, would all like Israel to close up shop and turn the Land of Israel into the Islamic Republic of Palestine. Will Jews be allowed to live in this Republic or will they be expelled to the West or Birobidzhan?[52] What would life for the Palestinian residents of the Republic look like? To understand why giving up the Land is an untenable option, we need to consider our rights to the Land, a point we will explore in Part 3.

If we do remain in Israel, what can we do to end the cycle and achieve lasting peace? In what follows, we will explore three halachic principles fundamental to the Rebbe's approach to this question. These principles firmly cohere with those of realpolitik and with military tactics used in counterterrorism since the dawn of post-World War II insurgencies.[53]

PART 2

Effective Military
Solutions
for Lasting Peace

Standing strong brings peace.
THE REBBE[1]

INTRODUCTION TO PART II

THE REBBE'S APPROACH to making peace for Israel and its neighbors is guided by three core halachic principles, which are intended to be applied sequentially. The first is to establish military deterrence, demonstrating that any aggression will be countered with a decisive response. This emphasizes that aggression is futile and will end with the aggressors' neutralization. Effective implementation of this principle precludes the need for further action, maintaining security through deterrence. This is the topic of **Chapter 4**.

Should this deterrence prove insufficient, the second principle is to proactively neutralize emerging threats. This principle demands a vigilant response against those who express hostile intentions, as explored in **Chapter 5**. If these measures don't swiftly resolve the issue, the strategy requires the implementation of the third principle: "until it is subdued."[2] **Chapter 6** delves into the intricacies of this principle and its application in various scenarios. This entails a comprehensive offensive to entirely dismantle the enemy's capacity for warfare, and ensure that it does not return in the future.

Non-military solutions such as ceasefires, endless talks, international peacekeeping, and Land for Peace agreements, though seemingly humane, have practically resulted in increased deaths on **both** sides.[3] Israel's enemies cynically exploit ceasefires and Land for Peace as tools to intensify their terrorism against Israel in a gambit to weaken and destroy it. Ironically, if **military** strategies can end the cycle of conflict and establish lasting peace, this shows that these more aggressive tactics are the truly **peaceful** solutions.

Who Determines the Appropriate Military Response?

Before considering military responses, it's crucial to determine **who** should decide the nature of these responses. Military action has political ramifications, so politicians will understandably have an opinion. In Israel's conflicts, political leaders often lean towards moderation due to political sensitivities. In contrast, military experts advocate decisive action, on the grounds that this will reduce casualties and strengthen Israel's strategic position. Post-conflict, politicians tend to propose concessions, while military experts argue against them and are particularly vocal about maintaining territory.[4]

The debate centers on a tension between two key points: (a) exercising restraint to maintain regional stability and avoid upsetting the international community, specifically the U.S., a crucial ally and arms provider, vs. (b) taking decisive military action to eliminate threats and reduce the overall number of casualties.[5]

According to *halachah*, the principle of *pikuach nefesh*, or "saving lives," is paramount in warfare decisions. Under these laws, one should **only** rely on an expert opinion when making decisions pertaining to questions of life or death.[6] This principle is typically spoken of in the context of medicine, where it means relying on relevant medical specialists.[7] However, *pikuach nefesh* applies in matters of war and national security as well. In such instances, the expert opinion should come from military specialists, not politicians.[8]

In general, *halachah* requires seeking advice from a military expert before undertaking military actions that could put Jewish lives at risk. However, in emergency situations where lives are at imminent risk, *halachah* dictates that one should take preemptive, life-saving military action first and seek expert military advice only afterwards.[9]

Based on this halachic principle, the Rebbe stressed that in matters of war, decisions should be guided exclusively by **active** duty military experts who speak purely from a military perspective and not by politicians or diplomats.[10] He noted that political considerations in Israel's conflicts have led to preventable deaths and turned military victories into ultimate defeats.[11] This has implications for military operations[12] and territorial concessions. Ceding land is not merely a diplomatic issue, but also a military concern, given land's strategic value.[13]

In what follows, we will see that the Rebbe's military guidance, rooted in *halachah,* corresponds with both classical and modern military strategy. On the other hand, strategies such as "Ceasefire Now" and "Land for Peace" directly serve the tactics employed by terrorist groups globally to overpower superior military forces.[14]

CHAPTER 4
Credible Deterrence

If someone comes to kill you, rise up
to kill them.

TALMUD, BERACHOS 58a

The First Military Principle

THE TALMUD TEACHES:[1] "If someone comes to kill you, rise up [take preemptive actions] to kill them [first]." This principle applies to both individuals and the Jewish nation's collective security. It dictates that Israel should not only respond to immediate threats, but also take preemptive action when facing dangers such as enemies amassing weapons or preparing to attack. This approach advocates preemptive strikes as a preventative,[2] not offensive, war. It follows that when Israel demonstrates its readiness to confront threats, it **deters** enemies, thereby preventing full-scale wars.[3]

Despite the diplomatic discomfort, Israel must show that it does not fear its enemies' weaponry and propaganda. Rather, Israel should summon inner strength and confidently neutralize its adversaries.[4] Such an approach will prevent war, as the enemy will not want to engage such a powerful foe.[5] As the Rebbe put it:[6]

When the enemy knows that the Jewish people are a nation that responds [to aggression] with [unwavering resolve and] ferocity, they will be so terrified that they will not [even contemplate] initiating a war. This accords with the teaching that "If someone is coming to kill you, rise up to kill them first." The very fact that we "rise up" [and demonstrate our readiness to defend ourselves] strikes fear into the [hearts of our] enemy.

This principle also demands the maintenance of a strong army, with divisions posted at probable flash points to deter possible attacks.[7] In the Rebbe's words:[8]

*When the Jewish people follow Jewish law and project strength, fear will befall their enemies. As the Torah teaches: "And all the nations of the world shall see that the name of G-d is called upon you, and they shall fear you."[9] [This fear will not only deter them] from attempting to attack Jews but will also cause them to "flee before you on seven paths."[10] In other words, they will flee from the Land of Israel and areas vital to Israel's security. This [outcome] will ultimately benefit the terrorists themselves, as they will avoid harm by having already fled the area. [Embracing this approach, rooted in halachah and a display of resolute strength,] is the **only** path to ensure true peace.*

Judaism is fundamentally a peace-loving religion and does not advocate killing, despite the perennial antisemitic canards claiming that "the Jews" seek to harm or kill non-Jewish people.[11] Even if a non-Jewish group persecuted and murdered Jews in the past, we must behave peacefully towards them, as they may have had a change of heart. However, when a nation sets out a vendetta against the Jewish people and evinces murderous hatred, then we have a moral obligation to engage in our own self-defense.[12]

Case Studies

Having laid out the principle of credible detterence let us consider several concrete case studies in which Israel applied it and cases in which it did not. Applying this principle consistently saved lives, while failing to do so cost lives.

A | The Six-Day War:
Successful Application of the Principle

The Six-Day War did not occur in a vacuum. Egypt and Syria, with support from Russia, had been threatening Israel in the months leading up to the war. Ahmad Shukeiri, Chairman of the PLO at the time, said of the Jews in Israel: "Those who survive will remain in Palestine, but I imagine that no one will survive."[13]

On June 2, 1967 the Israeli army struck the hostile armies, reclaiming the ancestral Jewish lands of Judea, Samaria, the Golan Heights, the Gaza strip, and the Sinai Peninsula. Israel crippled the air forces of all its regional enemies, including Jordan, Egypt, Syria, and Iraq. Miraculously, the war ended in six days with a total rout of the surrounding enemies who had much larger armies, territories, and populations. What appeared to be a serious existential threat to Israel evaporated in the face of a bold preemptive strike. This also gave Israel deterrence against future attacks, positioning it as a fierce enemy to be reckoned with.

B | The Yom Kippur War:
Failure to Apply This Principle

Prior to the Yom Kippur War, Israel's defense of the Sinai Desert, bordering Egypt, relied heavily on the "Bar-Lev Line," a complex system of fortifications. Two years before the war's outbreak, the Rebbe had already begun to sound the alarm about the Bar-Lev Line. As he wrote in a 1971 letter to General Aharon Yariv, then head of Aman, the IDF's military intelligence:[14]

Since you touched on the issue of the interim agreement [with Egypt], I hope you'll permit me to express [my thoughts] on a topic [that has been of] great confusion to me for about three years now. It is well known and accepted by all experts without exception that in our era, defense systems like the Maginot Line[15] and similar approaches — relying on fortifications and army platoons constrained in bunkers, etc. — are simply not effective. Especially in the age of fighter jets, paratroopers, and so on, and particularly when the front stretches for several hundred kilometers (if one includes the Suez Canal front and the Mediterranean front).

Rather, the strength of the army is in its mobility and the ability to move it swiftly from place to place using mobile units[16] for rapid deployment across varied terrain.

This holds true even when there are several footholds in the natural landscape — such as mountains, hills, etc. — in the rear of the defensive line. All the more so in the desert. Yet despite all this, vast sums and enormous efforts were invested in this line of defense.

Granted, [in constructing the Bar-Lev line] there was also a psychological benefit in saving the soldiers there from boredom,[17] a very serious problem in such a situation, but it's not plausible to say that this is why the line was built.

The Rebbe sounded the alarm that Israel was using a highly vulnerable defense strategy on the Egyptian border, one that had already been proven ineffective in World War II.

While the defense strategy was weak, Israel did have advance warning of the attack. Yet, despite Israeli intelligence indicating an imminent Egyptian offensive, Israel chose not to launch a preemptive strike to avoid being seen as the aggressor.[18] When Egypt attacked, its forces overwhelmed the Bar-Lev Line in under two hours and proceeded to make serious incursions into the Sinai. The Rebbe characterized the fact that they did not go further as a miracle.[19] He explained:[20]

It is a great miracle, even greater than the miracles of the Six-Day War, that when the Egyptians crossed the Suez Canal and the Bar-Lev Line, they did not advance further.[21] Nothing would have stopped them on their way to Jerusalem and Tel Aviv. They might have pressed further, G-d forbid, and the Syrian army might have done the same. The fact that they did not is nothing less than a miracle. The U.S. even thought that Israel might be done for.

The greatest proof that this is a miracle is [the case of] the formidable Maginot Line, built by the French in World War II. The Nazis came with their tanks and overwhelmed the Maginot Line with the exact same military strategy used here, conquering all of France. Moreover, in France, the Nazis needed to pass through many cities with military garrisons. In contrast, in the Yom Kippur War, the Egyptian army only had to traverse a desert and were faced with a [much] smaller number of defenders.

Commenting on Israel's failure to strike preemptively, the Rebbe continued:

We must listen to military experts, not diplomats. The diplomats and politicians, disheartened due to the exile,[22] did not accept the advice of military experts, who suggested calling for an immediate draft. Had the army mobilized the reserves, this may well have created a deterrent effect and there might have been no war.

The political hesitation stemmed from the fear that a preemptive strike would provoke other countries' condemnation and even withdrawal of support. Israel thus refrained from attacking. As a result, Israel suffered the loss and permanent injury of thousands of soldiers, along with the irreparable trauma and sorrow of thousands of widows and orphans.[23]

On Yom Kippur itself, military experts asserted that in order to prevent the war and save Jewish lives, it would be necessary to publicly call up the reserves.[24] Tragically, however, the Israeli government rejected this recommendation in order not to be seen as aggressors.[25] The Rebbe explicitly noted that this was a failure in applying the principle of "If they are coming to kill you, rise up to kill them."[26] After witnessing the tragedies of the war, caused in large part by her hesitation, Golda Meir, then Prime Minister, said in retrospect: "If, G-d forbid, such a situation were to recur, we must discount the international community's opinion and go to war."[27]

C | The October 7, 2023, Simchas Torah Massacre: Failure to Apply This Principle

In the recent Israel-Hamas war, Israel's billion-dollar border defenses, including a wire fence[28] equipped with lookout towers, were quickly breached by attackers using explosives, wire cutters, and bulldozers,[29] allowing Hamas to easily overpower the limited Israeli forces present.

What makes October 7 even more tragic is that, just as in the Yom Kippur War, the Israeli military establishment had advance warning of Hamas' military training at the border for over a year, yet took no action to stop it.[30] In the months, weeks, and days preceding the attack, the all-female lookout staff at Nahal Oz military base sensed the attack coming and reported troubling signs, but no one took their concerns seriously. Ultimately, only two members of the unit, Yael Rotenberg and Maya Desiatnik, returned home. The rest were either murdered or kidnapped by Hamas.

Yael reports that a week before the attack, she observed strange behavior from her lookout post. Armed men with maps started massing at the border and digging trenches. She reported it up the chain of command and was told that it was farming activity and should not be a cause for concern. She pushed back, specifying two particular spots where terrorists were massing with maps, yet the Israeli military command did nothing. Ultimately, the terrorists attacked from these two locations. "It's angering," she says, "we reported, we saw it coming, and we were the ones murdered."

Maya shares: "We knew something would happen, it was just a

matter of time. We would joke — **where** will the attack happen? There was a certain area that seemed really problematic. I reported it to the higher ups and they simply said, 'There's nothing we can do about it.'"

Even more alarming, Israeli military intelligence had received detailed reports of Hamas' plans. Drafts of these plans had circulated since 2016 and only became sharper with time, but the establishment did not believe that Hamas would actually carry out the attack. Preemptive strikes and more formidable border security could have prevented the disaster.[31]

What would an approach guided by the principle of "rise up to kill them" have looked like? First, it would have involved more vigilant defenses than mere reliance on a fence that could be easily overwhelmed. Second, it would have entailed taking warnings from the lookouts more seriously. It also would have demanded that the Israeli army neutralize the Hamas militants openly preparing to invade Israel.[32] More fundamentally, this approach would have demanded that the Israeli army not withdraw from Gaza altogether in 2005, given the prevalent terrorist threats and militant groups in Gaza already then.

D | Operation Defensive Shield: Partial Application of This Principle

The Second Intifada began in 2000. The following two years saw a dramatic increase in terror attacks targeting Israelis. Notably, the number of injuries and deaths reached its peak in 2002, before starting to decline in 2003.[33] As can be easily demonstrated, this decline directly correlated with a shift in military policy.

In 2002, the Israeli army launched Operation Defensive Shield (*Chomat Magen*). This operation involved the IDF invading the Palestinian stronghold cities of Bethlehem, Jenin, Ramallah, and Shechem (Nablus). During these invasions, the army neutralized many terrorists and confiscated weapons, deterring the population from engaging in violence. Suicide bombings and attacks precipitously dropped after Defensive Shield. In addition, the Israelis constructed a concrete barrier around Judea and Samaria which has prevented many terrorist infiltrations and attacks, as evidenced by the precipitous drop in terrorist attacks since 2003.[34]

Operation Defensive Shield was thus an important step in applying the principle of deterrence. However, it only temporarily ameliorated the terrorism problem, rather than fully resolving it.[35] This is because after Operation Defensive Shield, Palestinian populations rearmed, given that the IDF only sporadically polices the population.

E | Judea and Samaria:
Failure to Apply This Principle

The extent to which current Israeli policy allows a certain number of Israelis to be killed instead of exercising a zero-tolerance policy is well illustrated by a moderate Israeli intelligence officer's take on the current conflict.[36] When asked how we could deal with the conflict, he said: "Look, the public can tolerate a Fogel family from Itamar [tragedy][37] once in a while. But what happened in the Gaza Envelope [on October 7th, 2023,][38] is beyond the public's tolerance level."

The Fogel family lived in the community of Itamar in Samaria. One Shabbos evening, two teenage terrorists infiltrated their home and brutally slaughtered the entire family. According to this officer's perspective, the government tacitly sacrifices some residents of Judea, Samaria, and the rest of Israel[39] on the altar of international opinion. Israel decides as a matter of policy to allow a certain number of Jews to be killed with only surface level responses until the number of murders passes some threshold of "tolerance."[40] This leads to the worst outcome for everyone involved — Palestinian terrorism continues and Israel responds with counterterrorism operations, creating a hostile situation for everyone. International opinion remains largely unchanged, despite Israel's restraint.⁴¹ The international community consistently condemns Israel for its mere presence in Judea and Samaria and for doing anything at all to defend itself.

The Rebbe bemoaned the constancy of unaddressed terrorism. But sadly, in the decades since the Rebbe commented on the situation, terrorism has remained a constant scourge and only become more serious. Terrorist attacks in Israel, and most prominently in Judea and Samaria, are a weekly, if not daily, occurrence. Nearly any range of time since the year 2000 would show that terror attacks are a constant scourge, but for the sake of illustration, consider the staggering number of attacks in the first three months of 2024.⁴² In January, there were a total of **515 attacks**. Some attacks included:

January 7: In the Wadi Hermiya attack, a 30-year-old Israeli Arab man was murdered in a terrorist shooting attack and a Christian Arab woman was seriously injured and died three weeks later.

January 12: A terrorist cell infiltrated the Adora settlement in the Hebron Hills, injuring two Jewish residents. The three terrorists were neutralized.

January 15: Two Palestinian terrorists from Bani Na'im perpetrated an attack in Ra'anana, in which they stabbed a driver, stole her vehicle, and then carried out stabbing and ramming attacks, injuring over 18 people and killing a woman in her 70s.

February saw **475 attacks**. Some notable ones included:

February 16: A terrorist from Shu'afat opened fire on a bus stop at the Ram Junction,⁴³ killing two men and injuring four others, two seriously.

February 22: Two Palestinian terrorists opened fire at vehicles on Israel's Route 1 near Ma'ale Adumim, killing one person and injuring 11, including two critically.

February 29: A Palestinian security officer shot and killed two Israelis at the Eli gas station, in a shooting attack.

In March, there were **493 attacks**. Some major incidents include:

March 14: In the Beit Kama Junction stabbing attack, a terrorist from Rahat entered a shopping complex and stabbed four people, killing one and lightly injuring three others before being neutralized.

March 16: 2 terrorists from Hebron entered the Jewish neighborhood in Hebron and fired at children and homes. One attacker, an imam at a local mosque, was killed by IDF forces while shooting at children.

March 22: In a sniper shooting attack targeting a minibus at the Parsa Junction, a soldier was killed, and six Israelis were injured, two of them seriously. The terrorist was killed by an attack helicopter after a nearly five-hour manhunt.

March 28: Three Israelis were injured in a shooting attack on Route 90. The terrorist, an officer in the Palestinian Authority, turned himself in to the IDF the following day.

March 31: A 20-year-old civilian and a soldier were injured in a stabbing attack at the central bus station in Be'er Sheva by a terrorist from the Israeli Arab town of Rahat.

On the same day, in the Gan Yavne attack, an attacker from Dura in the Hebron district stabbed 3 Israelis in a shopping mall. One was critically injured and succumbed to his wounds several days later. The two others were seriously injured. The attacker was killed.

In 2023, excluding the October 7 massacre, Palestinian terror attacks murdered 44 Israelis and wounded 128. The violence reflected enhanced capabilities of militant groups like Hamas and Islamic Jihad to strike Israeli civilians despite Israeli security measures. The frequency and severity of attacks made 2023 the worst year of terror against Israelis in recent memory.[44] While attacks vary from year to year, these statistics demonstrate that Israeli civilians, especially in

Judea and Samaria, live under the constant shadow of terror.

The Israeli army's strategy against terrorism currently resembles a cat-and-mouse game. Israel captures terrorists, but often releases them soon after in negotiations. Moreover, it does not address the large stores of Palestinian weapons and violent rhetoric. This is an open secret. One night, during the 2023 Israel-Hamas War, an IDF soldier serving in the special forces in Judea and Samaria shared:[45]

> *We confiscate weapons from time to time. Often, when we make arrests, we search their phones. In their camera rolls, they have pictures where they are posing with all sorts of weapons, including heavy machine guns. We know exactly what they plan on using them for... but we cannot do anything about it because the government's policy ties our hands.*

As the Rebbe often said in response to earlier iterations of this same policy, the change must happen on a policy level. The government and the IDF must acknowledge that allowing our enemies to hold heavy quantities of weaponry which could easily be turned on vulnerable Israeli populations is unacceptable. Persistently adopting a tougher stance, similar to Operation Defensive Shield but with greater vigilance and perseverance, could end the cycle of violence, bringing safety to Israeli roads and sparing both Jewish and Arab families from loss. This decisive approach against terror will pave the way for a new era of mutual prosperity.

Summary

The principle of credible deterrence has proven to be a crucial factor in Israel's security. The case studies presented demonstrate that when Israel boldly confronts threats and takes decisive action, as exemplified by the Six-Day War and Operation Defensive Shield, it can deter enemies, prevent deadlier encounters, and save countless lives.

However, when Israel hesitates to apply this principle out of concern for international opinion or a desire to avoid being seen as the aggressor, the consequences can be tragic. The heavy losses of the Yom Kippur War, the October 7, 2023 Hamas attack, and the ongoing violence in Judea and Samaria serve as stark reminders of the price of inaction in the face of imminent threats.

As we look to the future, it is clear that Israel must embrace the principle of credible detterence to neutralize those who seek to harm it, with unwavering strength and resolve. By maintaining a powerful deterrent force, taking threats seriously, and acting preemptively when necessary, Israel can create an environment where its enemies dare not attack, paving the way for a new era of security and prosperity for all inhabitants of the region.

CHAPTER 5

Proactive Defense

*And even if they have not yet come but merely **intend** to come, Jewish defenders must preemptively take up arms [and neutralize them].*

REMA ON CODE OF JEWISH LAW 329:6

The Second Military Principle

A SECOND FUNDAMENTAL principle highlighted by the Rebbe is the proper assessment of risk, based on the Code of Jewish Law.[1] As established in the previous chapter, the Torah obligates preemptive defense efforts to be made in the face of adversity. Rooted in the halachic principle of pikuach nefesh, Jewish law goes further to actually detail the evaluation of potential dangers and gives clear guidance as to what risk is substantial enough to not be ignored under any circumstances. On a religious level, this obligation overrides almost all other commandments and allows for the suspension of Shabbos observance to take **proactive** measures against even **potential** attackers.

Legal Origins

The Talmud[2] discusses how Jews should respond to enemies who come to attack a city and the assessment of risk which must be performed in terms of violating Shabbos. If foreign forces besiege a Jewish town on Shabbos, the appropriate response depends on the motives of the assailants. If the enemies merely come to steal, it is not necessarily permissible to resort to armed defense. If, however, they intend to injure or kill, or even if they come with unspecified intentions,[3] the town's inhabitants must defend themselves, even if doing so involves violating the laws of Shabbos.[4]

Moreover, towns situated near the border are obligated to take up arms and violate Shabbos, even if the invaders' sole motivation is to steal seemingly **insignificant resources,** such as straw or hay. This is due to the strategic importance of border towns and the risk of minor conflicts escalating into more serious threats. In such a scenario, a proper show of force may deter future, potentially more dangerous, attacks. For these strategic reasons, maintaining control of these locations is paramount, even if it requires violating Shabbos. In the Rebbe's words:[5]

> The said psak din [legal ruling] deals with a situation where gentiles besiege a Jewish border-town, ostensibly to obtain "straw and hay," and then **leave**. But because of the **possible** danger, not only to the Jews of the town, but also to other cities, the Shulchan Aruch [Code of Jewish Law] rules that upon receiving news of the gentiles (even only [of] **preparations** [they are making]), the Jews must mobilize **immediately** and take up arms, even on Shabbos. This ruling is in accordance with the rule that "pikuach nefesh [saving lives] supersedes [the prohibitions of] Shabbos."

To emphasize this point, the Talmud then relates that as a young man, King David risked his life to lead a Jewish militia against the Philistines who were raiding the grain floors at the town of Ke'ilah.[6] Even though the Philistines were only coming to steal resources, G-d instructed David to strike the Philistines since Ke'ilah was a border town.

Notably, the Talmud issues this ruling regarding the protection of communities outside of the Land of Israel, clearly establishing that the key guiding principle at play is saving lives, not defending our ancestral homeland.[7] In the Rebbe's words:[8]

> *This psak din has its source in the Talmud (Eiruvin 45a), where the Gemara cites as an illustration of a "border-town" under the terms of this psak din — the city of Neharde'a in **Babylon** (present day Iraq) — clearly **not** in Eretz Yisrael. I have emphasized time and time again that it is a question of and should be judged purely on the basis of, pikuach nefesh, not geography.*

The Halachic Verdict

The Code of Jewish Law[9] codifies the Talmud and Maimonides' rulings as follows:

> *In a case where non-Jews besiege Jewish cities, [the course of action depends on the attackers' intentions]. If their intent is merely to steal or plunder property, we are not permitted to violate Shabbos in order to fight them. However, if their aim is to cause us harm, or even if their intentions are unclear, we [must preemptively] confront them with weapons and desecrate the Shabbos to fight them off. When it comes to a border city, the rules are more stringent. Even if the enemies are coming for insignificant items, such as straw or hay, we are obligated to desecrate Shabbos to fend them off.*

Rema, a leading authority on Jewish law, extends the ruling to apply even to the threat of an enemy merely **intending** to come and attack or plunder. He writes:[10]

> *And even if the attackers have not yet arrived but merely **intend** to come, Jewish defenders must preemptively take up arms [and neutralize the threat].*

Shemiras Shabbos KeHilchasah,[11] a major contemporary guide on Shabbos observance, states that in present-day Israel, it's imperative to violate Shabbos laws in order to defend the land against intrusions. This is because even if the intruders merely intend to steal, the situation could potentially turn dangerous. The intruders might realize that Shabbos and holidays are more vulnerable times for attacks, resulting in more severe threats.[12]

Practical Application:
Indirect Risk to Life Cannot Be Ignored

The Rebbe explained that the current security conditions render the entire Land of Israel a "border town,"[13] necessitating constant vigilance and readiness to act against threats.[14] This precludes territorial concessions that could endanger Jewish residents. Moreover, the Code of Jewish Law mandates arming and training the populace for defensive purposes.[15]

The Rebbe notes that if the Shabbos prohibitions are suspended in such a case, then all the more so is there a halachic imperative to engage in preemptive offense on an ordinary weekday. This is to dissuade our sworn enemies who, as *Rema* puts it, "have not yet come... but intend to come" to launch attacks against strategically important areas. This ruling applies to all of modern day Israel, with a particular emphasis on Judea and Samaria, which are of paramount importance for national security.[16]

Israel is intrinsically in a state of siege, surrounded by hostile nations. Unlike the adversaries described in the Talmud and Code of Jewish Law, who only sought resources like "straw" and "grain," these enemies explicitly express their intent to seize the land and annihilate its Jewish inhabitants.[17] Consequently, Jews who can take up arms must do so, even without the directives of a *beis din* (Jewish Court of Law), a king, or any local Jewish government. They must violate Shabbos not only once the enemy has arrived, but even when they have hostile intenions.[18] The Rebbe taught:[19]

We must revisit the Talmud's teachings regarding Neharde'a, [a city outside the Land of Israel that was][20] home to a diverse Jewish population. [Despite the city's location and demographic composition,] the Talmud establishes a single, [crucial] criterion: Will the Land be easily conquerable? If the answer [to this question] is affirmative, the Talmud determines that this [situation] places Jewish lives at risk. [In such a scenario,] there is an immediate imperative to take [decisive] action without [delay or the need to] seek outside opinion.[21]

Clearly, in order to save Jewish lives, we must not give away territory to our enemies in exchange for elusive promises of peace. Instead, we must defend strategically valuable territory. This demonstrates that the primary importance of holding land is not due to the Land's holy status, but Jewish security.

Well-Meaning Passivity Is Not an Option

In response to those who take a more thoroughgoingly spiritual view, suggesting we should simply pray for safety in Israel and not take concrete defensive measures, the Rebbe countered:[22]

*Some argue that since Jews require Divine assistance in order to be saved, they should focus on reciting Psalms and studying Torah instead of arming themselves and violating Shabbos. However, the Code of Jewish Law [unequivocally] rules that we must **also** arm ourselves and go out to fight.*

Similarly:[23]

We are obligated to act in accordance with the Code of Jewish Law, echoing the example set by Jacob, who, while starting with prayer, also prepared himself for war by "going out against them with weapons."

Reinforcing this point even further[24]

The Beis Yosef [the author of the Code of Jewish Law,] was familiar with the verse, "the voice is the voice of Jacob."[25]

Moreover, he himself studied Torah with great dedication and intensity, surpassing today's Torah scholars. Nevertheless, he still ruled that in such a situation, we must "confront them with weapons and desecrate Shabbos," since G-d wants us to operate within the natural order.

There is no need to formulate new rulings; we must simply follow the clear ruling of the Code of Jewish Law, which [instructs us] to go forth armed, even in exile.

"Sec. 329" and Land for Peace

Section 329 of the Code of Jewish Law fits with the preemptive stance we explored previously. It extends further, stressing the urgency of eliminating imminent threats. Another important point that section 329 of the Code of Jewish Law emphasizes is the importance of territorial integrity, stating that we must defend the border so that "the land not be opened up for easy conquest." This shows that not only is Land for Peace a bad policy, but also in violation of Jewish Law.[26] As the Rebbe expressed:[27]

*I am completely and unequivocally opposed to the surrender of any of the liberated areas currently under negotiation, such as Judea and Samaria, the Golan, etc. The simple reason [for my opposition], and the only reason, is that surrendering any part of them would contravene a clear psak din in Shulchan Aruch (Orach Chaim, sec. 329, par. 6,7). I have repeatedly emphasized that this psak din has **nothing** to do with the sanctity of Eretz Yisrael, or with the days of Mashiach, or the Geulah [Redemption], and similar considerations, but solely with the rule of **pikuach nefesh** [saving lives].*

Let's consider several case studies which demonstrate that territorial integrity is critical in order to provide security.

Case Studies

I reiterate: **Every** *military expert I know of who was asked,*
answered without exception, that **any** *territorial concession*
in Judea, Samaria, and the Golan **literally amounts to**
putting lives in danger, without any doubt in the matter.
THE REBBE[28]

A | The Gaza Withdrawal

As we saw previously, the Gaza withdrawal turned Gaza into a
terror base from which to launch much deadlier attacks on Israel
than they had before the disengagement. The events of October 7,
2023 leave no doubt that this is the case.

B | Maintaining the Golan Heights

In 1967, Israel reclaimed the Golan Heights from Syria.[29] Although
Syria and the international community have repeatedly
demanded it back,[30] Israel refuses to return it. The Golan Heights
plays a significant role in Israel's defense strategy for several
reasons:

1. Strategic Location
The Golan Heights is situated on a plateau overlooking Northern
Israel. Before Israel recaptured the Golan Heights in 1967, the area
was used as a base for repeated attacks on Israeli communities
in the Hula Valley and around the Sea of Galilee. Controlling the
Golan Heights has eliminated these security threats.

2. Early Warning System
The elevation of the Golan Heights allows for early detection of
incoming attacks from Syria, such as artillery or aerial threats,
providing Israel with crucial response time.

3. Terrain

The Golan Heights' rugged terrain acts as a natural barrier, making any ground assault from Syria, similar to the one they launched in the Six-Day War, more challenging.

4. Water

The Golan Heights is a key source of water for the region. Controlling this area ensures Israeli access to these vital water resources and prevents Syria from threatening Israel's primary water supply, the Kinneret.

Thus, despite international pressure, our principle indicates that Israel must hold onto the Golan Heights to ensure its security.[31] Consider the following analysis of the Golan Heights' importance to Israel's security, presented by a contemporary geographer:[32]

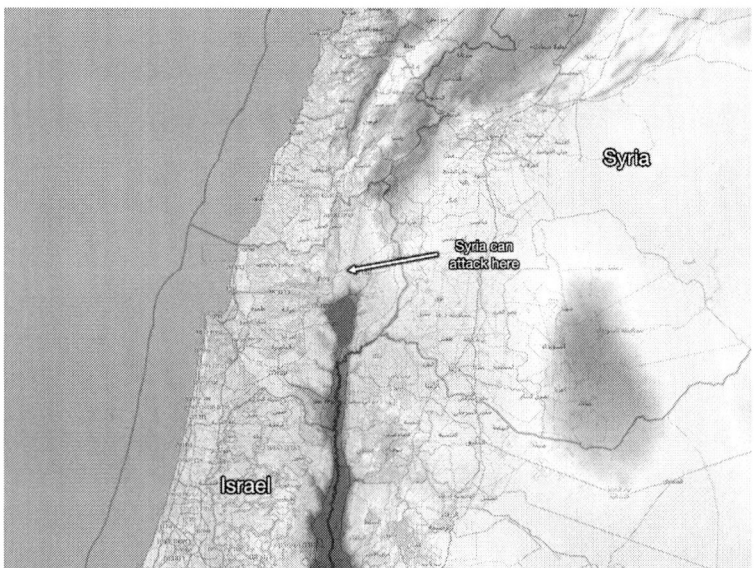

The border separating Israel and Syria is narrow, but it remains the one easy entry point between the sea and the mountains forming the Golan Heights. It used to be narrower before the 1967 Six-Day War, when Israel took over the Golan Heights. But now that Israel controls this area, it has access to the mountains

overlooking this pass and the Syrian plain. This is one of the reasons why Israel took it at the 11th hour of that war.

In order to attack Israel from that point of entry, Syria needs to prepare militarily in the area undetected and attack the mountains and the valley at the same time.[33] If it does succeed, it then faces a second set of hills, with its own set of defenses, to which its army would be fully exposed. Even if it succeeds, it then needs to extend its logistics to take over the coast and fight in the hills of Galilee, Samaria, and Judea, while Israel can easily move its forces around. This is awfully hard.

Meanwhile, Syria's capital — Damascus — is a stone's throw away from the Golan Heights.... Given the difficulties that Syria would have invading Israel, and how much Israel can keep control of its approach, it's very unlikely that Syria would repeat an attack on Israel, and if it did, it would probably not be an existential threat.

Of course, if Israel **did** cede the Golan Heights, this would jeopardize its security. The Golan Heights' strategic significance has become even more critical since the Syrian Civil War began in 2011. This war — which has had ripple effects across the world, displacing millions of refugees — has also destabilized the region.

Jihadist groups hostile to Israel flourish in Syria, while Iran has cemented itself in the region supporting the Syrian regime.[34] Although ISIS and Iran (among other hostile groups) are fighting against one another, both are hostile to Israel. If the Golan Heights was important for Israel's security in the past, the rise of these more volatile enemies just beyond the Golan Heights makes retaining the region even more crucial.[35]

C | Maintaining Judea and Samaria

Judea and Samaria, which Israel reclaimed during the Six-Day War, are crucial for Israel's security. Consider the following:

1. Strategic Depth

These areas provide Israel with strategic depth,[36] which is particularly important given the narrow width of Israel's pre-1967 borders. Broadly, this means that Israel now has expanded borders, population centers, and military installations which strengthen its position, making it less vulnerable to attacks to begin with and better able to fend off attacks if they do occur.[37]

2. High Ground

The elevated terrain of Judea and Samaria overlooks key Israeli population centers and infrastructure. Control over these areas provides a defensive advantage.

3. Buffer Zone

Judea and Samaria act as a buffer between Israel and potential threats from the east, notably Jordan. Although Israel now has a peace treaty with Jordan, these areas still serve as a strategic buffer due to Jordan's lax control, which has allowed a significant influx of weapons into Judea and Samaria. This impacts Israelis living in these regions by allowing for more frequent and deadlier terrorist attacks. Nevertheless, given that Israel has general military control of the region, hostile forces are unable to orchestrate major attacks without Israeli interference. Control over the Jordan valley is even more important given that much of Jordan's populace is anti-Israel, a fact highlighted by the large-scale anti-Israel riots that have been held there since October 7, 2023. Although Jordan is currently under an authoritarian monarchy, if the regime were to be overthrown by the majority, Israel could face threats from Jordan. Finally, terror groups in Judea and Samaria are financed by Iran.[38] Were Israel to withdraw, Iranian military operatives would likely proliferate in the region, much as they did in Syria, threatening Israel's security.

4. Control of Vital Resources

Judea and Samaria provide control over and access to the region's ample water resources.

However, perhaps, if we made peace with the Palestinians, then none of these factors would matter. The problem with this argument is that Israel successively granted greater autonomy to Palestinians since the Oslo Accords in 1993. This autonomy correlated with a large increase in both the frequency and force of terror attacks. The Rebbe had foretold this in years of talks, urgently predicting that autonomy would only lead to increased attacks.[39]

In 2006, when Hamas won the Palestinian elections and took control in Gaza, they declared all previous peace agreements, including the Oslo Accords, void.[40] This demonstrates the instability of the Land for Peace strategy. Consider the following presentation and graphics which illustrate Israel's vulnerability to attack without Judea and Samaria:[41]

Israel is extremely exposed without the protection of the mountains of Judea and Samaria. Most of Israel is extremely narrow, flat coastal plains, which can easily be attacked from the mountains. Controlling Judea and Samaria allows Israel to utilize their height to deploy early warning platforms to intercept incoming missiles or air fighters. It is thus not in Israel's interest to give up control of Judea and Samaria. They are easy to defend, hard to conquer, and in the hands of hostile forces, serve as a good base from which to launch attacks against Israel's coastal plains.

D | The Sinai Withdrawal

Israel captured the Sinai Peninsula on two occasions. The first was during the 1956 Suez Crisis. However, due to international pressure, Israel withdrew in 1957. Israel captured the Sinai again in the 1967 Six-Day War. However, following the Camp David Accords, Israel returned the Sinai Peninsula to Egypt.

The Rebbe strongly objected to Israel's decision to relinquish the Sinai Peninsula, arguing that doing so compromised Israel's security, putting Jewish lives at risk.[42] He presented several arguments to support his stance, all of which have stood the test of time:[43]

1. Power Ensures Peace

Land offers strategic power, which makes a country less susceptible to attacks, thereby engendering a state of peace. At the end of the War of Attrition in 1970, after a ceasefire with Israel, Sadat's predecessor, Nasser, moved military forces to the Sinai.[44] Similarly, Sadat could have used his later treaty as a Trojan horse to compromise Israel's security. Therefore, the peace treaty was a strategic error. Moreover, Sadat violated the terms of the treaty soon after they were signed.[45] If Egypt ever chooses to attack Israel, it is now in a much stronger position than it would have been without having control over the Sinai, which comes with access to airfields, oil fields, and additional strategic territory.[46]

2. Peace as a Ploy

The Rebbe depicted the Camp David Accords as a cynical Egyptian ploy, leveraging both the Jewish desire for peace, as well as U.S. geopolitical interests, to receive concessions from Israel through "peace" instead of war.[47] By the time Sadat came to make peace, Egypt had lost four wars against Israel and Israel had captured the Sinai Peninsula twice. Given these circumstances, it did not appear that Egypt could credibly hope to win a war against Israel. Therefore, Sadat may have chosen to take via "peace" what he could not have through war.[48]

There are numerous reasons to doubt Sadat's sincerity in his commitment to the peace treaty. Firstly, in 1975, Sadat changed Egypt's Armed Forces Day to October 6, commemorating the day Egypt attacked Israel in 1973, setting off the Yom Kippur War. Sadat maintained this designation during and after the negotiation and ratification of the Camp David Accords, and it continues to be marked in Egypt to this day.[49]

More strikingly, only seven months after signing the Treaty with Israel, Sadat issued a presidential decree founding "the 6th of October City." This city commemorates the Egyptian attack against Israel. It is a curious choice to commemorate an attack on a nation with which one has recently made peace.

Even if Sadat himself was sincere – and the previous evidence implies he was not – the Egyptian public certainly did not embrace Israel.[50] While Israelis flocked to visit Egypt following the ratification of the Treaty, Egyptians continued to show disdain towards Israel. As the Rebbe noted:[51]

> The only "achievement" secured in the "Peace Treaty" was allowing Jews to visit Egypt and look at beautiful buildings and the ancient ruins. In other words, [the agreement merely facilitated a superficial] exchange of tourists between the two nations. However, upon examining the tourism [statistics, it becomes evident that] very few Egyptians visit Israel. In contrast, if not for the difficulties of securing an entry visa, hundreds of thousands of Israelis would flock to visit Alexandria and other Egyptian cities, spending tens of thousands of shekels in the process.

Moreover, the local Egyptians reacted to Israeli concessions by shaming Israel. For example, when Israel withdrew from El-Arish in the Sinai on June 25, 1979, the Israeli newspaper *Maariv* reported:[52]

> After 12 PM on Friday, it was not pleasant to be an Israeli in El-Arish. The Shabab [Arab youth] pushed against the lines of soldiers and the military police and shouted: "Ya,[53] Sadat, with you in death and blood." Close to 3 PM in the afternoon, all the signs that mentioned Israel in El-Arish had already been uprooted. Avi Farhan, who brought his family to say goodbye to El-Arish, was forced to flee the capital of Sinai after being 'honored' with a string of curses from youths, who also tried to push his car off the road.

This reaction indicates that the peace treaty did not change Egypt's public perception of Israel. Similarly, after the Gaza disengagement in 2005, the Arab residents of Gaza defaced and destroyed all traces of Jewish presence.[54]

3. Regional Instability

Peace treaties in the Middle East are very fragile affairs. First, the totalitarian leaders of these nations can change their minds at any moment, rendering any treaty unstable. Second, Middle Eastern nations are prone to sudden changes in leadership that can lead to the rise of radical governments, as was the case in Iran.[55] This fear materialized in the case of Egypt when, shortly after the peace treaty's signing, an assassin killed Sadat.

Sadat's successor, Hosni Mubarak, had a lengthy tenure (from 1981 to 2011). Thankfully, Egypt did not pose a security threat to Israel during this period, as Mubarak did not instigate any attacks. However, the Arab Spring in 2011 led to populist uprisings that deposed Mubarak, replacing him with Mohamed Morsi, who was affiliated with the Muslim Brotherhood (the organization from which Hamas emerged).

This could have escalated into a serious security concern for Israel,[56] but a military coup soon ousted Morsi, who was replaced by Abdel Fattah el-Sisi, a military leader whose present policy considers conflict with Israel unnecessary. This record demonstrates the instability of Middle Eastern governments, a point that the Rebbe consistently emphasized[57] and which has been backed by military analysts and recent historical trends.[58] Should Egypt's unstable regime fall, elements within Egyptian society could use the Sinai to threaten Israel.[59]

Despite the general stability which has thus far characterized Sisi's rule, in 2014, a branch of ISIS infiltrated the Sinai desert and began to carry out terrorist attacks, primarily against Egyptian targets.[60] While this branch of ISIS has posed a relatively minor threat to Israel,[61] had Israel been in control of the region, this group would likely not have taken hold to begin with. The lax security in Sinai since Egypt's reoccupation has not only enabled the smuggling of weapons into Gaza, enabling Hamas to rearm,[62] but also facilitated sporadic terrorist attacks against Israel.[63]

Those most harmed by the terrorist presence in Sinai, however, are the local population, who suffer from frequent attacks and the fallout of clashes between terrorist groups and the Egyptian military. Many Arab residents of the Sinai Peninsula remember the Israeli presence in the Sinai as a "Golden Age."[64]

4. Dangerous Concessions for a "Piece of Paper"

Israel's withdrawal from the Sinai Peninsula involved losses of both strategic and economic assets. All it received in return was a "piece of paper,"[65] a cold truce which can be violated at any time. Let's explore the key assets Israel relinquished:

Oil Fields: One of the most significant losses for Israel was the oil fields in the Sinai. Israel had discovered and developed the Alma oil field, as well as others in the region, which supplied a substantial portion of its oil needs.[66] Ceding these fields to Egypt meant Israel had to find alternative, more expensive sources of oil, which seriously damaged the Israeli economy.[67] Furthermore, this loss made Israel far more vulnerable to international pressure, since Israel could then be forced into security compromises under threat of oil being withheld.[68] Ceding control of the oil fields also exposed the Egyptian peace treaty as a ploy. To this day, Egypt celebrates the anniversary of reclaiming the oil fields from Israel.[69] What it could not take by war, it took by peace. The Rebbe repeatedly bemoaned this mistake, noting:[70]

> In this day and age, oil is an indispensable vital **weapon**, for without it, planes and tanks are put out of action as surely as if they had been knocked out.[71] Sure enough, before long, the Government found it necessary to demand from the USA urgent oil deliveries, because the reserve would last only a few **days**. Moreover, prominent members of the Government **publicly**

*admitted that it was a serious mistake to have surrendered the oil wells. Be it also noted that since the surrender of the oil wells in Sinai — according to the **Government's figures** — some 2-1/2 billion dollars was paid by it to Egypt for oil from the very same wells that had been surrendered. Not to mention the fact of having to buy oil elsewhere also, at exorbitant prices.*[72]

Military Bases and Infrastructure: Israel had invested in military bases, air force bases,[73] and infrastructure in the Sinai Peninsula, which were either dismantled or abandoned when they left the region. This resulted in a significant investment loss and posed a security risk.[74] Additionally, Israel lost an important air force base that had played a critical role in the famed Entebbe hostage rescue operation.[75]

Tourism and Real Estate: The Sinai Coast, especially areas like Sharm El-Sheikh, had been developing into a tourist destination under Israeli control. Israel's withdrawal meant a loss of investments in tourist-related infrastructure and revenue.[76]

Relocation and Compensation Costs: Israel incurred substantial costs in forcibly removing Jewish civilian residents and relocating military personnel from the Sinai. This included the costs of building new homes, communities, and infrastructure in other parts of Israel. The government also had to compensate Sinai's Jewish residents for their lost homes and livelihoods. Furthermore, removing Sinai's Jewish residents ethically breached promises the Israeli government had initially made to encourage settlement in the region.[77] The expulsion also exploited the young Israeli soldiers who had joined the army, risking their lives to protect the Jewish people — and who were instead commanded to hurt their fellow Jews by evicting them from their homes.[78]

5. Setting a Dangerous Precedent

The Camp David Accords and Sinai withdrawal marked the first time Israel gave away "Land for Peace" and the first time Israel forcibly evicted its citizens from territory that it evacuated for "peace" with its erstwhile enemies. This set a dangerous precedent for the future concerning areas of vital strategic and ancestral significance such as Judea, Samaria, Gaza, and Jerusalem.[79]

The Sinai withdrawal thus substantially cost Israel strategically, economically, and morally.[80]

In an English letter addressed to a member of the *B'nai B'rith Messenger*[81] staff, the Rebbe distills his views on the Camp David Accords:[82]

> *Sadder still, there appeared some Jewish leaders who, for the sake of peace, or rather the illusion of peace — and frightened by threats of further violence in the midst of a hostile and callous world — were prepared to and actually did surrender portions of our land, in the ill-conceived belief that our enemies would thereby be appeased. Moreover, contrary to all experience and common sense, which have demonstrated again and again that every act of appeasement and concession only invites stronger pressures to yield to even more avaricious demands, there are still those among our own people who persist in following this dismal course. The so-called Camp David Accords are only the culmination of the first phase of this ill-fated and self-defeating policy.*
>
> *As you may have heard, when the Camp David negotiations were initiated, I considered it my sacred duty to call attention to the true nature of this disastrous expediency. There was no basis in law, nor in justice, nor in reality, to give in to pressure to sign an accord and treaty by which one party gives all and the other party takes all; namely, first giving away tangible and vital resources in terms of territory, fortifications, air fields, oil wells, and the dismantling of settlements, etc., all vital to its security, while the other gives in return no more than promises, such as the establishment of communications, exchange of ambassadors, and "normalization" of relations, all of which could be revoked at any moment under one pretext or another. I warned that far from bringing real and lasting peace, this "accord" would only whet our enemies' appetite*

for more "grabs," encouraged by the weakened security position of their adversary. I also warned that it was folly to put one's trust in the USA's part of this agreement, for it was obvious that the USA was leaning heavily towards the Arab position.

Since the signing of the Camp David Accords and Treaty, the consequences it has spawned have turned out to be even worse than I feared. Now, some 18 months later, everyone can clearly see that Egypt never intended to keep its promises fully. Right from the moment it took over one segment of Sinai after another, it broke its pledge to keep these zones demilitarized, though for the sake of expediency this matter has been hushed up. Even at this moment, Egypt is busily engaged in aggressive military preparations (the construction of tunnels under the Suez is but one glaring example). This should come as no surprise, given the record of broken Egyptian pledges in the period following the Yom Kippur War, and ever since 1948. At the same time, it is demanding, and obtaining, from the U.S. an ever-increasing supply of the most sophisticated weaponry, not to mention what is going to such other "moderate" Arab states as Saudi Arabia, Jordan, and even Iraq.

Such is the "even-handed" policy of our U.S. Government. Be it also noted that even in regard to its own obligations in connection with the Camp David Accords, particularly the assurance of oil supplies to compensate for the surrender of the oil wells in Sinai—developed with Jewish ingenuity and resources—it has found a convenient loophole, claiming that the situation is not "critical" as stipulated, which obliges the country to spend millions of dollars in overcharges on the open market, thus putting a critical squeeze on the economy of Eretz Yisrael, which is in dire enough straits as it is.

A Litany of Arguments Against Land for Peace

The Rebbe's key argument against Land for Peace centers around pragmatic considerations not at all tied to Israel's intrinsic holiness. That said, the Rebbe also emphasized that G-d miraculously returned the entire Land of Israel, and particularly Judea and Samaria, to Israel's control. Therefore, giving up this Land would demonstrate profound ingratitude towards G-d on Israel's part.[83] The Rebbe had multiple layers of reasons as to why Israel should not give away land. As he summarized his talks on Land for Peace in a letter:[84]

> I spoke of the prohibition to concede land based on the ruling of the Code of Jewish Law, irrespective of the Land's sanctity.
>
> I also spoke of the Land's sanctity.
>
> I also spoke of the [military] victory which occurred through open miracles [as a result of which giving away Land would demonstrate ingratitude].[85]
>
> Each of these points responds to different questions and claims:
>
> The **first** is the practical question of conceding the territory in Judea, Samaria, and the Golan. My response was based on the well-known hostility of Jordan and Syria, [given which, conceding the Land would be dangerous]. Moreover, since all of this territory is on the border, relinquishing it would violate a clear ruling in the Code of Jewish Law with respect to pikuach nefesh (saving lives), [a ruling] which applies even in a case of a remote possibility of danger to life. And in the Talmud's terms, [it holds] even in Babylon.
>
> The next question was with respect to the unfortunate Camp David Treaty, where some claimed that in order to be upstanding we need to uphold it. To this, I responded that a treaty can only be signed on that which belongs to a person; but one cannot relinquish what does not belong to them, for the Land of Israel is an eternal inheritance for the eternal nation. And, similarly, there are other answers for different questions. But as stated, with respect to the practical question, the most grave and serious concern relates to pikuach nefesh, and therefore I asked many times not to blur the issue with other concerns.

Summary

In an effort to save lives, The Code of Jewish Law (*Orach Chaim*, 329:6) guides us in the adherence to two key principles:

1) The imperative of constant vigilance, military readiness, and preemptive strikes against enemies with hostile intentions.

2) The importance of holding onto land for security purposes and the fallacy of the Land for Peace doctrine, which makes Israel more vulnerable to attack.

CHAPTER 6

Fully Neutralize Threats

You shall lay siege to the city that is waging war against you until it is subdued.

DEUTERONOMY 20:20

The Third Military Principle

Halachic Foundations

THE TORAH TEACHES:[1] "You shall lay siege to the city that is waging war against you until it is subdued." Shammai,[2] a Mishnaic sage, interprets the verse "until it is subdued" as a directive to continue fighting until the enemy surrenders. Maimonides codifies this as *halachah*.[3]

The Rebbe's Critique of Israeli Military Strategy

The word "subdued" means that the enemy must be brought to the point of **submission**.[4] Therefore, the Rebbe vocally advocated against the Israeli government's tendency towards limited

75

military operations over conclusive victories. The Rebbe called for a decisive approach. Once engaged in conflict, it is crucial to persist until the enemy is subdued, removing any future threat. This stance is more than just strategic; it is a moral and religious imperative to avoid prolonged conflict and additional loss of life.

Practical Implications of "Until It Is Subdued"

The Rebbe viewed this principle as having far-reaching implications for a broad range of military objectives and security policies:

1. The Ethics of Warfare

"Until it is subdued" emphasizes the importance of avoiding limited ground operations in urban environments, as they can be costly and counterproductive. Instead, it advocates for siege tactics and precision airstrikes. This aims to undermine local civilian support for terrorist groups by minimizing collateral damage and disrupting their operations and supply lines. By increasing the pressure on these groups while limiting the risks to friendly forces, it seeks to compel their ultimate surrender, leading to a swift resolution of the conflict without the need for large-scale urban combat operations.[5]

2. Ending Low-Level Terrorist Attacks

Persistent terrorist attacks against Israel necessitate a decisive response. The alternative would be a lenient approach that avoids prosecuting terrorists. The Rebbe firmly endorses the first option, emphasizing the necessity of imposing maximum punishment to deter future attacks. This aligns with the principle of pursuing the enemy "until it is subdued."[6] The Rebbe reasons that a softer approach would only embolden terrorists, thus perpetuating the cycle of violence.

Security operations must be comprehensive, eliminating threats to all Israelis and establishing lasting security, actualizing the biblical promise of "you will lie down [to sleep] and have no fear."[7]

Scripture warns us against adopting an indecisive stance, telling us:[8] "And those [hostile people] that you allow to remain shall become stings in your eyes and thorns in your sides, and they shall harass you in the land in which you live."

3. The Alternative: "Mowing The Grass"

The alternative to attacking an enemy "until it is subdued" is an approach referred to in works of military strategy as "containment."[9] In Israel's conflicts with Hamas and Hezbollah, this policy has been explicitly articulated and adopted, referred to by Israeli military theorists as "mowing the grass." This prescribes recurring, limited responses to persistent terrorist threats.[10] It involves tactical operations aimed at temporarily weakening terrorist capabilities without fully eradicating them. It fails to provide a long-term solution for eliminating belligerent entities such as Hamas and Hezbollah, who have thus far only emerged strengthened.

4. The Only Way to Honor the Memory of the Fallen

The Rebbe stresses that containment squanders resources and lives, allowing the enemy to return and inflict more damage. Conversely, fully subduing the enemy validates the expenditure of resources and honors the memory of those who perished in battle, as it paves the way to lasting peace. As the Rebbe put it:[11]

> Soldiers died in order to defend and conquer these territories which are vital for national security. They laid down their lives with the simple faith that by doing so, they were defending the Land of Israel and the Children of Israel. It follows that if we give away these territories, then the Jewish soldiers who fell (each of whom is "an entire world") made a pointless sacrifice.

This is not merely theoretical. In the course of writing this book, during the 2023 Israel-Hamas War, I was privileged to spend time with many active duty soldiers in the IDF. One soldier shared: "If we return to the status quo in Gaza after the war, allowing a hostile Palestinian government to take over again, I feel like all my friends who died, young men with wives and children, with dreams and aspirations, will have died in vain."

Since 1973, the Rebbe's call for a decisive approach has often been disregarded by Israel's military and political leadership, as well as by many in the general public, particularly those not under direct fire. The October 7 massacre has led to a paradigm shift, with even Professor Eitan Shamir, one of the key articulators of the "mowing the grass" strategy, moving towards a stance more aligned with the Rebbe's view.[12] In the following case studies, we will explore the consequences of not fully neutralizing threats.

Case Studies

A | Compassionate Jewish Naivete: Israel and Aram

Before delving into contemporary case studies, let's journey back 3,000 years to the ancient Kingdom of Israel.[13] The Biblical Book of Kings[14] recounts how the Aramean king, Ben-Hadad,[15] along with thirty-two allies, laid siege to Samaria, the capital of the Kingdom of Israel. He sent messengers to King Ahab, the Israelite King, with the message: "Your gold and silver, your women and children — are mine." Ahab responded by offering to pay taxes to Aram, yet Ben-Hadad still threatened invasion. Encouraged by one of G-d's prophets,[16] the Israelite Kingdom heroically defeated Ben-Hadad and his allies.

The prophet warned Ahab that despite Aram's defeat on the battlefield, they would attack again the following year. Indeed, Ben-Hadad regrouped with a more formidable army, but once more, G-d granted the Israelite army a victory. Ben-Hadad fled, but his advisors told him: "The Jews are a merciful people. If you surrender, they may spare your life." Ben-Hadad's men came to Ahab wearing sackcloth[17] and begged for mercy. Overjoyed at the Arameans' interest in peace, Ahab agreed to a peace treaty, sparing Ben-Hadad's life.

Ahab quickly overlooked Ben-Hadad's hostility, referring to him as "his brother" and agreeing to a trade agreement. After three years of quiet, this episode of misplaced trust ended with another war against the Aramean armies. In this battle, the Aramean forces, acting on Ben-Hadad's orders, killed Ahab and routed the Jewish armies.

The moral of the story, says the Rebbe, is that Israel must not relent in battle until it has rendered the enemy incapable of future aggression. The Rebbe emphasizes that the Torah's stories are not mere historical tales; they are eternal, actionable lessons that we must learn from and apply to our present reality.[18] The Rebbe laments how contemporary Israel has mirrored Ahab's naivete, failing to apply this crucial lesson of decisive victory and trading it for a false sense of "justice."[19] This ancient story sets the stage for examining similar patterns in Israel's more recent conflicts.

B | The Yom Kippur War: Damascus and Cairo

During the Yom Kippur War, the Rebbe advocated decisive Israeli military action, urging the IDF to capture the Syrian capital, Damascus. The Rebbe argued that doing so would humble the Syrian government and send a powerful message to never again attack Israel.[20] It would also serve the immediate goal of securing the northern front, allowing Israel to focus all its efforts on defeating Egypt. The Rebbe suggested a similar approach to Cairo, with the aim of undermining Egypt's military capabilities and establishing deterrence.[21] Defense Minister Moshe Dayan and Chief of Staff General David Elazar echoed the recommendation to conquer Damascus.[22] However, Prime Minister Golda Meir vetoed this course of action.

In response to her decision, the Rebbe drew a parallel to the forty years the Jewish people spent wandering in the desert, a situation that could have been avoided had it not been for their slave mentality. He saw a similar mindset in modern Israel's surrender to Western pressures, leading to unnecessary tragic outcomes.[23]

Syria has posed a minimal threat to Israel since the 1973 Yom Kippur War, largely due to Israel's aerial superiority and Syria's internal conflicts. In 1982, during the First Lebanon War, Israel decisively defeated the Syrian Air Force in the largest air combat engagement in modern military history,[24] and since 2011, Syria has been embroiled in a bloody civil war that has sufficiently absorbed its resources, preoccupying it from attacking Israel. Nonetheless, the Rebbe's recommendation for a more assertive approach at the time remains a point of reflection.

Despite Israel's successful defense and strategic gains, which positioned it to capture Damascus and advance towards Cairo, the Yom Kippur War ended with a ceasefire. While Israel emerged tactically victorious, the Arab narrative framed the conflict as a defeat for Israel.[25] This promoted a perception of Israeli vulnerability among its adversaries. The war's end resulted in a lingering narrative of half-measures. This was a deviation from the principle of "until it is subdued" which, if applied, could have significantly altered the region's geopolitical landscape in Israel's favor. Reflecting on the war in a letter to then Chief Rabbi of the United Kingdom, Rabbi Immanuel Jakobovits, the Rebbe wrote:[26]

> Another recent development bore out a view I expressed during the Yom Kippur War. I urged then, on the basis of halachah, to pursue the enemy ["until it is subdued"] (Deut. 20:20; and see also Num. 33:55), namely, to take Damascus — **not** for occupation, but to ensure that it "never" again would pose a threat. It was **then** also common knowledge that Soviet advisors were present there, with headquarters, etc. Only a few hours of occupation would have been sufficient to accomplish the task. But for "strange" reasons, it was not done. The results of the failure are evident, and have been particularly underscored recently by the military actions that were necessary to counter Soviet penetration.

C | The First Lebanon War

After the Yom Kippur War, Israel's military focus shifted.[27] Its neighboring countries with conventional armies had learned that engaging in full-scale war with Israel only led to their defeat. Cooperating with Israel had also proved beneficial for Jordan's national interests. Consequently, the primary threats were no longer state actors such as Egypt, Syria, and Jordan, but rather terrorist organizations, most notably the PLO.

As we have seen previously, beyond their hostility towards Israel and frequent terror attacks, the PLO did not play nicely with other Arabs nations. In Jordan, the PLO engaged in mischief including the hijacking and detonation of Western civilian airplanes on Jordanian soil,[28] as well as bids to overthrow the government, culminating in an assassination attempt on King Hussein of Jordan. This led King Hussein to mobilize the Jordanian army to expel the PLO. 10,000 Syrian soldiers came to the PLO's aid, but Hussein repelled them. Facing pressure from other Arab countries, Hussein allowed the PLO to relocate to Lebanon through Syria. By 1971, he had expelled the PLO along with many Palestinian civilians from Jordan.[29]

After relocating to Lebanon, the PLO continued their hostility. They used Lebanon as a base for launching attacks against Israel and played a key role in sparking the Lebanese Civil War in 1975, which eventually led to their expulsion by Lebanese and Syrian forces in 1991.[30] In 1982, following years of terrorist attacks by the Lebanon-based PLO,[31] the Israeli military invaded Lebanon with the objective of fully neutralizing the PLO. Then Prime Minister Menachem Begin described the operation's objective as achieving a "forty-year peace."

Originally named "Operation Peace in the Galilee," this military campaign sought to bring peace to Northern Israel by ending the ongoing attacks from Lebanon. Over time, however, it became the first conflict in a series of military operations, eventually becoming known as the "First Lebanon War." The "Second Lebanon War" took place in 2006, and at the time of writing, it appears that it may, G-d forbid, imminently be followed by a "Third Lebanon War," given Hezbollah's intensive military and rocket arsenal buildup as well as their constant acts of aggression and provocation. The First Lebanon War has broadly been described as a failure, drawing comparisons to the United States' unsuccessful campaigns in Vietnam and Afghanistan.[32]

On June 6, 1982, Israel invaded Lebanon. By the end of the first day, Israeli forces had advanced approximately 17 miles into Lebanese territory, and by the fourth day, they had reached the outskirts of Beirut, the Lebanese capital. The objective was to capture territory up to Beirut within 96 hours and then support the establishment of a new government. Within a few days, Israel had decimated the Syrian Air Force and repelled the PLO. Both the Syrians and the PLO pleaded for a ceasefire. Capitulating to international pressure, Israel agreed to a ceasefire on the sixth day of the war, before its soldiers could enter Beirut and eliminate the PLO.[33] The ceasefire allowed the PLO the time to strengthen their position. The Rebbe addressed the war, beginning by acknowledging G-d's miraculous intervention:[34]

> Once again, G-d has shown us open miracles, granting the Jewsih people a remarkable advantage [in battle]. [The success achieved by the Jewish forces surpassed all] expectations, with numerous soldiers bearing witness to open miracles.

However, the Rebbe also continued to point out the critical missteps that followed Israel's resounding victory:

> Some individuals [advocate] repeating the mistakes made in previous wars, arguing that we should halt the current military operation and refrain from completing the original plans, which aim to ensure that Jews can live safely throughout Israel. They [base their reasoning] on fear of international pressure. However, we must follow the advice of our military experts, as they are the only ones with relevant expertise in this matter. They have unanimously agreed that it is imperative to see the operation

through to its conclusion. This is the only pragmatic approach to ensure the safety and peace of the Jewish people in Israel.

From the conflict's onset, Israel faced intense political pressure to end the war. The U.N. passed a resolution demanding that Israel remove its forces from Lebanon. However, the Rebbe noted that the United States had tacitly given its support for the war, given that President Reagan was traveling and could thus avoid addressing the war directly. As the Rebbe stated:[35]

The United States is the only country whose opinion matters, as it provides [substantial] financial and military aid that considerably strengthen Israel's position.[36] In principle, [this support] could have allowed the Israeli army to have free reign. However, anxious politicians, deeply entrenched in a psychological state of exile, curbed the military's advance. Their fears were unfounded, since the United States had subtly given a timeframe within which Israel could have taken action. By failing to act swiftly, Israel lost this [valuable] window of opportunity.[37]

With its hands tied by politicians, instead of advancing forcefully, the IDF plodded cautiously forward during ceasefire windows and fought reactively, not proactively. This led to the IDF suffering heavy losses.[38] Israeli soldiers became easy targets for the Syrian army. Meanwhile, over 12,000 PLO terrorists, including their leadership, fortified themselves in Beirut.

The Rebbe lamented the Israeli government's decision to prevent the IDF from achieving the war's objectives:[39]

Merely initiating action is insufficient; it must be executed effectively and seen through to completion. Previous wars demonstrated that failing to finish the job not only prevents the operation from achieving peace and tranquility but also leads to another war a few years later. Even in the interim period, there is no peace and tranquility. Despite these unfortunate lessons, politicians are pushing to [prematurely] end "Operation Peace in the Galilee," even though they could have [already] [successfully] concluded the operation had they taken decisive action.

As the war carried on, Syria continued to violate the terms of the ceasefire, compelling the IDF to advance further. By this stage, the IDF had surrounded Western Beirut, cutting off its water and electricity supply. IDF planes dropped leaflets over Beirut, advising the residents to evacuate the area. Nevertheless, the war plodded on. In the Rebbe's words:[40]

Instead of finishing the operation, the government is busy with meetings. [Meanwhile,] each day that the operation drags on, more soldiers are wounded and even killed, G-d forbid.

The Rebbe advocated avoiding urban combat, urging the IDF to instead exert pressure externally by surrounding Beirut and threatening its destruction. This aimed to minimize Israeli casualties and compel the PLO to surrender without further bloodshed. The Rebbe criticized the Israeli government's misplaced focus on futile negotiations. As he put it:[41]

Regarding the claim [of Israeli politicians and international commentators] that completing the operation is only possible by entering the city, which will lead to soldiers dying: It is foolish to say that there is no other way to conquer such a small territory. There is no need to conduct a slow invasion when the operation can be finished from outside without entering the city at all.

[The most effective strategy is to] surround the terrorists from all sides and turn the area into a "mound of ruins"[42] without sending in a single soldier. We need merely notify the civilians to move to the other side of Beirut or leave the city altogether. By doing so, the operation can be completed without endangering a single Jewish life, or causing injury to anyone, not even the PLO. When [the terrorists] truly believe that this is not an empty threat and understand that we fully intend to turn their haven into a "mound of ruins," they will immediately and unconditionally surrender. This [approach] is the only way to ensure that there

are no casualties on either side and to guarantee hope that future wars will not be necessary. [Implementing] this strategy will bring true and lasting peace.

The Rebbe expressed frustration over the military cabinet's lack of decisive action. He argued that the cabinet should be composed of two or three individuals capable of finishing the job quickly. The Rebbe proposed delivering a heavy blow to Beirut, while simultaneously protecting Israeli soldiers from the thicket of urban warfare.[43] Infantry combat in densely populated urban settings, such as Beirut or contemporary Gazan cities, poses uniquely complex challenges for military forces due to the following factors:

Constrained Battlespace: Narrow streets, multistory buildings, and limited lines of sight constrain maneuverability and fields of fire.

Threats from Above and Below: The positioning of enemy combatants within tall buildings and underground tunnels facilitates attacks from unexpected angles.

Propensity for Ambushes: The dense urban terrain, offering ample cover and concealment, aids the enemy in ambushes and sudden strikes.

Civilian Proximity: The close intermingling of civilians makes it difficult to distinguish combatants from non-combatants. Therefore, urban warfare inevitably increases casualties. This allows for reams of photographs of dead civilians and destroyed property to be utilized by enemy propaganda machines. It also enables the practice of "lawfare," where international courts are weaponized against Israel.

Limited Technological Advantages: Essential technology such as sensors, air power, armor, and artillery are less effective in close-quarters combat situations.

The Rebbe's criticism extended beyond the First Lebanon War, identifying a recurring pattern in Israel's military history. He compared it to a failed surgical procedure, repeatedly started and stopped due to ignorant people's fears, leading to a cycle of incomplete military operations and ongoing conflict. This approach, the Rebbe argued, dishonors the sacrifices made by soldiers and ignores the nation's security needs. As he said:[44]

> [The question of] whether the war in Lebanon should have been started in the first place is a matter of debate. However, now that the government has dragged itself and the army into this conflict, it is imperative that they see it through to its conclusion. The government's hesitation can be illustrated with the following metaphor:
>
> [Imagine] a patient undergoing a critical surgical procedure. A fearful and weak-hearted observer, upon witnessing the first few drops of blood, cries out in panic, "Please, stop [the surgery]!" [As the surgeons] begin their work, [the observer, unable to bear the gruesome scene he is witnessing, interjects once more,] "Stop the procedure, allow the patient to heal and regain his strength. You can always perform a second operation later." Of course, [if the surgeons were to listen to this misguided advice,] the surgery would remain incomplete, [as the observer would continue to protest,] "The patient is losing too much blood; it's bad for them." As a result, the surgery would be carried out in a piecemeal fashion, [with no clear resolution in sight].
>
> If someone suggested such a method to medical professionals, he would be ridiculed. Yet, this is precisely the strategy being employed [when it comes to the lives and safety of] of three million Jews in Israel. [The consequences of this misguided strategy have been demonstrated repeatedly].
>
> In 1956, an **"operation"** was started in Sinai.[45] However, a fearful and weak-hearted individual [namely, Israeli politicians,] intervened and ordered them to stop. They didn't want to listen to him, so this individual called a conference where he declared, "[The decisive military approach] is not democratic! We need

86

a second opinion. We need to seek world opinion." This same scenario repeated itself time and time again.

*A **second** "operation" began in 1967 [the Six-Day War], and history repeated itself. In 1973, a **third** "operation" [the Yom Kippur War began], and once more, the same pattern emerged. Now, we find ourselves in the midst of the **fourth** "operation," [known as the First Lebanon War]. Hundreds [of lives] have already been sacrificed, may G-d avenge their blood, and hundreds more have been wounded. [In response], several individuals have put forth a [supposed] "solution," [claiming] that the best way to bring about a peaceful resolution is to leave all the bacteria [festering] inside the wound, merely shifting it from one area to another. [This approach] is taken with the misguided hope that, given time, the patient will [somehow] heal on their own.*

[After having simply relocated the bacteria, failing to address the root cause of the terrorism,] those in power will [undoubtedly] make a conference. They will travel around the world, attending conventions, waiting to see what unfolds next.[46]

The Rebbe contended that such an approach would obviously fail, yet its proponents would apply it and then travel the world engaging in 'peace' conferences, with the futile hope that they would be effective. The Rebbe continued:

*These experiments are being conducted on three million Jews, may G-d protect them. There are always changes. In this world, nothing remains exactly the same. But **essentially**, the problem has not changed. Here we have the same situation, the same people who are responsible to fix it, the same people or their disciples who are obstructing the process, and the same arguments. They proclaim that this path leads to peace, to justice. [They assert that] this is the way to appear virtuous in the eyes of the world. They say we have to take into account that we are not "a nation who dwells alone"[47] — we need the world's approval.[48] And nevertheless, they are being allowed to* *[continue to] lead the three million Jews by telling [such] lies. All the lengthy debates are irrelevant. The responsibility falls on two or three people. If you do not allow them to complete the campaign swiftly, then the outcome will be like the outcome caused by the Prime Minister who stopped the offensive during the Yom Kippur War.* She later wrote in her memoirs: *"I won't forgive myself for the rest of my life. The dead and injured will stand before my eyes as long as I live."*

Unfortunately, the Rebbe's comments then are just as pertinent now, and we can further expand on his remarks to note the following:

The **fifth "operation"** was the **South Lebanon conflict**, which lasted from 1985 to 2000.

The **sixth and seventh "operations"** were the **First and Second Intifadas**, respectively, spanning from 1987 to 2005.

The **eighth "operation"** was the **Second Lebanon War** in 2006.

The operations in Gaza then began:

The **ninth "operation"** was by **Operation Cast Lead** in 2008-2009.

A **tenth "operation"** followed with **Operation Pillar of Defense** in 2012.

The **eleventh "operation"** unfolded as **Operation Protective Edge** in 2014.

The **twelfth "operation,"** which took place in 2021, was **Guardian of the Walls**.

Each of these Gaza engagements followed the same troubling pattern. Now, we find ourselves in the midst of the **thirteenth** operation, the **Israel-Hamas War**. Once more, the familiar echoes of past operations reverberate as we witness a continuation of this long-standing cycle.

The protracted First Lebanon War evolved into a grueling war of attrition. Constrained by ceasefire agreements, the Israeli army faced repeated attacks from the PLO and the Syrian army. The rising number of casualties among Israeli soldiers sparked protests from the Israeli government's political opposition. Finally, on August 1, 1982, two months into the conflict, Israel launched a major offensive against Beirut. The offensive reached a climax on August 12 when the Israeli Air Force bombed the city, prompting local Muslim leaders to request that the PLO leave. That same night, PLO leader Yasser Arafat agreed to leave Beirut.

In the words of then Minister of Defense Ariel Sharon:[49]

> We needed to convince the terrorists to leave Beirut, which could only be accomplished through bombing the city. Arafat continued to lie and play games until we heavily bombed Beirut. And it worked! The night after we began bombing, he accepted our terms and left.

Finally, three months after the war began, the PLO and the Syrian army left Beirut.[50]

This phase of the war highlighted significant Israeli military achievements: dismantling the PLO's military infrastructure in Lebanon and neutralizing the Syrian army's threat. However, these successes were eclipsed by the drawn-out nature of the conflict, diverging from Israel's original military strategy.[51] Israel's indecisive stance at the most critical juncture of the war led to a complex political and military situation, marked by the avoidable loss of many Israeli and Lebanese lives and only a partial achievement of the war's objectives.

The Rebbe shared that a certain Israeli general once visited him and shared an observation that he had heard from an American colleague. The U.S. general had blamed the failure of the Vietnam War on political interference in military decisions. He maintained that had the U.S. military leadership been allowed to execute their strategies without political constraints, the outcome might have been very different. This situation mirrored Israel's situation in its wars with Lebanon. If Israel had taken the advice of its military experts and conquered the city of Tyre,[52] a victory in Lebanon could have been more easily secured. After drawing this parallel, the Rebbe highlighted a crucial difference:[53]

> *The contrast between the Vietnam War and Israel's wars with Lebanon is stark. For the United States, the Vietnam War was a distant[54] conflict, with limited direct impact on its civilian population and economy. In contrast, Israel's survival hinges on the outcomes of its wars. Lebanon, located on Israel's northern border, poses an immediate threat to Israeli civilians.*

Israel eventually withdrew most of its forces from Lebanon in 1985. Following this scaleback, the Palestinians in Lebanon and the Syrians, who were once allied against Israel, went to war against each other in what is known as the War of the Camps. Meanwhile, Israel maintained a limited security zone in Southern Lebanon, but faced hostilities from the newly formed Hezbollah, an Iranian-backed Islamist militia. Hezbollah's persistent attacks killed many Israeli soldiers in the security zone, prompting Israel to unilaterally withdraw from Lebanon in 2000, a move that Hezbollah hailed as a major victory.

D | The Second Lebanon War

While Israel's unilateral withdrawal from Lebanon may have temporarily satisfied Hezbollah's demand to "liberate occupied lands," it ultimately transformed Hezbollah into an ominous threat. This escalation was marked by Hezbollah's development of a substantial arsenal of long-range rockets, the training of a cadre of militants skilled in infiltrating Israel, and the construction of an extensive network of tunnels.[55] When undertaking the First Lebanon War in 1982, Israel had hoped to restore security to Northern Israel's residents. However, its subsequent withdrawal in 2000 resulted in an increased security risk for Northern Israel, as it allowed Hezbollah to gain strength and consolidate its presence.

The Second Lebanon War, which took place in 2006, was triggered by a cross-border raid by Hezbollah in which terrorists killed and abducted Israeli soldiers.[56] This escalated already heightened tensions due to Hezbollah's growing military capabilities and influence in Lebanon. The ensuing 34-day conflict saw extensive Israeli air strikes and a ground offensive, while Hezbollah persistently bombarded Northern Israel with rockets. The conflict resulted in significant loss of life on both sides and caused significant infrastructure damage.[57] The war ended with a U.N.-brokered ceasefire (UNSC Resolution 1701), which called for Hezbollah's immediate disarmament and the establishment of a 20-kilometer (roughly 12-mile) demilitarized buffer zone in Southern Lebanon. Despite these agreed upon terms, once the ceasefire was finalized, Hezbollah refused to disarm or leave the designated buffer zone.

After the war, the Israeli government's military strategy was widely criticized, while Hezbollah declared the conflict's outcome a "Divine Victory."[58] In the aftermath of the war, Hezbollah evolved into an even more formidable threat, far surpassing the danger posed by the PLO in 1982. The threat from Hezbollah escalated beyond what it was before Israel's withdrawal in 2000 and became even more significant than it was at the end of the Second Lebanon War in 2006.[59]

The ongoing conflict in Lebanon underscores the risks of not fully defeating an enemy, thereby enabling them to regroup and pose an existential threat. Following the October 7 attacks, around 80,000 Israeli citizens from Northern Israel have been displaced as a result of Hezbollah's threat.[60] Without decisive action against Hezbollah, their safe return remains uncertain.

E | Judea and Samaria:
Operation Defensive Shield

As previously discussed at length, Operation Defensive Shield in Judea and Samaria, launched in 2002, demonstrated a proactive approach to confronting the enemy. However, it fell short of fully applying the principle of "until it is subdued." The ongoing concern is the presence of weapons in key areas populated by Palestinians, such as Ramallah, Jenin, and Hebron. This state of affairs poses a continuous threat to Jewish communities in Judea, Samaria, and Israel as a whole.

In the 22 years since Operation Defensive Shield, there has been a persistent pattern of violence against Jews residing in Judea and Samaria. The continued armament of Palestinian communities and their potential for large-scale attacks on Jewish towns and cities heightens the danger. To prevent the recurrence of incidents like the October 7 attack, Israel should proactively target and disarm Palestinian strongholds in Judea and Samaria, eliminating both weapons and terrorist entities.

F | The Gaza Wars

1. Years of Unrest

During British rule over the Gaza Strip (1920-1948), local Arabs grew increasingly hostile towards both Jewish immigrants and Jews who had been living in Gaza for generations. This hostility ultimately led to Arab riots, looting, and murder. In the aftermath of Israel's victory in the 1948 War of Independence, Egypt took control of Gaza, using it as a hub for Palestinians, many of whom had been displaced during the war. In 1967, Israel took control of Gaza in a defensive war against Egypt. It established Jewish towns in the region, collectively known as Gush Katif. Nonetheless, Gaza retained its (hostile) Palestinian majority. Between 1993 and 2005, Gaza was a center of anti-Israeli terrorism, serving as a base for Palestinian terrorists carrying out suicide bombings and missile attacks against Israel.

2. Disengagement: More Violence

Israel's 2005 withdrawal from Gaza, intended to reduce tensions, was followed by Hamas' electoral victory in 2006 and the subsequent Gaza Civil War, leading to Fatah's violent expulsion by Hamas.[61] Crushing Fatah was only the beginning of Hamas' reign of terror in Gaza. In June 2006, Gaza-based Palestinian terrorists kidnapped Israeli Corporal Gilad Shalit. Israel responded with restrained military operations. This began a local cycle of violence that eventually culminated in the 2023 conflict.

3. The First Gaza War (2008-2009): Operation Cast Lead

These military operations, artillery exchanges, and border skirmishes ultimately led to the First Gaza War, or "Operation Cast Lead."[62] Following international outcry, Israel relented to a ceasefire and withdrew from Gaza, leaving it damaged but still under Hamas control. This withdrawal gave Hamas the opportunity to restock its arsenal and fortify its defenses. Meanwhile, the international community pledged $4.5 billion[63] in aid to rebuild Gaza.

4. Second Gaza War (2012): Operation Pillar of Defense

The ceasefire following the First Gaza War was short-lived, as Hamas continued to launch rockets and build tunnels into Israel. This led to Operation Pillar of Defense, a week-long campaign marked by heavy missile attacks from Gaza and Israeli counter-strikes.[64] The conflict ended with an internationally brokered ceasefire, bringing a temporary halt to the violence.

5. Third Gaza War (2014): Operation Protective Edge

In 2014, the kidnapping and murder of three Israeli teenagers in Judea and Samaria by Hamas terrorists prompted the IDF to arrest most of Hamas' active militants in the region.[65] Hamas retaliated with a barrage of thousands of rockets and mortars from Gaza into Israel, leading Israel to counterattack by bombing Gaza. This was followed by an Israeli ground offensive in Gaza, known as Operation Protective Edge, with the objective of dismantling Hamas' military capabilities. Although the IDF successfully demolished many terror tunnels and dealt a severe blow to Hamas' infrastructure, they failed to decisively cripple Hamas and eventually withdrew from Gaza.

6. Fourth Gaza War (2021): Operation Guardian of the Walls

On Jerusalem Day in 2021, Gaza-based terrorist organizations Hamas and PIJ fired a barrage of almost 4,400 rockets into Israel. Israel responded with airstrikes on over 1,500 terrorist targets in Gaza, including launch sites, command centers, and weapons' caches, as well as by neutralizing hundreds of terrorists. However, despite this response, the terrorist organizations in Gaza managed to maintain their operational capabilities.[66]

7. Looking Toward an Uncertain Future

Clashes continued between Israel and Gaza with intervals of rocket attacks and border skirmishes, followed by IDF response with airstrikes. These intermittent attacks and exchanges of fire continued until October 7, 2023, when various Gazan groups, led by Hamas, raided Israel. They took 238 hostages, brutally murdered over 1,200 Israelis, and violated many of the women and girls. Israel responded with heavy airstrikes on Gaza, followed by a ground offensive.

The question has now become: Will this be the final Israel-Gaza war? Does Israel possess the inner fortitude to take bold action and alter the status quo? Or will Israel once again fail to decisively end the cycle of violence, paving the way for future conflicts?

Although Israel has devastated Gaza, if it allows Gaza to be rebuilt under an autonomous Palestinian government, we can be certain, barring miracles, that the cycle of violence will perpetuate. To consider just how real a possibility this is, consider the following comments from a soldier who fought in the 2023 Israel-Hamas War. In early April 2024, I met up with a friend who had served as a tank gunner in the Gaza war. He had briefly returned from fighting in Khan Younis and was set to soon return to begin the Rafah incursion. "Sure, we devastated the place," he said, "but there's been no fundamental policy change. I'm going to bet that twenty years from now, there will be another Gaza war."

Defeating Terrorists
and Restoring Peace

As we have seen, the Rebbe emphasized the necessity of a decisive military approach to deter and defeat terrorist groups. This strategy includes not only military action, but also Israel's projecting an unwavering determination to confront and neutralize its adversaries, thereby preventing attacks in the first place. But is there any precedent for such an approach? Has it proved successful elsewhere in the world?

If we consult recent military history, there are numerous examples of non-state terrorist groups around the world conducting reigns of terror against civilian populations. These groups are often hosted by sympathetic (or terrorized) local populations. Can such groups be defeated? Let's explore two case studies from around the world.[67] Notably, both groups are "terrorist," but neither are Islamist.

A | Peace in Sri Lanka:
The Case of the Tamil Tigers

Sri Lanka endured over 25 years of civil war, finally ending in 2009, fueled by ethnic tensions between the Sinhalese majority and the Tamil minority. Some Tamils formed a militant group, known as the Tamil Tigers, seeking to establish an independent state. From 1983 until 2002, the Tigers engaged in terrorism and controlled significant territory in Sri Lanka's northern and eastern regions. The Tigers were notorious for their use of suicide bombers and child soldiers, as well as for pioneering the use of women in suicide attacks.[68] The Tigers were far more formidable than Hamas has ever been[69] and enjoyed vast streams of international aid and support.[70]

In 2002, international mediators brokered a ceasefire, leading to a temporary halt in hostilities. However, several rounds of peace talks failed to produce a lasting agreement. The ceasefire collapsed in 2006, leading to renewed heavy fighting. In response, the Sri

Lankan government launched a massive military offensive against the Tigers, successfully recapturing its territory. This time, despite appeals from the international community and the Tigers for ceasefires, the Sri Lankan government did not budge.[71] The conflict culminated with the Sri Lankan military defeating the Tigers decisively in 2009. [72] Since then, the once fierce Tigers have ceased to exist, and thus can no longer terrorize the Sri Lankan population.

B | Ending Gang Violence in El Salvador

To further prove the point that the Rebbe's principles of credible detterence, proactive defense and fully neutralizing threats are effective, let's consider another example. This case study, along with the tale of the Tigers, shows that these principles are effective against domestic terrorism across ethnic and cultural lines. In recent years, El Salvador has experienced a victory in its battle against gang violence, primarily driven by President Nayib Bukele's aggressive tactics to combat violent gangs like MS-13[73] and Barrio 18.[74]

Before Bukele's presidency, El Salvador grappled with one of the world's highest homicide rates, largely due to gang violence. The gangs were deeply rooted in Salvadoran society, committing extortion, drug trafficking, and brutal violence. The government's previous efforts, including the "Gang Truce of 2012,"[75] had limited long-term success.

Upon assuming office in 2019, Bukele launched a forceful and comprehensive initiative to address gang violence. His approach, known as the "Territorial Control Plan," established enhanced law enforcement and military intervention in gang-dominated areas, culminating in the establishment of the "Terrorism Confinement Center" and the arrest of over 71,000 suspected gang members.[76] This unyielding approach resulted in a significant drop in homicide rates and weakened the gangs' influence.[77]

Securing Stability:
National Security Overrides External Pressure

Both Sri Lanka and El Salvador faced condemnation from the international community, including the U.N.[78] and media outlets like Al Jazeera,[79] for their seemingly aggressive strategies. However, by prioritizing national security over external pressures, both nations successfully achieved peace and improved public safety. These examples suggest that were Israel to adopt similar tactics against terrorist threats,[80] it would lead to a more tranquil and stable environment, allowing both sides of the conflict to return to peaceful, productive lives.

Counterarguments

Let's consider three potential counterarguments to this heavy-handed approach towards terrorism:

Argument 1: The humanitarian cost of implementing such a strategy is too high.

Sri Lanka fought unrelentingly[81] to crush the Tigers. El Salvador declared a state of emergency and rounded up large numbers of people with gang tattoos without fully investigating their gang affiliations. If Israel were to adopt similar approaches, it would extract a great human cost.

Reply: Terrorist groups thrive on exploiting humanitarian concern and international law, weaponizing it to their advantage.[82] The first step in effectively combating these groups is to recognize this exploitation. One must then take decisive action to quell the terrorists and undermine their popular support, thereby bringing about peace. Prioritizing humanitarian concerns can be a red herring if restraint will perpetuate the cycle of violence, leading to more humanitarian crises for all parties involved. Instead, decisively neutralizing violent groups leads to the most humanitarian outcome and makes peace.

Consider the situation in Gaza. Every time Israel has granted Gaza greater autonomy, the Palestinian government of Gaza has perpetrated more serious attacks. These attacks lead to more Palestinian casualties since Israel must retaliate to defend itself. This leaves Israel with two humanitarian options with respect to Gaza's population:

1) Maintain tight control over Gaza to prevent it from being a launchpad for serious attacks, thereby protecting Israeli citizens and, by extension, Gazans.

2) Allow indiscriminate attacks from Gaza, putting Israelis in harm's way and ultimately risking the dismantling of Israel altogether.

So, if Israel has the right to exist, then option (1) is the only practical choice.

Argument 2: The Israeli military lacks the necessary capabilities to completely defeat Hamas or other Palestinian terrorist organizations.

Reply: Israel does, in fact, have sufficient military power to defeat Hamas. If Israel were to fight an uncompromising war against the Gaza Strip, Hamas and the local populace would be forced to surrender, breaking the cycle of conflict and paving the way for positive growth.

Argument 3: The international community will not allow Israel to eliminate Hamas and other such hostile terror groups.

Reply: The international community has stood by as numerous humanitarian crises have unfolded globally. When Sri Lanka and El Salvador addressed their domestic terrorism issues, there were complaints from the international community. However, these concerns had little impact and both countries are now enjoying greater prosperity as a result. Israel must conduct a cost-benefit analysis. If Israel preemptively ceases fire or withdraws from Gaza and Lebanon such that active terrorist groups can fortify and others can form, Israel will be forced, yet again, into war against an emboldened, empowered enemy. Israel faces a decision: either to go for another round and risk the lives of both its own citizens as well as those of the Palestinians, or to ignore international opprobrium and proactively dismantle terrorist infrastructure now. A further concern is that in the future, Israel may not have the power and military capabilities to finish the job; additionally, they may face even stronger international pressure and opposition. If Hamas maintains its stronghold in Gaza and the world's political landscape shifts, becoming even more hostile to Israel, Israel may lose its opportunity to act.

—————⚬—————

The pacifist approach imagines that terrorism can be defeated without resorting to war. This is a dangerous misconception and, as demonstrated in Part 1, it ultimately leads to more terror. Not only are half-hearted efforts unhelpful, they are also damaging, as they enable the enemy to hold out, leading to prolonged conflict and additional deaths. The enemy and its supporting populace will only stop their aggression if they believe that further warfare is no longer beneficial to their interests.

Conclusion

Military strength and strategy, while important, are not the ultimate keys to a successful outcome. Victory is granted by G-d, not by our own abilities.[83] On the other hand, G-d created a natural world and wants us to operate within its principles. As such, we must strike a balance between faith and practical action.

After careful consideration, we see that the only way to end the cycle of violence is for Israel to take decisive military action, ensuring that the enemy will not be able to regroup to fight another day. Ideally, this should be accomplished through military deterrence, stopping the battle before it starts. This deterrence should stem from a formidable military force and the perception that Israel will use it unqualifiedly if provoked. If that image of deterrence is compromised and Israel is attacked, it must retaliate until the enemy has been completely neutralized. While other strategies may appear to be more benevolent, they ultimately perpetuate the cycle of conflict. We must end the cycle and **make peace**.

But, what right do we have to be in Israel in the first place? What justifies our fight for the Land? And are there more critical dimensions to winning this war than just military policy? We will explore these questions in Part 3.

The Rebbe speaking at a "*farbrengen*," a chassidic gathering, at the Chabad movement's central synagogue, 770 Eastern Parkway in Brooklyn, New York. The Rebbe delivered hundreds of hours of public talks on Israel's security from this platform. (Velvel Schildkraut, JEM)

The Lubavitcher Rebbe, Rabbi Menachem Mendel Schneerson, became the leader of the Chabad movement in 1950. (JEM)

The Rebbe in a moment of contemplative prayer.
(Chaim B. Halberstam, JEM)

THE REBBE CORRESPONDED and met with the State of Israel's leadership since its inception. Many Israeli leaders would visit the Rebbe when they came to New York.

The Rebbe escorts Israeli President Zalman Shazar through 770 in 1971. They are surrounded by an honor guard from the NYPD. (Velvel Schildkraut, JEM)

The Rebbe with Shazar in his office, in one of the many meetings they would share over the years. (Velvel Schildkraut, JEM)

THE BEGINNING OF 1967 was marked by sharp tension as Arab nations prepared their armies, threatening the destruction of Israel. On June 5, 1967, Israel launched a preemptive strike against its enemies, miraculously defeating their armies and reclaiming large parts of the ancestral Jewish homeland.

Israeli paratroopers at the Western Wall after liberating it in the Six-Day War. The Rebbe described this as a gift from G-d. (David Rubinger, Israeli Government Press Office)

The Israeli army prepares to scale the Golan Heights in the Six-Day War.
(Yosef Levitah, IDF Spokesperson's Unit)

Swedish U.N. peacekeepers evacuating at the onset of the Six-Day War. As the Rebbe noted, the fact that belligerent forces could banish peacekeepers highlighted their ineffectiveness.

IDF 14th Armored Brigade advances in the Sinai Desert during the Six-Day War. (Alex Agur, IDF Spokesperson's Unit)

AFTER THE SIX-DAY WAR, the Israeli government built a system of fortifications along the bank of the Suez Canal called the Bar-Lev Line. As early as 1970, the Rebbe sounded the alarm over the ineffectiveness of reliance on static fortifications. Tragically, on October 6, 1973, the Egyptian army easily overran the fortifications.

Chief of Staff Haim Bar-Lev (center) with commander Mordechai "Motta" Gur (left) during a debriefing following a raid targeting terrorist positions in southern Lebanon, 1970.
(Yaakov Hanani, IDF Spokesperson's Unit)

Bar-Lev Line Fortifications, October 26, 1970.
(IDF Spokesperson's Unit)

The Bar-Lev Line in 1973.
(IDF Spokesperson's Unit)

EGYPT ATTACKED ISRAEL on Yom Kippur 1973. In the early hours of the war, the Egyptian army advanced rapidly, killing and capturing many Jewish soldiers. The Israeli army fought heroically to turn the tide of the war. The Rebbe assessed Israel's failure to strike preemptively as a grave mistake that cost lives, and its subsequent military victory as a miracle.

A woman mourns at the grave of an IDF soldier killed during the Yom Kippur War. (Dan HaDani, National Library of Israel)

Efraim Hamiel, then an IDF officer, prays the morning prayer while wearing tefillin in the Sinai Desert during the Yom Kippur War. (Avi Simchoni, IDF Spokesperson's Unit)

Major General Ariel Sharon (wearing a head bandage) during the Yom Kippur War holds a map of Operation "Abirey Lev" (the IDF's plan for crossing the Suez Canal). To his left are Defense Minister Moshe Dayan and Chief of General Staff Haim Bar-Lev. (IDF Spokesperson's Unit)

IDF Tank crosses the Suez Canal during the Yom Kippur War advancing into Egypt. (IDF Spokesperson's Unit)

IN NOVEMBER 1977, Anwar Sadat, the president of Egypt, flew to Israel in an unprecedented move by a leader of an Arab nation. Sadat addressed the Knesset, offering a peace treaty in return for major territorial concessions. The sitting U.S. President Jimmy Carter and Secretary of State Henry Kissinger rushed to broker a treaty, but the Rebbe warned that concessions would be a bitter mistake for Israel.

Yitzchak Shamir listens with consernation as Sadat addresses the Israeli Knesset. Shamir was one of the few members of the Knesset who voted against participating in the Camp David accords. (Knesset)

Sadat and Menachem Begin speak over dinner in the King David Hotel. Note the Swastika symbols on Sadat's tie. Sadat had been a lifelong admirer of Hitler. (Yaakov Saar, Israeli National Photo Collection)

Sadat confers with U.S. Secretary of State Henry Kissinger. As the Rebbe put it: "Kissinger is America's Secretary of State, not Israel's. He does what he believes to be in America's best interest." (CIA)

The IDF forcibly extracts a Jewish resident of the Jewish town of Yamit as part of the Camp David agreements to cleanse the Sinai of Jewish people. (Beni Tel Or, Israeli Government Press Office)

PRIME MINISTER MENACHEM BEGIN came to consult the Rebbe and receive his blessings before the fateful Camp David Accords in the summer of 1977.

The Rebbe greets Begin outside 770 Eastern Parkway.
(Velvel Schildkraut, JEM)

The Rebbe receives Begin in his office. After a press conference, the Rebbe and Begin met privately for an hour.
(Chaim B. Halberstam, JEM)

THE REBBE EXPRESSED consistent love and admiration for the soldiers of the IDF. In 1976, the Rebbe addressed a delegation of disabled IDF veterans who traveled to America to participate in the paralympics. After the address, the Rebbe individually greeted each disabled soldier, as well as their wives and children. In his talk, the Rebbe noted that the soldiers should be referred to not as "the IDF's wounded," as was their name in IDF bureaucracy, but rather the "IDF's distinguished."

(Yossi Melamed, JEM)

THE REBBE PASSIONATELY encouraged the efforts of the IDF. More broadly, he emphasized the key importance of credible military deterrence and proactive defense.

The Rebbe meets with Lieutenant Colonel Yisrael Yarkoni, an IDF war hero, on January 7, 1973.
(Velvel Schildkraut, JEM)

Rabbi Itzik Neimark, one of the Rebbe's emissaries to Hebron, participates in an IDF battlefield evacuation drill during the 2023 Swords of Iron War. (Rabbi Itzik Neimark)

THE REBBE TAUGHT that the key to developing morale in the IDF is connecting to Jewish tradition and practice.

IDF soldiers dance with Torah scrolls on Simchas Torah in Hebron while held by yeshivah students. (Rabbi Itzik Neimark)

Rabbi Itzik Neimark, one of the Rebbe's emissaries to Hebron, reads the Megillah for a group of soldiers. (Rabbi Itzik Neimark)

A young Chabad boy offers a soldier a Lulav and Esrog on the Sukkos Holiday. (Rabbi Itzik Neimark)

"And all the nations of the earth shall see that the name of G-d is called upon you, and they shall fear you." (Deuteronomy 28:10) A soldier takes a moment to put on tefillin and recite the Shema prayer. (Rabbi Itzik Neimark)

A young soldier studies the daily portion of Chumash while on a break from combat in Gaza during the 2023 Swords of Iron War.

Rabbi Avraham Yaakov Friedman, the Rebbe of Sadigura, at the completion of a Sefer Torah dedicated to Jewish children. An influential Chassidic leader, he enjoyed a close relationship with the Rebbe, and discussed central issues relating to Judaism's perspective on Israel's security with him. (Levi Friedin, JEM)

The Rebbe meets with the Ashkenazi and Sephardi Chief Rabbis of Israel in 1983. (Yossi Melamed, JEM)

Lieutenant Rabbi Uriyah Durani, leads his platoon in a combat training exercise during the Swords of Iron War. (Rabbi Uriyah Durani)

"We must confront them with weapons..." (Code of Jewish Law, sec. 329). Rabbi Mordechai Stambler, a Chabad high school teacher and activist in Samaria, participates in an IDF drill fending off an invasion in an Israeli border town. (Rabbi Mordechai Stambler)

THE REBBE EMPHASIZED the importance of childhood education as the key to cultivating a strong and proud Jewish people who can formidably face opponents. In 1980, the Rebbe inaugurated Tzivos Hashem, "The Army of G-d," an international Jewish youth movement.

"From the mouths of children and infants, you have established might" (Psalms 8:3). The Rebbe placed a strong emphasis on encouraging children's education and spiritual development. Here the Rebbe meets with a young father and two of his children. (Chaim B. Halberstam, JEM)

A young boy in a Tzivos Hashem uniform receives Havdalah wine from the Rebbe in 1981. (Levi Freidin, JEM).

A young girl leads thousands of children at a 1990 Lag BaOmer rally outside 770 in reciting the Twelve Pesukim (Torah verses), with the Tzivos Hashem logo in the foreground. (JEM)

SARAH NACHSHON is a modern legend. Her resoluteness led to the re-establishment of Jewish presence in Hebron in 1975 after it had been interrupted in 1929, following the Hebron riots. In 1980, Nachshon, along with other courageous women, defied the Israeli government's restrictions and retook Beit Hadassah, an abandoned Jewish building in Hebron. This led to an expanded Jewish community in Hebron. The Rebbe pointed to Nachshon as a paradigm of courage, and encouraged others to learn from her.

Sarah Nachshon and her children smile in Beit Hadassah, while a soldier guards the campus. (Nachshon Family)

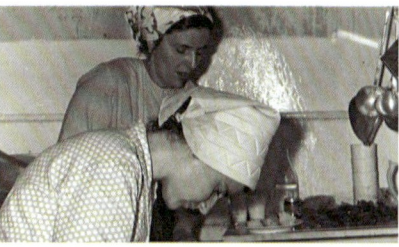

Sarah Nachshon and Miriam Levinger preparing food in Beit Hadassah, c. 1980. (Jewish Community of Hebron)

Baruch and Sarah Nachshon meet with the Rebbe in 1992. (Chaim B. Halberstam, JEM)

An elderly Sarah Nachshon prays at the Cave of the Patriarchs, c. 2011. (Flavio, Hebron Portraits)

THE REBBE'S INFLUENCE was not limited to one political or spiritual camp. He met with leaders from across Israel's political spectrum. The Rebbe corresponded with and met Yitzchak Rabin and Shimon Peres, both of whom would come to symbolize Israel's left wing in the 20th century, and who implemented policies that were at odds with the Rebbe.

Shimon Peres, then a young Member of Knesset, waits to meet the Rebbe in 1966. (JEM)

Yitzchak Rabin, then Israel's Ambasador to the United States sits with Chassidim while waiting to meet with the Rebbe in 1972. Rabin would go on to become Israel's Prime Minister just two yeras later. (JEM)

The Rebbe meets with Ran Adelist, founder of "Peace Now," in 1991. Although the Rebbe vocally criticized Peace Now since its inception in 1978, here, the Rebbe and Adelist meet and discuss Israel's security policies. (JEM)

The Rebbe meets with Elyakim Rubinstein a distinguished Israeli diplomat and jurist, then a member of the Yitzchak Shamir government, in 1990. Rubinstein complained of intensive American pressure on Israel to make concessions. The Rebbe responded: "If one wants to accomplish something with the United States, he must demonstrate unwavering conviction."
(Chaim B. Halberstam, JEM)

The Rebbe predicted that autonomy agreements would lead to Jewish people being expelled from parts of Israel. That prediction tragically came to fruition with the Oslo Accords. Here, an "Area A" sign warns Israelis to avoid the area.

Shlomo Nakdimon, author of First Strike, a history of Israel's attack on Iraq's Osirak Nuclear reactor, presents a copy of his book to the Rebbe in 1990. (Chaim B. Halberstam, JEM)

Ariel Sharon, an Israeli general and war hero turned Prime Minister, enjoyed a longstanding relationship with the Rebbe. (Chaim B. Halberstam, JEM)

The Rebbe meets with
U.S. Senator Joseph Lieberman
and his wife Hadassah in the Fall of 1990.
(Levi Freidin, JEM)

The Rebbe meets with Yosef Ciechanover in 1989. Ciechanover served in a wide variety of political roles from 1957-2016. He and the Rebbe corresponded extensively.
(Chaim B. Halberstam, JEM)

While Prime Minister Yitzchak Shamir never met the Rebbe, the two corresponded and communicated extensively. The Rebbe's influence was responsible for Shamir staying in power. Here, Shamir and Uri Zvi Greenberg, an Israeli poet and politician, join a 1977 Chabad gathering in Israel. (Levi Friedin, JEM)

The Rebbe shares a smile with Benjamin (Bibi) Netanyahu on Sukkos 1987. Netanyahu enjoyed a close relationship with the Rebbe. In 1984 shortly after becoming Israel's Ambassador to the United Nations, the Rebbe told Bibi: 'You will go into a house of lies. Remember that in a hall of perfect darkness, if you light one small candle, its precious light will be seen from afar, by everyone. Your mission is to light a candle for truth and for the Jewish people.' Netanyahu has gone on to become Israel's longest-serving Prime Minister, a role he currently occupies. (Levi Freidin, JEM)

LARGE PORTIONS of the Land of Israel remain unsettled or in perpetual dispute. The Rebbe argued that instead of allowing an uneasy status quo to continue indefinitely, the Israeli government must resolutely support and facilitate settling the entire Land of Israel. He approvingly cited the example of "Tower and Stockade," a project of the Haganah in the 1930s where pioneering youth and families would construct new Jewish towns in a single night.

Residents of Kfar Chabad farming the land in 1950. (Boris Carmi, National Library of Israel)

Israeli pioneers building a "Tower and Stockade" community at Kibbutz Amir in 1939. (Zoltan Kluger, National Library of Israel)

Volunteers on trucks carrying building materials to establish the new "Tower & Stockade" Kibbutz Ein Gev at the Sea of Galilee in 1937. (Zoltan Kluger, National Library of Israel)

The Fogel Family, a young couple and three of their five children were tragically murdered on a Friday night in 2011 in their home in the Samaria town of Itamar, Israel. The Rebbe's strident security policies were intended to prevent such tragedies.
(Alex Kolomoiski)

A distraught Tamar Fogel cries as she attends the funeral of her parents and three younger siblings. (Abir Sultan, Flash 90)

The Rebbe receives Ron Nachman, Mayor of the city of Ariel in Samaria. Nachman apprises the Rebbe of progress in developing the city on April 2, 1989. (Chaim B. Halberstam, JEM)

The Rebbe offers a warm smile during a *farbrengen*. (Levi Friedin, JEM)

The Rebbe takes a reflective moment during a *farbrengen*. (Levi Freidin, JEM)

MAKE PEACE

PART 3
The Soul
of the Struggle

When your child asks you in time to come:
"What is the meaning of these commandments
that the L-rd our G-d commanded you?" tell him:
"G-d took us out of Egypt, to bring us to the Land
that He promised our forefathers. And G-d
commanded us to follow these commandments
for our own good in all times."
DEUTERONOMY 6:20-24

INTRODUCTION
TO PART III

WHAT ARE WE, as Jews, doing in the Land of Israel altogether? How do we justify our presence and ongoing struggle for the Land? Addressing these questions can help us clarify **why** we should adopt the proactive military strategies outlined in Part 2. By establishing our claim to the Land, we uncover a deeper dimension of the conflict. Ultimately, in the battle of competing ideologies and narratives surrounding the Land of Israel, the group that will prevail is the one with the most coherent and compelling narrative, the deepest ideological conviction, and the confidence to unapologetically assert their position. **Part 3** explores each of these critical elements.

Chapter 7 explores two aspects of the Jewish people's claim to the Land of Israel. First, it explores the historical basis for this claim. Then, it delves into various contemporary narratives regarding ownership of the Holy Land, including Islamist perspectives, Western Social Justice arguments, international legal frameworks, and finally, the Torah's narrative. The chapter analyzes how these narratives are used to either support or challenge Jewish claims to the land. Ultimately, it argues that the Torah provides the most stable justification for the Jewish people's claim to the Land of Israel.

Chapter 8 examines the arguments of those who disagree with the claim about the Torah's view advanced in chapter 7. Some argue that Torah values and principles actually require the Jewish people to concede parts of the Land. Others believe the Torah obligates Jews to relinquish the Land entirely. And some hold that even if Jews may live in the Land, the Torah forbids them from defending their presence there.

The chapter carefully analyzes these arguments, which often cite Torah passages or Jewish ethical concepts, demonstrating how they rely on selective readings of Jewish sources and fail to grasp the full complexity of the Torah's teachings on the Jewish relationship to the Land. By presenting a more comprehensive understanding of the Torah's view, the chapter demonstrates how these arguments do not represent the Torah perspective on the Jewish people's connection to the Land and their responsibilities to it.

Chapter 9 explores the crucial role of ideology in conflict dynamics, a factor that is often overlooked. Having established that the Torah provides a solid foundation for the Jewish people's claim to the Land of Israel and the obligation to defend it, this chapter focuses on how ideology determines a group's willingness to persevere in the face of adversity. The Rebbe clearly illustrates this point by examining Israel's Islamist adversaries who draw strength from their deep commitment to religious ideology.

For the Jewish people to triumph in this ongoing struggle, the Rebbe explains that they must embrace a level of commitment and dedication that matches that of their adversaries. If they succumb to the prevalent Western cultural trends that prioritize leisure and entertainment, Israel will find itself ill-equipped to overcome an enemy fueled by a willingness to sacrifice everything for their cause. On the other hand, if Israel and the broader Jewish community wholeheartedly embrace their own ideological wellspring — the Torah and its commandments (*mitzvos*) — they will be able to summon the strength and resilience needed to prevail over their foes and secure lasting peace.

The Jewish Claim
to the Land

G-d appeared to Abraham and said,
"I will give this land to your offspring."

GENESIS 12:7

Remember Abraham, Isaac, and Israel, your servants, to whom
you swore and said, "I shall multiply your offspring like the stars
of the heavens. And this entire Land of which I have spoken, I
shall give your offspring, and they shall inherit it forever."

EXODUS 32:13

GIVEN THAT THE conflict centers around the Jewish people's presence in Israel, let us discuss why the Jews have a right to be there to begin with? Perhaps they should go back to Moscow, Brooklyn, Egypt, Birobidzhan, or wherever they came from. What is their claim to this land?

The History

The Divine Promise

The Jewish people's connection to the Land of Israel begins with the Biblical Patriarch Abraham approximately 4,000 years ago. In the Torah, G-d commands Abraham to leave his homeland and migrate to the Land of Canaan,[1] which He promises to give to Abraham and his descendants as an eternal inheritance.[2] Once Abraham arrives in the Holy Land, G-d tells Abraham:[3]

> Look around from where you are, to the north and south, to the east and west. All the land that you see I will give to you and your offspring forever.

G-d reaffirms this promise declaring:[4]

> I have given this land to your descendants, from the river of Egypt to the great river, the Euphrates — the land of the Kenites, Kenizzites, Kadmonites, Hittites, Perizzites, Rephaites, Amorites, Canaanites, Girgashites, and Jebusites.

G-d further emphasizes the eternal and unconditional nature of this promise in the Covenant Between the Parts (*Bris Bein HaBesarim*), promising:[5]

> I will establish my covenant as an everlasting covenant between Me and you and your descendants after you for the generations to come, to be your G-d and the G-d of your descendants after you. The whole land of Canaan, where you now reside as a foreigner, I will give as an everlasting possession to you and your descendants after you; and I will be their G-d.

This promise is then passed down to Abraham's son Isaac[6] and grandson Jacob, the other patriarchs of the Jewish people. G-d assures Jacob:[7]

> I will give you and your descendants the land on which you are lying. Your descendants will be like the dust of the earth and you will spread out to the west and to the east, to the north and to the south. All peoples on earth will be blessed through you and your offspring.

Settling the Land

After G-d miraculously brings the Jewish people out of slavery in Egypt and leads them through the desert under Moses' guidance, He reiterates His promise to give them the Land of Israel on numerous occasions. As they prepare to enter the land, G-d declares:[8]

> See, I have given you this land. Go in and take possession of the land the L-rd swore He would give to your fathers — to Abraham, Isaac, and Jacob — and to their descendants after them.

Following Moses' passing, Joshua leads the Israelites in conquering the land of Canaan, defeating the Canaanite kings and taking possession of the land.[9] This marked the fulfillment of G-d's longstanding promise to their forefathers, as recorded in the book of Joshua:[10]

> So Joshua took the whole land, according to all that the L-rd had said to Moses; and Joshua gave it as an inheritance to Israel according to their divisions by their tribes.

The book of Joshua concludes[11] by emphasizing the comprehensive nature of this fulfillment:

> The L-rd gave to [the people of] Israel all the land which He had sworn to give to their fathers, and they took possession of it and dwelt in it. The L-rd gave them rest all around, according to all that He had sworn to their fathers. And not a man of all their enemies stood against them; the L-rd delivered all their enemies into their hand. Not a word failed of any good thing which the L-rd had spoken to the house of Israel. All came to pass.

From Joshua's time and on, the Jewish people were predominant population in the Land of Israel, until the Roman conquest 1,500 years later, in the first century CE. In 70 CE, the Romans destroyed the second Jewish Temple in Jerusalem. Despite this tragedy, Jews still remained the dominant population in Israel for several decades.

The Exile and Diaspora

However, things took a turn in 132 CE, when the Jews launched the Bar Kochba revolt against Roman rule. They fought heroically until 135 CE, when the Romans brutally suppressed the rebellion, massacring and exiling a significant portion of the Jewish population. This marked the beginning of the present Jewish exile, known as the Diaspora, which saw Jewish communities dispersed across the Middle East, North Africa, and Europe. The Diaspora's dynamics and persecution caused Jewish people to flee across the world, and hence the existence of large Diaspora communities across the world to this day.

Nonetheless, even during this prolonged exile, a small but continuous Jewish presence has remained in the Land of Israel. Throughout the nearly 2,000 year exile, Jews in the Diaspora have retained a deep connection to the Holy Land and many, driven by this heartfelt yearning, made the difficult journey to resettle in their ancestral homeland.

A map of the Jewish Diaspora:[12]

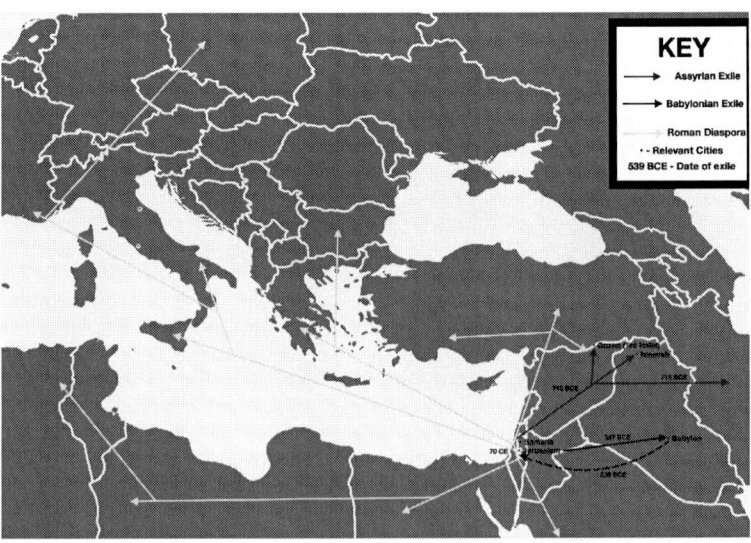

The Land of Israel changed hands repeatedly during this period, with the region remaining sparsely populated. Following the end of Roman rule, the Byzantine Empire took control of the Land until the rise of Islam in the 7th century.[13] From that point onwards, a succession of eight ethnically diverse and warring Muslim empires fought over the land. This era was punctuated by a two-century interlude of Christian Crusader rule. The Muslim Egyptian Mamluks reconquered the Land from the Crusaders in 1260. They retained the Land until 1516 when they were defeated by the Ottoman Turks, who subsequently held the Land for 400 years. During these eras, the Land's political landscape was in a constant state of flux. By the early 20th century, the total population of the Land of Israel had dwindled to levels even lower than those during the Roman period.

The following graph depicts the demographic decline along the Mediterranean coast over time, providing a stark visual representation of the Land's diminished population during the absence of Jewish sovereignty.[14]

Population of the Levant over Time

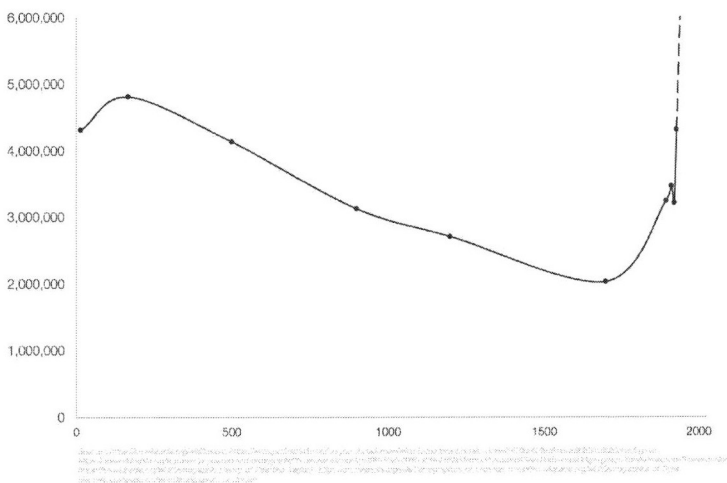

The Great Return

The late 19th century marked a turning point in the history of the Land of Israel, as many Jews began to return to their ancestral homeland. In 1917, amidst the turmoil of World War I, the British Empire conquered the Land of Israel from the Ottoman Empire. The British government subsequently issued the Balfour Declaration in 1917, promising to support the establishment of a Jewish homeland in the region. This commitment was further reinforced in the 1939 Peel White Paper, in which the British pledged to found a Jewish homeland in the Land of Israel.

The Arab street rejected these proposals, responding with violent riots. Although individual Arab landowners continued to sell land to Jewish buyers, the Arab leadership staunchly opposed Jewish presence in the Land. By 1947, the United Kingdom had given up on managing or resolving the escalating conflict. It transferred the responsibility for determining the region's future to the U.N., which, in an attempt to address the competing claims of both peoples, proposed a plan to partition the Land into two separate states, one Jewish and one Arab. The Jews accepted the partition; the Arabs did not. Against this backdrop, Israel declared independence.

In 1948, soon after Israel declared independence, five Arab nations, dissatisfied with the U.N.'s proposed partition plan and maintaining that the entire territory from the river to the sea was Arab land,[15] invaded Israel in an attempt to annihilate the Jewish state. On the eve of the invasion, Azzam Pasha, the General Secretary of the Arab League, ominously predicted:[16]

> It will be a war of elimination and a dangerous massacre which history will record, similar to the Mongol massacre or the wars of the Crusades. We will sweep them [the Jews] into the sea.

Despite overwhelming odds, Israel emerged victorious, defending its territory and reclaiming portions of biblical Israel. In the aftermath of the war, Judea and Samaria came under Jordanian control, while the Gaza Strip fell under Egyptian governance. Notably, neither Jordan nor Egypt attempted to establish a Palestinian state in those regions or extend citizenship to the Arab residents living there.

Nearly two decades later, in the 1967 Six-Day War, Israel once again found itself facing a formidable Arab coalition. In a stunning military campaign, Israel not only repelled the attacking forces, but also reclaimed the Gaza Strip, the Golan Heights, Judea, and Samaria — all parts of biblical Israel. These newly acquired territories included historically significant Jewish cities such as Jerusalem, Hebron, and Shechem (Nablus) – the heartland of Jewish Israel.

Can History Alone Establish Ownership?

With this background information, let us begin to evaluate the most convincing argument for the land's ownership. As Jews, we may know with conviction that this is our land and the land of our ancestors, but how can we articulate it convincingly to the world at large? How can we effectively respond to those who challenge the legitimacy of our presence in our G-d-given homeland?

If we judge by historical precedent alone to determine the rightful owner of the Land of Israel, then the seven Canaanite nations who inhabited the region in ancient times have the strongest claim as they are the earliest documented residents of the region.[17] However, since these nations no longer exist, the Jewish people stand as the next candidate for "nation with the most ancient claim to the land."[18]

Some claim that Muslims should be granted the rights to the land as they held it for an extensive period more recently. However, Israel's Muslim rulers were not a monolith. Although the Land of Israel was under Muslim rule from 635 until 1917 CE, Muslims conquered the region from Christian rulers. Furthermore, Muslim rule over of the Land was not continuous, either politically or ethnically, as a succession of different Muslim groups vied for control, with eight separate Muslim empires governing the Land over the course of approximately 1,000 years.[19] In many instances, contemporary Islamist claims to the land are at variance with facts and history.

For one example of the absurdity of such competing historical claims, let us reflect on the Rebbe's comments on the ongoing conflict over the Cave of the Patriarchs.

Located in the ancient city of Hebron, the Cave of the Patriarchs is a Jewish heritage site where the Jewish Patriarchs and Matriarchs are buried. Jews have prayed at the site for over 3,000 years.[20] However, under Muslim rule, the synagogue that once stood at the site was replaced with a mosque and Jews were barred from entering.[21]

In 1967, when Israel regained control of the Cave of the Patriarchs, the Israeli government chose to allow both Jews and Muslims to pray in the structure built atop the cave. The government apportioned the larger section of the building to Muslim worshippers, while designating a smaller section for Jewish prayer.

Despite this attempt at peaceful coexistence, the area has regularly been marred by violence, as local radicalized Muslims have carried out numerous terror attacks targeting Jewish worshippers. These attacks have persisted from 1968[22] up until the time of this writing.[23]

Reflecting on the ongoing territorial dispute, the Rebbe notes:[24]

> The Muslims argue that the Jewish people cannot take a part of the Patriarchs' Cave since the Muslims have been there for 1,000 years. However, from this argument [of antiquity] itself, the opposite point is demonstrated: Surely, the Muslims cannot take a portion

of the Patriarchs' Cave from the Jews, since the Jewish people's ownership precedes the founding of Islam by over 1,000 years.

Articulating the Jewish Claim to the Land

After all the raw historical facts, the question of who has a legitimate claim to the Land of Israel ultimately comes down to **narrative**. What story do you tell? What story do you live by? And why should others accept it?

In what follows, we'll briefly explore some of the many narratives underlying the competing claims to the land of Israel and the different conclusions drawn from each perspective.[25] After considering these varying viewpoints, we will explain why the Torah's narrative provides the Jewish people with the most solid and enduring claim to the Land, not only for Jewish opinion, but also with respect to the world at large.

A | The Islamist Narrative

According to this set of narratives,[26] the Land of Israel[27] is Islamic land which belongs to what is referred to in Islam as the *Ummah*, or the global community of Muslims.[28] As such, it is part of *Dar al-Islam* (the domain of Islam).[29] Although Islamist doctrine may allow for Jews residing within the boundaries of a Muslim-governed Israel, it precludes Jewish sovereignty over the land. Osama bin Laden encapsulated this narrative in his "Letter to the American People":[30]

> *If you want a real settlement that guarantees your security in your country and safeguards your economy from being depleted in a manner similar to our war of attrition against the Soviet Union, then you have to implement a roadmap that returns the Palestine land to us, all of it, from the sea to the river, it is an Islamic land not subject to being traded or granted to any party.*

This narrative, based on certain interpretations of Islamic texts, dismisses Jewish historical claims and leaves no room for a Jewish state **anywhere** in Israel. According to this narrative, "from the river to the sea, Palestine will be free."[31] This narrative is held by Hamas,[32] Hezbollah,[33] the Islamic Republic of Iran,[34] al-Qaeda, ISIS, and many other Islamist groups in the Middle East and the world over.

Not only does this narrative hold significant appeal for Islamists, but it also resonates with other parties. Those sympathizers may not personally endorse the Islamist narrative, but they do believe in the right of its advocates to fight for their cause. Additionally, in order to appease Islamists and avoid confrontation, certain parties and Western nations are willing to make concessions at Israel's expense.

B | The Western Social Justice Narrative

The Western Social Justice narrative putatively advocates for justice and peace.[35] Its proponents tend to view conflicts as struggles between powerful oppressors and the weak oppressed.[36] They rally to offer their support to the perceived weaker party. In the context of the Israeli-Palestinian conflict, this narrative frequently portrays Israel as the powerful oppressor and the Palestinians as the victims, casting a negative light on Israel's actions. As the Rebbe frames the argument:[37]

> Some argue that it is just and moral to give more land to the Arabs, especially since they are deeply impoverished while the Jews have progressed and flourished.
>
> Others make the further claim that handing over all the territories to the Arabs is an act of justice and righteousness and, as such, the entire Land of Israel should be given to the Arabs.

Despite the inherent contradictions[38] between the Western Social Justice and Islamist narratives, the former can be exploited to serve the latter's interests, weaponizing it against Israel.

The Western Social Justice narrative vocally declaims Judea and Samaria as "occupied territories." Taken to its logical conclusion, this perspective suggests that Israel, due to its perceived power and success, has no legitimate claim to exist. Moreover, the fact that many Jews lived in Europe for most of the past millennium and that the United Kingdom, a historically colonizing nation, granted the Land to the Jewish people, allegedly taints the Jews' possession of Israel with the label of "European Colonialism." Consequently, this narrative ultimately implies that Jews should be forced out of Israel.

This narrative can implicitly reach the conclusion that Israel should not exist by advocating its withdrawal from Judea and Samaria, which would make Israel's security untenable.[39] Alternatively, it can reach this conclusion more explicitly by saying that Israel has no right to exist at all.[40] Either way, it ultimately reaches the same outcome.

In many respects, this social justice narrative can be even more damaging than the Islamist one. This is particularly true given the fact that many Muslim countries have moved on from the "Palestinian issue" as a cause for conflict and are now interested in establishing peaceful relations with Israel, rather than using the Palestinians as a tool to undermine Israel's legitimacy. Nonetheless, the Western Social Justice Warriors, in their various incarnations, refuse to let the issue rest, perpetuating the conflict rather than facilitating a resolution where all parties can live in peace and prosperity.[41]

Foreseeing the popularity of certain arguments in contemporary discussions, the Rebbe astutely noted that this narrative leads to absurd conclusions. He pointed out that if applied consistently, this narrative would require many established nations, particularly the United States,[42] to "close up shop" and relinquish control to the indigenous populations who originally inhabited these lands. This notion, which was debated over half a century ago, has reemerged in recent times, despite its impracticality. As the Rebbe put the point:[43]

If the argument for Israeli sovereignty over the disputed territories is based on the premise that the land rightfully belongs to the Jewish people, having been unjustly seized by foreign invaders who expelled them, then one could argue that Native Americans have a similar claim to Washington D.C. After all, the land on which the nation's capital now stands was once inhabited by indigenous tribes before European colonizers arrived.

However, despite the fact that some Native American activists have indeed made such claims, the notion of displacing the U.S. President from Washington and installing a Native American leader in his place is not given serious consideration.

C | The International Law Narrative

Some argue that Israel's right to exist is based on international law and recognition from the international community. This view highlights the U.N. Resolution that ratified Israel's establishment. However, this narrative is weak. While the U.N. endorsed the State of Israel's formation, it has since called for Israel to return to its precarious pre-1967 borders, a move that would severely compromise Israel's security. Thus, basing Israel's right to exist on the approval of the U.N. and international consensus exposes it to existential threats.

Over the years, the Rebbe often discussed the perils of the Jewish people basing their claim to the Land on international recognition. For instance:[44]

Although one gentile [Balfour] asserted that a Jewish homeland should be established, 140 other gentiles[45] maintain the opposite position! Who determined that this individual [Balfour] possessed the authority to make such a decision? (This assertion is indeed accurate. Balfour does not have the right to determine that the Land of Israel belongs to the Jews. Rather, it is a matter of "G-d granting it to them [the Canaanite nation] when He so desired, and then taking it from them and bestowing it upon us according to His will").

The current difficulties we face stem from the fact that the Jews predicated their claims on the 'Balfour Declaration'!

Moreover:[46]

When Balfour and his contemporaries made their declarations, the validity of their statements was confined to their own lifetimes and tenures as ministers. During that period, they were obligated to honor their commitments. However, they later came to regret their decisions, as the conflicts with the Arabs began to emerge during Balfour's lifetime.

Throughout his years of commentary on the matter, the Rebbe routinely discussed the U.N.'s anti-Israel resolutions. For example, U.N. General Assembly Resolution 3379, adopted on November 10, 1975, which determined that "Zionism is a form of racism and racial discrimination." Moreover, the Rebbe frequently discussed U.N. Resolution 242, the resolution adopted unanimously by the U.N. Security Council on November 22, 1967, in the aftermath of the Six-Day War. It called for the withdrawal of Israeli armed forces from territories occupied in the conflict and the termination of all its territorial claims.[47] Thus, Israel clearly cannot rely on the international community for its claim to legitimacy.

Furthermore, consider these striking facts, well-formulated by a contemporary political commentator, that demonstrate how precarious relying on narratives of international law or acceptance is:[48]

From 2015 to 2022, the U.N. General Assembly adopted resolutions on Israel 140 times, and on countries of the rest of the world put together only 68 times. Similarly, from its creation in 2006 to 2022, the U.N. Human Rights Council adopted 99 resolutions against Israel, but only 61 against Syria, Iran, Russia, and Venezuela combined.

It's difficult to understand this by referencing Israeli behavior.

What you have is a confluence of prejudices coming together at the U.N. There is most obviously the Muslim world taking the side of its co-religionists. Combine that with leftist and third worldist dislike of societies seen as powerful and successful, along with old fashioned antisemitism, and you get an international community that cares more about the sins of Israel than those of everyone else in the world combined.

Imagine that you're living in a town where the police are always arresting you for jaywalking and trying to make sure you get a long prison sentence. At the same time, they ignore the crimes of murderers and rapists. It would be irrational to think "well, if only I stopped jaywalking, they would leave me alone." It's clear that the cops are out to get you, and the jaywalking is just a pretense.

Remarkably, Israel has managed to avoid U.N. sanctions and even possible military interventions, largely thanks to the United States' veto power in the U.N. Security Council. This underscores the precarious nature of relying on the international community and international law to legitimize Israel's existence, as it is vulnerable to shifting global dynamics and political whims.

Setting the U.N. aside, the forces that facilitated the establishment of the State of Israel are relevant only while they are in power. Other global actors, such as the United States, disregard the U.N., which diminishes the impact of its complaints.[49]

D | It Doesn't Matter: Realpolitik

Perhaps having a claim to the Land of Israel simply does not matter. Several Muslim countries, including Egypt, Jordan, the United Arab Emirates, Bahrain, and Morocco have established diplomatic relations with Israel since doing so is in their geopolitical interests. Additionally, other Arab countries cooperate with Israel and have even defended it, as demonstrated by Saudi Arabia's defense against Yemenite Houthi missile attacks during the 2023 conflict.[50] Moreover, when Iran launched its unprecedented missile and drone attack against Israel, Jordan's air force participated in taking down the projectiles, and opened its airspace to Israeli warplanes. Similarly, Saudi Arabia and the United Arab Emirates aided Israel logistically.

Israel serves the United States' interests as a friendly country located in a strategically important region, and serves as a ballast against extremist groups in the Middle East. So, perhaps, as long as Israel serves other countries' political interests, whether or not its existence is technically justified is irrelevant, since other countries would in any case refrain from attacking it and might even defend it. Thus far, it seems that the most stable narrative underlying Israel's right to exist is "might makes right" — it can exist because it serves the interests of powerful nations. But even this is precarious, since nations' interests can evolve over time.[51]

Choosing the Torah's Narrative

We have thus explored several narratives: the first two were ideological and in a certain sense both religious.[52] The third is legal but based on a mix of ethical assumptions and political expediency, and finally one based on realpolitik. The Rebbe explained, however, that there is only one stable narrative that underlies Israel's right to exist: the Torah's narrative.

Surely, when we speak to the world at large, we must present an argument that actually holds its weight. Relying solely on proof from international agreements or U.N. recognition will not grant us the support we wish to achieve from global opinion.[53] As we have demonstrated, other narratives often lead to the conclusion that the Jewish people do not have a rightful claim to the Land of Israel and, as such, it must be returned to those who inhabited it centuries ago.[54] In order to defend our claim to the Land, we must know and speak our truth..

119

Telling it to the World

Rashi's First Teaching

Rashi, the foremost Jewish biblical commentator, observes that the Torah begins with a lengthy historical narrative of the world's creation. He questions why the Torah, a text consisting primarily of laws, begins with a story. He concludes that the narrative teaches a critical lesson: The world belongs to G-d — He created it — and He chooses to give portions of it to whomever He sees fit. As *Rashi* puts it:[55]

> *"He declared the power of His actions to His people, giving them the inheritance of nations."[56] Meaning, if the nations of the world say to the People of Israel, "You are robbers because you conquered the land of the seven Canaanite nations," Israel can respond, "The entire earth belongs to G-d; He created it and gave it to whomever He saw fit. By His will He gave it to them [the nations], and by His will He took it from them and gave it to us [the Jewish people]."*

Understanding Rashi's Context: The Crusades

The Rebbe notes that given *Rashi's* historical context, his comment is all the more striking:[57]

> *Our ability to influence nations lies in our commitment to speaking the truth. We must offer the response that Rashi gave hundreds of years ago. Rashi intended that it be publicized even in his own time, when there were severe decrees against the Jewish people. Although Rashi knew what the Jewish people's enemies were capable of, he nonetheless showed that we can quiet even them with the Torah's teachings.*
>
> *Rashi lived during the time of the Crusades.[58] During that period the Jewish people endured immense suffering akin to the atrocities committed against them in Nazi Germany —*

120

may such horrors never occur again. Yet, despite the adversity faced by Jews, Rashi instructed his primary audience of young children[59] just beginning their Torah studies with the following teaching: When a non-Jew accuses you of being "robbers" who conquered territories, respond by citing the Torah, which states, "He declared the power of His deeds to His people, to give them the inheritance of nations."

Rashi explains to the five-year-old that the importance of being able to articulate his Jewish identity and knowledge extends beyond the confines of his Jewish school or home environment. He emphasizes that the child must be prepared to provide thoughtful responses to anyone who may inquire about his faith, regardless of the setting or the identity of the person asking.

Rashi's Significance in the 20th and 21st Century

Rashi empowered the next generation to find solace and affirmation in the Divine promise of the Promised Land, even in the face of oppression. While *Rashi* made these confident comments in bleak times, G-d has now given the Land back to the Jewish people.[60] As the Rebbe puts it:[61]

G-d gave this Land to the Jewish people in a miraculous manner, as Rashi notes at the beginning of his commentary on the Torah, "He chose to give it to them, and has now chosen to give it to us."

More explicitly:[62]

G-d performed an open miracle, to the extent that every Jew, and even the nations of the world, say, "G-d's hand has done this."[63] [The miracle being referenced is] the Jewish people's victory in the Six-Day War where, in a completely supernatural manner, G-d returned the Jewish people's eternal inheritance not just in a spiritual sense, but in a physical one [as well]. G-d took the Chosen Land, which had been in the possession of idolaters, and gave it to the Chosen people.

As members of the Jewish community, we need to ask ourselves: What are we doing here? The answer lies in the fact that G-d promised us the Land in the Torah and has miraculously returned it to us now. This is the only reliable foundation for our claim to the Land. As the Rebbe teaches:[64]

G-d told Abraham at the Covenant Between the Parts (Bris Bein HaBesarim) [65] *that his descendants would inherit the Land [of Israel]. G-d later reaffirmed this promise to Abraham's son Isaac*[66] *and grandson Jacob.*[67] *When their descendants returned to the Land under Joshua's leadership, the Jewish people conquered it, fulfilling G-d's promise and establishing it as their eternal inheritance.*

The Land of Israel Vs. The State of Israel

More than Semantics

Given that the Torah's narrative is the most stable basis for the Jewish claim to the Land, the Rebbe emphasizes the importance of referring to Israel as the "Land of Israel" not merely the "State of Israel." This distinction is not merely semantic; it aligns with the biblical narrative[68] and underscores that our claim to the Land is rooted in an **ancient, Divine promise** rather than in **modern nationalism**.[69] We must confidently assert our claim to the Land as truth, without any qualifications and with childlike sincerity.[70]

It is critical to view our claim to the Land of Israel through the Torah's lens. As the Rebbe put it in a 1969 letter to Geulah Cohen:[71]

Some, including myself, do not use the term, "The State of Israel." This is because: The Land of Canaan was given as an inheritance to the People of Israel starting from the Covenant Between the Parts with Abraham our forefather. In place of the name "Land of Canaan," the name "Land of Israel" was established, a designation lasting several thousand years. This is how the Land is referred to in the Torah and in the common parlance of the Jewish people from young to old. Such matters are not subject to a vote or a majority decision that can change from time to time, which could lead to unforeseen negative consequences.

Viewing the Jewish people's claim to Israel through a nationalist lens weakens their claim, as it indicates that Israel is a new entity, founded only in 1948. The Rebbe emphasizes this point, stating:

Moreover, changing this name weakens the People of Israel's claim to ownership of the Land of Israel, including even the limited area that was liberated in the year 5708 [1948], since the new name gives it a character of novelty, innovated in 5708. Consequently, the claim of ownership over the Land of Israel also begins then. This is the opposite of the Torah's stance and Rashi's teaching at the beginning of his commentary on the Torah.

The Rebbe emphasizes the significance of *Rashi's* commentary, noting that Jewish children customarily begin studying Scripture at the age of five:

And I emphasize this, for it has been the custom of our people for generations that a five-year-old begins [studying] Scripture, meaning that Rashi's words are addressed to the Children of Israel starting from the age of five years old.

Rashi's commentary provides a powerful response to those who challenge the Jewish people's right to the Land of Israel:

If the nations of the world say to Israel, "You are robbers for conquering the lands of the seven nations," the Children of Israel will answer, "The entire earth belongs to the Holy One, blessed be He; He gave it to them by His will and He took it from them by His will and gave it to us."

The Rebbe notes that this ancient response, rooted in the teachings of the Torah, remains the most effective answer to the challenges posed by other nations in contemporary times:

> *Surely you know that this was indeed the claim of quite a few nations of the world in our era as well, and I did not find a single successful response to that claim other than the most ancient traditional response in the words of our Sages which we mentioned.*

The Holy Land

The biblical narrative not only clarifies our claim to the Land for ourselves, but also helps others understand and acknowledge it. For those who hold the Bible in high regard, either because of their faith or as a key aspect of cultural heritage,[72] the assertion that the Land of Israel historically belongs to the Jewish people is particularly compelling.[73]

The Bible's influence is evident in the global recognition of Israel as the "Holy Land,"[74] a name tracing back to the Bible, which describes it as a land that receives special attention from G-d:[75] "a Land upon which the L-rd, your G-d's, eyes are upon from the year's beginning until [the] year's end." This argument is particularly persuasive for an American audience, given the country's foundation on Biblical values[76] and a history of Bible-affirming presidents. The Rebbe observed that even Jimmy Carter, a U.S. president known for pressing Israel to make concessions, taught Sunday school Bible classes, highlighting the deep-rooted Biblical influence within American culture.[77]

Relevant Even to Those Who Are Not Bible Believers

The Rebbe contends that regardless of whether individuals adhere to the Bible or acknowledge it as part of their cultural legacy, it remains essential for Jews to confidently assert their claim to the Land of Israel. This claim is not based on international law or the aftermath of the Holocaust,[78] but on the Biblical promise. When

Jews genuinely believe in and assert this claim, it commands respect and support, independently of external validation.

The Rebbe reinforces this argument with a story from the Talmud about Geviha ben Pesisa, an ancient Jewish lay-person.[79] The story illustrates how asserting the Jewish claim to the Land of Israel based on the biblical narrative can be effective even when engaging with those who do not share the same faith. When several nations asserted their rights to the Land of Israel in front of Alexander the Great, Geviha, representing the Jewish people, successfully defended their claim using Torah verses. Although Alexander, as a pagan, did not regard the Bible as G-d's ultimate word, he nevertheless respected Geviha's conviction and clarity. This illustrates the Rebbe's point that when a Jew truly believes in the Torah and proudly declares its teachings, it can deeply resonate even with those who do not share the same faith, influencing global decision-makers and deterring those who challenge the Jewish claim. By speaking the Torah's truth, Geviha played a crucial role in affirming the Jewish claim to the Land.[80] His example serves as a powerful reminder to contemporary Jews that they must boldly assert their G-d-given right to the land, even in the face of international skepticism.

The strength of basing our claim on the Torah is that it is irrefutable.[81] If we ground our claim solely on the fact that G-d gave us the Land, as stated in the Torah, no one can undermine it.[82] This is encapsulated in the Torah's description of the Jewish people as "You are children of the L-rd, your G-d,"[83] indicating that, like children who inherit their parents' assets, the Jewish people are the rightful heirs to that which G-d has bestowed upon them.[84]

Adhering to the Torah's narrative also undermines the "Land for Peace" argument. According to this argument, Israel is just another nation-state, subject to typical diplomatic rules, which includes the possibility of ceding land. However, recognizing Israel as the Holy Land, Divinely bestowed upon the Jewish people, nullifies any governmental authority to negotiate away this ancestral heritage. This shifts the discourse from political bargaining to recognizing a historical and spiritual inheritance that transcends conventional statecraft.[85]

The Rebbe in His Own Words

Distilling the Biblical Narrative

The Rebbe succinctly distills the Torah's narrative and its implications in a letter to a member of the *B'nai B'rith Messenger* editorial staff:[86]

> *Following Jewish custom, I will begin with a prefatory remark apropos the name of your publication—"B'nai B'rith Messenger." As the name implies, its purpose is to convey a message to its readers and through them to their families and friends, who are B'nai B'rith, "Children of the Covenant." The reference is, of course, to the covenant between G-d and His people, beginning with the first Jew, our father Abraham. According to this covenant, G-d assured Abraham,[87] "Unto your seed I have given this land. . ." This G-d reaffirmed again before the birth of Isaac:[88] "And I will establish their generations for an everlasting covenant . . . and I will give unto you, and to your seed after you, the land of your sojourn, all the land of Canaan, for an everlasting possession."*

> *Since the Bible is held sacred not only by Jews but also by Christians and Muslims, no one can honestly question the Jews' title to the Land of Israel. Indeed, in accordance with this covenant, G-d led our people out of Egyptian bondage into the Promised Land, and our people took possession of it and, since the time of King David, made Jerusalem the eternal capital of their land, long before any of the present-day world capitals came into being. With a brief interlude of 70 years — the Babylonian exile — our people dwelt in the Land of Israel for 1,340 years ([from] 2488—3828),[89] and even after G-d saw fit to send our people into the present exile and dispersion, there has always, up to the present day, been a Jewish presence and yishuv [settlement] in our land, while all Jews*

throughout the Diaspora have longed and prayed (three times daily) for our return to our homeland and everlasting possession — "May our eyes behold Your return to Zion in mercy."[90]

Yet, of late, our title to Eretz Yisrael has been challenged by the very nations who, by force of arms, repeatedly sought to rob us of our everlasting possession....

Jews Must Proudly Express Their Divine Right to the Land

And here is where my request comes in. I do not know what you and the editor and publisher of the B.B.M. [B'nai B'rith Messenger] think as individuals, about the situation outlined above; nor am I adequately familiar with the position which the B.B.M. has advocated in the past. I do believe, however, that a publication that carries the banner of B'nai B'rith, and which is now in its 84th year, has the primary obligation to carry the message of the Divine covenant to its numerous readers, many of whom are leading personalities in various Jewish communities — the message of the Torah, Torat Chaim [the Torah of life] and Torat Emet [the Torah of truth], namely: that Eretz Yisrael is ours by Divine covenant, as indeed is recognized by all who believe in the sanctity of the Bible; and the "facts of life" and "truth" are that Jews are not "occupiers" or "aggressors" in their homeland, but that what has passed into our hands is only a restitution of what is rightfully ours by Divine will and grace, not by the "false grace" of the United Nations.

We cannot afford to be generous and give away any part of our tiny land in response to the threat of force, since retaining every last inch of it is a matter of vital security for its three and a half million Jews, men, women and children, as well as for our Jewish people as a whole.

Influencing the Home Front

Despite the fact that a Torah based claim will, all things considered, be more effective when addressing hostile audiences, the Rebbe expresses skepticism that any argument will move Israel's most staunch opponents. Instead, he considers the long term impact of narrative on the morale of Jewish youth.[91]

> I do not deceive myself in thinking that arguments of justice and fairness will win over the U.N., the Vatican, etc. The most influential factor [for the Jewish people to prevail] is the morale of the youth (including the IDF), the students in the U.S. (and surely also other countries).[92] The approach that this is about "the State of Israel that was founded with the approval of the U.N. in the year 5708" (and not about the Children of Israel who returned to the Land of Israel, the land of their inheritance, from the time of Joshua, — an unending inheritance, even if it was forcibly taken) harms the vital interests of even the State of Israel to the point that it led to deaths. This is what compelled me to speak about these matters, which others should have sounded the alarm about.

The Rebbe emphasized that educating young Jews to see their connection to the Land of Israel as a G-d-given heritage stretching back three millennia would inspire them to fight for it more passionately than if their claim was based solely on modern events like the 1947 U.N. declaration and 1948 War of Independence. Grounding Israel's significance in ancient Jewish history and tradition is key to instilling an enduring commitment to the Land in the next generation.[93]

Summary

In this chapter, we presented a comprehensive analysis of the Jewish historical and spiritual connection to the Land of Israel. We evaluated and challenged various contemporary narratives, including those of Islamists, proponents of Western Social Justice, and the international community. We argued that the Torah's narrative, grounded in Divine promise and historical continuity, is the most stable and legitimate basis for the Jewish claim to Israel. This perspective not only reaffirms the Jewish right to the Land, but also provides a moral and spiritual framework for understanding Israel's existence and defending its legitimacy in the face of global scrutiny and political challenges.

However, there are some Jewish groups who offer a different perspective on what the Torah says regarding the Land of Israel. These groups offer Torah-based arguments for territorial concessions of varying degrees. In the following chapter, we will examine these alternative arguments in detail and then dismantle them.

Correcting Jewish Misconceptions of the Claim to the Land

Justice, Justice, shall you pursue; in order that you live and inherit the Land that the L-rd, your G-d, is giving you.

DEUTERONOMY 16:20

I have made you swear, daughters of Jerusalem... that you not stir up or awaken the love, until the time is right.

SONG OF SONGS 2:7, 3:4, 8:5

Peace, Justice, and Integrity: Investigating Jewish Social Justice

IN THE PREVIOUS CHAPTER, we explored the Torah's narrative and its clear support for the Jewish people's claim to the Land of Israel. However, some argue that Jewish values and Torah teachings actually demand ceding parts or all of the Land of Israel. These arguments often appeal to Jews who are not committed to the Torah as a whole, but value key Torah principles such as peace and justice. These Jews are often attracted to some form of the Western Social Justice narrative due to its apparent emphasis on these virtues.

Many of these Jews are individual activists, while others have founded or joined organizations based on the premises of "peace" and "justice" which advocate failed and dangerous policies such as Land for Peace, unilateral disengagement, unconditional ceasefires, and the like. The "peace" and "justice" in question usually entail Israeli withdrawal from Judea and Samaria, a generally permissive attitude towards Arab violence, attempts to delegitimize Israel's defense forces and documenting its "war-crimes" or "apartheid policies," and even advocating dismantling the Jewish state.

The key progenitor of such organizations[1] is "Peace Now," founded in 1978 on the very laudable premise of achieving peace **now**, and not just at some point in the distant future.[2] Yet, despite its noble ambitions, it has advocated many misguided policies based on the premises of the Western Social Justice narrative. Just three months after Peace Now launched, The Rebbe addressed the organization in a public talk:[3]

> An organization known as "Peace Now" has recently been established with great publicity. The members of this movement argue that the only way to [achieve] peace is to give the Arabs everything they demand!

Pragmatic Arguments for Peace Now

Within the broader group of Jewish organizations that promote conceding parts of the Land of Israel, there are various positions. More conservative organizations — such as Peace Now — tend to voice pragmatic arguments for territorial concessions, such as the need for security, demographic concerns, or international pressure. More radical groups openly advocate for a complete end to Israel as a Jewish homeland.

To better understand the perspective of the more conservative concessionary rhetoric, it is instructive to examine an exchange between the Rebbe and Ran Adelist,[4] a founder of Peace Now. This exchange, which took place in 1990, highlights the pragmatic arguments often used by such organizations to justify territorial concessions:[5]

> Ran Adelist: *I would really like to know if the Rebbe is still of the opinion that we need to keep all the territories — namely, Judea, Samaria, and Gaza — regardless of public opinion.*
>
> The Rebbe: *If I can influence you, then I hope you will accept this premise: All of the Land of Israel belongs to the People of Israel, and anyone who gives a part of it to someone else is robbing the People of Israel.*
>
> Adelist: *Even if that leads to a war against the world?!*
>
> The Rebbe: *Those who want to fight against the People of Israel don't need a specific reason; they want to harm Israel regardless of how Israel behaves. I come from Russia, where there were always blood libels against Jews, not because the Jews were guilty, but because the gentiles sought to libel and harm [the People of] Israel.*
>
> Adelist: *Is it not possible that the gentiles will ever make peace with us?*
>
> The Rebbe: *It doesn't matter what you or I do. If they have the ability [to harm us], you and I cannot prevent them. Only the Holy One, blessed be He, can protect us. Moreover, the Holy One, blessed be He, doesn't need my encouragement to protect Israel because every Jew, wherever he is, and all the more so in the Land of Israel, is G-d's only son. Do not waste time looking for reasons to give away parts of the Land of Israel.*

In this exchange, Adelist suggests to the Rebbe that on pragmatic grounds Israel should relinquish territories so that it will not be harmed by the international community. The Rebbe responded that concessions would not help, arguing that hatred towards the Jewish people has been a persistent historical phenomenon with deep-rooted causes that go beyond any specific Jewish policies or actions.[6]

Fundamental Arguments for Peace Now:
Peace and Justice as Core Values

Peace Now and its ideological descendants' arguments tend to be more **moral** than pragmatic, based on the premises that "peace" and "justice" are fundamental values.[7] As the Rebbe framed it:[8]

> In addition to these pragmatic arguments, they also proclaim "Peace Now!" Their claims have the force of the value of peace, which is so fundamental that "the entire Torah was given to make peace in the world."[9] Moreover, they demand not just peace, but "peace **now**" — such that **now** there will be "peace upon Israel."[10]

Purportedly, not only will concessions satisfy the Torah value of "peace," but they will also satisfy the Torah value of "justice":[11]

> Furthermore, they shout that handing over all the territories to the Arabs is an act of **justice** and **integrity**, and consequently, all the territories of the land of Israel should be given to the Arabs.

Such policies however, are destructive:

> "Peace Now" is bringing [destruction] upon the Jews and upon the Land of Israel. They are "destroyers and demolishers"[12] of the Jewish people and of the land of Israel, may the Merciful One save us.

The Rebbe adds that the fact that their policy is destructive to Israel is evident from the fact that their supporters are interested in destroying Israel as a Jewish state:

> (The fact that their policy is destructive is demonstrated by the fact that the communists and the Arabs joined them [in their activism].)

What further belies the claims of Peace Now is that while peace is a fundamental Torah value, peace can only be had with a viable partner. The history of terrorism since the Six-Day War demonstrates that concessions to the Arabs have only encouraged further violence. As the Rebbe expressed it:[13]

They shout "Peace Now" and, indeed, there is nothing greater than peace, yet — "'There is no peace,' says the L-rd, 'for the wicked.'"[14] The intentions of the PLO are known. They confirmed these intentions again at a recent gathering — they intend to expel all the Jews from the entire land of Israel!

This is no secret — they say it openly, it has been printed everywhere; everyone knows about it. This is nothing new — they [the various Arab movements] have been proclaiming this for 32 years (since 1948)! So, it is clear that any agreement made with them will not lead to peace!

Even when concessions are made, on condition that they sign a piece of paper that they are making peace for now — as "Peace Now" wants — not only does this not help, but instead endangers the Jews [by creating an illusion of peace that will be exploited in the future].

Some people err, thinking that terrorism began recently. This is a lie! Terrorism has unfortunately been going on every month since the Six-Day War. This is because the Arabs were emboldened when they realized that the Jews were afraid and had sent emissaries [saying] that they wanted to concede [territory]!

And so it went: Every time the Jews conquered something from the Arabs, they pursued the gentiles to return what they conquered, all in the name of peace, justice, and integrity.

Each time, this attitude [further] empowered [the local] Arabs. [This continued] until it reached the point that they killed a Jew, a yeshivah student, in Hebron, in the center of the city![15]

The Rebbe asserts that the approach of conceding to the Arabs in exchange for a piece of paper promising peace has led to a "real danger to the Jews and to the land of Israel":

The aforementioned evidence makes it clear that "Peace Now" endangers the Jewish people and the Land of Israel. Nonetheless, they continue to demand conceding more territories to the Arabs in exchange for a piece of paper on which it is written that they are making peace.

We can see where the approach of concession to the Arabs leads. Even if [Peace Now and elements of the Israeli government and population] delude themselves that in the meantime they will have "peace now" — this is meaningless. It is obvious that [the policies they advocate] lead in an undesirable direction, since the Arabs' intention is not peace, but to expel all the Jews from the Land of Israel!

Thus, the Rebbe argues that the Peace Now's approach of concessions to Israel's enemies, despite their stated intentions and history of terrorism, is misguided and dangerous. He maintains that such concessions will not lead to lasting peace or justice but will instead harm the Jewish people and the Land of Israel.

Similarly, the Rebbe argues that the hostile Arabs' demands and actions demonstrate that they do not truly want peace:[16]

Their arguments are senseless. There is no one with whom to make peace, because they do not want peace! The Arabs say explicitly that they want the Old City of Jerusalem, Shechem (Nablus), Hebron, and more! Yet, Jews insist, "Peace Now" — that the only way to achieve peace is by giving them everything they demand.

Taking a More Holistic Torah Perspective

The Rebbe asserts that the response to the regrettable conclusions drawn based on this mix of pragmatic concerns and appeal to the Torah values of "peace," "justice," and "integrity" is to take a holistic approach to the Torah's value as opposed to a piecemeal one:[17]

Some might conclude that "the people who dwell in the land are strong"[18] and thus we must concede. Others might make the ethical claim that territories should be given to the Arabs from

136

the perspective of justice and integrity. However, the authentic Jewish approach is to turn to the eternal wisdom of the Torah and the Code of Jewish Law for guidance.

The Code of Jewish Law was given by the Holy One, blessed be He, who governs the world and knows all the calculations of justice and integrity. Moreover, He is the essence of goodness, and "the nature of good is to do good."[19] Therefore, by following the path of the Code of Jewish Law, there will undoubtedly be true good for all the people of the world.

The Rebbe further criticizes those who claim that the Torah demands concessions at the expense of Jewish lives:[20]

They say that concessions are the justice and integrity that the Torah demands of every Jew. They shout that this is the Torah's teaching! When others inquire, "How can you make concessions — doing so will put Jewish lives at stake?!" They respond that it is forbidden to diverge from the path of justice and integrity.

The Rebbe dismantles this argument made in the Torah's name:

*We need not rely on their wisdom. One merely needs to open the Code of Jewish Law, which rules that even when one only **hears** that enemies are approaching and even when they are coming for mere straw and stubble — one must confront them with weapons, so that they will not capture the city, making the entire land more vulnerable.*

Whose "Peace" and "Justice"?

The Rebbe explains that Peace Now and similar organizations ultimately derive their approach from prevailing cultural narratives over native Jewish values, recasting Jewish values to align with the dominant culture. The Rebbe notes that this is not a new phenomenon, but instead has been a recurring pattern across Jewish history. In any given time period, there have been conflicts between Jews who remained faithful to native Jewish tradition and Jews who lacked confidence in their tradition, preferring to imitate the dominant local culture.[21] As the Rebbe put it:[22]

> *Throughout Jewish history, there have always, broadly speaking, been two sorts of Jews. Some did everything to fit into the dominant culture, while others followed the Torah path. While many in the pacifist camp claim to fight for Jewish values, when we study their position more deeply, we see that it just follows the prevailing cultural narrative. In this respect, they are like the Hellenizing Jews[23] in the Chanukah story. The Hellenizers had no conviction and constantly gave in to all of the dominant culture's demands. In contrast, Jews who held strong to their convictions ultimately succeeded and garnered respect from the non-Jews.*

The Antidote: Robust Jewish Education

Peace Now, as well as other organizations or individuals who recommend ceding the Land of Israel, have adopted values other than the Torah's. Their arguments are not logically based, but instead depend on narratives and values. Had they been educated according to the Torah's teachings, or if they can be educated to receive the Torah's teachings now, then they would fundamentally accept the Jewish people's right to the Land. As the Rebbe explains:[24]

> *Some Jews wonder: "Why should we fight for the Land of Israel? We have no genuine right to it. Our presence in the land is unjust. The Arabs were here first; we expelled them from the Land." Based on this reasoning, these Jews conclude that we should leave Israel, move to other lands, and enjoy a pleasant life there.*
>
> *This line of thinking comes from imbibing foreign ideologies. People who think this way have usually never heard of the concept of the "sanctity of the Land of Israel." The Land of Israel does not belong to the Jews because of the Balfour Declaration or the U.N. Partition Plan and its promise of a national homeland for the Jews.*

*Our claim to the Land of Israel derives **only** from the fact that the One G-d, Who gave the one Torah to His one nation, gave the Land to us. The Land of Israel is the only place where a Jew can fulfill and study the Torah in its full form.*

Had we taught this truth to these Jews, then their sons and daughters would not ask:

"Why did you settle Arab lands?"

"Why did you displace the Arabs?"

"Why are we fighting wars when we could just give all the Land away to the Arabs and relocate to a peaceful place in some other land, where we can 'be like all the other nations?'"[25]

One who has had a traditional Jewish education would not ask these questions. Such education makes one clearly recognize that this is the Land that G-d gave to Abraham, Isaac, Jacob, and their descendants for all time. It belongs only to the Jewish people.

If we were to explain this point to assimilated Jews, their arguments would fall away and they would cease to aid the enemies of the Jewish people.

If more Jews come to this recognition, they will also be able to share it with the world at large.

Without the Torah, the Jews Will Ultimately Leave Israel

The Rebbe argues that any narrative not based in the Torah's teachings will ultimately lead Jews to conclude that they should leave the Land of Israel. As he shared:[26]

Someone once asked me, "How can you justify your claim — which you even want stated at the U.N. — that the Land of Israel belongs to the Jewish people because G-d said to our forefather Jacob, 'You shall spread out to the west, the east, the north, and the south,' and, 'I will give it to you and your descendants'?[27] This happened when Jacob was on his way to Haran, exhausted from his journey, and he lay down to sleep. Are you saying that just because Jacob had a dream, the Land of Israel belongs to the Jewish people?"

I replied, "Prophecy occurs during sleep. Jacob, even in his sleep, dreamed of G-d."

The gentiles understand that the Land of Israel belongs to the Jews. Now, it remains only to convince the Jews themselves. The gentiles know that the Arabs' connection to the Land of Israel only began when they arrived a few hundred years ago. The Jews' connection to the Land of Israel began at the time the Torah was given, and even before that, when the Holy One, blessed be He, the G-d of Abraham, Isaac, and Jacob, gave the Land to the Jews. So, even a gentile knows that the Land of Israel belongs to the Jews and that Jacob's dream is the true reality.

Yet the Jew claims to not believe this! Well, then, what are you doing in the Land of Israel? Go abroad! You'll be better off there. Indeed, there are many 'yordim' [those who leave Israel] who abandon the Land of Israel, most of whom do not believe [in the Torah's assertion of the Jewish right to the Land]."

The Rebbe argues that the Torah's narrative alone provides stable ground for the Jewish claim to the Land of Israel. Without a thoroughgoing commitment to the Torah narrative, even some among the Jewish people will reach the conclusion that they should leave the Land.

Divinely Mandated Exile

We have explored one popular set of Jewish arguments, based on the Torah values of "peace" and "justice," which maintains that we should make concessions ranging from giving away parts of Israel to relinquishing it entirely. While at first glance, these sentiments are laudable, careful inspection shows that they are pragmatically dangerous and that they do not cohere with the Torah's view. Notably, the arguments founded on "peace" and "justice" most often come from Jews who are assimilating into the prevailing Western culture.

Yet there is another set of arguments often advanced in the Torah's name which opposes Jewish self-defense and is in favor of concessions. Unlike the first cluster of claims we explored, this second group of arguments tends to be championed by Jews who are deeply committed to Torah study and practice. However, a careful analysis of Torah sources and the current reality reveals that these concepts are being misapplied in a way that endangers Jewish lives and contravenes Jewish law.

Briefly, the arguments against Jewish self-defense, which are often extended to the point of saying that Jews should altogether relinquish the Land of Israel, are based on the following two Talmudic passages:

A | The Three Oaths

The Talmud[28] teaches that G-d issued three oaths concerning the Jewish people and their relationship with the nations of the world:[29]

1) The Jewish people are not to ascend to the Land of Israel "as a wall" — namely forcefully and en masse.[30]

2) The Jewish people are not to rebel against the nations.

3) The nations are not to subjugate the Jews excessively.

Some cite the first two oaths as proof that the Jewish people may not defend themselves and must acquiesce to all demands the non-Jewish nations make, be they demands of the West, the Muslim world, or the Palestinians. They argue that any form of Jewish self-defense would constitute a violation of these oaths.

Others go further, claiming that the Jewish people's presence in the Land of Israel is altogether illegitimate given that they came to Israel "by force." Instead, the Jewish people must wait for the arrival of *Mashiach*, when G-d will miraculously redeem them and give them the Land; until then, they are not permitted to establish a sovereign state in the Land of Israel.

B | Do Not Provoke the Nations

Another argument advanced against Israel's right to self-defense is the Talmudic teaching,[31] "Do not provoke a small gentile." Some interpret this to mean that the Jewish people may not assert their rights to the Land or defend themselves, since doing so will provoke "the small gentile" (the Palestinains and other less powerful countries, such as the many powerless and war torn countries that routinely vote against Israel in the U.N.). They argue that such actions will also provoke "the great gentile" (the United States and other dominant world powers) who enjoins Israel to make territorial concessions and restrain or withhold defensive measures.

The Rebbe's Response

While some loudly proclaim these two Talmudic teachings to present a valid argument against Israel's right to exist or to defend itself,[32] the Rebbe offered a number of arguments refuting the relevance of these teachings to contemporary policy. In the following sections, we will delve into the Rebbe's arguments and explore how to properly understand these Talmudic teachings.

A | *Pikuach Nefesh* Overrides These Concerns

The Rebbe notes that both the "Three Oaths" and the admonition against provoking the gentiles are irrelevant given the concern of *pikuach nefesh* (saving lives). Neither of these arguments are cited in the Code of Jewish Law. The Three Oaths are mentioned in a non-halachically binding *Midrash* — and a matter of debate at that — while the statement against provoking the gentiles is a piece of Talmudic advice.

In contrast, the Talmud and Code of Jewish Law clearly rule that Jews living in any location have an obligation to defend themselves when their lives are threatened. Thus, the Rebbe maintains that while one could have hypothetically made the argument of the Three Oaths to discourage a concerted effort by Jews to leave the Diaspora and settle in Israel, such arguments became irrelevant once historical circumstances forced a sizable Jewish community to move to Israel.[33]

The Rebbe strongly emphasizes this point in his teachings:[34]

> There is no reasoning with those who advocate concessions — thus, we should pay them no heed. Rather, we must protest against their claim and clearly state that theirs is not the Torah view! This view is contrary to the clear ruling in the Code of Jewish Law that one must take up arms and not allow them [enemies] to approach a city near the border, even if it is outside the Land of Israel. This has no connection at all to the dicta they invoked — not to the prohibition of "lo techanem,"[35] "do not provoke a small gentile," and not to [the matter of] the Three Oaths. Rather, there is only one, essential factor, that of saving many Jewish lives [pikuach nefesh].

The Rebbe repeats this view, underscoring the paramount importance of *pikuach nefesh* and calling on people to stop mixing confounding variables into their discussions of the Jewish people's presence in the Land of Israel:[36]

> I keep reiterating: There are those who are convinced that the issue of defending the land is connected to the "Three Oaths," "Zionism," and the "coming of Mashiach." So it must be emphasized: Defending the land has absolutely no connection to these concepts!... This is a matter of pikuach nefesh, plain and simple!

B | Examining these Arguments Through the Lens of 20th-Century History

The Rebbe dismantles the relevance of the principles of the Three Oaths and "do not provoke" by providing historical context for the Jewish people's presence in Israel.

The Rebbe begins his analysis by referencing the Holocaust. He notes that the argument to not provoke the nations was applied before the founding of the contemporary State of Israel. During the Holocaust, when it became evident that the Nazi regime was slaughtering the Jewish people in Europe, some Jews attempted to lobby the U.S. government to bomb the train tracks that the Nazis were using to transport European Jews to the concentration camps. However, other Jews rejected this idea on the ground that doing so would "provoke the gentiles." As the Rebbe puts it:[37]

> We cannot, G-d forbid, repeat the mistakes of the past, when, out of fear of provoking Washington, the terrible decrees were allowed to happen. There were Jews [at the time] who said, "We must be silent; we must not start up with Roosevelt." When others responded, "Jews are in danger! Trains are traveling to concentration camps," those who said not to engage the government retorted, "Do not provoke a small gentile!"[38]

> This timidity contributed to the fact that the United States ultimately did not bomb the railroad tracks leading to the camps, as demonstrated by reliable historical documents. The United States had the opportunity to take action, and yet some Jews mistakenly said that we could not contend with Washington. So no action was taken.

> Now, some of the Jewish leadership and their disciples who have influence over policy in the Land of Israel are not ashamed to use their influence in the same misguided way. They urge Israel not to defend itself and promote U.S. foreign policies that leave Israel vulnerable to harm.

No matter how many [repentive] fasts they undertake,[39] they cannot atone for the harm they caused by insisting that no one should say a word against Washington. Not only does this approach not help, but it manifests the verse, "your destroyers and demolishers will come from within you."[40]

The Rebbe argues that the historical record demonstrates the tragic consequences of misapplying the teaching of "do not provoke a gentile." This approach can, and has, led to countless Jewish deaths, which is an unforgivable sin and a violation of the paramount principle of *pikuach nefesh*.

The principle of *pikuach nefesh* played a crucial role in shaping the Jewish people's relationship with Israel throughout the 20th century, justifying both Jews moving to Israel and the subsequent imperative to remain and defend the land.

In the early 20th century, as Europe became increasingly unstable and war-torn, many Jews sought refuge in the Land of Israel. The primary motivation for this wave of *aliyah* (immigration to Israel) was not nationalist ideology, but rather the urgent need to escape persecution and mortal danger.

Rabbi Shalom Wolpo,[41] one of the key expositors of the Rebbe's teachings on Israel's security, clarifies the distinction between establishing a Jewish state for nationalist purposes and immigrating to Israel to save lives:[42]

The approach of establishing a state for the purpose of Jewish nationalism, [to institute] a Jewish kingdom, is fundamentally flawed. This is because, besides the fact that this government is not based on the laws of the Torah, the very idea of conquering the Land during the time of exile and establishing Jewish rule in it through rebelling against the nations contradicts the Three Oaths. This is the meaning of the oaths not to rebel against the nations and not to "ascend as a wall" to conquer the Land of Israel in order to supposedly bring redemption before its time.

However, in that time [in the early 20th century], immigration to the Land of Israel for the purpose of saving lives was halachically mandated, as doing so saved lives. When the Arabs and others later came to interfere with the Jewish immigration, halachah obligated the Jewish people to form an organized Jewish defense force and "confront them with weapons." Similarly, there was a halachic obligation to ensure the livelihood of the land's inhabitants. Therefore, there is no contradiction between supporting saving lives through the orderly immigration of Jews to the Holy Land and the war against the enemies who come to exile us, G-d forbid, and the principle of "they shall not ascend as a wall."

Once the Jewish people were already in Israel as a result of the practical reality, then the prohibition to leave the Land took hold.[43] As Rabbi Wolpo continues:

All this was true in 1948, and all the more so in our time, when the question of the Three Oaths is completely irrelevant. This is because once one is already in the Land of Israel, they are forbidden to leave it, in accordance with the ruling of Maimonides that it is forbidden to leave Israel for foreign lands. We are not talking about conquering the land or establishing Jewish rule in the land anymore. There are millions of Jews in the Holy Land and the gentiles want us to put these millions of Jews in mortal danger. It is forbidden to listen to them and one must strongly oppose their agenda. The current situation has no connection at all to the Three Oaths — not to the oath not to "ascend as a wall" and not to the oath not to rebel against the nations.

Relating to Zionist Leaders: A Pragmatic Shift

In this context, although the leaders of the Chabad movement opposed the Zionist movement, when it was primarily a nationalist ideology in Europe,[44] their stance took on a more complex character once the nascent Zionist groups became active in Israel. This shift was particularly pronounced after the Holocaust, when a Jewish presence in Israel became imperative to protect and preserve Jewish life.

Recognizing the critical role played by the Jewish settlers in the Land of Israel, the Rebbe Rayatz, the sixth Lubavitcher Rebbe, began to express support for their important work. While maintaining Chabad's traditional opposition to the secular, nationalist aspects of Zionism, the Rebbe Rayatz acknowledged the vital importance of establishing a safe haven for the Jewish people in their ancestral homeland.

On the second day of Rosh HaShanah in 1947, 243 days[45] before the State of Israel was founded, the Rebbe Rayatz addressed the efforts of young Jews working to secure Jewish settlements in Israel and establish a state in light of the impending British withdrawal and the coming Arab onslaught. He exclaimed:[46]

> In the Holy Land, may it be built and established, there are young people who are sacrificing themselves for the Jewish people. They are doing great work, may the Almighty strengthen them and grant them success. While they must improve their observance of practical mitzvos, such as observing Shabbos, putting on tefillin, and keeping kosher, and so on, they are just human beings with shortcomings. The greatest efforts must be made to bring them closer to the fulfillment of practical mitzvos. However, for the good they do with their passionate Jewish self-sacrifice, all Jews — regardless of their affiliations — should bless them and declare: "May their hands be strengthened!"

Thus, despite taking issue with the lack of halachic observance on the part of the key players in the Jewish *yishuv*[47] (community) on the eve of the State of Israel's founding, the Rebbe Rayatz nonetheless applauded their self-sacrifice on behalf of the Jewish people.

Israel's Victory in 1948: A Miraculous Act of G-d
In 1948, after Israel miraculously defeated five Arab armies, the Rebbe saw this as further proof against the contemporary relevance of the Three Oaths. Moreover, the Rebbe perceived Israel's continued victories in its wars despite formidable odds

as clear indications that G-d decided to return the Land to the Jewish people with open miracles. In the Rebbe's words:[48]

> The obligation to retain the Land does not at all contradict the prohibition against "ascending as a wall" [en masse] and rebelling against the nations — "Do not provoke a small gentile"— because in this case, we are talking about something that the Holy One, blessed be He, gave to the Children of Israel in a supernatural manner. Everyone admits, the Jewish people did not receive the Land in return through their own abilities, G-d forbid, but rather miraculously.
>
> Since we are now at the end of the exile, [right] before the redemption, the Holy One, blessed be He, gave the Children of Israel additional parts of the Land of Israel. **And, therefore, the Children of Israel must be in those parts of the Land of Israel.**

The open miracles surrounding the Jewish people's reclamation of their ancestral lands make it such that giving away the Land demonstrates profound ingratitude toward G-d. As the Rebbe stated:[49]

> We are in the time of exile and, as such, there are parts of the Land of Israel that have not yet been given to the Children of Israel; with regard to these areas, the command, "Do not provoke a gentile" applies. But here we are talking about areas of the Land of Israel that have already been given by the Holy One, blessed be He, to the Children of Israel through open miracles and, therefore, this has nothing at all to do with the matter of "Do not provoke a nation" — this is not a provocation at all, because these areas were given to the Children of Israel by the Holy One, blessed be He!

Rabbi Wolpo further highlights the miraculous nature of the Jewish people reclaiming their ancestral lands, illustrating why the Three Oaths do not apply to the contemporary reality:[50]

> This Talmudic statement has no relevance to the conquest of

Jerusalem during the Six-Day War. The oath not to "ascend as a wall" is an instruction about the manner of the redemption from exile — meaning, it is a directive not to attempt, during the time of exile, to bring the redemption before its time by ascending with a strong hand to conquer Jerusalem. However, once a Jewish community is already living in the Holy Land, it is obvious that conquering Jerusalem for the security of those living in the Land of Israel has no connection to the Three Oaths. For they are not doing this to hasten the end [of exile], but only for security purposes.

This was especially the case during the Six-Day War, where there was no intention at all to conquer Jerusalem. On the contrary, [Israeli leaders] called on the King of Jordan many times not to go out to war against them. Afterwards, when he did not heed the call and attacked Israel and Jerusalem,[51] they fought against him in a defensive war.[52] In the tumult of battle, the commanders advanced and conquered Jerusalem. The political leadership did not intend to take this action or achieve this outcome.

There was no intention of bringing the redemption before its time. Rather, it was something that the Holy One, blessed be He, gave us against our free will and against the will of those who planned the war's objectives. Through Divine providence the course of the defensive war against the enemies necessitated, from a military and security standpoint, the conquest of Jerusalem and all the other territories.

Supporting the Jewish Settlement in Israel: A Response to Critics

In a letter to Zalman Shazar, Israel's president from 1963-1973, the Rebbe reiterated the importance of basing our claim to the Land on the Torah's narrative and true Jewish values:[53]

Some criticize me for my support of Israel saying: "Why did you invoke the Torah concepts of the Land of Israel, the Holy Land, and the Covenant Between the Parts and mix in the Almighty — with respect to the modern state!" After all, those who strove for the establishment of the State of Israel, those who stood and now stand at its head, and those who speak in its name proclaim that it is a State founded in the year 5708 [1948] in the areas the British left and from which the Haganah [a precursor to the IDF] expelled the Arabs (or entered and took possession without opposition). The representatives of the nations of the world (led by the Communists in the U.N.)[54] agreed to approve the establishment of a State.

The Rebbe's religious opponents critique him for defending this G-dless enterprise. The Rebbe responds that he is merely applying the appropriate religious concepts to the situation at hand.

I respond that this framing is completely false. The Jewish people's presence in Israel is not new; rather, in the year 5708 [1948], they liberated an important part of the Land of Israel [which was historically theirs] (and also conquered a certain area outside of it, adding to the Land of Israel)....[55]

C | Concessions Are a Greater Provocation

The rationale behind the principle of "do not provoke a small gentile" is that engaging in provocative behavior will lead the gentile to retaliate.[56] Given that this is the case, the Rebbe explains that this rule does not apply with respect to Israel's security. He argues that in the context of Israel's security, concessions themselves are a provocation.

The Rebbe's reasoning is that if Israel, as a nation, is resolute in asserting its rights, then other countries will respect that position. In contrast, if Israel makes concessions, it will simply "provoke" other countries to demand even greater concessions.[57]

Summary

We have shown that despite claims to the contrary, the Torah narrative does in fact endorse the Jewish people's claim to the Land of Israel. Moreover, the various arguments presented in the Torah's name against our claim to the Land or our right to defend it hold no merit. Israel's policies must be based on the paramount importance of protecting Jewish lives, settling and securing the G-d-given land, and dealing with reality as it is, rather than on misconceptions about what will appease those who cannot be appeased. Only a resolute stance combining authentic Jewish values and hard-nosed realism can provide a path to true and lasting peace.

We have thus stated (and defended) our narrative. But having a narrative alone is not sufficient in order to win the battle. To achieve victory, we need to communicate our narrative passionately and cultivate that passion within ourselves and, even more importantly, within our children. The next chapter will explore the role of ideology and the critical need to cultivate passion for the Land of Israel purely within the framework of the Torah and its commandments.

The Ideological War: The Torah Is Our Greatest Weapon

You have established [our] strength
from the mouth of children.
PSALMS 8:3

And all the nations of the world shall see that
G-d's name is called upon you,
and they will fear you.
DEUTERONOMY 28:10

Fighting Fire with Fire

CLARIFYING OUR CLAIM to the Land of Israel leads us to the soul of the conflict. While military strategy is essential, success in modern warfare extends beyond physical engagement. It ultimately lies in unwavering dedication to our cause and the readiness to make sacrifices for it.

We have presented the Torah's perspective on military strategy and the Jewish right to the Land, demonstrating why these views are logical and offer the best chance at having a secure and prosperous Israel for all its inhabitants. However, the key element in the struggle for the Land of Israel is not military tactics or even narrative; instead, it is the strength of our ideological commitment.[1]

In this chapter we will explore the Rebbe's analysis of Israel's enemies' intense fervor, particularly those driven by Islamist extremism. The Rebbe argues that we can only overcome such a formidable enemy with a parallel or greater commitment to our own ideology — the Torah and its *mitzvos*. The key to driving this ideology is Jewish education and outreach, and the most critical focus of this education and outreach must be children.

Hizb Allah:
The Party of G-d and
Terrorism's Ideological Roots

It can be tempting to dismiss Israel's enemies — the PLO, Syria, Hamas, Hezbollah, and Iran, among others — as mindless thugs who engage in violence for its own sake. In fact, their actions emerge from a calculated, complex ideology. Israel's enemies at its founding were motivated by Arab nationalism. But over the years, a newer, more formidable enemy began to form. From 1950 onward, a young group of passionate Muslim clerics began to fervently study traditional Islam, fusing it with political ideology. Some adopted Marxist narratives about class struggle and connected them with Islamic narratives.

Islam became the narrative of the oppressed, while moderate Arab regimes, secular regimes with Muslim polity, and most of all Israel and the United States, took the role of the oppressor. This ideology slowly took hold in various locations, particularly among young scholars congregating in Najaf, Iraq. Finally, in 1979, this brand of fierce Islamist purism burst into the public sphere with the Iranian Revolution. In this revolution, Ayatollah Khomeini led a movement which overthrew the Shah of Iran, Muhammad Reza Pahlavi, who had been an ally of the U.S. and Israel. Overnight, the Imperial State of Iran became the Islamic Republic of Iran.

At its inception in 1979, the new Republic made use of violent gangs who called themselves "Hezbollah." The name "Hezbollah" is an anglicized version of the original Arabic *Hizb Allah*, meaning "party of G-d."[2]

While both the Sunni and Shi'ite[3] strains of Islam have given birth to radical terrorist groups (Hamas is associated with the Sunni, while Hezbollah is Shi'ite), the Islamic Republic of Iran is Shi'ite.[4] During the Lebanese Civil War (1975-1990), fundamentalist Shi'ite militias, inspired by Iranian clerics, began to form. Out of these militias, Hezbollah of Lebanon, the most famous Hezbollah terrorist group, was formally born in 1982. Since its inception, Iran has closely directed and funded it.[5]

In addition, Iran uses Hezbollah in Lebanon as a key player in its "Axis of Resistance,"[6] which includes branches of Hezbollah in many other countries, all of whom follow the Shi'ite interpretation of Islam. However, Iran has also welcomed Sunni groups, such as Hamas, into its Axis of Resistance. Notably, the Arabic word for "resistance," "*muqawwama*," is what the "m" in Hamas stands for. Lebanese Hezbollah too, embraces *muqawwama* as one of its central tenets.[7]

The groups which make up the Axis of Resistance are not just terrorist groups. Instead, they are entire ideologies which strive to create an Islamic State.[8] Hezbollah in Lebanon, for example, is a political party, provides healthcare services and, most importantly, funds three large educational networks throughout Lebanon through which it inculcates its ideology into children.[9]

Since the inception of the Islamic Republic of Iran, its terrorist groups have been a menace to the West, with Hezbollah perpetrating one of the deadliest attacks on the U.S. Marine Corps ever in 1983.[10] Nonetheless, few fully anticipated the depth of the danger that radical Islam posed to the world, and fewer considered strategies for fighting it. In what follows, we will explore one Jewish strategy for neutralizing such a dangerous foe.

King David's Warriors

The ideological trends that formed today's most fearsome threats to Israel began coalescing in the 1950s, only fully revealing themselves in more recent times. But one possible antidote has a long history of its own.

At the turn of the 20th century, Czarist Russia entered its sunset years, and diverse ideologies sent the world into upheaval. Competing political and intellectual movements swirled, upending the world order. Examples include Marxism, Socialism, Anarchism, Nationalism, and Progressivism, among others.

Against this turbulent backdrop, in 1897, the fifth Lubavitcher Rebbe, Rabbi Sholom Dov Ber Schneerson, known as the Rebbe Rashab, formed a *yeshivah* called *Tomchei Temimim Lubavitch*. The students of this *yeshivah*, the *temimim*, would form an ideological vanguard to teach a passionate Judaism. They would revitalize and protect the Jewish people from the period's dangerous ideological stormwinds.

On Simchas Torah 5661 (1900), amid the fraught turn of the century, the Rebbe Rashab delivered a watershed talk to the *yeshivah* students of *Tomchei Temimim*. This talk continues to form a central mission statement for Chabad *yeshivah* students to this day.[11] In it, the Rebbe Rashab called upon the *yeshivah* students to become *Chayalei Beis David* (Warriors of the House of David),[12] referring to the ancient warriors who fought for Judaism's legendary King David.[13]

The Rebbe Rashab explained that *yeshivah* students could no longer suffice with concern just for their own spiritual welfare. In those turbulent times, the *yeshivah* students needed to become ideological warriors, bearing the banner of passionate Torah-allegiant Judaism and inspiring the entire Jewish people.[14] They needed to teach Jews to proudly embrace their Judaism, not the "-isms" (the varying ideologies) of the time.

From an Elite Force to a People's Army

The Rebbe Rashab formed an "elite force" of young men who would go on to spread the Torah's teachings. His son and successor, the sixth Lubavitcher Rebbe, the Rebbe Rayatz, continued to support and develop this "army," creating a separate division for young women called *Achos Temimim*.[15] Yet he also worked to extend the educational project far beyond this elite force.

He had the inspired young *yeshivah* students set up networks of schools and expand the ranks of young Jews with a basic religious education. Joining the Rebbe Rayatz in his efforts, the Rebbe further advanced this project. During the Rebbe Rayatz's lifetime, in 1941, the Rebbe took charge of the newly founded *Merkos L'Inyonei Chinuch*, a Jewish educational institute that aimed to spread Jewish awareness among quickly assimilating Jewish youth and communities.[16]

Tzivos Hashem: G-d's Army

When the Rebbe assumed the helm of the Chabad movement's leadership in 1951, basic Jewish education remained a priority, as did strengthening the ranks of the *yeshivah* students. In addition to the term coined by the Rebbe Rashab, "Warriors of the House of David," the Rebbe popularized a military term which first appears in the Torah:[17] *Tzivos Hashem* — "G-d's Army." The Rebbe Rayatz had used the term as an extended metaphor to discuss the Jewish people's mission in the world and their capacity to defeat evil, much like an army overcomes its enemies.[18] Over the years, the Rebbe continued to use the term *Tzivos Hashem* in reference to the entire Jewish people's responsibility to overcome evil.[19]

Rallying the Troops

The Rebbe would also repeatedly use the term *Tzivos Hashem* in public adddresses to mothers, telling them of their great responsibility in raising the next generation of G-d's army, Jewish children.[20] But in 5733 (1972), the Rebbe addressed the children themselves. In the months preceding the Yom Kippur War, the Rebbe called for children's prayer rallies to "vanquish enemies and avengers."[21] Then, in 5736 (1975-1976), the Rebbe introduced the "Twelve *Pesukim*" (Twelve Torah Passages), a selection of twelve Torah and Talmudic passages that were to be memorized by every Jewish boy and girl.[22] At the onset of the year 5741 (1980-1981), the Rebbe called for children's prayer rallies on special occasions, such as before Rosh HaShanah, during the Ten Days of Repentance, and during the festival of Sukkos, to be held throughout the world, especially at the *Kosel* (the Western Wall in Jerusalem), *Maaras HaMachpelah* (the Cave of the Patriarchs in Hebron), and *Kever Rachel* (Rachel's Tomb in Bethlehem).[23]

Making It Official

On the Fast of Gedaliah, 5741 (1980), the Rebbe concluded his talk by speaking about the Land of Israel and the "*Tzivos Hashem*" who defend it.[24] Later that month,[25] the Rebbe formally launched *Tzivos Hashem* not just as a concept, but as a youth movement that would eventually become a global force, reaching Jewish children all around the world.

At this inaugural rally of the *Tzivos Hashem* movement, much of the groundwork the Rebbe had laid was on display. A selected group of children, representing countries from around the world, led the assembled children in reciting the Twelve *Pesukim*. The children also sang the song "*Utzu Eitzah*," a biblical verse which speaks of the futility of plotting to harm the Jewish people. In full, it reads: "Contrive a scheme, but it will be foiled. Formulate an evil plot, but it will not prevail. For G-d is with us!"[26] The Rebbe had encouraged children to sing this verse at gatherings for nearly a decade[27] and consistently invoked it when praying for Israel's security.[28] At this groundbreaking rally, the Rebbe explained to the assembled children that they were now soldiers in *Tzivos Hashem*, the Army of G-d.[29]

Throughout the course of the year, the Rebbe continued to encourage *Tzivos Hashem's* activities.[30] *Tzivos Hashem* became a persistent theme in the Rebbe's teachings, and the movement continues to thrive and expand today.[31]

Making the Connection

In 1980, during a conversation with Israeli journalist Motti Eden, the Rebbe candidly shared his perspective on the ideological war for the Land of Israel, highlighting our enemies' formidable strength.[32] In this discussion, the Rebbe explicitly connected the ideological shifts in the Middle East which we have studied and the role of *Tzivos Hashem* in responding to them.

In the course of the conversation, Eden inquired about the Rebbe's emphasis on children's rallies, noting that these gatherings, where children would recite Torah verses and prayers, often preceded major events critical for Israel's security. For example, the Rebbe repeatedly called for such rallies in the months leading up to the Yom Kippur War.[33]

In response to Eden's question, the Rebbe explained the deeper motives behind these gatherings. He explained that Israel's precarious security situation necessitated such rallies. The Rebbe's focus was not on military concerns, but rather on the ideological shifts unfolding in the Middle East. He observed a growing trend among Middle Eastern nations towards heightened religious devotion, marking a departure from the more pragmatic approaches of the past. The Rebbe noted that this increase in religious fundamentalism had given rise to a more relentless adversary, underscoring the importance of the rallies as a crucial measure to counteract this escalating ideological threat. In the Rebbe's words:[34]

> *Arabs are increasingly embracing religious devotion. Four decades ago, Arab leaders — especially the senior figures who held sway over the younger generation could be influenced with modest incentives. Today, the scenario is starkly different. The younger*

Arab generation exhibits a level of fanaticism and zeal for their religion and independence that surpasses any form of religious leadership seen in previous generations. Their youthfulness only intensifies their fervor. They are impervious to any material inducement, be it money or honor. Their commitment is to Allah, to self-sacrifice. In their eyes, nothing holds higher glory.

Secular Zionism's Decline

In stark contrast to the Islamic world's surging ideological zeal,[35] the Rebbe lamented the erosion of the once-robust spirit that had sustained Israel prior to the founding of the State and during its formative years:

Unfortunately, our Jewish youth are heading in the opposite direction. Thirty years ago, the fact that Israel was a "pioneering" country was highly valued. No one needed to be convinced to be a pioneer; people would come on their own and demand [that they be granted the opportunity]. They would request land in the Negev, eager to contribute to the pioneering project through their own labor and sacrifice. Now they are saying, "Enough! We have lived under pressure for thirty years. We deserve a fun, peaceful life."

The pioneering ethos and spirit of self-sacrifice that once characterized Israel have been supplanted by a culture lacking firm ideological commitment,[36] one which values comfort and an "easy life." This, compounded by the fact that Israel's allies are also losing their own ideological core, has created a global perception that Israel is a weak country. In the Rebbe's words:

The problem with this weakness is that it is witnessed by all the nations surrounding Israel, as well as by London, Washington, Paris, and Russia. [The hostile nations] have succeeded [in this exploitation of Israel]. This is because the government in Washington is also not strong, [being afflicted by the same Western pursuit of pleasure,] and it is just looking for the easy way out so that [the U.S. government] can sleep peacefully and soundly.

The Rebbe maintained that trying to recreate idealism out of pioneerism would prove ineffective, as it would be insufficient to counteract Israeli society's impulse to relax:

> The bond [between the Jewish people and the Land] cannot be formed by trying to recreate pioneerism. Today's Israeli is not interested in pioneering. He is tired; he wants a few years of rest. He is still an idealist, but he rightfully demands a break between one crisis and the next.

Instead, the Rebbe held that the antidote to this growing problem lies in immersing Jews, especially Jewish children, in the Torah's teachings, especially the teaching of G-d's giving the Holy Land to the Jewish people. Teaching and inspiring them with the Torah's messages is the only strategy that will motivate them to defend their claim to the Land and equip them to face the ideological threat. As the Rebbe put it:

> The first and most crucial item is that we need to change the perspective of the [Jewish] youth regarding their personal connection with the Holy Land. They are a single continuum of 30 generations of Jewish men and women. 35 or 40 generations ago they entered the Holy Land which was given to them as an eternal inheritance. Jews living in the Land of Israel are not engaging in theft; there is no injustice here. The Arabs came into play [over] a thousand years later, and eventually departed, showing little interest in the Land.[37]

> A young boy or girl, however, does not have the patience for these rhetorical concepts; they need something concrete that they can participate in. So, you must tell them that the Torah verse, "Hear O Israel, the L-rd is our G-d, the L-rd is One," was not only addressed to someone named Israel who stood at Sinai 3,000 years ago, but that it was meant for this [child here today:] Avraham, Moshe, or Shlomo, who lives in Tel Aviv on such and such a street, and it was he who G-d had in mind when He said, "Hear, O Israel." And if the child's name is Yisrael [Israel], then it

certainly fits the purpose. Subsequently, you can explain to him that the Torah of Truth teaches that "Out of the mouths of babies and infants, You have established might to silence foes and avengers."[38] "Babies and infants" refers to Jewish boys and girls at [around] the age of four or five. Someone who is 70 and sitting in the Knesset is not a child, so he cannot avert the danger.

The Rebbe saw Islamist fundamentalism expanding at an alarming rate. Such fervor must be accounted for in our broader strategy. Attempts to bribe Islamist fundamentalists are futile. Our strength lies in unwavering faith, as this is the only language they comprehend.[39] And this unwavering faith will be most impactful when it is inculcated into Jewish youth.

Elsewhere, the Rebbe explains that the verse, "Out of the mouths of babies and infants, You have established might to silence foes and avengers,"[40] possesses not only a spiritual quality, but also a pragmatic one. "Might," or "power," stems from our worldview, which is shaped by our education. If we teach children to be proud of and connected to the Land — to claim it as their Divine inheritance — they will be prepared to fight for it. Conversely, a weak ideological foundation leads to a lack of "established might."[41] Yet Torah study should not be limited to children; instead, we should foster a culture of Torah study, empowering the entire Jewish people, young and old, to firmly assert their claim to the Land.[42]

In a 1976 address, the Rebbe expressed similar concerns about the rise of strong religious fundamentalism among the Muslim youth, asserting that the only way for Jews to triumph in the battle for the Land of Israel is by them cultivating a similar, if not greater, religious fervor:[43]

The Israeli political establishment treats the Arabs of today as if they were the Arabs of 25 or 30 years ago. They overlook the emergence of a new generation, one uninterested in monetary incentives. Bribes have no effect on them. As this younger generation assumes leadership, our strategies must evolve. The government, however, continues with its outdated approach.

The Rebbe observed this generational shift becoming evident as early as the 1970s. On October 3, 1976, the eve of Yom Kippur, hundreds of local Arab high school students violently stormed the Jewish synagogue at the Cave of the Patriarchs, burning Torah scrolls and desecrating other sacred items.[44]

In addressing the importance of the ideological fervor to decide conflicts, the Rebbe cited the verse, "G-d will grant His people strength and bless them with peace."[45] He emphasized that strength precedes peace, meaning to achieving peace requires the projection of power. While military prowess might be an overt expression of this power, its true source lies in the study and practice of the Torah.[46]

We must fight fire with fire. Reciting biblical verses not only generates Divine blessing, but also instills conviction in Jewish children. We can only counter faith with faith. Israel and many Jewish people have become spiritually complacent, while our enemies are true believers. Hedonistic, weak people, produced by the decay of Western values, will quickly be overcome by the burning fire of the faithful. Therefore, children's rallies and bolstering Jewish education are crucial for nurturing true believers who will staunchly defend the Land.[47]

Deradicalization

While Israel cannot dictate education across the entire Middle East, the Rebbe maintained that Israel has a responsibility to oversee Arab education within its borders, including in Judea, Samaria, and Gaza. He expressed concern that the Israeli government's hands-off approach had allowed the development of a formidable enemy within Israel itself:[48]

The Arabs who live within the State are allowed to do whatever they want. They can say anything they wish, print whatever they

want in the newspapers, and educate their children as they see
fit. Consequently, a new generation of Arabs is emerging. These
are not the Arabs of the past, who could be swayed by money
or [material] comforts. These youths are growing up with an
education that glorifies self-sacrifice for their values.

Israel should not tolerate education that actively undermines
its right to exist. To frame the point more sharply, consider the
following suggestion for combatting extremism offered by a
contemporary political philosopher:[49]

Require all Islamic schools to register and all Islamic teachers
and scholars to be licensed by the State. Prohibit them from
promoting violence. Pay them for their good work.

Mitzvos as Spiritual Armor: The Secret of Jewish Military Morale

The Torah has the power to shape young Jews into individuals
prepared to fight and sacrifice for the Land. But what about those
already on the battlefield? In a *sichah* delivered only 38 days after
the end of the Yom Kippur War, where Israel had been badly
surprised and sustained serious casualties, the Rebbe reflected on
the key elements of a successful military strategy. He posited that
performing *mitzvos* boosts morale, a crucial factor in any war. The
Rebbe began by analyzing the nature of warfare, explaining that
the people operating advanced instruments are more essential
to winning a battle than the weapons themselves:[50]

Contemporary warfare has completely changed. In the past, mili-
tary strength was determined quantitatively. The army with more
weapons and soldiers would win the battle. Today, the calculus has
changed entirely, and wars are won by the army with more sophis-
*ticated weaponry. The type of weapons matter, but the **soldiers***
[employing the weapons and] fighting the war matter even more.

The critical determinant of a soldier's success is their inner state, their perspective and frame of mind. In the Rebbe's words:

> The soldier's inner psychological and spiritual state determines their ability to perform in war. The attitude of the soldiers and the population determines their ability to be victorious. As the verse goes,[51] "The weak shall say, 'I am mighty,'" and that perspective will allow him to be victorious. So, even if one is militarily advanced, but feels weak and uninspired to defend against attackers, they are vulnerable to defeat.

The Rebbe then honed in on the special application of this teaching to Jewish soldiers, who can and must derive their strength from the Torah:

> This is true of any army; how much more so when dealing with Jewish soldiers who are defending the Land of Israel — the key to their victory is their perspective:[52] "If G-d is not watching the city, the watchman watches in vain."

While physical military strength is critical, we also need to remember that G-d ultimately determines the outcome. Therefore, in addition to constantly training and maintaining its vigilance, the army must constantly work on bolstering its faith. As the Rebbe expressed it:

> Soldiers cannot be ready to fight just once a year. Instead, they must be constantly vigilant and must constantly train. Similarly, we must inculcate the perspective that "G-d watches the city."[53] This means having faith in G-d at all times. Our primary strength comes from the fact that "we invoke the name of G-d."[54] We must foster that perspective at all times. In order to make this a bit easier, from time to time, G-d shows us open miracles in battle. Throughout Israel's history, many wars and battles seemed to have naturally been headed towards disaster for the Jewish people, yet G-d rescued them.

The Rebbe then connected this faith with the important military concept of "morale,"[55] illustrating how the Jewish tradition provides us with an array of similar concepts:

> An army needs "morale" in order to succeed. Unfortunately, our conceptual dictionary and nomenclature have devolved such that when choosing words and concepts, we default to using non-Jewish terms instead of native Jewish ones. So, today we discuss "morale" instead of Jewish terms such as "strength of spirit," "emunah" (faith in G-d), "bitachon" (taking security in G-d), and the like.[56] Nonetheless, the concept is now commonly called "morale," so I too will use the word "morale."

Cultivating these traits will not only aid us in battle, but will also instill fear in our enemies, leading them to recognize that enmity towards us is futile. The Rebbe explained:

> If we have the right morale and the right weaponry, our enemies will not even consider attacking in the first place as they will know with certainty that they will be defeated. So long as we are [spiritually] "healthy" and have no doubts about G-d Who "guards the city," we will succeed in our military endeavors.

> To boost morale, we need more than superficial entertainment.[57] We require individuals who can provide soldiers with meaningful inspiration, leaving them motivated enough to inspire others.

The Rebbe continued, presenting a historical survey in which he argues that the only durable path towards Jewish staying power is through a Judaism that is allegiant to the Torah. Whenever Jewish groups deviated from this path, prioritizing prevailing cultural values (the idolatry of the times)[58] over Judaism, they either assimilated completely or eventually returned to a Torah-aligned path. In the Rebbe's words:[59]

> Judaism is the oldest, most enduring tradition. There must be some secret to its continuity. We see that no secular ideology across the ages accounts for Jewish staying power, neither language nor clothing. The only thing that gives the Jewish people their resilience is the Torah with its mitzvos that demand

concrete actions.

These action-oriented mitzvos, [coupled with] faith in G-d, are the only factors that protected the Jewish people for thousands of years. If someone were to come and claim that they have some new invention, a new way of doing things, one need only consult the annals of Jewish history to find some parallel and see that similar attempts have ended in failure: either [these breakaway groups embracing "new" ideas and methods] have reintegrated into traditional Judaism or they have dissolved into the dominant culture.

Just as with respect to physical weaponry, we must consult the relevant experts [for instruction], so too with respect to psychological and spiritual "weaponry" — we must consult the relevant experts [Torah scholars and teachers]. One might ask: What is the connection between putting on tefillin and morale? When it comes to medicine and weaponry, the relevant question isn't if it makes sense to the layman, but rather if it works. Does it yield results? Similarly, when we look at the track record of action-oriented mitzvos, we see that they are the only tool that guarantees Jewish continuity. They **work,** so we must use them; then, in our spare time, we can theorize about why they work. When we make our community and our army bases holy [by] following in the Torah's ways,[60] then we will receive the blessing of: "The L-rd, your G-d, walks in the midst of your camp to save you and to deliver your enemy to you."[61]

Thus, the Jewish people's secret weapon is observing the mitzvos. When we do so, then "awe and terror will befall our enemies."[62] Now, if we can get both the soldiers and the population to engage in Torah and mitzvos, there will be no wars to begin with.

Material weaponry must be expertly crafted and skillfully wielded. However, on a more profound level, spiritual weaponry empowers physical weaponry. This is not only true on a theoretical level; rather, it is empirically observable.[63]

With respect to physical weaponry, we are careful to test it out *before using it, even if it should theoretically work. Similarly, when it comes to spiritual or psychological "weaponry," we cannot suffice with theories; rather, we must actually test the "weapons."*

The fact that these "weapons" work is an open secret, but only Jews are capable of effectively wielding them; they are of no use to our adversaries. As the Rebbe explained:[64]

When our enemies know that Jews are a fierce enemy who strikes back they will be so terrified that they will not go to war to begin with. Putting on tefillin has the spiritual quality of striking this fear.

In a private audience with Israeli Air Force General Ran Ronen Pekker,[65] the Rebbe and Pekker agreed on the importance of strengthening the Jewish people's faith through education. The Rebbe stressed that while integrating this perspective into the education of Israeli children is crucial, it is equally critical to share it with adults, as waiting until the next generation grows up will be too little, too late.[66]

Jewish Unity Through the Torah Scroll

The Rebbe also promoted building ideological fortitude through the Torah with his "Letter in the *sefer Torah* (Torah scroll)" campaign, designed specifically for IDF soldiers.[67] In this campaign, the Rebbe explained that a letter in the *sefer Torah* not only symbolizes Jewish unity, but also has the power to boost morale and instill fear in our enemies. As he put it:[68]

Registering our soldiers for a letter in the Torah [scroll] strikes fear within [the hearts of] our enemies. For when they know that every soldier is united with 304,805 other Jewish soldiers (corresponding to the number of letters in the sefer Torah), not only will our enemies flee, but they will not attack to begin with, as they will realize they are facing a formidable enemy.

Conclusion

We have demonstrated that strengthening our ideological resolve is the only way to emerge victorious in the war over the Land of Israel. The key to bolstering Jewish ideological fortitude lies in studying the Torah and observing its *mitzvos,* with a particular emphasis on educating our children about their connection to the Land through the Torah's timeless messages.[69] Furthermore, *mitzvah* performance will increase soldiers' morale. And ultimately, no matter how powerful our weapons and technology are, the only thing that guarantees our ability to overcome threats like Hezbollah are armies like *Tzivos Hashem.* Because the true battle is one of the spirit.

All this may prove effective in cultivating the Jewish people's connection to the Land and allowing them to stand strong against their enemies. But what happens when the "nations of the world" — the U.N., the U.S., and others — question Israel's claim to the Land and its defensive military actions? We do not live in a vacuum, and fierce ideology not grounded in realpolitik can have disastrous results. How can we expect others to respect our ideology when their convictions are so different from our own? The following two chapters will explore these questions.

PART 4

Pragmatic Policy and Domestic Governance

Some trust in chariots and some in horses, but we trust in the name of the L-rd our G-d.
PSALMS 20:7

Do not rely on miracles.
TALMUD, PESACHIM 64b

INTRODUCTION
TO PART IV

ISRAEL INCREASINGLY WAGES public relations battles in the chambers of foreign governments, the United Nations, the streets of major international cities, and on social media platforms. The international community holds strong divergent opinions about what Israel should and should not do in its defense and relationship with its neighbors. How should Israel navigate this complex landscape and respond to pressure?

Chapter 10 offers the Rebbe's analysis of the psychological factors that lead to Israel's capitulation and provides deep-rooted solutions in the face of international pressure.

Building on these insights, **Chapter 11** explores the underlying dynamics of Israel's international relations, with particular emphasis on its relationship with the United States, a power which supports Israel but also restrains it. The chapter explains why, from the perspective of realpolitik, Israel should remain resolute in the face of political pressure.

To this end, **Chapter 12** discusses the critical importance of the Israeli government actively encouraging Jewish people to proudly settle the entire Land of Israel, particularly areas which are known to the world as "occupied territories."

However, this raises questions of governance. Israel did not immediately assert sovereignty over these ancestral Jewish homelands after the Six-Day War, leaving them in an ambiguous state. **Chapter 13** argues that from a pragmatic standpoint, Israel alone should govern them. Any other form of governance will cause further tragedy for both Israel and the Palestinians.

Continuing on the topic of policy and governance, Israel faces serious domestic terrorism. Terrorists are often imprisoned and then released in a cycle of prisoner exchanges for kidnapped Jews. **Chapter 14** offers practical guidance on the rules of engagement and prisoner exchanges, which often become the topics of international discussion and scrutiny.

Chapter 15 transitions from discussing questions of how to deal with our enemies to explaining how our relationship with one another impacts our national security. It explores two dimensions of **Jewish Unity** and their relevance to Israel's security. Disunity emboldens enemies, while unity deters them. Secondly, the chapter emphasizes that every Jew, even in the diaspora, is united with the Jews of Israel. This connection demands that all Jews educate themselves and take appropriate action to promote Israel's security and well-being.

CHAPTER 10
Cultivating Confidence

Be bold as a leopard.
ETHICS OF THE FATHERS 5:20[1]

*We were like grasshoppers in our own eyes —
and so we were in their eyes.*
NUMBERS 13:33

IN THE PREVIOUS CHAPTER, we explored the Rebbe's insight that the struggle for the Land of Israel is not merely a physical battle, but ideological and spiritual as well. The Rebbe emphasized the importance of returning to authentic Jewish values as the key to prevailing in this conflict. Building on this point, we will delve into the Rebbe's analysis of the psychological factors that undermine Israel's resolve, leading to self-defeating policies.

Israel has time and again acted against its own interests in areas such as: poor military decisions, dangerous concessions to enemies, capitulating to international pressure, and a weak stand against internal terrorism. At the root of these self-sabotaging behaviors, the Rebbe discerned a lack of Jewish pride and an assimilationist tendency. This "exile mentality" undermines the Jewish people's ability to assert their interests. Those afflicted with this mindset are reluctant to take the strong stand necessary for security. To counter this, the Rebbe prescribed cultivating an attitude of Jewish pride and confidence in the Jewish people's Divine mission.

In the coming pages, we will explore the Rebbe's insights into the psychological dimension of the struggle for Israel. We will uncover the root causes of the challenges facing the Jewish people in their quest for security in their homeland. More importantly, we will delve into the Torah based tools the Rebbe offered to transform these mindsets. These provide a framework for fortifying Jewish pride, resilience, and determination. Not only can these tools help resolve the conflict in Israel, they can also serve as a guide for cultivating an authentic Jewish perspective and countering the scourge of antisemitism wherever it may arise.

The Challenge

Checking our Values

The Rebbe argues that the root cause of concessions is a lack of Jewish pride. Instead of embracing their identity, some Jews seek validation from non-Jewish sources. The Rebbe articulates this point:[2]

> The root of all these troubles lies in following the approach that "the House of Israel is like all the nations"[3] — believing that the Jewish people need to adopt the ways of the gentiles. [In reality,] the Jewish people are a "light unto the nations," [exemplars of moral and spiritual leadership].[4] Yet, they act in the opposite manner, striving to imitate any practice they see among the gentiles.

Jewish tradition offers wisdom that the Jewish people can share with the world. However, many Jews feel drawn to imitating non-Jewish culture. The Rebbe elaborates, explaining that Israel's decisions are influenced by misguided concern over potential international responses rather than by Jewish values and identity:[5]

This behavior stems from an inferiority complex and fear of the non-Jewish world — the "foreign god"⁶ within the Jewish psyche. It manifests as a constant obsession with the question: "What will the gentiles think?"

A Jew who falls into this mindset is in a deep state of internal exile. While the Jewish people as a whole are in a physical exile, such an individual also exiles his own soul.

Therefore, he seeks validation from the non-Jewish world. When a gentile gives him attention, engages him in conversation, or bestows upon him the "privilege" of a handshake or pat on the shoulder, he is willing to sacrifice everything, G-d forbid, to please the gentile.

The Rebbe contrasts this attitude with the ideal Jewish self-concept of a confident individual who fulfills G-d's bidding. He laments that some Jews' commitment to Judaism is confined to the private sphere, while in public matters they act as if G-d does not exist:

This behavior is the opposite of [the proper Jewish self-concept, characterized by commitment to G-d's Will and dedication to fulfilling His commandments, acting as] "the mighty ones who do His bidding, to obey the voice of His word."⁷

In his private life, he may be a religious Jew; but when it comes to communal matters, he acts as if the Creator of the world does not exist, G-d forbid!

The core issue is whether one recognizes G-d's sovereignty over all worldly powers. The Rebbe asks: Do we truly believe in a Master of the Universe,⁸ Who is the "Master" of Washington, London, Paris, and all other world capitals?

Some Jews capitulate with the following rationale:

What does the Code of Jewish Law have to do with politics? It is impractical [and irrelevant in this context]. When it comes to worldly affairs, I am the "wise one" — the diplomat who knows how to find favor in the eyes of the gentiles.

The Rebbe articulates the underlying question: Should Israel's diplomatic approach be guided by a Jewish perspective, or should it align with prevailing political trends?

The dispute is not merely about conceding a portion of Israel. The core disagreement [revolves around]: Is there a "Master of the Universe"?

The Rebbe argues that the real question is whether the Jewish people truly believe in the Torah's teachings, or merely pay lip-service. The Rebbe expresses a prayer that the Jewish people will adopt confidence rooted in faith and that this shift will positively impact Israel's global standing.

May each and every one of the Children of Israel conduct themselves in a manner of "the mighty ones who do His bidding, to obey the voice of His word," knowing that when one behaves according to the directive of the Code of Jewish Law, they are under the protection of the Creator and Ruler of the world, and "the hearts of ministers and kings are in G-d's hands!"[9]

The Rebbe asserts that adopting a proud, authentically Jewish perspective is not only morally correct, but also leads to favorable practical outcomes. By following G-d's Will, the Jewish people merit Divine intervention in world affairs, shaping events positively.

Low Self-Esteem

The Rebbe identifies a mindset of inferiority and fear as the root cause of most of Israel's challenges. He argues that this mindset leads to compromising Jewish security and self-respect in a misguided attempt to appease the non-Jewish world. The Rebbe asserts that some Jews' sense of inferiority is so pervasive that they become incapable of asserting Jewish interests:[10]

There are Jews whose inferiority complex towards gentiles and gentile culture is so profound that they are unable to free themselves from this feeling.

This inferiority complex undermines Israel's security policies, leading to actions that contradict Torah values:[11]

As a result of this "inferiority complex" and terrible fear of gentiles and gentile culture, these individuals act contrary to G-d's Will and the teachings of the Torah in all matters relating to the security of the Land of Israel.

Like Grasshoppers:
All a Matter of Self-Perception

The Rebbe looks to the biblical story of the spies as a paradigm for understanding Israel's contemporary concessions. In this narrative, Moses sends spies to scout out the Land of Israel before leading the Jewish people to conquer it.[12] The spies returned with a disheartening report: "We were like grasshoppers **in our own eyes**, and so we were in their eyes."[13]

The Rebbe[14] offers profound insight into the psychological dynamics at play. He suggests that the ancient inhabitants of the Land viewed the Israelites as "grasshoppers" precisely because that is how the Israelite spies perceived **themselves**. The spies' own feelings of inferiority shaped how they were seen by others.

In contrast, Joshua and Caleb, the dissenting spies who ultimately led the Jewish people into the Land of Israel, exhibited a different attitude. They confidently declared: "G-d is with us"[15] reflecting deep faith in Divine support.

The Rebbe identifies the contemporary "spies" as those who advocate for defeatist mindset when it comes to governing the Land of Israel:[16]

The contemporary "spies" are those who advocate governing the

Land of Israel with the mentality of "we were like grasshoppers in our own eyes" [like the biblical spies]. This mindset is [characterized by] fear towards the gentile nations, just as the "men of stature" were perceived [as a threat] by the spies.

The Rebbe's critique suggests that this "grasshopper" mentality, which prioritizes appeasing gentiles over asserting Jewish rights, is a form of spiritual and political weakness. It mirrors the failure of the biblical spies who, consumed by fear, lost faith in G-d's promise.

The Rebbe acknowledges the gravity of the pressure Israel faces from the international community:

The gentile nations are the majority, and exert immense pressure on Israel. Let no one claim that this pressure is insignificant. The pressure is constant and overwhelming, often manifesting as [threats to withhold vital aid,] money, and weapons.

Despite the gravity of the pressure, the Rebbe counsels the leadership to learn from Caleb and Joshua's faith.

Yet despite this [overwhelming] pressure, Caleb and Joshua [resolutely] declared:[17] "If G-d is with us, we will prevail, no matter the odds."

The Rebbe argues that projecting an inferiority complex to the nations creates a self-fulfilling prophecy, emboldening them to demand more concessions. He suggests that the nations would have accepted Jewish control of Israel if not for the fear projected by Jewish leaders:[18]

Indeed, it is evident that the gentiles would have made peace with the Jewish people's [rightful] ownership of the Land of Israel — if not for the fact that they saw the Jewish people themselves behaving in a manner of "we were like grasshoppers in our eyes," and therefore, "so we were in their eyes."

In his discussions of Peace Now, a movement we explored in Chapter 8, and their concerns that Israel needed to make concessions in order to be spared from Islamist aggression and international pressure, the Rebbe often compared the organization to the biblical spies. He saw their approach as stemming from a lack of faith and a willingness to compromise on Jewish values out of fear.[19]

A Leaf Rustling in the Wind: Overestimating Threats

The Torah warns that if the Jewish people fail to follow G-d's Will, they will be punished with irrational fear, vividly characterized as:[20] "The sound of a driven leaf will send them fleeing as though from a sword." The Rebbe saw this as a metaphor for the unwarranted weight given to threats against Israel, such as the withholding of aid, economic boycotts, political isolation, and the like. While these threats sound ominous, they often amount to mere rhetoric. Just as a rustling leaf poses no real danger and should not provoke terror, these threats should be recognized for what they truly are — largely insubstantial. The Rebbe expressed his hope that the Jewish people not fall victim to this irrational fear and instead face challenges with courage and faith:[21]

> May it be G-d's Will that the Jewish people cease to fear "the shadow of the mountains"[22] [challenges that appear daunting]. In truth, these are not real "mountains" at all; they are merely the "sound of a driven leaf"— a detached leaf separated from the tree that gives it life. The Torah acknowledges that there may be some among the Jewish people who, G-d forbid, succumb to the fear. It may be so intense that they convince other Jews to share their trepidation. However, the Torah clarifies: a Jew must not fear the "sound of a driven leaf"!

The antidote for this irrational fear lies in realizing its baseless nature, and understanding that one should fear only G-d. The Rebbe emphasizes this point by citing the Biblical Joseph:[23]

> The only legitimate fear is fear of G-d, as [exemplified by] Joseph's

declaration: "I fear [only] G-d."[24] When one fears the Holy One, blessed be He, this nullifies all other fears. This holds true even if the fears are substantive. How much more so does it apply when the fears are [as insubstantial as] a "driven leaf" — and in our case regarding threats facing the Jewish people, the fears are even less significant than that.

Fear can undermine even the most powerful warrior. It erodes morale and paralyzes one's ability to act decisively in the face of adversity. The Rebbe recognizes the corrosive effects of fear and the need for the Jewish people to overcome it. When the Jewish people realize that many of the threats they face are of no substance, they can dispense with fear.

Exile of the Soul

As we have seen, the Rebbe labeled this lack of self-esteem, fear, and tendency towards making concessions an "exile of the soul." On a simple level, exile refers to being displaced from one's physical home. However, following earlier Chassidic thought, the Rebbe expanded the concept of exile to encompass a spiritual and psychological dimension — a state of being exiled from one's ideal spiritual space.[25] This mindset of inner exile, of being trapped within non-Jewish values, conceptions, and hierarchies, is the ultimate reason Jewish people continue to make self-destructive decisions. The key to overcoming this predicament is a psychological paradigm shift, a resolution to break free from this exile. Jewish people who find themselves "stuck" in this detrimental mindset must first recognize it. Then they can take active steps to liberate themselves from its grip, including turning to G-d in prayer and beseeching Him to grant them the strength and clarity to break free. As the Rebbe expressed these points:[26]

There are Jews who have entered a state of profound inner exile, whether they reside outside the Holy Land or within it. [This exile manifests as] an "inferiority complex" and an overwhelming fear of gentiles and gentile culture, which leads them to act contrary to the will of G-d and Torah in all matters relating to the security of the Land of Israel. May it be His will that "a spirit from above will flow upon them"[27] and they will cry: "carry me out of Egypt!"[28] May they beseech the Holy One, blessed be He, to extract them [from this exile] and raise them above all limitations and boundaries!

The Solution

Developing Inner Resolve

The Rebbe's antidote to psychospiritual maladies he diagnosed consists of cultivating an alternate mindset based on Jewish values. This process begins with the chassidic ethos of inner resolve and not allowing oneself to be swayed by external opinions.[29] The Rebbe illustrated this principle with the example of Joshua and Caleb, who stood firm in their faith and conviction, even in the face of the overwhelming majority of the spies' cowardice. The Rebbe noted that the Code of Jewish Law codifies the Rabbinic teaching to "be bold as a leopard,"[30] emphasizing that one must not be fazed by anything.[31]

The Rebbe further reinforced this idea by invoking the biblical example of Mordechai, who stood strong in his commitment to Jewish values and defied the powerful Haman. Mordechai's unwavering stance serves as a paradigm for the core mindset that Jewish people must cultivate in order to ensure their security in the Land of Israel.

This attitude is characterized by strength, confidence, and the ability to respond with resolve when bullied into making concessions that undermine Jewish interests. The Rebbe emphasized that the ultimate source of this strength is an unshakable commitment to the Torah, which is the true source of Jewish power.

A | Do Not be Daunted

Sarah Reclaiming Hebron as a Jewish Burial Ground

As an illustration of this mindset, the Rebbe cited the actions of women who played a pivotal role in reestablishing the Jewish settlement in Hebron, nearly 50 years after the Jewish community had been expelled following the tragic 1929 Hebron massacre, perpetrated by the city's Arab residents. Although Israel reconquered Hebron during the Six-Day War in 1967, the Israeli government initially forbade Jews to resettle the city.

Sarah Nachshon, a courageous Chabad woman and pioneering resident of the Jewish settlement in Kiryat Arba on the outskirts of Hebron helped break the restrictions on Jewish settlement in Hebron.[32] On March 5, 1975,[33] Sarah and her husband Baruch, a famed Chabad artist, celebrated the birth of their ninth son. As residents of Kiryat Arba, they gave their son a *bris milah* (circumcision) at the Cave of the Patriarchs. The *bris* was celebrated with fanfare, although the Israeli army arrested Baruch for performing the *bris* ceremony which included wine, offending Muslim sensibilities.

Tragically, just five months later, in the summer,[34] the infant, Avraham Yedidyah, passed away from sudden infant death syndrome (SIDS). Sarah made the resolute decision to bury her son in Hebron despite the government's strict prohibitions. Her heroic actions created the first significant crack in the long-standing ban on Jewish presence in the city. Nachshon recounts her experience:[35]

> When my five-month-old son, who was born in Hebron and received his circumcision at the Cave of the Patriarchs, passed away, I decided that I must bury him in the Old City of Hebron. I conveyed my wishes to Rabbi Moshe Levinger, the Rabbi of Kiryat Arba, who transmitted my request to the Prime Minister's office. Prime Minister Yitzchak Rabin and Defense Minister Shimon Peres expressly forbade the burial. I was not sure what to

*do. I called Rabbi Gedalia Koenig[36] of Jerusalem, who encouraged
me to act upon my wishes. He told me that the cemetery was the
key to the city. "If you take back the cemetery," he said, "you will
have taken back Hebron." This gave me the strength to follow
through.*

*On my way from the hospital in Jerusalem to Hebron, soldiers
stopped me. After two hours had passed, the Head of IDF's Central
Command arrived and told me that I had two choices: "Either bury
your son in Jerusalem or Kiryat Arba, since we intend to relinquish
the Old City of Hebron to the Arabs." Incredulous, I responded, "How
can you relinquish Hebron? It is one of the holiest cities in Israel!"
He told me, "No fairytales, please. Forget about it." I decided that
no matter what, I would take my son [to Hebron]. Many soldiers
came to prevent me from driving further, so I got out of the car
and began to walk down the highway towards Hebron. I passed
roadblock after roadblock. Finally, they said that the Defense
Minister [Shimon Peres] had relented and allowed the burial — as
I heard over the soldier's radio, "Let the madwoman from Hebron
go [and bury her son]." At that point, the soldiers drove me to
the cemetery. It was dark when we came to the cemetery. Many
soldiers and residents attended the burial. I spoke at the burial
and said, "Abraham purchased a burial plot for his wife Sarah here
in Hebron. My name is Sarah, and I have now brought my son
Abraham to be buried in Hebron, more than 3,000 years later."*

Nachshon's determination served as a step for Jewish people to
return to Hebron.[37] However, her contributions to the rebuilding
of Jewish life in the city did not end there.

Beit Hadassah: Reclaiming Hebron as a Living Jewish City

Beit Hadassah, a building in Hebron purchased by Jews in 1893,
had served as a hospital, providing free medical care to both Jews
and Arabs, until Arab mobs vandalized it in the 1929 Arab riots.
Beginning in 1975, a group of *yeshivah* students began to clean the
abandoned building, and attempted to resettle it.[38] However, the
Israeli government, concerned about provoking the international

community and the Arab world, repeatedly removed them from the premises and ultimately jailed them. This struggle lasted until 1979.

In response to the government's restrictions on Jewish residence in Hebron, a group of courageous Jewish women and their children decided to make a bold move. The group was led by Sarah Nachshon and Miriam Levinger,[39] a prominent leader of the Jewish movement Gush Emunim, which worked to resettle Jewish communities in Judea and Samaria. These 15 brave women, along with their 35 children, moved into Beit Hadassah and remained there for ten months, defying the government's orders and asserting their right to live in the historic Jewish city. As Sarah Nachshon tells the story:[40]

> It all began during a gathering at Rabbi Moshe Levinger's home, which my husband Baruch attended. These gatherings were held frequently to strategize how we could ensure a Jewish presence in Hebron. In 1979, we were deeply concerned about Hebron's future, especially after Begin signed the Camp David Accords and banished the Jewish settlement at Abu Rhodes in the Sinai Desert.[41] With Yamit, also in the Sinai, scheduled to be cleared out next, we feared that Hebron and Kiryat Arba would follow.

> My husband proposed that we establish a settlement in Hebron to cement the Jewish claim. We decided that women would lead this effort as Begin, being a gentleman, would not forcibly remove women. The following morning, Miriam Levinger came to my door and we began discussing the details. Due to the government tapping our phones, we went from door-to-door to gather women who would join us, and collected supplies.

> One night, at 2 A.M., we loaded our children and supplies into a truck and drove to the street behind Beit Hadassah. With the help of yeshivah students from Yeshivat Nir in Kiryat Arba, we climbed up a ladder and went through a window to get into the building. Once inside, the children began singing, which surprised the soldiers guarding the building outside. They asked, "How did you

get here?" to which one of the three-year-old children innocently replied, "The Patriarch Jacob carried us in on a ladder."

The women and children lived in Beit Hadassah without running water, and since the government would not permit them to reenter once they left, they stayed. Ultimately, this brave protest led the government to partially capitulate and allow some Jewish settlement in Hebron, paving the way for the admittedly limited Jewish presence in the city today. In the early months of their time in Beit Hadassah, the Rebbe approvingly referred to the bravery of Sarah Nachshon and the women who were with her as the antithesis of the spies' fearfulness. As he said:[42]

May it be G-d's will that, at the very least, [the Israeli government] will learn from the "righteous women of Israel" who "cherish the Land"[43] and the Code of Jewish Law. [These women] conducted themselves in a manner contrary to [the perspective of the biblical spies who said,] "we were like grasshoppers in our own eyes." These [courageous] women conquered Hebron![44]

Several months into their stay in Beit Hadassah, Nachshon began to have doubts. Although the women and children had stayed in the building for months, no progress appeared to have happened. Uncertain of how to proceed, she sent a letter to the Rebbe requesting guidance. The Rebbe responded in a public address, saying:[45]

Today, I received a letter from a woman who has been living in Beit Hadassah in Hebron for months, with many young children. [Shockingly,] she is being disallowed from living in Hebron by fellow Jews! The army, which engages in self-sacrifice to protect Israel, has been deployed to forbid more Jews from entering Beit Hadassah, a building that everyone, even the Arabs, admit belongs to the Jews! The army does not allow any Jewish men into the building. This woman asked me — how much longer will this last? What can I answer her? She tells me that she is there with other righteous Jewish women.

The Rebbe had a dilemma. While he valued Nachshon's self-sacrifice, he could not tell young women and children to keep living in substandard conditions. The Rebbe continued, stating that the government was shirking its responsibility. He went on to draw a parallel to a biblical story:

> This situation is reminiscent of the Torah's story about the daughters of Tzelafchad, who approached Moses, the leader of the generation, and requested an inheritance in the Land of Israel. Even Moses, [the great spiritual leader and prophet,] did not know what to answer them. He told them, "I must bring your question to G-d." The Holy One, blessed be He, responded to Moses, saying, "The daughters of Tzelafchad are correct. Give them an inheritance in the Land."[46]

The Rebbe concluded:

> If the women in Hebron have such great affection for the Land of Israel, the People of Israel deserve to conquer Judea and Samaria.

Nachshon recalls that the Rebbe's encouragement gave her the resolve to remain in Beit Hadassah with her children for several more months. Ultimately, as a result of the women's tenacious insistence on remaining in Beit Hadassah, the government allowed the space to be reclaimed by Jewish people. This served as another important stepping stone toward renewing the Jewish community in Hebron.[47]

B | Mordechai Did Not Bow

As mentioned briefly above, the Rebbe furthered his case of cultivating fearless confidence by appealing to the Biblical example of Mordechai, a paradigm case of standing up to non-Jews in positions of political authority. The book of Esther chronicles how the wicked Haman, the viceroy of the mighty Persian empire, demanded worship from all the king's ministers. Only Mordechai, a proud Jew in the king's court, refused to bow before Haman.[48] This defiance enraged Haman, who then plotted to kill not only Mordechai, but all the Jews in the empire. Ultimately, Mordechai emerged victorious; Haman was executed and Mordechai replaced him as viceroy.

Mordechai's example demonstrates the power of Jewish confidence in the face of adversity. Mordechai refused to bow, even though Haman was very dangerous. The Rebbe suggests that Jews should emulate Mordechai's example and not be intimidated by contemporary "Hamans" — hostile people in positions of political power. By remaining steadfast in their faith, Jews can overcome even the most formidable challenges just as Mordechai did.

The Rebbe's advice has many applications. For example, the Rebbe advises that when asked to relinquish territories, the Israeli political establishment should not continue its previous policy of concession. He urges them to instead adopt a resolute stance, drawing inspiration from Mordechai's unwavering determination:[49]

> In order to rectify the mistakes of the past, from now on, [the Israeli government] must conduct itself in a proper manner. No more territories should be handed over and the border must be strictly guarded. When they are faced with demands to hand over territories, they must stand firm, [embodying the spirit of Mordechai,] who refused to "kneel or bow down" [in the face of pressure].

The Rebbe's view is that a strong, confident attitude is the antidote to the psychological issues that lead to concessions. The Rebbe commented on this point in response to Israel's protest against the Carter administration's vote against Israel in a 1980 U.N. Security Council resolution. After tremendous outcry from the Jewish community, Carter backpedaled. Commending the Jewish people for speaking up in their own defense, the Rebbe declared:[50]

Since the Holy One, blessed be He, performed such an overt miracle in our times [namely, that a great world power capitulated to a small state], the correct response is not complacency. On the contrary, the Jewish people must continue with unwavering resolve, "neither kneeling nor bowing down!"

And as the Rebbe expounded on the point elsewhere:[51]

The People of Israel must stand firm and embody the principle of "neither kneeling nor bowing down" in relation to the integrity of the Land of Israel. They cannot be intimidated by pressure. Instead, they must approach this pressure with the mindset of "Hatch a plot and it will be foiled; speak your piece, but it will not stand, for G-d is with us."[52]

If the Jewish people cultivate this perspective, "the fear of the Jews will befall their enemies."[53] When the Children of Israel conduct themselves as true "Jews," rejecting idolatry [which can manifest as the prevailing culture] and embracing the entire Torah, their fear falls upon all the nations surrounding them, eliminating the need for war.

This is the only path to establishing genuine peace, as it is written, "And I will make peace in the land." When the nations of the world see the people of Israel standing firmly in all matters related to the observance of Torah and mitzvos, "neither kneeling nor bowing down," it moves them to respect the People of Israel.

C | Jewish Power

The Rebbe's antidote to the pressure on Israel to make concessions was always to stand firm against the pressure. The ultimate source of the ability to do so, according to the Rebbe, is the Torah and an uncompromising commitment to its values. To articulate this point, the Rebbe considers the verse:[54] "The L-rd will give strength to His people; He will bless His people with peace." The *Midrash* explains that "strength" refers to Torah.[55] Commenting on this point, the Rebbe observes:[56]

> Consider the verse: "The L-rd will give strength to His people." The Midrash explains that this verse refers to the Torah, which has several names. Why does this verse specifically use the term "strength"? Why not simply say, "The L-rd will give the Torah to His people"?
>
> [The choice of the word "strength" is significant.] It demonstrates that although "the Holy One, blessed be He, found no better vessel for holding blessing for [the People of] Israel than peace," peace must be prefaced with "The L-rd will give strength to His people." [True peace can only be achieved when the Jewish people are imbued with the strength that comes from Torah.]
>
> It is insufficient to merely study and observe Torah. Rather, one must embody the Torah with "strength" — with firm, unwavering commitment. Moreover, it is said, "There is no strength except Torah." This means that a Jew's strength and fortitude come from the Torah and nothing else — not from a position of power, honor, nor money.
>
> When we conduct ourselves in this way, [fully committed to the Torah and its values,] the second part of the verse will also be fulfilled: "The L-rd will bless His people with peace."

Summary

In this chapter, we explored the Rebbe's analysis of the psychological factors undermining Israel's resolve in the struggle for the Land of Israel. The Rebbe diagnoses the root causes of self-defeating policies: a lack of Jewish pride, an assimilationist tendency, and an "exile mentality." The exemplar of these challenges are the Biblical spies who spurned G-d's gift of the Land.

The Rebbe's prescription for overcoming these challenges is to cultivate authentic Jewish pride and strength. Many of the apparent challenges are illusory, a mere "leaf rustling in the wind." Others are real, but a resolute mindset and tapping into the well of Torah values allows us to overcome them. This empowers us to tap into an infinite source of resilience and courage.

We are called to emulate the Biblical heroes, Joshua and Caleb, who stood up to the majority of cowardly Jewish leaders, thus inheriting the Land. We must learn from Mordechai, who was fearless against mortal danger at the hands of one of the world's most powerful political leaders. Finally, we can learn from the contemporary example of Sarah Nachshon and the women who accompanied her who stood strong in their faith against a government that capitulated under international pressure.

CHAPTER 11

The International Community and the Politics of Self-Interest

Assyria will not save us.

HOSEA 14:4[1]

Seek the welfare of the city that I have exiled you to, and pray to G-d on its behalf, for in its peace, you will have peace.

JEREMIAH 29:7

IN THE PRECEDING CHAPTER, we discussed the importance of the Jewish people expressing confidence in their right to the Land of Israel. However, even if we cultivate confidence, Israel is a smaller country that relies on the United States and other countries for its safety.

This poses a significant challenge when the United States, a primary provider of weapons and hard military deterrence for Israel, demands concessions and threatens to withhold aid. In such cases, Israel may feel compelled to make compromises that will harm security. How can Israel assert its position while navigating its dependency on the United States?

The Rebbe addresses these concerns by analyzing the politics of self-interest. He notes that the U.S. State Department, presidents, and other government arms, like any nation, will prioritize their own strategic interests. This suggests that, provided a strong Israel is in America's interests, America's threats to withhold aid from Israel are unlikely to result in disastrous consequences.[2]

However, this also implies that Israel cannot depend solely on American assistance and should develop independent alliances and contingency plans. Israel should not make significant security concessions based on the assumption that America will intervene in a crisis. While the U.S. has been a steadfast ally, it will ultimately act in alignment with its national interests, which may not always accord with Israel's. Therefore, Israel must be prepared to make decisions that prioritize its own security, even if they do not always gain American approval.

Introducing the Special Relationship

The global perception is that the United States and Israel are allies. This perception has numerous geopolitical ramifications, shaping the way other nations view and interact with both countries.[3] However, it is essential to critically assess this partnership.

America has provided over $150 billion in defense aid to Israel since the Six-Day War in 1967.[4] The U.S. Air Force and Navy offer a deterrent, making hostile powers think twice before attacking Israel. For instance, at the beginning of the 2023 Israel-Hamas War, the U.S. deployed two carrier strike groups to the Middle East[5] and intercepted long-range missiles targeting Israel.[6] Moreover, on April 13, 2024, when Iran launched an unprecedented attack on Israel — the largest drone attack in history, involving 170 drones, 30 cruise missiles, and 120 ballistic missiles — the U.S. led a coalition to aid Israel in downing the projectiles.

Throughout the conflict, the U.S. continued to demonstrate its strong support for Israel by increasing munitions shipments to the country. Moreover, President Joe Biden's visit to Israel at the beginning of the war, despite mounting international pressure, served as a symbol of the United States' commitment to its ally's security.

While Israel appears to benefit from this relationship, U.S. aid often comes along with pressure to exercise military restraint. Since the Yom Kippur War in 1973,[7] this pressure has taken various forms, including urging ill-fated peace negotiations, land concessions, and premature ceasefires. These pressures prevent Israel from achieving decisive victories,[8] compromising its security. American leaders often state: Comply with our demands or risk losing military and diplomatic support.[9]

This places Israel in a serious predicament. On the one hand, complying with U.S. demands costs Israeli lives. On the other hand, American support seems crucial, in which case refusing these demands might result in even greater losses. This raises a fundamental question: Should Israel conduct itself as a vassal state, reliant on the more powerful United States, or should it assert its autonomy in decision-making?

In what follows, we will explore the Rebbe's analysis of the underlying dynamics of the U.S.-Israel relationship. By understanding the true character of the relationship, Israel can make better security decisions, preserve the life of its citizens, and make peace in the land.

America First

An often overlooked point in understanding the United States' relationship with Israel is that the United States prioritizes its own perceived interests.[10] U.S. demands serve U.S. goals. It's also important to note that the U.S. government is composed of various groups and departments. These groups generally have highly divergent visions and interests, further complicating the relationship.

It's perfectly natural for America to prioritize its own interests — this is a characteristic of any well-governed nation. Jewish citizens in the United States should take pride in their country, express gratitude, and demonstrate patriotism, as exemplified by the Rebbe, who acknowledged America as a *medina shel chessed* (a country of kindness).[11] Nevertheless, Israel must understand its relationship with the U.S. for what it is. As the Rebbe succinctly stated:[12] "Kissinger[13] is America's Secretary of State, not Israel's. He does what he believes to be in America's best interest."

Be a Strong Partner

The United States needs a strong partner, not a feeble friend. Israel must avoid constantly seeking U.S. approval, as this can undermine the relationship by portraying Israel as weak.[14] When Israel appears overly reliant on U.S. support, it may encourage U.S. policymakers to make demands that are not in Israel's best interests. Regrettably, as we explored in the last chapter, low self-esteem often leads Israel's leaders to quickly capitulate. The Rebbe illustrated this point when he criticized the behavior of some of Israel's leaders:[15]

> These Jews lack the strength and pride that should be inherent in every member of the Jewish people. When such a Jew sees a gentile smiling at him, he completely loses his composure and is ready to do anything to please. In exchange for a [mere] smile (or even a half-smile) from the gentile, he is prepared to endanger three and a half million Jews,[16] regardless of the consequences!

The United States uses Israel as a pawn in its geopolitical strategy, while Israel is pleased when U.S. officials refer to it as a "good boy."[17] While Israel may think that compliance leads to approval, displaying vulnerability risks turning Israel into a liability for the U.S. The Rebbe explained the psychology behind this:[18]

> If Israel wants a place on the international stage and desires that nations respect it, then it must be strong by their standards. [Nations] do not rush to make peace with those [they perceive as weak and] powerless.

196

Concessions do not bring peace closer. Every concession weakens the conceding side. When Israel refuses to yield, the other parties involved in the conflict [will concede, since they] are in greater need of resolution than Israel.[19]

However, this only holds true when a nation demonstrates tangible strength, not when it relinquishes resources and territories.

The Rebbe further emphasized that Israel's strength would yield increased American support:[20]

We will receive all of the arms already promised [by the United States], and even more than promised, when we make it clear that this matter is not up for discussion: it is non-negotiable. We must state this clearly. This [position] is not our own idea, theory, or desire; rather, [it is rooted in a Divine promise found in the Torah and G-d, not the U.S., is the source of our strength. As the Torah tells us,] "He is the One Who gives you might."[21] This is what G-d said in His holy Torah, in the Bible, which is accepted by the entire world.

Furthermore, the Rebbe emphasized that displaying strength will cause the United States to regard Israel as a reliable partner, serving its geopolitical interests in the Middle East. As he put it in a 1991 conversation with Ron Nachman, the Mayor of Ariel, a Jewish city in Samaria:[22]

Israel's welfare is in the United States' best interest. Israel acts as a front-line defense against America's enemies, such as Iran and Syria, as well as hostile countries and non-state actors throughout the Middle East who want the United States to fail. If we look at the speeches of U.S. presidents, we see a persistent theme: A strong Israel is necessary to counter Syria and Iran's influence. These countries oppose the U.S. no less than they oppose Israel, and perhaps even more.

Historically, Israeli strength has attracted American support. The most notable example is the 1967 Six-Day War, where Israel decisively defeated its Arab adversaries using unadvanced weapons and having far fewer soldiers. This led the U.S. to perceive Israel as a valuable ally, particularly against Soviet-aligned hostile nations.[23]

However, since forming this strategic relationship with the United States, Israel has capitulated to U.S. and international pressure, achieving only limited success and merely fending off enemies, allowing them to survive, regroup, and to fight another day. Consequently, Israel has not achieved a decisive military victory since the Six-Day War.[24]

The United States appears to give with one hand and take away with the other when it comes to Israel. While the United States provides Israel with advanced military technology, it pressures Israel into diplomatic arrangements which either make the technology useless against Israel's enemies[25] or restrain Israel from using it to achieve decisive military victories. This contradictory approach derives from certain elements in the U.S. government, particularly the State Department and individual presidents, who use Israel as a pawn on their geopolitical chessboard. Unfortunately, Israel often lacks the confidence to object to this treatment.

Understand and Escape Geopolitical Chess

In 1969, two years after the Six-Day War and amidst Israel's War of Attrition with Egypt, students from the youth village in Be'er Yaakov, a town in central Israel, wrote to the Rebbe asking if they could hope for peace in their lifetime. He responded that according to the way of the world, the outlook was bleak. Nonetheless, the Rebbe counseled optimism.

Peace requires both sides to want it. But why would Israel's Arab neighbors desire it? It would mean acknowledging that the

Land belongs to the Jewish people and relinquishing their own territorial claims, a concession that would be difficult for them to accept. The Rebbe articulated his thoughts as follows:[26]

> *True peace can reign only when it is based on the goodwill of both parties. I see no reason for our Arab neighbors to want true peace, as it would entail definitively relinquishing both recently conquered territories and territories conquered twenty years ago. Similarly, it will be difficult for them to accept that the Jewish people living in the Land of Israel have every right to live there unconditionally.*

Moreover, the Rebbe argued that the constant state of war and tension in the region served the local Arab states' interests, as well as the Palestinians'. The ongoing conflict helped draw international sympathy and financial support for their cause, making it less appealing for them to seek a resolution to the conflict. He elaborated on this point, stating:

> *On the other hand, the war profits the Arabs, as it allows them to request aid from [global] powers outside the region. The rulers of Arab states stir up competition between the global powers in order to receive aid, assistance, gifts, and more.*

The Rebbe astutely observed that corrupt Arab states, terrorist groups, NGOs (non-governmental organizations),[27] and liberation organizations strategically pit different interest groups against one another to maximize the financial payouts they receive. Perpetuating the conflict serves the interests of these groups by maintaining a steady stream of perverse incentives. The Rebbe continues:

> *They will not have access to any of this [financial support] when the tension in the region subsides and life enters a normal routine. [Once peace is established and daily life returns to normal, the arrangements that currently provide them with funding from external powers will cease.[28]]*

Beyond the malevolent interests that drive Israel's Arab

neighbors to perpetuate the state of war, the Rebbe suggests that international powers have perverse incentives of their own. These foreign actors, he contended, deliberately manipulate the conflict, using Israel as a pawn in a complex game of geopolitical chess. The Rebbe articulated this perspective, stating:

> Additionally, and perhaps this is an even more significant point, some powers outside the Middle East, especially the major ones, [namely, the United States and Russia] seem to have a vested interest in perpetuating tension in the region and ensuring that it remains divided among several peoples, regimes, and kingdoms. This fragmented geopolitical landscape opens the door for foreign powers [specifically the U.S. or Russia] to exert influence and even dominion by aligning themselves with one of the factions. However, if peace were to prevail among the peoples in this strategically vital area and they were to cooperate with one another, it would reduce the potential for foreign powers to assert control or even maintain their influence over this critical zone.

The Rebbe lays bare the machinations of international powers who seek to maintain a precarious balance of power in the Middle East. By ensuring that no single country in the region becomes too powerful, these foreign actors can exert control and shape outcomes to their advantage.[29] The United States and Russia, in particular, have a vested interest in perpetuating the tensions that characterize the Arab-Israeli conflict.

Despite the bleak geopolitical assessment, the Rebbe counseled optimism:

> Despite all of the aforementioned factors, no Israeli man or woman should ever despair [or lose hope in the possibility of] peace, G-d forbid. The Jewish people's entire existence throughout the generations, including their current presence in the Holy Land, completely transcends the natural order. By all economic and political standards, such a small and weak nation

should not exist, let alone occupy such a position as it does now, standing at a point where the interests of mighty empires collide, located at the crossroads of several continents and the most powerful blocs in the international arena.

The Rebbe reminds us that the Jewish people's existence defies conventional wisdom. Despite their small size and apparent weakness, the Jewish people have thrived, even as they find themselves at the center of conflicts between great powers. The Rebbe continues, painting a vivid picture of the Land of Israel's turbulent history:

It is astounding that throughout history, even in the most ancient times, the Land of Israel has been a focal point of conflict between all the nations and kingdoms during their [respective] reigns, such as Egypt, Assyria, Babylon, Greece, Rome, and so on. The inhabitants of Israel only enjoyed peace and tranquility during brief periods when the People of Israel were faithful to G-d and walked in His ways, [following] the way of the Torah and the Commandments, as [was the case] during the days of David and Solomon.[30]

Despite the challenges and tribulations that have beset the Jewish people, the Rebbe remained steadfast in his faith:

The Land of Israel is described as having "the eyes of the L-rd, your G-d, upon it from the beginning of the year to the year's end,"[31] and "Behold, the Guardian of Israel neither slumbers nor sleeps."[32]

Therefore, just as [the Holy One, blessed be He, has done] until now, He will continue to protect His people Israel from all troubles and distress. The more the foundation of the existence of the People of Israel — "a single nation in the Land"[33] — is based on living daily life according to the teachings of the Torah given by the One G-d, the more our security in our Holy Land will increase, culminating with the fulfillment of the [Divine] promise: "And you shall dwell securely in your land, and I will make peace in the

Land, and you shall lie down with none to frighten you."[34]

The Rebbe asserts that the Jewish people's well-being is inextricably linked to their adherence to the Torah and their faith in G-d. The more the Jewish people ground themselves in the Torah's teachings, the greater their security in the Holy Land will be, until the ultimate fulfillment of G-d's promise of lasting peace and tranquility.

It is important to have a clear eyed perspective of the perverse machinations of countless players on the geopolitical chessboard. With this awareness it might seem that little Israel has no chance. Yet, the Jewish people's existence transcends the natural order — so long as it taps into its supernatural source of strength, the Torah and its commandments.

Performative Politics

Having articulated the point that in many respects, Israel is a pawn on America's chessboard, it is worth further considering America's motivations. When analyzing America's diplomatic efforts with Israel, it's essential to consider the extent to which the U.S. government's motives align with its stated concerns for other parties in the region. For instance, is the United States sincerely invested in Palestinian self-determination or Egypt's sovereignty over the Sinai?

The United States focuses on securing its own geopolitical interests. Its role in negotiations beyond this scope is performative not substantive — aimed at projecting its image as a fair mediator concerned with the welfare of all parties. This helps the U.S. enhance its diplomatic prestige.

There are several instances where the U.S. made ostensible demands of Israel, only for it to later emerge that these stipulations were more performative than genuine:

A | The Suez Crisis (1956)

The Rebbe offered a penetrating critique of Israel's 1956 withdrawal from the Suez Canal,[35] a decision made under intense pressure from the United States. In the Rebbe's words:[36]

> Some years after Israel's initial retreat from the Suez Canal, the United States questioned why Israel had acquiesced so readily, implying that Israel should have mounted greater resistance. The United States needed to threaten Israel with sanctions for the sake of performative politics, but it had expected that Israel would not yield to these threats.

> The current situation in the region is disastrous. Israel's behavior is analogous to that of an individual deliberately setting his own house ablaze to collect insurance money. He attempts to rationalize this act by arguing that without the fire, there would be no insurance payout to collect.

> Similarly, Israel's withdrawal from the Suez had disastrous consequences, and the rationale behind the decision — avoiding American sanctions and receiving American aid — is analogous to burning one's house down in order to obtain insurance money.

The Rebbe highlights the short-sightedness of Israel's decision to withdraw from the Suez Canal. By capitulating to American pressure and prioritizing short-term gains, Israel undermined its own long-term security.

B | The Camp David Accords (1978)

The Rebbe saw the demands put forth by various players in the Camp David Accords on behalf of the Palestinian people as largely performative.

Egypt and the Palestinians

The Rebbe argued that Sadat's advocacy for Palestinian rights was a matter of political optics rather than genuine concern. He maintained that Sadat attempted to project the image of a strong leader championing the Palestinian people on behalf of the Arab world, rather than a sincere desire to secure their autonomy.

The Rebbe contended that Israeli opposition to territorial concessions would align with Sadat's true preferences. Beneath the veneer of public demands, Sadat sought to bolster his own standing without altering the regional balance of power:[37]

> *Sadat will make big demands, but we should not be concerned. This is the nature of negotiations. One puts forth ambitious demands that exceed what they realistically anticipate receiving to create room for negotiation. Moreover, all of Sadat's demands, beyond what he seeks for his own country, are mere lip service. Given that the other [Arab] countries opposed his decision to visit Israel to begin with, he is politically beholden to advocate for the Palestinians' cause.*
>
> *However, helping the Palestinians does not advance his interests and may weaken his position. Therefore, if Israel were to respond politely and firmly, that they cannot cede land because doing so would endanger Jewish lives, Sadat would be pleased. [As this would provide him with political cover he needs, while allowing him to focus on securing the concessions that are truly essential to Egypt].*

The Superpowers and the Palestinians

The Rebbe further noted that the pressure exerted on Israel by the United States and the Soviet Union was political posturing rather than sincere commitment to the Palestinian cause. He argued that their insistence on Israeli concessions was intended to appease Arab states. As the Rebbe elaborates:

> *Furthermore, the pressure that the U.S. and USSR are exerting on Israel is insincere. Their push for Israeli concessions primarily stems from the pressure placed upon them by Syria and Lebanon. The same holds true for their demands regarding the*

so-called "Palestinians." The nations of the world only care about the Palestinians to the extent that the Arab countries have made them an issue. In reality, these nations do not care about the Palestinians; they are interested in access to the Arab countries' vast oil reserves.

Thus, when we display strength and confidence, asserting that "Judea and Samaria are non-negotiable, as ceding this land would jeopardize the lives of Jews in Jerusalem, Bnei Brak, Hadera, Haifa, Tel Aviv, and all of Israel's cities," the international community will ultimately accept our position and even be pleased. They will have fulfilled their obligation by advocating for the Palestinians, and we will have done ours by defending our interests. With this understanding, we can all look forward to a world of peace and proceed in harmony.

By understanding the political calculus of world leaders, Israel can secure agreements that work to its advantage. Similarly, with respect to American pressure, the Rebbe asserts:[38]

The U.S. government is pressuring Israel to surrender territories because the United States itself is under pressure to secure [favorable] oil prices [from the Arab states].[39] However, [the U.S. government] privately hopes that the Jewish people, as a "wise and understanding nation,"[40] will act with reason and resist such demands, recognizing that the long-term security and stability of Israel must not be compromised for the sake of short-term political expediency. History demonstrates that conceding territory does not lead to lasting peace but instead invites further pressure for additional concessions, [as Arab states and other actors perceive territorial compromise as a sign of weakness to be exploited rather than a gesture of goodwill to be reciprocated.]

Foreign nations act out of self-interest rather than altruism. While they may publicly voice concern over various issues, they only take action when doing so serves their own objectives. Consequently, the commitment expressed by many countries to the Palestinian cause is more about advancing their own geopolitical interests than a genuine concern for the well-being of the Palestinian people themselves.

Does "America" Pressure Israel?

As discussed previously in this chapter, it is important to recognize that "America" is not a monolithic entity, but rather a complex network of competing interest groups operating within the framework of the government. The State Department, for instance, may have different priorities and objectives to the Department of Defense, and both may diverge from the agenda of the sitting president. Therefore, the pressure exerted on Israel does not come from the United States as a whole, but rather from factions and individuals within its governing structure.[41]

This point is especially relevant when considering the policies of different U.S. administrations. With each change in presidency, new agendas come into play, often centered around the personal legacies that the presidents wish to establish. However, these priorities may not hold significance for their successors. Bearing this in mind, Israel should navigate through challenging administrations by collaborating with allies in the U.S. government who share its long-term interests, instead of yielding to short-term pressures that compromise Israel's security.

More importantly, Israel must remember that achieving peace in the region is not the foremost concern for the United States. If a president determines that brokering peace in Israel would require an excessive effort, they would shift their focus to issues that are of greater concern to the American electorate.

The Rebbe emphasized this point extensively in his analysis of the Camp David Accords, which were presided over by President Carter. However, similar arguments can be applied to the actions and motivations of other American presidents.

The Rebbe maintained that one of Carter's key motivations in advancing the Camp David Accords was to secure a significant foreign policy victory that would bolster his chances of winning the upcoming presidential election.

To illustrate this point, the Rebbe stated:[42]

> *The president of the United States at the time wanted to achieve a "peace agreement" between Israel and Egypt to salvage his personal prestige, calculating that through doing so, he would [improve his prospects of being] reelected as president. Therefore, regardless of the specific contents [of the agreement], the parties involved [were pressured] to leave Camp David with a [signed] "peace treaty" in hand.*

The Rebbe further elaborated on the political context surrounding the Camp David Accords, highlighting the pressure on President Carter to secure an agreement:[43]

> *At that time, the political climate was such that the president of the United States needed to secure an agreement signed by the three countries — Israel, Egypt, and the United States — in order to demonstrate his prestige ahead of the [upcoming] elections. For him, the specific content of the agreement was of little consequence; his primary concern was ensuring that he did not leave [the negotiations] without a signed agreement from all three countries. Therefore, had Israel stood firm, refusing to relinquish control of the oil fields and strategic territories that were vital for its security, the "peace treaty" would have still been concluded.*

One could view the Camp David Accords as political theater where Carter stood to lose the most if an agreement was not reached. The Rebbe elaborated on this, noting the asymmetric consequences for the Egyptian delegation:[44]

> *As the negotiations progressed and the Israeli and Egyptian delegations arrived at Camp David, it became clear to even the*

most casual observer that if the delegations parted without real results, it would not have harmed the Egyptian representatives in the slightest. Sadat had done everything in his power [to pursue peace]: He had traveled to Jerusalem and then to Washington, offering peace in the name of Egypt and all the Arab countries. He [could claim that he] did everything in his power [to pursue peace], but did not succeed in bringing about resolution to the conflict.

Likewise, the failure of the talks about giving the territories of Judea and Samaria to the Palestinians did not harm the Israeli representative either. Israel had no reason to discuss matters concerning Jordan [namely the status of Judea and Samaria, which had been previously held by Jordan] with Egypt. Moreover, both Jordan and the Palestinians had made it clear that Egypt did not represent their interests, so the Israeli representative had no incentive to engage in discussions with Egypt about this issue.

However, the United States was compelled to take action to prevent the delegations from dissolving before signing the papers [of the peace agreement]. Since the president of the United States had invested his full authority in the process, inviting the delegations to his capital, he needed to show that the United States was a dominant power capable of brokering a resolution. Failure to do so could have had negative repercussions for his prospects in the upcoming elections. Therefore, he had to exert pressure on both sides to sign a peace agreement, regardless of its contents. [For Carter, the primary objective was] to secure the signatures of both parties, [rather than the substance of the agreement].

Moreover, the Rebbe noted that much of the agenda behind the Camp David Accords came from actors within the State Department, rather than from the Executive branch:[45]

Those who signed this agreement[46] reversed 40 years of Israeli security policy and ultimately regretted their decision Why did they acquiesce to this agreement? They succumbed to pressure that was largely for show, as President Carter himself did not believe Israel would ever agree to such terms. His pressure tactics were primarily intended to fulfill the State Departments demands.

Can Israel Truly Rely on America for Security?

A common argument put forth by those who advocate for Israel making concessions is that the United States will guarantee Israel's security. The thinking goes that the United States will intervene on Israel's behalf should it find itself in danger.[47] This fails to take into account America's weak track record with respect to its allies.

A | The Suez Crisis

The capricious nature of U.S. foreign policy in the Middle East is evident in the United States' inconsistent approach to the Straits of Tiran, a waterway of strategic significance to Israel, situated between the Sinai Peninsula and Saudi Arabia.

During the 1956 Suez Crisis, the Eisenhower administration warned Egypt that any attempt to blockade the straits would be considered an act of aggression. The subsequent promulgation of the Eisenhower Doctrine in 1957 further reinforced the United States' commitment to defending the nations of the Middle East against communist threats, including situations like the Tiran blockade.

A mere decade later, in 1967, Egypt once again imposed a blockade on the straits. However, the United States, under the leadership of President Lyndon B. Johnson, advised Israel to refrain from taking military action, highlighting the unpredictable nature of American foreign policy.[48]

B | Abandoning Taiwan

From the end of the Chinese Civil War in 1949 until 1978, the United States had recognized Taiwan as the sole legitimate government of China. Taiwan was an ally against communist expansion in Asia. With American support, Taiwan held China's seat in the United Nations until 1971. However, by the 1970s, the PRC had emerged as a significant global power and the United States began to see the benefits of establishing diplomatic relations with the mainland.

In 1972, U.S. President Richard Nixon made a historic visit to the PRC. This visit was followed by years of negotiations, which culminated in the establishment of diplomatic relations issued on December 15, 1978. The agreement was officially announced by U.S. President Jimmy Carter and PRC leader Deng Xiaoping.

As part of the agreement, the United States recognized the PRC as the sole legitimate government of China and acknowledged the PRC's position that there is only one China, with Taiwan being a part of it. Consequently, the United States terminated its mutual defense treaty with Taiwan and withdrew its military personnel from the island. The shift in U.S. policy towards the PRC was a pragmatic move to counter Soviet influence and establish a new strategic relationship with a rising global power.[49]

During this time, the Rebbe expressed opposition to Israel's participation in the Camp David Accords. He pointed to America's abandonment of Taiwan as a portent, showing that U.S. would abandon weaker countries when doing so serves its interests.[50]

C | Failure at Camp David

After Israel signed the Camp David Accords, the United States failed to fulfill several of its commitments to Israel. For instance, despite promising to help Israel develop oil fields and to provide grants, America did not honor these pledges.[51]

D | Further Cases of the U.S. Abandoning Allies

The United States has a history of abandoning erstwhile allies when political expediency or shift in public opinion dictate, extending beyond the Rebbe's explicit commentary on Israel. Here are a few notable examples:

Vietnam (1975): The United States left Vietnam. This culminated in the defeat of the South Vietnamese government, which had been supported by the United States, at the hand of the North Vietnamese forces.

Iran (1979): During the Iranian Revolution, the United States faced a critical decision regarding its support for Mohammad Reza Pahlavi, the Shah of Iran, who had been a long-standing ally in the Middle East. The Carter Administration chose not to intervene to maintain his regime. As a result, the Shah was forced to flee the country and was replaced by a hostile Islamist regime led by Ayatollah Khomeini.[52]

Kurdish Forces in Northern Syria (2019): The United States withdrew its troops from Northern Syria in a betrayal of its long-standing Kurdish allies. This left the Kurdish forces, who had been partners of the United States in its fight against ISIS, vulnerable to attacks.[53]

Afghanistan (2021): After maintaining a military presence in Afghanistan for 20 years, the United States withdrew its troops. This led to a swift takeover of the country by the Taliban, raising concerns about the future of Afghanistan and the fate of those who had collaborated with the U.S. or depended on its support.

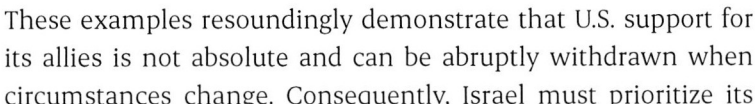

These examples resoundingly demonstrate that U.S. support for its allies is not absolute and can be abruptly withdrawn when circumstances change. Consequently, Israel must prioritize its own security interests, even if doing so may lead to a reduction in U.S. aid. This trade-off is necessary, as relying too heavily on U.S. support could lead Israel into a dire existential crisis, wherein U.S. aid and arms would be of little use.[54] The Rebbe expressed this sentiment:[55]

> Many of the security challenges that currently face Israel are the result of years of Jews believing that they have nothing to fear from the numerous nations that wish to annihilate us, since they maintain that our "good friends" in Washington will protect Israel from harm.
>
> This belief is astounding, given that we are surrounded by millions of people who wish to annihilate us. Nonetheless, powers in the Israeli government assure us that there is nothing to fear, not because they rely on G-d, but because they rely on someone sitting in Washington. They believe that the U.S. president will do everything in his power to ensure that no one harms Israel and, therefore, they do not pray to G-d for protection. Instead, they flatter the Americans for aid. Moreover, they foolishly think that America will sacrifice its own interests to save Jews.

While Israel must prioritize its own security interests, this does not mean that it should refrain from engaging in diplomacy with the United States. As the Rebbe clarifies:[56]

> Although we rely on G-d, He wants us to work within the natural order. [It is appropriate and necessary for us] to travel to Washington and engage in diplomacy.

Remaining Independent

While much of the modern State of Israel's narrative is based on the claim of independence, in reality, Israel is heavily dependent on United States aid.[57] What if that aid were to be withheld?

Strategic Partnerships

To ensure its long-term security, Israel cannot view itself as a mere client state of the U.S. Instead, Israel must diversify its diplomatic relationships, taking into account the possibility that the U.S. might withdraw its support. According to the Rebbe, an effective contingency plan would focus on developing relationships with countries that share Israel's goals.[58] These countries could include European nations such as Germany, France, and Hungary, as well as Asian powers like India.

Balance of Power

Beyond minor partnerships, the Rebbe encouraged Israel to cultivate ties with major global powers, such as Russia and China, to reduce its dependence on any single nation.[59] The Rebbe noted that Egypt had markedly enhanced its geopolitical position by engaging with both Russia and the United States. Israel could employ a similar strategy.

Furthermore, Israel should continue to pursue strategic partnerships with regional powers such as Saudi Arabia and the United Arab Emirates. These countries share a common interest in allying with Israel to counter the Iranian threat and regional instability it brings.[60]

Sourcing Weapons

In a similar vein, the Rebbe advocates for Israel to diversify its sources of military equipment. By relying on the U.S., Israel leaves itself vulnerable to American pressure. Should the U.S. decide to withdraw military support, Israel could find itself lacking the means to defend itself.

To mitigate this risk, the Rebbe recommended that Israel invest in developing its own domestic arms industry and diversifying its sources of armament. By doing so, Israel bolsters its negotiating position with the United States and reduces its susceptibility to external influence. A self-reliant Israeli military would compel the U.S. to engage with Israel more seriously.

The Rebbe spoke favorably about Israel's sourcing weapons from a diverse range of countries, including Germany.[61] He maintained that this would ensure Israel's access to military equipment, preventing it from becoming reliant on a single supplier.

The Lavi Fighter Jet

During the 1980s, Israel initiated the Lavi program,[62] aiming to create the world's most advanced fighter jet. The Lavi project successfully progressed through various stages of development and testing, showcasing Israel's technological prowess. However, Israel ultimately scrapped the Lavi program due to intense pressure from the United States.

The U.S. government opposed the Lavi project, as it saw the Israeli fighter jet as a competitor to American-made fighter planes in the global market. By pressuring Israel to abandon the Lavi project, the United States aimed to preserve its market share. The cancellation of the project kept Israel dependent on American-made combat aircraft. This limited Israel's strategic flexibility and also made it more susceptible to American influence and pressure. The Rebbe criticized the decision to cancel the Lavi project as he had seen it as a positive step in the direction of arms independence.[63]

Justifying Israel's Firm Stance: Case Studies

When articulating its position on security matters to the U.S. government, Israel must underscore that its stance is firmly rooted in the halachic principle of *pikuach nefesh* — the imperative of safeguarding life above all else.

After communicating this position, Israel must remain steadfast in upholding it, even when faced with pressure to capitulate. Yielding on a matter that has been declared inviolable would undermine Israel's credibility and invite further attempts at coercion. If Israel were to back down after taking such a principled stance, it would send a message that its positions can be altered. This would undermine Israel's ability to advocate for its security needs in the future, as its declarations would be perceived as subject to change.

The Rebbe observed that:[64]

> *Yielding to pressure only invites more pressure, creating a vicious cycle. [The path forward is to] take a principled, unwavering stance from the outset — not out of mere obstinacy, but by asserting our G-d-given rights to the Land, an unassailable truth that lies beyond dispute.*

History provides numerous examples that support the Rebbe's view, demonstrating that when Israel has remained resolute in its commitment to its security needs, it ultimately earned the respect and support of the U.S. government.

A | Israel's Nuclear Program

Israel's nuclear program serves as a powerful example of the Rebbe's view that Israel must prioritize its own security interests above all else. When confronted with American pressure to abandon its nuclear ambitions, Israel refused to capitulate. By standing firm, Israel not only maintained its nuclear capabilities, but ultimately gained U.S. support for its program as well. This validates the Rebbe's perspective on the importance of being firm in the face of external pressure when it comes to matters of national security.[65]

The Rebbe observed:[66]

> *It is widely acknowledged in the corridors of power in Washington,*

Moscow, and the capitals of the Arab world that Israel has been engaged in the development and production of nuclear weapons. This capacity has been in Israel's possession for a number of years, and its nuclear arsenal continues to expand and evolve at a steady pace.

Initially, the United States and other global powers sought to deter Israel from pursuing these nuclear ambitions and exerted pressure to this end. However, when Israel responded with unwavering determination, making it clear that it would forge ahead with its nuclear program regardless of external opposition, those applying pressure retreated, contenting themselves with a perfunctory denial of the program's existence.

Subsequently, the pressure dissipated entirely. Remarkably, some of the very Western nations that had initially implored Israel to abandon its nuclear aspirations are now actively contributing to Israel's nuclear program through various means of support.

B | Israel and Saddam Hussein's Nuclear Program

A further striking example of Israel standing up for its own interests in the face of American pressure, and eventual retrospective American approval of its actions, is Israel's 1981 bombing of Iraq's nuclear reactor.[67] This case illustrates several key points in the Rebbe's teachings about Israel's relationship with the international community, which we will explore in detail:

1) Israel must prioritize its own security interest.

2) The international community cannot be relied upon to protect Israel and will turn a blind eye to, or facilitate, parties that seek to harm it.

3) The United States puts its perceived interests ahead of Israel's, even if doing so may jeopardize Israel's security.

4) Israel can afford to look out for its own interests, since international and American condemnation is often more performative than substantive.

5) Threats to that are minimized by the international community are nonetheless very real and must be addressed decisively.

6) In retrospect, the United States comes to appreciate Israel's actions.

With these points in mind, let's explore the story. Saddam Hussein, Iraq's brutal dictator, posed a serious threat to Israel — from the beginning of his rise in Iraqi politics in 1970, intensifying when he became the country's leader in 1979, and only ending when the United States toppled his regime in 2003. Throughout his rule, Saddam pursued nuclear ambitions and openly threatened Israel. The United States consistently expected Israel to refrain from responding to Saddam's threats, weapons' development, or even blatant attacks. However, following such a policy could have been disastrous for Israel. Israel's decision to stand up for its own security, despite American disapproval, ultimately helped stall its volatile enemy.

In 1980, just one year after becoming Iraq's President, Saddam Hussein instigated the Iran-Iraq War, which lasted eight years and claimed over a million lives by some estimates. Throughout his rule, Hussein demonstrated his brutality, most notably during his 1988 Anfal campaign against the Kurdish people of Iraq.[68] During this campaign, he used chemical weapons, such as mustard gas, against civilian populations to maintain Iraqi control over the Kurdish regions. Saddam's callous actions demonstrated that he was determined to enforce his will at any cost. His willingness to kill large numbers of people to achieve his goals proved that his threats were not mere bluster.

Saddam's Nuclear Ambitions

Iraq's nuclear program began in 1950, but only gained significant momentum in 1973, when the Iraqi government acquired the Osirak nuclear reactor from France. Throughout the 1970s and 1980s, Saddam invested heavily in developing Iraq's nuclear program, and by 1981, the country was on the verge of developing a nuclear weapon. This raises the question: Why did Saddam pursue nuclear weapons so enthusiastically?

Historians studying Iraq-Israel relations offer insights into this matter. They note that initially, the international community did not perceive Iraq's nuclear research as a serious threat:[69]

> Iraqi officials generally claimed that the program was geared toward peaceful purposes, and in 1980, U.S. intelligence officials found "no hard evidence that Iraq has decided to acquire nuclear explosives."

However, a careful examination of the evidence, including information released after America's seizure of Saddam's archives following its 2003 invasion, shows that this was not the case. The claim that Saddam's primary motivation in acquiring the Osirak reactor was to produce nuclear power cannot be taken seriously given that Iraq was the world's sixth-largest producer of crude oil at the time. With such abundant oil resources, Iraq would have not needed to pursue nuclear energy as an alternative source of energy.

Saddam's Antisemitism

Saddam's animosity extended beyond regional conflicts with Iran and internal struggles with the Kurdish population. He expressed extreme antipathy towards Israel and professed a desire to "free Palestine," envisioning an Arab-controlled territory spanning from the Jordan River to the Mediterranean Sea. This aligned with his pan-Arab ideology, which saw all Arabs as one nation under his leadership.

However, Saddam's hostility towards Israel was not merely political; it was rooted in his deep-seated hatred for Jews. He believed that Jews and the State of Israel sought to harm him, Iraq, and the entire Arab nation. This hatred and paranoia fueled his pursuit of nuclear weapons.

Saddam refused to even verbally countenance Israel's existence. According to Amatzia Baram, a leading expert on Israel-Iraq relations, Saddam said he would only meet Israel's prime minister to demand that the Jews leave the Middle East altogether.[70] Some claim that Saddam's harsh rhetoric was mere posturing meant to distract the Iraqis from their own woes and direct their anger towards the Zionist enemy. However, Daniel Chardell, a scholar of Saddam's regime, argues that this reading is inaccurate. Saddam was a thoroughly convinced enemy of the Jewish state.[71]

> Above all, Saddam's relations with the United States were inextricable from his perception of Zionism and its "entity," the state of Israel. Not unlike other Baathists[72] of his generation, Saddam entertained the antisemitic theory that Jews exercised outsize influence over Western media and finance, enabling them to dictate U.S. policy toward the Middle East. To the very last, Saddam held fast to his conviction that Zionism was the root of the Arab world's rot. All "bad things" that had befallen the Arabs traced back to the Jewish state, he told his American interrogator in 2004. "Everything that happened to us was because of Israel." One might interpret these as the words of a defeated, delusional despot who was desperate to lay blame for his own errors at the feet of his favorite scapegoat. But Saddam's remarks reflect an apparently genuine and remarkably consistent set of convictions dating back to his young adulthood. He took it as an article of faith that Zionist circles worked in tandem with Western imperialists to keep the Arabs in a perpetual state of internecine conflict, economic underdevelopment, and scientific backwardness.

Hussein's hatred for Israel and Jews is confirmed by his recommended reading for members of the Iraqi government to learn about Jews. Baram writes:[73]

> *At a meeting of the party leadership in the mid-1990s, Saddam said that in order to understand Israel ("the Zionist entity" was the more common term), it was worth reading closely "The Protocols of the Elders of Zion."[74] There was general agreement to this, and the president promised to distribute copies to all the members of the leadership for purposes of a thorough discussion in the near future.*

Further articulating the point of Saddam's Jew hatred, Hal Brands and David Palkki, two scholars of Saddam's regime, write:[75]

> *Iraqi records make clear, there was no clean divide between anti-Zionism and antisemitism in Saddam's thinking. Saddam often referred to Israelis as "the Jews," and antisemitic ideas were ubiquitous in his private comments on Jews and Israel. Discussing Israeli politics, Saddam referred to "the Jews" as nefarious, clever characters. "This is the way the Jews are," he said. "I mean, they are smart, or, rather, wicked." The sense that Jews and Israelis were devious individuals motivated by sinister designs was a virtual article of faith within the Iraqi regime.*

Given this context — an unstable leader who expressed hatred for Israel and demonstrated his readiness to engage in deadly wars with unconventional weapons targeting civilians — Saddam was a frightening enemy.

Iraqi Nuclear Power as a Tool to Create "Rivers of Blood"

A study of Saddam's archives today leaves no room for doubts as to his plans once obtaining a nuclear bomb. Nuclear weapons were a critical piece in Saddam's plan to destroy Israel. Saddam intended to wage a conventional war using combined Iraqi, Syrian, and Jordanian ground forces. Nuclear weapons would serve as a tool to counterbalance Israel's nuclear capabilities. Brands and Palkki document Saddam's chilling vision of a war against Israel in an essay backed by copious citations from Saddam's meetings.

They write:

> On March 27, 1979, Saddam Hussein, the de facto ruler and soon-to-be president of Baathist Iraq, laid out his vision for a long, grinding war against Israel in a private meeting of high-level Iraqi officials. Iraq, he explained, would seek to obtain a nuclear weapon from "our Soviet friends," use the resulting deterrent power to counteract Israeli threats of nuclear retaliation, and thereby enable a "patient war" — a war of attrition — that would reclaim Arab lands [according to him, all of Israel]. As Saddam put it, nuclear weapons would allow Iraq to "guarantee the long war that is destructive to our enemy, and take at our leisure each meter of land and drown the enemy with rivers of blood." Saddam envisioned that this war would cost Iraq some 50,000 casualties, to say nothing of Israeli losses.

The evidence presented thus far clearly demonstrates that a nuclear-armed Saddam would have posed a threat to Israel. In May 1981, when discussions about Saddam's nuclear reactor were at their peak, and Libya's megalomaniacal dictator Muammar Gaddafi sought nuclear weapons as well, the Rebbe commented:[76]

> The state of the world is such that one madman can come and, with the push of a button, cause destruction throughout the entire world! It is only by G-d's grace that this does not happen.

Given Saddam's animosity towards Israel and his explicit intention to use nuclear weapons against the Jewish state, Israel's survival was at stake.

America Counsels Restraint

Despite Saddam's fearsome posturing and dangerous tendencies, the American government was reluctant to support an Israeli attack on Iraq's nuclear reactor. The United States had recently delivered advanced F-16 fighter jets to Israel, but they stipulated that the planes could not be used without American permission. Within Israel itself, the government was divided on whether to attack the reactor. Notably, the primary concern was not the military feasibility of the operation, but rather negative international reaction, particularly that of the United States.[77]

Operation Opera

As the Iraqi reactor neared completion, time was running out for Israel to take action. Prime Minister Begin and his cabinet made the weighty decision to proceed with destroying the reactor. On June 7, 1981, on the eve of Shavuos, eight Israeli F-16 fighter jets took off from Etzion Airbase in the Sinai desert[78] as part of Operation Opera, aimed at destroying Iraq's Osirak nuclear reactor.

The mission was meticulously planned and executed. The planes evaded detection by the radar systems of the countries they flew over, including Jordan, Saudi Arabia, and crucially, Iraq.

Each of the Israeli F-16s was equipped with two 2,000-pound bombs. Upon reaching the reactor, the pilots initiated a well-choreographed bombing run, severely damaging the reactor and rendering it non-operational. Miraculously, the mission was completed without any Israeli casualties,[79] and all aircraft returned safely to Israel. This operation was a significant success and a crucial step in neutralizing Iraq's nuclear threat.[80]

The International Reaction

The deed was done. How would the international community react? In the aftermath of Israel's strike, Israel provided the following statement to the international community:[81]

> For a long time, we have followed the construction of the Osirak nuclear reactor. Sources of unquestioned reliability told us that it was intended for the production of atomic bombs. The goal for these bombs was Israel. After the Iranians slightly damaged the reactor, Saddam Hussein remarked that it was pointless for the Iranians to attack the reactor because it was being built against Israel alone.

The atomic bombs that this reactor would have been capable of producing, were of the type dropped on Hiroshima. Within a short time, the Iraqi reactor would have been in operation and hot. In such conditions, no Israeli Government could have decided to blow it up. This would have caused a huge wave of radioactivity over the city of Baghdad and its innocent citizens would have been harmed. We were therefore forced to defend ourselves against the construction of an atomic bomb in Iraq, which itself would not have hesitated to use it against Israel and its population centers. Two European Governments were helping the Iraqi dictator in return for oil to manufacture nuclear weapons. Once again we call on them to desist from this terrible and inhuman act.

Despite its reasonable explanation for its actions, Israel faced a torrent of global condemnation. Even Egypt, then ostensibly at peace with Israel, criticized the bombing,[82] as did the United States. As one author summarizes:[83]

Iraq and France complained bitterly. The Soviet Union and other nations chimed in. A New York Times editorial stated, "Israel's sneak attack on a French-built nuclear reactor near Baghdad was an act of inexcusable and short-sighted aggression."[84] In the immediate aftermath, the U.S. suspended deliveries of F-16s to Israel "for the time being."

Jeane J. Kirkpatrick, U.S. delegate to the U.N., said the "diplomatic means available to Israel had not been exhausted," and the U.N. Security Council "strongly condemned" Israel's destruction of the reactor in a unanimous vote.[85]

President Reagan's Reaction

Despite the wave of global condemnation, the sitting U.S. President, Ronald Reagan, privately sympathized with Israel:[86]

Showing his positive sentiments for Israel, [Reagan] confided in his diary on June 10[87] that, if Congress found that Israel had indeed violated the agreement, "I'll grant a Presidential waiver. Iraq is technically still at war with Israel & I believe they were preparing to build an atom bomb."

Nonetheless, Reagan was also personally terrified of the possible repercussions of Israel's attack — how Saddam and the Arab countries would react — writing in his diary,[88] "I swear I believe Armageddon[89] is near."

Exploring the U.S. Government's Reaction

We have seen that Reagan supported Israel's attack. However, other actors in the U.S. government did not. The attack seemed to hamper U.S. strategic policy. Some officials were concerned that Israel's actions had angered the Arab countries, which would hurt oil prices, and by extension the American economy. It would also weaken American geopolitical power in the region. The Rebbe taught many times that the United States' calculus in dealing with Israel, and indeed all foreign countries, was one of self-interest. Their official response to Israel's defensive move proved as such. As a result of its "losses," the U.S. administration chose to punish Israel. As one analysis puts it:[90]

The Reagan administration was put on the defensive. In an effort to assuage Arab anger, it suspended the delivery of six F-16 aircraft to Israel and voted in support of a U.N. Security Council resolution condemning the raid, infuriating Israeli officials who insisted that they had acted in self-defense. The administration [also] doubled down on a controversial arms package to Saudi Arabia.

Some U.S. government officials raised the possibility of cutting off American aid to Israel altogether. The analysts suggest that their anger came from concerns over how the Israeli attack and the perceived U.S.-Israel connection would hurt America's standing with the Arab countries. Yet they also note that some of the U.S. condemnation was bluster meant to shield Israel from real consequences.[91]

So, we see that according to leading analysts of the period, U.S. condemnation:

1) Did not come from the entire administration — the President himself supported Israel.

2) Was more performative and strategic than sincere.

3) Came from a desire to protect U.S. strategic interests.

4) Was, in certain respects, intended to shield Israel from more meaningful consequences.

The Rebbe's Reaction to the Bombing:

In the short term, it appeared that Israel's preemptive attack against a dangerous enemy isolated it from the international community. The cacophony of criticism was deafening. Some wondered: Was it worth the cost? Would Israel become an international pariah? The Rebbe was unfazed, and observed that the criticism was a mere performance in the service of American geopolitical interests. On 9 Sivan, four days after Israel's preemptive strike, the Rebbe opined,[92] "The United States is very pleased with Israel's actions in bombing the atomic reactor in Iraq, but of course it cannot express its joy openly." While reading Reagan's diaries partially confirms this assessment, we will see that American retrospectives fully affirm it.

A few months later, in a letter to Rabbi Immanuel Jakobovitz, the Rebbe noted that Israel's bombing of the reactor was a generally positive development and an indication of the proper attitude Israel should adopt in international relations. As the Rebbe wrote,[93] "The bombing of the nuclear reactor in Iraq... shows a salutary departure from the policy of appeasement and subservience."

The Aftermath of Opera:
The Nuclear Program Continues

In the aftermath of Operation Opera, Saddam redoubled his nuclear efforts. Nonetheless, Israel's operation significantly set back his progress. In 1990, Saddam made a gamble that would severely set back his nuclear program once again. Saddam's government was in crippling debt to the neighboring oil-rich Arab country Kuwait. Moreover, Kuwait's oil production was hurting Iraq's economy by lowering the price of oil. With this in mind, Saddam conquered Kuwait in two days, annexing it to Iraq. Not willing to cede his country, the Kuwaiti king and his Saudi Arabian allies, alarmed by Saddam's power grab, appealed to the international community to restore Kuwaiti sovereignty. The international community answered the call, and set out to dislodge Saddam during the 1991 Gulf War.

The First Gulf War

The United States, Saudi Arabia, the United Kingdom, and Egypt assembled a large multinational force to remove Iraq from Kuwait. The lead-up to the war was tense. Saddam had chemical weapons which he had used on civilian populations. With this in mind, the American-led coalition prepared for a large number of deaths. In the months preceding the war, Saddam began threatening an uninvolved country: Israel. Israel's home-front command began issuing gas masks and the population was cautioned to enter bomb shelters with their gas masks on in the event of an air raid. While terror of a new holocaust raged, the Rebbe counseled calm, assuring the Jewish world that Israel would not be harmed.[94]

On January 17, 1991, Saddam launched Scud missiles at Israel. All in all, he launched 42 missiles at Israel. Yet only two people died as a direct result of the missile strikes. 4,100 buildings were, however, damaged, and 28 were completely destroyed. Saddam had chosen to send conventional missiles and even some missiles with concrete in their warheads instead of chemicals. This lowered the casualty rate considerably.

While in the first Lebanon War, the Rebbe had counseled quick and decisive attacks, and the Rebbe retrospectively argued that failing to preemptively strike in the Yom Kippur War had been a strategic error, in this case, the Rebbe did not publicly recommend that Israel strike Iraq. Instead, the Rebbe's general counsel was that Israel had nothing to fear and that the war between the international coalition and Iraq would ultimately aid Israel. Israel did not need to get involved in the war.[95]

While high-ranking Israeli officials suggested attacking Iraq, particularly after they had sent the first round of missiles, Israeli military command recommended against attacking. They reasoned as follows: The United States was fighting the war together with a coalition of Arab countries, most prominently Saudi Arabia and Egypt, but also with others, including Syria, the United Arab Emirates, and even the Afghani militants who would one day form the Taliban. If Israel attacked Iraq, this could destabilize the coalition by exciting the antisemitism of America's Arab allies. Beyond their military assistance, the large coalition of Muslim allies were crucial as they served to delegitimize Saddam's regime.

Shamir explained his rationale for not attacking as follows:[96]

> The primary concern is the weapons of mass destruction the Iraqis possess. Only the U.S.-led Coalition forces have the capability to effectively neutralize these weapons, which are dispersed across Iraq.

The Rebbe, while not explicitly stating whether Israel should participate, said,[97] "May the Holy One, blessed be He, help the United States and allow it to succeed in its war in Iraq." In retrospect, Shamir reflected on the Rebbe's influence on him during this critical time, partially crediting the Rebbe with his decision not to go to war:[98]

> I led a policy of restraint and prevented Israel's intervention in the [Gulf] war. This was despite the sense of anxiety and helplessness that prevailed, and the opposing view that advocated for Israel to take initiative. One of my sources of encouragement during those days was the Lubavitcher Rebbe, who sent reassuring messages about the war's outcome and its implications for Israel,

lifting many spirits.

What is particularly notable about the Gulf War in clarifying the Rebbe's position on Israel's security is that it demonstrates that the Rebbe did not advocate for reckless displays of strength. Instead, he was a careful strategic thinker who knew how to counsel restraint when it was the strategically warranted move. The critical point is that the Rebbe did not counsel restraint in response to political pressure or moralizing rhetoric, but in response to the factors that would enhance Israel's security.

The American coalition ultimately won the war against Iraq, neutralizing Saddam as a threat and leaving Israel relatively unscathed. Notably, the Iraq war prompted a serious American reevaluation of Israel's 1981 bombing, retrospectively vindicating it.

An American Retrospective

Two scholars present the total reversal in American messaging on Israel's raid in the aftermath of the Gulf War:[99]

> Contemporary accounts from 1981 correctly portrayed the raid as an act that met with wide reproach in the United States. The 1991 Gulf War, however, prompted a reevaluation of the episode by former Reagan administration officials and by well-established nonproliferation experts. Gerard C. Smith, President Carter's special representative for nonproliferation, who in 1981 testified before Congress "critically on the Israeli attack," reconsidered his position in 1993, candidly admitting that he "was wrong" and now favored "military actions" against possible [nuclear] proliferators.
>
> After the Gulf War ended, Defense Secretary Dick Cheney tacitly embraced the Osirak raid, praising the Israeli air force for having destroyed Osirak and thanking it for making the "job much easier in Desert Storm." This reevaluation grew stronger after the 2003 U.S. invasion of Iraq and, in some cases, evolved into a revisionist narrative. Richard Perle, a former Reagan administration official

and former adviser to the Bush administration, repeatedly cited the raid as an exemplary operation and claimed that the 1981 condemnation was not genuine. Perle maintained that "the State Department of course got out the obligatory condemnation of Israel's unilateral action," but in fact "the president [actually] thought it was a terrific piece of bombing."

Similarly, in a 2002 New York Times opinion piece, we read:[100]

Even the Reagan administration, normally sympathetic to Israel, chose to "condemn" the attack; France declared it "unacceptable"; Britain denounced it as "a grave breach of international law." ... In retrospect, the condemnations were completely wrong.... Thank G-d that Menachem Begin overrode his own intelligence agency, which worried that the attack would affect the peace process with Egypt, and ordered the reactor destroyed. Otherwise, Iraq would have gained nuclear weapons in the 1980s, it might now have a province called Kuwait and a chunk of Iran, and the region might have suffered nuclear devastation.

C | Operation Orchard

Another similar, but far lesser known, Israeli military operation further demonstrates the value of Israel standing up for its interests irrespective of possible international condemnation. This time, Syria was developing a nuclear reactor, which would have been a serious threat for Israel. As the U.S. Air Force magazine tells the story:[101]

Years later, Israel carried out a preemptive attack against another nuclear site, but this time the world paid much less attention. In 2007, Israel and the US were aware of a nuclear reactor — and probably a nuclear weapons program — under development in Syria with North Korean assistance. That September, Israeli F-15s and F-16s destroyed the facility using Maverick missiles and 500-pound bombs.

More than a month later, US officials said the target was a partially constructed nuclear reactor. No other Arab nation criticized the raid, and the main international complaint came from North Korea.

Remarkably, three decades after the original nuclear disarmament provoked global outcry, Israel's second such strike barely evoked a whimper.

Respond to Pressure the American Way

In November 1989, Israel's Cabinet Secretary Elyakim Rubinstein apprised the Rebbe of the challenges of resisting pressure from then U.S. Secretary of State James Baker. In response, the Rebbe offered a critical perspective on dealing with the United States:[102]

If one wants to accomplish something with the United States, he must demonstrate unwavering conviction — not out of spite, but because there is no other way. It is unreasonable to expect Israel to act against its own survival.

The solution to these strained relationships lies in reversing the current strategy. Up to this point, the approach has been to compromise — not only on minor issues but on vital ones — without receiving anything in return.

This is contrary to the nature of the United States. The United States was founded on — and continues to thrive — by maintaining a strong stance on matters critical to its survival. It made no difference whether England and France opposed them, or even if the entire world stood against them. By holding their ground, they succeeded and continue to succeed to this day.

Summary

In this chapter, we delved into the Israel-U.S. relationship, exploring the challenges that arise from Israel's reliance on

American support. The United States has been a crucial ally to Israel, providing military aid and diplomatic backing. However, this relationship has also led to significant pressure on Israel to make concessions that compromise its security interests.

The Rebbe's perspective on this matter is that Israel must prioritize its own security interests above all else. He argues that yielding to American pressure sets a dangerous precedent, inviting further demands which undermine Israel's strategic position.

Instead of capitulating to American demands, the Rebbe advocates for Israel to take a firm stance on issues critical to its survival, even in the face of strong opposition from the United States or other world powers. By demonstrating unshakable commitment to its core interests, Israel can deter pressure and safeguard its long-term security. The Rebbe's approach is grounded in the belief that a principled, unwavering position, rooted in the Jewish people's G-d-given right to the Land of Israel, is an unassailable truth that lies beyond dispute. By asserting these rights and refusing to compromise on matters of existential importance, Israel can effectively convey the message that its security is non-negotiable.

The chapter highlights several examples where Israel's steadfast refusal to capitulate to external pressure has led to positive outcomes. Prime examples include the development of Israel's nuclear program, which Israel developed despite international pressure not to, and Israel's preemptive strike on Saddam's nuclear reactor in 1981. In both cases, Israel's resolute stance, driven by the imperative to protect Jewish lives, ultimately garnered grudging respect, and even support, from the United States and other global powers. These instances powerfully validate the Rebbe's perspective, demonstrating that when Israel prioritizes its own security interests and stands firm in the face of pressure, it can safeguard its future and contribute to regional stability.

The Rebbe also emphasizes the importance of Israel diversifying its diplomatic relationships and military resources to reduce its vulnerability to external influence. By cultivating strong ties with a wide range of global powers and sourcing its military equipment from multiple suppliers, Israel can mitigate the risks of overreliance on any single ally and maintain greater strategic autonomy.

Ultimately, the Rebbe calls for a delicate balance of self-reliance and unwavering commitment to Israel's security, while still engaging in necessary diplomacy with the United States and other nations. Israel must remain resolute in its positions and avoid compromising on matters of existential importance, even in the face of intense international pressure. At the same time, the Rebbe recognizes the value of maintaining a strong relationship with the United States, a "kingdom of kindness" that has historically shown goodwill towards the Jewish people.

To conclude, let us turn to a poignant quote that encapsulates the Rebbe's nuanced view of this complex issue:[103]

> Israel cannot afford to engage in a prolonged conflict with the United States, as it relies heavily on America's support, albeit self-interested, in the form of financial aid and military assistance. Moreover, since the United States is a "kingdom of kindness" and has a tendency to show goodwill towards the Jewish people, it is imperative that Israel strives to maintain a strong relationship with the United States in every way possible, except for those that lead to the opposite outcome [namely, actions that could harm Israel's security or vital interests].

By striking this delicate balance, Israel can navigate the complexities of its alliance with the United States, while remaining true to the principle of *pikuach nefesh* and ensuring the safety and well-being of the Jewish people in their G-d-given homeland.

CHAPTER 12

The Question of "Settlements"

Rise up and walk through the length and breadth
of the land, for I have given it to you.
GENESIS 13:17

How long will you put off going in to take possession of the
land which the L-rd, the G-d of your fathers, has given you?
JOSHUA 18:3

IN THE PREVIOUS CHAPTER, we explored the notion that American, and more broadly international, concern is driven by self-interested considerations. This has significant ramifications for a key aspect of Israel's security: the administration of Judea and Samaria, and ultimately of Gaza as well. These areas are highly contentious, with the U.N. and various non-governmental organizations worldwide vociferously proclaiming that Israel's presence in these territories violates international law. Every American administration from Jimmy Carter to Joe Biden has called for Israel to limit its presence in these lands, or even to withdraw entirely.[1]

Israel's control over Judea, Samaria, and Gaza strikes at the heart of Israel's security and the Jewish people's connection to their ancestral homeland. In Parts 1 and 2, we explored why relinquishing control over these territories would be a strategic disaster for Israel. The geographic advantages provided by these lands are crucial for Israel's defense, and any withdrawal would leave the Jewish state vulnerable to attack from all sides.

In Part 3, we explored the historical and religious ties that bind the Jewish people to the entire Land of Israel. The so-called "occupied territories" are an integral part of the Jewish people's identity and heritage, with roots that stretch back thousands of years to the foundations of Judaism. Given the strategic importance and the profound spiritual significance of these territories, the question becomes: Practically speaking, what should Israel do with these lands?

We have already discussed the danger of giving up these areas in the name of peace. As the disengagement of Gaza and the withdrawal from many areas in Judea and Samaria have shown, these concessions only embolden terror. But what should Israel do with the land it holds, yet is claimed by so many to be "illegally occupied"? The Rebbe offers an unequivocal and straightforward answer: Israel should settle them all, immediately.[2]

A Program of Maximal Settlement

The Rebbe articulated his view on the imperative of settling all the contested territories of the Land of Israel in a 1977 letter to Uri Zvi Greenberg, a renowned Israeli poet and activist:[3]

> Perhaps you have heard that I spoke of the absolute necessity to settle all the territories [with Jews] at once, particularly those disputed by the nations of the world. I maintain that the enemies of Israel, may G-d protect us, will only despair of their evil scheme [to take away the Land] when they see that we are genuinely sincere about the Land being ours.

The Rebbe advocated a proactive approach that leaves no room for doubt as to Israel's intentions. He recognized that hesitation or half-measures embolden Israel's adversaries, who interpret this as weakness.

In response to the claim that settling the Land will provoke outcry, the Rebbe counters that **any** Jewish settlement, regardless of its size or location, will inevitably lead to protest:

> As I have said numerous times, even those who fear protest have seen, both in the past and present, that the protest will be just as forceful whether they settle in one area or in the entire Land.

The Rebbe argued that since opposition is a foregone conclusion, there is no reason to limit settlement efforts. He urged Israel to seize the opportunity to establish Jewish presence throughout the entire Land. The Rebbe stresses that in order to materialize this approach, one must actively advocate for the settlement of the Land and rally others to this cause:

> If you agree with this assessment — and undoubtedly, as a resident of the Holy Land witnessing the situation firsthand, you recognize that it is correct — then you must raise your voice in the strongest possible terms to advocate for the comprehensive settlement of the Land. Your influence will undoubtedly sway many circles to heed your call. While the ideal course of action would have been to seize the opportunity immediately [after the Six-Day War], it is imperative that we act now.

In the talk the Rebbe references in his letter to Greenberg, he clarified that the call of the hour was to settle all of greater Israel's territories, basing this imperative on the Divine promise of the Land to the Jewish people:[4]

> The verse which states, "I have given your descendants this Land,"[5] teaches that we should pay no attention to the gentiles who dispute the Jewish people's ownership of certain parts of the Land of Israel, claiming, "You are robbers."[6] It is incumbent upon us to "Arise, walk through the land, covering its length and

breadth" [7] — to establish Jewish settlements in **all** areas of the Land of Israel, especially those that are disputed.

Furthermore, the Rebbe adds that for these settlements to be effective, they must embody the spirit of traditional Jewish character, following the example set by the Patriarch Abraham:

This settlement must follow the legacy of our forefather Abraham — for "the deeds of the fathers are a sign for the children" [8] — *who, when he journeyed through the Land of Israel, "built an altar to the L-rd."* [9] *Therefore, to emulate his example, we must establish vibrant Jewish communities in all those places, complete with [the essential institutions of] a study hall and a mikveh, which are the hallmarks of traditional Jewish life.*

The Rebbe further asserts that a policy of partial settlement will not appease the nations and will only invite increased diplomatic pressure on Israel:

We must not, G-d forbid, [inadvertently] invite pressure from the nations of the world by adopting the misguided policy of settling only certain areas [of the Land of Israel]. Such an approach would imply that we take into account the claims of those who dispute our right to the Land of Israel. There is no logical or practical basis for differentiating between settling a few isolated places and establishing a presence along the entire border and throughout all the territories. **In both cases,** *the international "uproar" will be* **to the exact same degree.**

When we [confidently] demonstrate the truth [of our claim to the Land of Israel], we will not encounter [significant] opposition. This is because, as G-d declares, "I have given this land to your descendants." [Notably,] this verse is formulated in the past tense, indicating that G-d has already bestowed [the Land upon us]. Since [Judaism emphasizes that] action [rather than mere theory] is of primary importance, [10] *our focus should be on the concrete steps needed to establish our presence throughout the Land of Israel. There is no need for us to make grandiose proclamations about our intentions. [Rather, we should prioritize tangible actions that establish our presence throughout the Land of Israel.]*

He predicts that Israel will ultimately enjoy international support and assistance:

By following this path, not only will the nations of the world not protest our actions, but we will also be spared from any casualties, G-d forbid — not even a single Jewish life, which is considered an entire world in itself, will be lost.[11] [Furthermore,] no one will even be injured, G-d forbid. In fact, this policy will lead to the fulfillment of [the verse,] "Praise the L-rd, all nations; extol Him, all peoples, for His kindness has overwhelmed us."[12] The "nations" and "peoples" of the world will eventually come to assist the Children of Israel, providing not only what they have already promised, but also with any additional assistance that the Jewish people may require during their remaining time in exile.

Take Action

The Rebbe advises that a small group of government officials who have the authority to implement such a settlement policy should do so, asserting that once the policy is executed, public opinion will be so overwhelmingly in favor of the decision that it will be officially approved by the Israeli legislature and judiciary. He wrote:[13]

It is astonishing and painful that this [course of action] has not been pursued until now. Under current [Israeli] law, the aforementioned settlement policy can be carried out in its entirety, in a substantial manner, literally within a single day — provided the decision is made and an order is issued to be fulfilled immediately by just two key individuals: the Prime Minister and the Minister of Settlements.

Even if the following day necessitates a discussion of this matter in a meeting of the entire government and various Knesset committees, it is virtually certain that once the [settlement policy has been] put into action, those in the government who [initially] opposed this course of action will [eventually] acquiesce. This is especially true when they witness the tremendous enthusiasm [and support] of the overwhelming majority of the Jewish people, both within the Land of Israel and throughout the diaspora, upon being informed of their settlement. However, as mentioned earlier, it is crucial that this process be carried out without any [unnecessary] commotion or publicity.

International Backlash

The Rebbe dismissed worries about international backlash, asserting that many segments of the international community already harbor deep-seated animosity towards Israel and the Jewish people, irrespective of the specific policies surrounding settlement. He argued that swift and comprehensive action in settling the land would reduce pressure on Israel rather than intensify it, as the world would come to view the establishment of settlements as an irrevocable reality. The Rebbe articulated his position as follows:[14]

Some suggest that resolute action by Israel will anger the international community. [However,] the international community is already [fundamentally] unhappy with the Jews. It is a basic principle that Esau, [an archetypal paradigm of non-Jewish nations,] harbors an inherent hatred towards Jacob.[15] Many in the non-Jewish world hold an intrinsic animosity towards the Jewish people as a matter of fact. [In order to minimize the pressure faced by Israel,] it is imperative that we swiftly settle all of Israel's territory in a single, decisive move; each moment we hesitate only invites further pressure. If our [primary] concern is angering others, [it is essential to understand that] they will be angry regardless of our actions. By taking decisive steps to establish an irrevocable reality on the ground, we can minimize the pressure we face.

The Rebbe illustrated his point by recalling a historical precedent: between 1936 and 1939, before the founding of the State of Israel, the Haganah, a precursor of the IDF, swiftly established 57 settlements throughout the Land of Israel in a series of overnight operations known as "Tower and Stockade." These settlements were created to enhance Jewish security and solidify the Jewish claim to the Land.[16] Building on this historical example, the Rebbe argued for decisive, rapid settlement of Judea and Samaria, stating:

> The State must actively support the efforts of all Jews who wish to settle in Judea and Samaria. This process can be accomplished overnight, requiring just a few hours to complete. Israel successfully executed a similar strategy under British rule, establishing settlements throughout the Land of Israel overnight. Now, with the full resources and authority of the State at their disposal, they can achieve this goal even more effectively — not as a temporary measure, but as a permanent settlement in the manner described by the Torah, involving entire families and providing all the necessary infrastructure for living and working. Given the swiftness with which this settlement can be established, no external pressure can hinder its implementation. Even if such actions were to temporarily strain Israel's relationship with the United States, Israel possesses the resilience to withstand a period without American assistance. Once the reality of widespread settlement is firmly established, international pressure will become irrelevant, and Israel will not be able to reverse the process. This is the only strategy that the international community will take seriously, as they will recognize the genuine commitment and conviction behind Israel's actions in settling the Land. Once we have taken action, they will have no choice but to accept it.
>
> There are additional reasons as to why the United States will ultimately accept Israel's settlement of Judea and Samaria. [While] the true reason lies in the principle that "the hearts of ministers and kings are in G-d's hands,"[17] on a pragmatic, political level, Israel serves as a bulwark against hostile Arab countries.

The Americans have thus far exerted pressure on Israel in an attempt to appease these Arab countries, believing that long-term pressure will yield the desired results. However, once facts on the ground have been established [through widespread settlement], no amount of pressure can undo them, and the pressure will [inevitably] cease. Moreover, the United States will secretly welcome [this development], as it will bolster Israel's position as a protective force against [hostile] Arab countries.

The Consequences of Indecision

The Rebbe decried the tragic consequences of Israel's failure to settle the entire Land. He argued that while Israel hesitates, fearing international condemnation, its enemies in the PLO settle the Land unimpeded.[18] The Rebbe taught that this lack of resolve creates a detrimental status quo, giving the impression that Israel does not have a legitimate claim to the Land.

In 1978, more than a decade after the Six-Day War, the Rebbe commented on Israel's minimal settlement efforts in Judea and Samaria. He noted that the government had severely restricted settlement in the Old City of Jerusalem and completely prohibited settlement in Hebron. The Rebbe passionately argued that these actions, or lack thereof, undermined the Jewish claim to the Land:[19]

The gentile rightfully questions, "If you have already conceded territories to us, why do you now refuse to hand over Jerusalem?" If Jerusalem truly belongs to the Jewish people, then why, for over a decade, did the government not permit Jews to settle there? They allowed Arabs to purchase homes and properties, but when a Jew sought to buy, they denied him the right. During the ten years [following the Six-Day War], only a handful of Jews managed to settle in the Old City of Jerusalem, and even that [was achieved] with great difficulty.

In Hebron, the city of the Patriarchs, [the government] did not allow a single Jew to settle.[20] When the Jews insisted and stood firm in their desire to live in the city of the Patriarchs, the government decreed that settlement was permissible only outside the borders of Hebron. To sweeten this bitter pill, they called the settlement "Kiryat Arba."[21]

The situation became so dire that when [several] Jews wanted to renovate the synagogue of our forefather Abraham located in Hebron, they were denied permission. Not only that, but the government even forced soldiers, who defend the borders with self-sacrifice, to evict [their fellow] Jews from the synagogue.

The Arabs themselves acknowledge that this synagogue belongs to the Jews. Moreover, in the Torah (which the gentiles also believe in as the "Bible"), it is written that our forefather Abraham, after whom this synagogue — by Divine providence — is named, purchased the Cave of Machpelah and its surroundings.

All of these tragic outcomes are a direct result of not allowing Jews to purchase land in Judea and Samaria, particularly in Hebron. In stark contrast, and this fact must be brought to light, the PLO is actively purchasing land and properties in Judea and Samaria, in Hebron and Shechem, with everything being registered in their names.

Demographic Concerns

Addressing concerns about the displacement of Arab inhabitants due to Israeli settlement, the Rebbe contended that such concerns are misplaced. He noted that there are plenty of uninhabited areas suitable for settlement, stating:[22]

Some argue that Israeli settlement will [inevitably] lead to the displacement of Arab residents. However, this assertion is false, as there is plenty of open, [unsettled] land that can be developed [without encroaching upon areas] currently inhabited by Arabs.

The Rebbe maintained that the ideal candidates for settling the

Land of Israel are those born within its borders. Responding to the claim that there are insufficient numbers of Jews to effectively settle the Land, he insisted that the Israeli government and Jewish culture as a whole must promote policies that encourage and facilitate an increase in the Jewish birth rate.[23] By doing so, a large population of native-born Israelis would emerge, equipped with the unique skills and understanding needed to settle the entire Land. The Rebbe passionately argued:[24]

> Rather than relying on the uncertain arrival of new immigrants, who may lack the innate connection to the Land and the skills required for its development, we must focus our efforts on increasing the birth rate [among the Jewish population]. We must proclaim that the Land of Israel has grown and is ready to be settled [and, as such, requires a larger population of native-born Israelis to do so]. I firmly believe that [if we promote this message,] the [Jewish people] will listen [and respond], resulting in tens of thousands, if not hundreds of thousands, of additional births. Those born in the Land possess an innate understanding and aptitude for its development, [making them the most valuable resource for its settlement.]

The Rebbe maintained that demographics are not immutable, but can be shaped by well-crafted social policy and public discourse. By implementing measures to encourage population growth and promoting a narrative that emphasizes the importance of settling the Land of Israel, it is possible to achieve positive demographic outcomes that will greatly aid the settlement process.

Summary

For nearly half a century, the question of Jewish settlements in Judea, Samaria, and Gaza has been a source of controversy and the focus of extensive diplomatic efforts. World leaders, presidents, and non-governmental organizations have invested immense time and resources in attempting to resolve this issue.

Amidst the web of political and legal considerations surrounding the settlement debate, the Rebbe offered a strikingly simple solution: Israel should settle the all vacant areas under Israeli control as swiftly and comprehensively as possible.

The Rebbe reasoned that once these settlements were firmly established and integrated into the fabric of the land, the international community would regard Israel's actions as irreversible, reducing the prospects of any successful challenges to its sovereignty over these regions.

As the debate surrounding Israeli settlements continues to this day, the Rebbe's call for action remains as relevant and urgent as ever. Despite the passage of time, previous territorial concessions, and the evolving political climate, it is not too late for Israel to heed his call for the unabashed settlement of all areas possible in Judea, Samaria, and Gaza, if Israeli control is successfully reestablished as an outcome of the current war. Foreign opposition will eventually evaporate, but Israel's security will be bolstered for generations to come.

CHAPTER 13
Governing Judea, Samaria, and Gaza

Solomon ruled over the whole region west of the Euphrates River, from Tiphsah to Gaza, over all the kings west of the Euphrates; and he had peace on all sides around him. During Solomon's reign, the people of Judah and Israel dwelt in safety, each person under their own grapevine and fig tree, from Dan to Beersheba.

I KINGS 5:4-5

ONE OF THE MOST contentious issues in the Israeli-Palestinian conflict is the question of who should govern Judea, Samaria, and Gaza. Since 1967, much of the discourse has suggested that Palestinian self-determination, entailing autonomous government and ultimately an independent state, is the most ethical outcome.

Palestinian peoplehood is a 20th-century construct. Even during four centuries of Ottoman-Turkish control that lasted until 1914, there was no "Palestinian" ethnicity and no idea of advocating for Palestinian statehood in these regions. After the Ottoman Empire's fall, these territories came under British rule. The United Kingdom renamed the area "Palestine". Palestinian identity began to develop during this period, partly in reaction to the growing

Jewish presence. After Israel's independence, Judea and Samaria came under Jordanian control, while Egypt governed Gaza. This persisted until the Six-Day War in 1967.

In the aftermath of the Six-Day War, Israel took control of the strategically important ancestral Jewish homelands of Judea and Samaria, and Gaza, which had sizable Arab populations. Beginning with peace talks with Egypt in the 1970s, the topic of Palestinian autonomy in these territories became a major issue.

Does Israel have an ethical imperative to offer the Palestinians autonomy?

As can be readily understood from much of the discourse in this book, the Rebbe held that Palestinian autonomy would not solve any underlying issues in the conflict. He was clear in articulating that such a move would bring disaster upon the Jewish people in Israel and harm the Palestinians as well. As such, the Rebbe passionately campaigned for absolute Jewish governance of the entire Land of Israel.[1] Three weeks after the Rebbe's passing in 1994, an autonomous Palestinian government, the PLO-based Palestinian Authority (PA), was inaugurated. Instead of peace, the PA has brought corruption and internecine violence to Palestinian enclaves in Judea, Samaria, and Gaza.[2] Moreover, Palestinian autonomy is responsible for a tremendous upsurge in terrorism that impacts both Jews and Palestinians, including nearly daily attacks and deadlier episodes such as the Second Intifada, the Knife Intifada, and the many Gaza Wars, culminating most recently in the 2023 Israel-Hamas War.

As the war proceeds and in its aftermath, Israel finds itself at a crossroads with respect to governing Judea, Samaria, and Gaza. This chapter explores the Rebbe's warnings against autonomy.

The History of Palestinian Autonomy

Shortly after Israel's victory in the Six-Day War, the United Nations called for Israel to return the newly reclaimed Jewish heartlands to Arab sovereignty.[3] Under this arrangement, Jordan would regain Judea and Samaria, while Egypt would take back Gaza. Until their defeat in the Yom Kippur War, the Arab countries had hoped to militarily reconquer these territories. Following this setback, they shifted tactics, elevating Palestinian national identity and autonomy as a tool to reclaim the lands under pan-Arab rule.[4] This became a major point of discussion during the 1978 Camp David Accords, which included talks of a five-year period of autonomy for Palestinians in Judea, Samaria, and Gaza. Beginning in 1978, the Rebbe extensively delineated the dangers of granting such autonomy.[5]

In 1991, the U.S. under President George H.W. Bush and Secretary of State James Baker pressured Israel to attend the Madrid conference[6] by making important financial assistance for Israel's large-scale absorption of Jewish immigrants from the collapsing Soviet Union contingent upon Israel's participation. The Israeli government under Prime Minister Yitzchak Shamir, facing economic challenges,[7] agreed to attend the conference.

The Madrid Conference led to the 1993 Oslo Accords, which divided Judea, Samaria, and Gaza into Areas "A"[8] (full Palestinian control), "B" (Palestinian civil control, Israeli military control), and "C" (full Israeli control), establishing Palestinian autonomy.

The Oslo Accords created the Palestinian Authority (PA) in 1994, transforming the Palestine Liberation Organization (PLO) into a quasi-state led by Yasser Arafat, a long-time terrorist. Despite formally renouncing terrorism, Arafat, along with his successor Mahmoud Abbas, continued to encourage and fund terror groups such as Fatah's Tanzim[9] and the al-Aqsa Martyrs' Brigades[10], as well as populist terror. The PA gained control over major Palestinian population centers in Judea, Samaria, Gaza, and Jericho, making these areas unsafe for Jews and leading to their deterioration due to corrupt governance and clashes between Palestinian clans.

The American Role in Autonomy Talks

The United States has consistently been the driving force behind the pressure for Palestinian autonomy in one form or another. During the Carter administration, the Rebbe expressed his shock at the President's alarming proposition for Palestinian autonomy:[11]

> *Just a few months ago, an Israeli delegation visited the United States to discuss the issue of Judea and Samaria. During the course of the dialogue, Washington put forward an utterly alarming proposition — granting the Arabs full civil jurisdiction over the territories of Judea and Samaria! When I heard this, I was shocked! How could the President of the United States, the leader of a "kingdom of kindness,"[12] even contemplate such a [misguided] idea? While it is true that we are enjoined to "seek the welfare of the city,"[13] especially in light of the President's recent call for education,[14] [this does not justify compromising our fundamental principles and the security of our homeland.] Such thinking is utterly misguided [and must be firmly rejected]!*

Since Carter's presidency, there has been a relentless push by successive U.S. administrations for Palestinian autonomy and statehood. Ronald Reagan quietly held talks with the PLO.[15] George H.W. Bush championed Palestinian autonomy in the 1991 Madrid Conference. Bill Clinton continued this trend with the 1993 Oslo Accords and the 2000 Camp David Summit. In 2002, George W. Bush introduced the Roadmap to Peace plan, calling for the creation of a Palestinian state. Barack Obama reiterated his support for a Palestinian State and strongly criticized Israeli communities in Judea and Samaria as "an obstacle to peace".

Although Donald Trump's approach was more favorable to Israel, his administration nonetheless put forward a peace plan in 2020 that included the possibility of a Palestinian state, albeit with limited sovereignty and conditional upon various factors, such as demilitarization and recognition of Israel as a Jewish state.

Joe Biden expressed support for the establishment of a Palestinian state. In 2021, he restored U.S. aid — which had been cut during the Trump administration — to the PA, signaling a continued commitment to Palestinian autonomy. In the following sections, we will explore why Israel should reject these repeated overtures for autonomy and discuss the alternative course of action that should be pursued.

Categorically Rejecting Autonomy

In 1992, Israeli Knesset member Moshe Katzav, a member of Yitzchak Shamir's government, visited the Rebbe. The Shamir government had recently agreed to attend the Madrid conference, and the Rebbe feared that they would succumb to American pressure and offer autonomy to the Palestinians. The Rebbe began the discussion by addressing the issue from a religious perspective:[16]

> Merely discussing autonomy desecrates G-d's Name. While it is a personal matter when individual Jews in Israel do not observe the Torah and its commandments, the autonomy plan amounts to the Israeli **government** declaring war against G-d and His Torah.

Given that the Torah teaches that Jews may not surrender the Land of Israel, the State of Israel giving away land would amount to a national rejection of the Torah's laws. Moreover, ceding land would jeopardize Israel's security violating the Torah's emphasis on the paramount value of life.

The Rebbe proceeded to explain that the "autonomy plan" was a Trojan horse for statehood — a point that is quite evident today, with the idea of a "two-state solution" now commonplace and the notion of dismantling Israel entering public discourse. The Rebbe continued:

> The claim that autonomy merely involves Palestinian self-administration over areas such as education and agriculture, while Israel retains control of foreign affairs and security, and that this [arrangement] would only be a trial, [misses the fundamental issue

at stake.] This is not a diplomatic matter, but rather a discussion about surrendering portions of the Land of Israel, G-d forbid.

The Rebbe then addressed the intense U.S. pressure on Israel to engage in "Land for Peace" negotiations. The Shamir government's rationale for participating in the negotiations was their need for financial guarantees from the American government to fund the absorption of a large wave of *aliyah* from the former Soviet Union. However, the Rebbe argued that agreeing to make even small concessions would lead to pressure on Israel to make larger concessions in the future.

As for the argument that due to the current immigration from Russia, we require [financial] guarantees from the U.S. government and must therefore consider their views — this [line of reasoning] is the first step towards surrendering portions of the Land of Israel. The very fact that [the proponents of concessions] admit that they are acting under pressure from the nations of the world is proof [of the dangerous nature of this approach]. [Once we begin to yield to pressure,] we will find ourselves subject to ever-increasing demands, with no end in sight. As our history has repeatedly shown, capitulating to pressure only invites further pressure.

Katzav noted that indeed, the American government appeared to be inching closer to endorsing Palestinian statehood, remarking:

Last year, President George [H.W.] Bush wrote that he opposed a Palestinian state. This year, he only wrote that he is not in favor of a Palestinian state, so we see a change here.

The Rebbe ruefully responded:

And we [clearly] see the direction in which the change is heading.

The Rebbe noted that the proposed autonomy would create a slippery slope, leading to relinquishing Jewish lands:

Currently, they speak only of a five-year plan, for they fear to explicitly state their true intentions of ceding portions of the

Land of Israel. Yet their ultimate aim is clear — to hand over parts of the Land of Israel. In my estimation, Shamir himself is well aware of this, even more so than I.

The Rebbe, acknowledging Shamir's past dedication to the Land of Israel, noted approvingly:

Shamir has [amassed] many merits in his defense of the Land of Israel, dating back to his days in the Irgun.[17] In those times, Shamir bravely fought against foreign rule over our land, yet now he speaks of surrendering parts of it.

The Rebbe then offered a resolute call to action:

In my opinion, the practical course of action [is clear] — we must ensure that Shamir immediately ceases all discussions of autonomy.

In an unparalleled statement, the Rebbe declared that if Shamir would not halt the autonomy talks, he would unleash the full force of his political influence to bring down the Shamir government:

I have always fought for the [establishment of a] government led by Shamir.[18] Just as I exerted every effort to ensure his leadership, if the government persists in this [misguided] direction, then I, Menachem Mendel, will be the first to fight with all my might against Shamir, striving for the disbandment of his government! Until now, only Shimon Peres stood in opposition to the Shamir government, but if Shamir continues down this path of entertaining discussions about autonomy, then I too will stand firmly against his government. If Shamir finds himself unable to withstand the pressure from the nations of the world, let him declare that he can no longer serve as prime minister!

The Rebbe, drawing upon the symbolic meaning of Shamir's name, continued:

Shamir, [in the Jewish tradition,] refers to a creature capable of cutting through the hardest of stones. So let Shamir, with all his

might, put a [resolute] "shamir" to the decision regarding these
talks of surrendering parts of the Land of Israel. [By doing so,] he
will completely shatter any thoughts of engaging in such matters
[which pose a grave threat to the integrity of our G-d-given land
and our Divine mission as a people].

Regrettably, Shamir had already engaged in discussions of autonomy with the Palestinians. The subsequent Israeli government, led by Prime Minister Yitzchak Rabin and Foreign Minister Shimon Peres, helped create the Palestinian Authority. In the forthcoming analysis, we will delve into the Rebbe's prescient warnings regarding autonomy and examine the consequences that have emerged as a result of this ill-fated path.

Autonomy as a Pathway to Violence

The Rebbe's Predictions

One of the gravest concerns the Rebbe raised regarding Palestinian autonomy was violence it would inevitably bring. Since the dawn of the 20th century, hostile Arab elements have persistently attacked Jewish communities in the Land of Israel. When Israel took control of Judea, Samaria, and Gaza in 1967, it finally had the means to ensure that these hostile populations could not perpetrate attacks against its citizens. However, Israel's weak response to terrorism and discussions of relinquishing these territories emboldened Palestinians to engage in increasingly frequent and intense terror attacks. The Rebbe warned against removing Israeli military oversight in these strategically crucial regions:[19]

If you wish to show respect to the other side, by all means, do
so. If you want to speak in a gentle tone, you are welcome to.
But do not compromise on security based on the notion that we
will have to rely on the Arabs in the Old City of Jerusalem [for
our safety]. When civil administration is handed over to them,

supervision over their actions will weaken, and one cannot begin to imagine the grave consequences that will result from this, G-d forbid!

Elsewhere, the Rebbe noted that given the frequency of attacks prior to autonomy, one could only anticipate escalation in such assaults if autonomy were granted:[20]

[Certain] Jewish "diplomats" attempt to downplay the gravity of autonomy, [asserting that it] amounts to nothing more than granting the Arabs civil administration and weapons for their police force. Although the true meaning of "autonomy" is known to all, G-d did not rely on people exercising common sense. Instead, He demonstrated in practice the dire consequences that unfolded in the territories and even in the Old City of Jerusalem. Even before being granted autonomy, provided with weapons for a police force, and being permitted to choose their own representatives — the Arabs began launching attacks against the [Israeli] army and the police force.

The Rebbe noted that while the government claimed that Palestinian autonomy would be limited, by granting autonomy Israel relinquises control over an actively hostile population and, as such, cannot dictate what the consequences of autonomy would be:[21]

[The government officials] delude themselves into thinking that since "they" will decide the extent of autonomy, "no less and no more," the Arabs will accept it because it was "agreed upon."

How It Played Out

We have already delved into the disastrous consequences of autonomy, but let us briefly review the tragic events that unfolded: After the Palestinians were granted autonomy in 1994, terrorist attacks escalated at an alarming rate, culminating in the Second Intifada, characterized by relentless suicide bombings which claimed thousands of innocent Israeli lives and instilled a sense of terror in the population. Only when Israel took decisive action through Operation Defensive Shield was some semblance of order restored. Defensive Shield, by necessity, partially undermined Palestinian autonomy, as it required Israeli soldiers to enter Palestinian-majority cities such as Bethlehem and Jenin. Israel also constructed security barriers and restricted Palestinian access to Israel. The Palestinians, given autonomy, made life unbearable for Israelis, compelling Israel to implement protective measures that made life more challenging for Palestinians.

In 2006, Hamas won the PA elections, but Israel and the U.S. prevented them from taking control in the West Bank. Since then, Abbas has led a corrupt, unelected, and unpopular government in the West Bank, while autonomy allowed Hamas to seize control of Gaza,[22] leading to repeated wars and ultimately Gaza's destruction in 2023.

Consider the following characterization, which is one among many that could be cited to describe life under the Palestinian Authority, discussing how the PA deals with dissidents:[23]

> *During the first intifada, the PLO purged more than 800 Palestinians. In the past month, gangs linked to Arafat have machine-gunned collaborators in Gaza, Ramallah, Nablus, Qalqilya, and even Manger Square in Bethlehem. Tanzim executed Bassam Eid, a 22-year-old in Ramallah, after his sister reported seeing him talking to an Israeli. After all, dialogue is forbidden. Executions are public, and meant to terrorize. Bodies are displayed to send a warning.*

> *Before journalists label victims of summary executions collaborators, they must ask why no trial, and what exactly Arafat's henchmen mean by the term. They may find that, to the Palestinian Authority, a collaborator is anyone who speaks of coexistence with Israel or questions into whose bank accounts hundreds of millions of dollars of aid money disappeared. But with*

little outrage over the killings of so-called collaborators, it should be no surprise the Palestinian peace camp has all but disappeared.

Or consider the reflections of another analyst on the challenges of Palestinian autonomy in retrospect:[24]

[Yitzchak Rabin, the Israeli prime minister who granted Palestinian autonomy, had said,] "Forms of Palestinian or Shi'i terror [exemplified by Hezbollah] and the intifada do not present a threat to the very existence of Israel. They are painful and they interfere with the normal way of life for many Israelis. But the Palestinians, the Shi'is, and the intifada are not threats to the very existence of Israel."[25]

To elaborate, by "painful," Rabin meant that the inevitable terror attacks would lead to Israelis being murdered or injured from time to time. By "interfere with the normal way of life," Rabin meant that the fear of being murdered or injured by terrorists, or of having one's house or car blown up, indeed interferes with living a normal life. Yet, in Rabin's opinion, all this was a worthwhile price to pay for "peace" as recognized on the international stage, since it would not lead to the State of Israel being dismantled. The analyst continues:

Rabin was right — but only up to a point. He was referring to Palestinian terror based largely in neighboring states [such as Jordan and Lebanon], where the Palestine Liberation Organization (PLO) had operated since the mid-1960s. Rabin did not fully comprehend the possible impact of terror from within a Palestinian quasi-state, operating from bases in immediate proximity to Israeli cities. The impact of this terror from 2000 onwards went well beyond the daily personal security of Israelis and posed a threat to Israel's economic security and its own domestic Arab-Jewish modus vivendi.

Will it be possible for Abu Mazen [Mahmoud Abbas] — or any leader for that matter — to rein in Palestinian terrorism when two-thirds of the Palestinian public supports suicide bombing operations against Israeli civilians, and when only 7 percent believe the new Palestinian leadership should accept the roadmap plan? Not surprisingly, a late April poll conducted by the Palestinian Center for Communications shows that less than two percent of the Palestinian public supports the new prime minister.

As it stands, more Palestinians believe the Palestinian goal is "to liberate all of historic Palestine" than "to end the Israeli military occupation and establish an independent Palestinian state based on U.N. Security Council resolution 242."

Not much has changed since this analysis was written.

Autonomy as Ethnic Cleansing

The Rebbe's Predictions

The Rebbe expressed deep concern about the consequences of granting autonomy to Arab communities in areas previously shared by Jews and Arabs. He argued that the hostile actions taken by Arabs against Jews before autonomy was granted indicated that autonomy would make these areas unlivable for Jews, amounting to ethnic cleansing of Jews from parts of Israel:[26]

We do not need to speculate about the implications of autonomy; we have already seen it in action. As soon as the Arabs were given a semblance of autonomy, they [immediately] drove the Jews out of their territory.

The Rebbe cautioned against the assumption that the relatively peaceful coexistence between Jews and Arabs in the immediate aftermath of the Six-Day War would continue once Arabs were granted autonomy over certain areas:

The government is deceiving itself. They allowed Arabs to settle among Jews immediately after the Six-Day War, and so they believe that this coexistence will continue even once the Arabs have been given autonomy, and even once the territories have been completely handed over to Arab control. The government thinks that under these circumstances, Jews will still be able to settle there. This [belief] is [utterly] naive.

To support his view, the Rebbe pointed to the Israeli government's reluctance to allow Jewish settlement in predominantly Arab areas, such as the Old City of Jerusalem and Hebron, even before autonomy was granted. He saw this as an indication that the government recognized the potential for violence in these areas:

The fate of Judea and Samaria and those who live there does not depend on the government that handed them over; it depends on the Arabs! Even now, before the Arabs have been granted autonomy, the government is afraid to allow Jews to live in the Old City of Jerusalem, [fearing that the Arabs will kill any Jews who settle there or that Jewish settlement will provoke Arab unrest.] There is no point in even discussing Jewish settlement among the Arabs in Hebron, as [the government] vehemently opposes it. Even in the Old City of Jerusalem, when a few courageous Jews snuck in and managed to establish a presence, the government only allowed them to remain due to public pressure. They were forced to permit these Jews to live there since they were already inside, but they refused to allow any additional Jews to settle there.

[If this is the situation now,] how much worse will it be after the Arabs are given autonomy?! This will, G-d forbid, make the entire Land of Israel vulnerable to Arab aggression and control. The government will be powerless to take action against the Arabs once they have autonomous rule. It is absurd to claim that after receiving autonomy, the Arabs will suddenly start considering the opinions of Jewish government officials. They will have no reason to do so and every incentive to assert their own interests at the expense of the Jewish population.

How It Played Out

Since the signing of the Oslo Accords in the 1990s, which divided the West Bank into Areas A, B, and C, travelers on highways in Judea and Samaria encounter large red signs, particularly along Highway 60. This highway, built on an ancient route dating back to Biblical times, spans from Beersheba to Hebron, continues to Jerusalem, and then extends into Samaria, passing through historic sites such as Shiloh and Shechem before ending in Nazareth. The red highway signs at the entry points to Area A display a stark warning in Hebrew, Arabic, and English:

This Road Leads To Area "A" Under The Palestinian Authority. The Entrance For Israeli Citizens Is Forbidden, Dangerous To Your Lives, And Is Against Israeli Law.

These signs serve as a sobering reminder that the Oslo Accords, which supposedly aimed to establish a framework for resolving the Israeli-Palestinian conflict, have not achieved their intended goals. Instead, they have led to the ethnic cleansing of Jews from ancestral Jewish lands. Similarly, in response to persistent security threats, Jewish towns that once employed Palestinians or allowed them access for shopping and recreation have now disallowed such access, citing the need to prioritize the safety of their residents.

Sarah Nachshon's daughter, Devorah Attia,[27] a lifelong resident of Kiryat Arba, a Jewish town near Hebron, shares her experience of the changing dynamics between the Jewish and Arab communities in the city before and after the establishment of the Palestinian Authority:

Before the establishment of the PA, we used to frequent the market in the Old City of Hebron. We would buy fruits, vegetables, and clothing, engaging in conversations with the local Arab merchants. Sure, there was an occasional stabbing, but we got along for the most part. However, at the outset of the Intifada, leading up to the PA's establishment, an elderly Arab storekeeper confided in my mother, saying, "It's no longer a good idea for you to come here. They told us that Mr. Berez [a reference to Israeli politician Shimon Peres] said that if the Arabs throw stones at the Jews, we will be granted our own state."

Attia notes the irony of the situation — the "peace" process has increased violence.

Creating an Enemy Army

The Rebbe's Predictions

The Rebbe strongly opposed the development of a Palestinian paramilitary police force, which was an integral part of the autonomy agreements. He counseled that this dangerous concession would arm Israel's enemies. In his words:[28]

Those who attempt to deceive the public [by claiming] that these actions will bring us closer to the long-awaited peace are [gravely] mistaken. It is impossible to achieve peace by pursuing actions that, G-d forbid, increase the risk of war by arming our enemies!

The Rebbe explained that it was foolish to negotiate with terrorists while engaging in the magical thinking that somehow they would be reformed.

From morning till night, these Israeli politicians proclaim that they are prepared for any arrangement: joint governance based on mutual trust, autonomy, and similar proposals. For them, the highest priority is to sit at a table with murderers and terrorists.

He painted a vivid picture of the consequences of such negotiations:

And what will be the result? It is clear to everyone, including the politicians themselves. We are dealing with murderers and terrorists who cannot be trusted, even after they make promises and sign agreements. A promise or a signed document from them has no more value than a mere scrap of paper! They sit at the negotiating table with a murderer to reach an agreement, while the murderer holds a knife and stabs them!

Elsewhere, the Rebbe expanded on his opposition to the creation of a Palestinian security force, warning that it would have deadly consequences:[29]

> *Any stipulations that the Israeli government sets regarding the nature of this "autonomy" are completely irrelevant, since there is another party involved. When Israel hands over the territories, G-d forbid, the other side will establish a police force. Since a police force must be armed, there will be no choice but to allow the police officers of the autonomous authority to possess weapons. And once they are armed, they will act without restraint and do as they please.*

How It Played Out

In the aftermath of granting autonomy to the PA, a "police force" was established, which consumes one-third of the PA's annual budget.[30] The Palestinian Authority Security Force (PASF) is a military organization, complete with soldiers who undergo military training, carry assault rifles, and travel in armored personnel carriers (APCs).

At first glance, the PASF appears to serve Israel's interests. They arrest Hamas members, eliminate some of the many terrorist cells scattered across Palestinian enclaves, and engage in limited security coordination with the IDF. However, upon closer examination, the situation is far more complex.

In 2006, Hamas would have taken control of the entire PASF had the United States and Israel allowed them to claim their electoral victory. The PASF only remains in nominal cooperation with Israel due to international intervention that overrode the majority of the Palestinian population's vote for Hamas.

While the PASF helps in suppressing Hamas and other terrorist groups in Judea and Samaria, their efforts are inconsistent.

Hamas continues to flourish in Hebron, while the PIJ, Hamas, and numerous other start-up terrorist groups thrive in Samaria. The PA security forces either choose not to police these groups or do so selectively.

Beyond its crimes of omission, more and more members of the PASF are committing active terrorist attacks against Jews in the Land of Israel. October 7, 2023 marked an inflection point. In the aftermath of those massacres, an unprecedented number of Palestinian Authority security personnel have been involved in terrorist attacks against Israelis. One of the most brazen attacks occurred on February 26, 2023, when Colonel Muhammad Mansara, a senior officer in the PA's Preventive Security Service, opened fire unprovoked on a group of Israelis at a gas station in the town of Eli. He murdered a rabbi and father of three, as well as a sixteen-year-old teenager, before he was neutralized.[31] However, this incident is just the tip of the iceberg.

Palestinian supporters openly boast that at least 50 PA security officers have been "martyred" in attacks on Israelis over the course of 2023 and early 2024. Among them were Lieutenant Colonel Jawad Rimawi, who was killed in a firefight with IDF troops in Jenin, and Colonel Mujahid al-Tamimi, who died in a shootout with Israeli forces in Shechem. Both officers were honored with official military funerals by the Palestinian Authority, complete with uniformed honor guards, highlighting the PA's support for their actions.[32]

The scope of PA security forces' engagement in terrorism has become so significant that Ronen Bar, the head of the Shin Bet security service, warned Prime Minister Netanyahu of the imminent danger of a mass "flipping guns" scenario.[33] This term, translated from a Hebrew idiom, refers to the possibility that the PA security force, ostensibly aligned with Israel, will suddenly turn against the Israeli army and Jewish communities en masse.

The Shin Bet's dire forecast appears to be gradually coming to fruition. In January 2024, a unit of armed PA policemen forced an IDF patrol to withdraw from the village of Biddya in Samaria, brandishing their weapons and blocking the soldiers' path. This incident occurred in Area B, where under the Oslo Accords, the PA has no authority to operate.[34]

Recent evidence points to the Palestinian Authority actively preparing for a full-scale conflict with Israel. Videos show PA security forces conducting advanced military training, including urban warfare stimulations, sniper training, paratrooping drills, and anti-tank missile firing practice, in various Muslim countries around the world such as Pakistan and Algeria. The PASF has no enemies which would justify such training — unless it views Israel as an enemy. These activities go far beyond the scope of routine policing duties suggesting a more sinister agenda.[35]

The situation is further inflamed by PA President Mahmoud Abbas's open praise of terrorists who have killed Israelis, whom he hails as "martyrs" and "heroes." Meanwhile, official PA media outlets and school curricula continue to actively promote hatred and violence against Jews. By transforming its security forces into a hostile army-in-waiting, while simultaneously pursuing hostile diplomacy against Israel, the PA pursues a two-pronged strategy aimed at undermining Israel.

A Step Toward Giving Israel Away

The Rebbe's Predictions

The Rebbe argued that any discussion of Palestinian autonomy was merely the first step towards relinquishing Jewish land. He warned that once the principle of autonomy was accepted, it would unleash an unrelenting torrent of pressure on Israel to relinquish more and more territory.

How It Played Out

In the 1970s, and even until the 1990s, it was possible for some to view the Rebbe's dire warnings as exaggerated or alarmist. Although a close examination of Palestinian and Arab rhetoric would have justified the Rebbe's perspective, the general public might have been inclined to believe two key assumptions: firstly, that the Palestinians and their supporters were willing to renounce violence, and secondly, that they were prepared to accept Israel's existence within the pre-1967 borders. These assumptions formed the foundation of the early peace movement in Israel and appeared to underlie Shimon Peres' efforts towards peace. This narrative also garnered widespread political support for the government led by Yitzchak Rabin and Shimon Peres, paving the way for the Oslo Accords.

However, in retrospect, what once required the foresight and analytical prowess of a visionary like the Rebbe should now be readily apparent to anyone who studies the history of Israel's relationship with the Palestinians.

The Rebbe's predictions that Palestinian autonomy would lead to relinquishing parts of Israel have been proven to be true. No concession has brought about peace. Instead, each concession whets the Palestinian appetite for more concessions. With each passing year, Palestinian activism becomes more trenchantly established. This global activism attempts to undermine Israel in every way possible – be it accusing Israel of war crimes, human rights' abuses, or other moralizing critiques. Palestinian government activists and their allies have fueled the BDS (Boycott Divestment and Sanction) movement and have led the charge against Israel in the United Nations and the ICJ. Had there been no Palestinian proto-state, Israel would be in a far stronger position. The moment that Palestinian autonomy was legitimized, it created a bottomless pit of demands for the "rights" of the Palestinian people. Ironically, if the so-called Palestinians were to choose to be peaceful residents of Israel, their human rights and living conditions would far outstrip what they could expect as citizens of the Palestinian Authority.

Practical Solutions: Assert Full Security Control

The Rebbe began speaking out about the dangers of granting Palestinian autonomy in the late 1970s and continued to speak publicly on the issue until 1992. Now, more than three decades later, Israel faces a crucial decision regarding the future of the territories it has controlled since the Six-Day War in 1967. As one analyst frames the issue, Israel can take many possible paths:[36]

> After two decades of postponing a conclusion and instead "managing" the conflict, the time has come for Israel to decide its vision for the Territories. Does it want to annex part of them (the settlement blocs? Area C?) in order to realize the vision of the connection between the people of Israel and the Land of Israel? Does it want to control the territories with a Palestinian population (in Gaza? in the major cities and towns of Judea and Samaria?) or create the reality of another political entity while maintaining freedom of security action?

The Rebbe offered clear practical advice regarding the territories. As Rabbi Pinchas Peli[37] recollected the Rebbe's comments to him in a meeting:[38]

> When it comes to Judea and Samaria, Israel must annex these territories, even though doing so will undoubtedly present challenges. This position is not based on mystical or visionary ideals, but pragmatism. When a nation conquers territory, it retains control over it. While absorbing several million more Arabs into Israel could create problems, these problems pale in comparison to the alternatives: the establishment of a hostile Arab state or federation of states along Israel's border, which would serve as a breeding ground for terrorism. Ideally, Israel

should have annexed these territories immediately following the Six-Day War. With each passing day, Israel's every action in Judea and Samaria becomes increasingly subject to international scrutiny and debate, largely because of Israel's attempts to curry favor with the international community.

In a similar vein, the Rebbe acknowledged that annexing the territories under Israeli civil control would prove challenging — but it was the best available option:[39]

Indeed, annexing the territories and absorbing their Arab residents will [undoubtedly] pose significant challenges for Israel. However, [we must ask ourselves:] Is it preferable to have a hostile Palestinian state on our doorstep, strategically positioned to attack us and wage constant war? While [annexing these lands] may be a fraught [and complicated] endeavor, it is ultimately better for these adversarial Arabs to live under Israeli governance and supervision [than to allow them to establish a belligerent nation at our borders].

The Rebbe advocated full military control over cities such as Hebron, Shechem, and Ramallah, arguing that reducing Jewish military oversight of the Arabs would not lead to greater peace and security:[40]

Some argue that in order to achieve peace and security, we must reduce Jewish military oversight of the Arabs. [However,] it is crucial to recognize that the discussion is not about remote areas such as the Sinai desert, located far from civilization, where we might question their ability to launch attacks. Instead, we are talking about cities such as Hebron,[41] Shechem, and Ramallah, which are all in close proximity to Jerusalem. [Remarkably,] some Jews still suggest that removing Israeli military oversight will lead to greater peace and security, despite the fact that doing so would enable our enemies to amass weapons. [It is important to note that] even under strict military supervision, our enemies manage to find ways to stockpile weapons.[42] If we were to relinquish military con-

trol entirely, we would have no means of monitoring terrorists and their weapon stockpiles, [leaving us vulnerable to attack.]

The Rebbe emphasized that retaining these territories is crucial for ensuring the safety of Israel's Jewish population. He criticized the suggestion to remove the army from these regions and hand over military and civil control to a hostile population:

Holding these territories helps guarantee the safety of Israel's Jewish population. Yet some argue that we should withdraw the army from these regions and hand over military and civil control to the Arabs. In effect, this would mean entrusting military control to individuals who are themselves terrorists, or whose [close relatives, such as their] fathers and sons, are terrorists. It is a fact that many officials [in these areas] are indeed related to terrorists.[43] [By relinquishing control to such individuals, we would be placing the security of Israel's Jewish population in the hands of those who seek to harm us.]

The Rebbe found it irrational that some Jews advocated reduced supervision of the hostile population, especially considering the weapons seized in Judea and Samaria even when there was supervision:

This decision is deeply misguided. Weapons were seized in Judea and Samaria even with active supervision in place, a reality the government tried to conceal from the public. [Yet the full picture] is worse than the limited details that were disclosed. Decision makers have access to the complete facts. Before reducing supervision of Palestinians in these areas, they must first provide transparency about the events that occurred there over the past decades, when there was supervision.

Reiterating comments he had made in the immediate aftermath of the Six-Day War, the Rebbe argued that instead of withdrawing, Israel needed to assert its control over the Land.

Even a decade ago, it was argued that if Jews did not settle all

266

of the liberated territories, it would spell disaster for Israel, G-d forbid. Leaving any portion of these lands unsettled, could only be interpreted in one way: [as a declaration] that the Jewish people have no legitimate claim to them!

The Rebbe stressed that this policy was not just about settling Judea and Samaria, but a matter protecting territories adjacent to densely populated Jewish areas:

This issue extends beyond settling Judea and Samaria, (or as they call it — the "West Bank,"[44] "Green Line,"[45] or "Red Line"[46] in attempts to partition the Land of Israel). It concerns territories right next to major Jewish population centers] home to over three million Jews (may they increase) — places such as the Old City of Jerusalem, Hebron, Shechem, Ramallah, and other locations in the heart of Jewish settlement in our Holy Land. Leaving these territories unsettled poses a literal, tangible danger, besides the fact that it sends the message that the Jewish people have no rightful claim to them!

Considering the Alternative

The Palestinian autonomy project stands at a critical crossroads. Negotiations throughout the 1980s resulted in the establishment of the Palestinian Authority in 1994, led by a terrorist (Yasser Arafat) and plagued by corruption. The PA then found itself in an uneasy coexistence with terrorist groups that flourished under its governance. Following Arafat's death, Mahmoud Abbas, a corrupt, Holocaust-denying politician, assumed control of the PA. As Abbas ages, the PA is becoming increasingly unpopular, corrupt, and unstable, posing a significant threat to Israel's security. To comprehend the gravity of the situation, let's examine the proposed leadership candidates for succession at the PA.

Marwan Barghouti, a favorite of Western media, is one potential future PA leader. Another candidate frequently mentioned is Mohammad Dahlan. While it is probable that a corrupt technocrat[47] from Abbas' inner circle will succeed him, let us consider each of these individuals as case studies of officials praised by Western media as credible candidates to head a Palestinian state that will putatively coexist peacefully with Israel.

Marwan Barghouti

Marwan Barghouti, often portrayed by Western media outlets as the "Palestinian Nelson Mandela" and the "most popular Palestinian leader alive," is touted as a potentially transformative figure in Palestinian politics.[48] However, it is crucial to examine his background and actions. In 2002, Barghouti was imprisoned for orchestrating the murders of at least 26 Jews. From behind bars, he has persistently advocated for violent uprisings against Israel.[49] Given his history and continued incitement, it is difficult to understand how Barghouti could be considered a stable partner for Israel, even if he enjoys popularity among Palestinians. While this notion may align with the media's idealistic vision, it remains far removed from the harsh realities on the ground.[50]

Mohammad Dahlan

Mohammad Dahlan is another potential candidate praised in Western media as having the potential to succeed the current leadership. However, Dahlan's history within the Palestinian government raises serious concerns about his suitability as a partner for peace with Israel. He is currently in exile in Abu Dhabi given his history of violent conflicts with Hamas and with Mahmoud Abbas' forces. But Dahlan has a storied history in Palestinian government.

In the aftermath of the Oslo Accords, Dahlan assumed control of the Palestinian security forces in Gaza. In 1997, evidence surfaced that he had diverted 40% of the taxes collected on imports at a single Gaza crossing, amounting to a staggering one million shekel per month, into his personal bank account.

In 2011, conflicts with Fatah forced Dahlan to flee Judea and Samaria, leading him to pursue an illustrious career serving the leaders of the Gulf states.[51] Given his troubled past, it is difficult to envision Dahlan as a credible partner in establishing a stable and peaceful Palestinian state alongside Israel. During his previous tenure in a similar role, Dahlan left behind a legacy of corruption and contributed to the Palestinian civil war.

It emerges, then, that the two figures heralded by international media[52] as potential future Palestinian leaders, Marwan Barghouti and Mohammad Dahlan, both present significant issues that undermine their ability to serve as reliable partners for peace. In light of this reality, it appears that Israel currently lacks a viable counterpart capable of governing a peaceful Palestinian state.

Consequently, from a purely security-oriented perspective, Israel must reassert complete military and civil control of Judea, Samaria, and Gaza to ensure its own safety and stability in the face of ongoing challenges posed by the Palestinian leadership vacuum.

Taming Gaza

During the current conflict, discussions about the future of Gaza, often referred to as "the day after," have been notoriously ambiguous. Israel has been criticized for failing to articulate a sufficient response to the challenges posed by the region. The Rebbe, however, offered clear guidance on Gaza.

At a 1991 meeting, an activist involved in developing Jewish settlement in Gaza approached the Rebbe, seeking a communal blessing. The Rebbe responded with the following counsel:[53]

> *[In Gaza,] absolute security and full control [must be maintained], without any form of capitulation. May your efforts be met with*

much success. The Hebrew meaning of "Gaza" implies taking a strong, courageous stance. However, if [control] can be achieved through pleasant and peaceful means, that would be the ideal approach.

Summary

The Rebbe's opposition to Palestinian autonomy was rooted in his understanding of the dangers it poses to Israel's existence. He foresaw that Palestinian self-rule would lead to a dramatic escalation in terrorist attacks, the creation of a hostile military force, and the relentless undermining of Israel's legitimacy on the international stage.

The Rebbe's warnings have proven tragically accurate in the years since the Oslo Accords. The Palestinian Authority has transformed into a breeding ground for terror and incitement. Confronted with this grim reality, Israel must summon the courage to embrace the Rebbe's vision of Jewish sovereignty over the entire Land of Israel. Although such actions will inevitably provoke condemnation, Israel cannot allow itself to be held hostage by hostile world opinion or the illusion of a peace process that has brought it to the brink of disaster. The paramount concern must be the security of the Jewish people.

CHAPTER 14
Addressing Domestic Terrorism

One who displays mercy toward the cruel will ultimately become cruel toward the merciful.

MIDRASH, KOHELES RABBAH[1]

IN THE OPENING CHAPTERS of this work, we discussed the Rebbe's principled approach to war. In this chapter, we will delve into a specific aspect of Israel's ongoing struggle: the war against domestic terrorism. Since its establishment, Israel has been beset by terrorism, most often perpetrated not by conventional military units, but by individuals nurtured in a hostile ideological environment or associated with one of the numerous terrorist groups that have emerged in Arab communities within and surrounding Israel.

This grim reality raises a crucial question: What is the most effective approach to dealing with these terrorists? The first consideration is the rules of engagement. Should lethal force be employed as the default response, or should every effort be made to capture terrorists alive? If terrorists are apprehended rather than neutralized, a second question arises: Can imprisonment serve as an effective deterrent to prevent these individuals from reoffending upon release?

Another question to consider in connection with imprisoning terrorists is prisoner exchanges. Throughout its history, Israel has held a significant number of terrorists in its prisons, convicted of crimes ranging from incitement to cold-blooded murder of Jewish civilians. Tragically, kidnapping has been a persistent weapon in the terrorist arsenal, targeting innocent civilians and low-ranking soldiers to use as bargaining chips for securing the release of imprisoned terrorists. The largest-scale incident of this nature took place on October 7, 2023. This tactic raises a moral quandary: Is it justifiable to release unrepentant terrorists, incentivizing further kidnappings and endangering more innocent lives, in order to rescue hostages?[2]

The Rebbe provides unambiguous moral guidance on navigating these complex questions:

Adopt a Zero-Tolerance Policy for Terrorists in Israel

The Rebbe often used the metaphor of surgery to illustrate the most effective approach to dealing with Israel's conflicts with its various enemies. The Rebbe argued that surgery can be performed in two ways: bit by bit or all at once. While the bit-by-bit method may seem less severe, it is ultimately more damaging and less effective. In contrast, performing the surgery all at once may appear more intense, but it leads to a quicker and more complete healing process.

The Rebbe applied the surgical approach to dealing with terrorism in Israel:[3]

> With respect to Israel, there are two options. The first is to inform the other side that we are unwilling to hand over the Land of Israel to them. Since this [itself] would anger them, we would not take action against the terrorists to avoid further provocation. Instead, we would wait and see if, after a week, they might be in a more amenable mood. Then, we would reiterate our position.

However, in practice, we would take no concrete action. As a result, armed terrorists would remain [entrenched] in the Old City of Jerusalem, Hebron, Shechem, Ramallah, and other areas, [posing a constant threat,] G-d forbid!

Alternatively, there is a second option. In one decisive move, we could remove all the terrorists, safe and sound, and send them away. After all, not all the tens of thousands of Arabs [residing in Judea and Samaria] are terrorists — [the actual perpetrators of violence are] only a handful of individuals. The majority of the residents [in these areas] are not engaged in terrorism; they simply desire to live in peace.[4]

In Lebanon, a small group of individuals are responsible for the unrest, yet their actions have led to the deaths of tens of thousands of people, G-d forbid. The same holds true for the terrorists in the Land of Israel. There are a few individuals in the Old City of Jerusalem, Hebron, Shechem, and Lod who are causing all the disturbances. We are aware of their identities and have the capability to deal with them, but we hesitate to do so, claiming that "one should not provoke a small nation," let alone a "large nation [— the United States]." As a result, we feel constrained from taking action against the terrorists, allowing Jews to settle there, or even allowing security personnel to be stationed in these areas; [this inaction is] all due to our apprehension of the international community's reaction.

The Rebbe's approach is straightforward: Deport all terrorists. If an individual identifies as a member of a terrorist organization, Israel must arrest and deport them. By imposing such consequences, the incidence of terror will rapidly decline, fostering a safer and more peaceful environment for all.

The Complexity of Prisoner Exchanges: A Reward for Terror

The Rebbe explains that when dealing with terrorists, civilian rules of engagement do not apply. Instead, we must adhere to the principle explored in Chapter 4: "If one comes to kill you, rise up to kill them [first]." In the context of active terrorists, this means that they should be neutralized rather than imprisoned. As early as 1968, the Rebbe cautioned Israeli government representatives:[5]

> You will pay dearly for imprisoning terrorists since, in the future, their [various allies] will demand concessions to release them and call for prisoner exchanges.

The Rebbe's prediction came to pass in 1978, when Palestinian terrorists[6] kidnapped Israeli soldier Avraham Amram.[7] Following a sustained public opinion campaign, the Israeli government agreed to release 76 convicted terrorists, including murderers, in exchange for Amram's safe return. The Rebbe strongly criticized the disproportionate prisoner exchange, arguing that it would embolden terrorist groups, set a dangerous precedent, and lead to the frequent release of convicted murderers.

The Rebbe began his criticism by noting the disproportionate nature of the exchange:[8]

> The United States and the Soviet Union have recently engaged in a prisoner exchange, but in that case, five prisoners were exchanged for two. In contrast, Israel has exchanged one individual for more than 70 prisoners.

The Rebbe then presented the core critique of such exchanges:

> The Israeli government itself had previously announced that refusing to capitulate to terrorist threats is a fundamental guiding principle, firmly supported by Jewish law and common sense. Furthermore, from a political standpoint, establishing a precedent of releasing terrorists will [embolden] terrorist organizations, encouraging them to take more hostages. Thus, we have no choice but to demonstrate that this strategy will not advance their objectives. Yet, in a shocking reversal, the government abandoned this principle, exchanging over 70 terrorists —

among them several known murderers — for a single hostage.

The Rebbe's foresight proved to be accurate, as the number of terrorists released in such exchanges escalated exponentially over time. In 1983, Israel freed 4,765 terrorists in exchange for six abducted Israeli soldiers. Just two years later, in 1985, Israel released 1,150 terrorists to secure the return of three kidnapped Israeli soldiers.[9] The trend continued in 2011, when Israel freed 1,027 terrorists in exchange for abducted Israeli soldier Gilad Shalit. Among those released as part of the deal was Yahya Sinwar, who had been serving a life sentence for orchestrating the abduction and murder of two Israeli soldiers and four Palestinians. While he was in prison, Israel treated Sinwar for a near-fatal brain tumor saving his life.[10] Tragically, following his release, Sinwar went on to mastermind further attacks, including the devastating October 7, 2023, massacre in Israel.

Beyond pragmatic considerations, Rabbi Shalom Wolpo articulates the Rebbe's principled opposition to prisoner exchanges on the following halachic grounds:[11]

Despite the unique circumstances surrounding prisoner exchanges, where the abductors are seeking to advance ideological goals rather than obtain financial gain, there might be grounds to discuss the halachic basis for prisoner exchanges. The baseline halachic principle teaches that one may not redeem hostages for exorbitant sums, as doing so would incentivize further abductions.[12] This principle, which allows for negotiations in hostage situations, was initially established in the context of cases where the abductors were solely seeking financial gain. However, when the negotiations involve exchanging hostages for convicted terrorists, capitulation is strictly forbidden due to the [overriding] principle of pikuach nefesh [safeguarding life]. The freed terrorists openly declare their intention to continue perpetrating attacks, rendering their release a clear and present danger [to innocent lives].

Blunting Prison's Deterrent Effect

The Rebbe vividly illustrates how both Israeli humanitarianism and the policy of prisoner exchanges have undermined the deterrent effect of prison sentences against terrorism:[13]

> No terrorist is genuinely concerned about [serving] time in an Israeli prison. On the contrary, incarceration is often a favorable outcome. Their basic needs, such as food, drink, and accommodations, [are well taken care of,] frequently surpassing the living conditions in their villages. Moreover, they are confident that within a short period, there will be a prisoner exchange in which hundreds of terrorists will be traded for a handful of Jews. These exchanges are not exceptional [cases], but rather a matter of established policy.

The staggering disparity between the number of terrorists exchanged and the few Jews released in return substantiates the Rebbe's perspective. Moreover, convicted terrorists in Israeli prisons receive excellent treatment on humanitarian grounds. A prime example is Marwan Barghouti, a terrorist mastermind discussed in the previous chapter. Barghouti has an extensive educational history, most of which he acquired while incarcerated in Israeli prisons. At the age of 18, Barghouti was imprisoned for his involvement with terrorist groups. During this time in jail, he completed his high school diploma and learned Hebrew.[14] Years later, when he was imprisoned again for orchestrating numerous murders, Barghouti pursued and earned his PhD within the standard timeframe of eight years, all while behind bars.[15] This suggests that Israeli prison provides terrorists with opportunities to further their education and achieve personal goals. Tragically, these accomplishments empower them to become even more effective terrorists should they be released, as is often the case.

The Cost of Not Credibly Punishing Terrorism

The Rebbe expressed grave concern over the heavy cost of Israel's inadequate response to domestic terrorism. He painted a grim picture of a nation plagued by rampant violence, where the government fails to effectively capture and prosecute those responsible for terrorizing its citizens. Even when terrorists are apprehended and imprisoned, they are often released in lopsided prisoner exchanges, undermining the deterrent effect of the justice system. This weakness in the Israeli security establishment emboldens terrorists and erodes the sense of safety among the Jewish population:[16]

> *The security situation in Israel has deteriorated to an alarming degree, leaving Jews in many areas living under the constant threat of violence. Terrorists brazenly murder [innocent] Jews, while the security establishment's efforts to apprehend them are [woefully] insufficient. [The government's reluctance to take decisive action stems from a misguided] fear of international backlash, worrying that the prosecution of terrorists will lead to condemnation and a tarnished reputation as an unpeaceful people. [This hesitation persists] even once terrorists have been captured and imprisoned, as the government [repeatedly engages in disproportionate prisoner exchanges,] releasing hundreds [of dangerous terrorists] in exchange for a small number of Jewish hostages.*

Commenting on the halachic status of disproportionate prisoner exchanges, the Rebbe observes that while it may be a matter of debate in the abstract, the Israeli government is concretely prohibited from engaging in such exchanges when doing so releases murderers who will go on to commit further acts of violence:

> *From a halachic perspective, one could argue in favor of such exchanges, as each Jewish captive is not merely important*

but is described as being "an entire world."[17] However, those who released the terrorists failed to establish clear guidelines defining the circumstances under which an exchange would be halachically permissible and when it would be forbidden from a national security standpoint. It is well-documented that many terrorists who were freed in prisoner exchanges have subsequently perpetrated additional terrorist attacks.

A review of Israeli government records and news articles confirms this disturbing trend, with the story of Yahya Sinwar serving as perhaps the most notorious example. Palestinians who are released in these exchanges are celebrated as heroes, further encouraging attacks against Israelis. The case of Mohammed Ibrahim Abu Ali, the murderer of Yehoshua Salome, a young *yeshivah* student murdered in 1980 whose death the Rebbe publicly mourned, illustrates this troubling phenomenon. Abu Ali spent 28 years in prison, during which time he rose through the ranks of Fatah and was elected to the Palestinian Legislative Council. Upon his release in 2008, he was greeted with a lavish reception, with his family preparing to slaughter seven baby camels, 40 sheep, and a bull to celebrate his return.[18] Such a hero's welcome for released terrorists serves to glorify violence and inspire future attacks against innocent Israelis. An overarching policy which facilitates such events jeopardizes Jewish lives, indicating the need for a revision in Israel's approach to punishing terrorism.

Summary

The Rebbe provided clear guidance on addressing domestic terrorism in Israel, recognizing that terrorism poses a grave threat to Jewish safety and undermines every aspect of life in the Land of Israel. The policies adopted thus far have been inadequate in addressing this issue. The Rebbe advocated a zero-tolerance policy, proposing that all identified terrorists be swiftly arrested and deported. Moreover, the Rebbe championed the implementation of stricter rules of engagement to neutralize terrorists.

The Rebbe vehemently criticized the practice of prisoner exchanges, arguing that such methods incentivize further kidnappings and attacks by releasing convicted terrorists who most often return to their violent ways. He also highlighted that the generous treatment afforded terrorists in Israeli prisons, coupled with the high likelihood of their release in a prisoner exchange. These factors, the Rebbe contended, blunt prison's deterrent effect, undermining its ability to effectively combat terrorism.

Drawing upon both halachic principles and pragmatic considerations, the Rebbe underscores the necessity of adopting a resolute stance against terrorism. He argued that the Israeli government's perceived weakness and willingness to engage in negotiations with terrorists have contributed to a deterioration of security and an escalation of attacks targeting Israeli citizens. The Rebbe calls for decisive action to neutralize terrorist threats and prioritize the safety and security of the Jewish people in Israel.

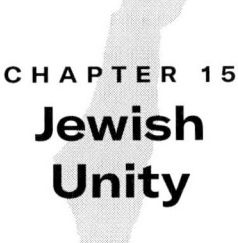

CHAPTER 15

Jewish Unity

Peace is Unity.

THE REBBE MAHARASH, RABBI SHMUEL OF LUBAVITCH[1]

Jewish Unity Fosters Peace and Security

HAMAS' DECISION TO strike Israel on October 7 was influenced by the significant internal discord that gripped Israel in the preceding year, fueled by intense political disagreements.[2] The divisions within Israeli society presented an opportune moment for Hamas to launch an attack, as a fractured nation is more vulnerable to external threats. To prevent such painful realities from recurring, Israel must prioritize the Torah ideal that Jewish unity fosters peace and security.

While there are differing opinions on matters critical to the Jewish state's character and security, the Rebbe[3] consistently emphasized that unity among the Jewish people brings about the fulfillment of G-d's promise to "**make peace** in the Land."[4] Throughout the years and in numerous contexts, the Rebbe reiterated that when the diverse segments of Jewish society unite to form a cohesive whole, harmony and peace will follow. With unity, the Jewish people will become a formidable force, causing Israel's enemies to turn against each other rather than attacking as a united front, as a brief examination of Middle Eastern history clearly demonstrates.[5]

It is important to hold steadfast opinions on matters critical to the Jewish state's character and security. Yet the Rebbe consistently emphasized that unity among the Jewish people and peace with our neighbors will be achieved when the Jewish people follow the Torah and its directives.[6] Disagreements may arise, and the Rebbe maintained that Torah-values must be vocally advocated for. However, internal Jewish disputes, even over legitimate matters, should never be accompanied by violence, unrest, or hateful rhetoric. Instead, the emphasis should be on the fact that we are one family.[7] As the Rebbe put it:[8]

> *Throughout Jewish history, there were eras when the Jewish people, despite being well-versed in Torah, faced defeat in battles due to internal strife.[9] This stands in stark contrast to the time of King Ahab when, despite the prevalence of idolatry, the Jewish people emerged victorious in wars because of their unity.[10] The crucial difference lay in their embrace of a spirit of togetherness, demonstrating love [ahavas Yisrael] and camaraderie among themselves.*

The Jewish People's Responsibility to Advocate for Israel

As English readers, many of whom are Jews living in the diaspora, we might question the relevance of achieving clarity on the Jewish claim to the Land of Israel and the ethics of Jewish warfare. It may seem like a concern exclusive to Jews residing in Israel, and we might hesitate to express our personal opinions on Israel's affairs. However, the Rebbe explains why every Jew has both the right and responsibility to educate themselves on these matters and to speak out:[11]

Every Jew has a portion in the Land of Israel.[12] Therefore, every Jew, regardless of whether they live in Israel or are religiously affiliated, has an inalienable connection to Israel. Each individual Jew is an integral part of the Land of Israel, making everyone's input significant. The fact that many of the Torah's laws apply specifically to Israel [and in the times] when the majority of the Jewish people reside there[13] highlights the importance of every Jewish person to the Land. Furthermore, this shared ownership represents a shared destiny, which unites the Jewish people.

The Rebbe further elaborates on this responsibility, particularly for those in positions of religious leadership:[14]

Rabbis in the diaspora have a particular obligation to make their voices heard in support of Israel, taking the necessary steps to defend its security. Failing to do so violates the [fundamental Torah] principle of "You shall not stand idly while your fellow's blood is shed."[15] Even if one's fellow Jew is [physically] distant, one has a responsibility to protect them, which, [in this context,] involves speaking out and advocating for Israel, as well as making informed decisions that prioritize its security.[16]

This responsibility extends to all Jews, regardless of their location, as the Rebbe emphasizes:[17]

Even in the diaspora, one must act for the sake of the Holy Land and support it in the manner prescribed by the Torah. By virtue of being born Jewish or properly converting, every Jew [automatically] belongs to a "kingdom of priests and a holy nation," whether they desire this status or not. Therefore, every Jew is obligated to act in accordance with the Torah's will and to speak out assertively in every place where they have influence. This is a Torah law [inherently] connected to the preservation of life [Pikuach Nefesh], and on this point, there can be no argument.

CONCLUSION

Realism about Redemption

One who prays must direct his eyes downward
and his heart upward.

YEVAMOS 105b

THROUGHOUT THIS WORK, we have explored the complex challenges facing Israel in its pursuit of enduring peace and security. By meticulously examining the historical context, ideological underpinnings, and practical realities of the conflict, we have arrived at a comprehensive understanding of the steps necessary to **end the cycle** of violence and **make peace**.

At the core of this understanding lies the acknowledgment that simplistic solutions, such as unconditional ceasefires, international mediation, or "Land for Peace" negotiations, have consistently failed to bring about the desired outcome. Instead, we must turn to the Torah's wisdom for guidance, embracing a strategic approach that prioritizes the protection of Jewish lives and the unwavering assertion of our G-d given right to the Land of Israel.

The Torah-based military strategy outlined in this book emphasizes three key principles: credible deterrence, proactive treatment of security risks, and subduing enemies until they no longer pose a threat. By adhering to these principles and rejecting the temptation to compromise under external pressure, Israel can defend its citizens, secure its borders, and pave the way for a brighter, more peaceful future for generations to come.

Equally important is the recognition that the conflict is not merely a territorial dispute, but a clash of ideologies. To counter the fervent zeal of Islamist extremists, Israel must kindle an equally ardent commitment to Jewish values and Torah teachings among its own people. This requires a concerted effort to prioritize Jewish education and nurture a deep connection to the Land of Israel among both Israeli youth and Diaspora Jewry.

In terms of practical policy, the Rebbe advocates for Israeli sovereignty over Judea, Samaria, and Gaza, the active encouragement of Jewish settlement throughout these lands, and the dismantling of the Palestinian Authority. Israel must adopt a zero-tolerance approach to domestic terrorism, reject disproportionate prisoner exchanges, and employ rules of engagement that prioritize the neutralization of terrorists.

Above all, we must emphasize the paramount importance of Jewish unity. By addressing internal disputes through peaceful dialogue and a shared commitment to Torah values, while encouraging all Jews to educate themselves on Israel's security challenges and advocate for policies aligned with the Torah's vision, we can create a unified front in the face of adversity.

The path to lasting peace and security for Israel is not an easy one, but by embracing the principles and policies the Rebbe taught, we can work towards a future in which the Jewish people can live safely and securely in their ancestral homeland. With unwavering faith in G-d's promises and a realistic approach guided by the Torah's wisdom, we can navigate the challenges of the present and usher in the Messianic era, a time of universal harmony and everlasting peace.

Making Peace Is Our Responsibility

The Rebbe is well known for his teachings about *Mashiach*, the great Jewish leader who will bring about an era of global peace, prosperity, and happiness. The arrival of *Mashiach* will mark the beginning of a time when all humanity will work together, using all available resources to pursue knowing G-d and promoting universal goodness throughout the world.

In the Messianic era, the Prophet Isaiah describes a utopian future where "the wolf will dwell with the lamb, and the leopard will lie down with the kid."[1] This symbolizes a time when the Jewish people will coexist peacefully and securely with nations that were once hostile towards them, represented in this verse as predatory animals such as "wolves" and "leopards." In this era, those formerly antagonistic forces and people will be transformed into agents of peace and prosperity.[2]

However, the world has not yet reached the Messianic era described by Isaiah, as evidenced by the ongoing cycle of violence in Israel and wars of greater scale across the globe. *Mashiach*, as a king who "wages G-d's wars," plays a crucial role in bringing about this era.[3] However, merely expressing a desire for peace or engaging in prayer and Torah study is insufficient. Rather, concrete action is necessary to truly usher in the Messianic era. Echoing the words of his father-in-law, Rabbi Yosef Yitzchak,[4] the sixth Lubavitcher Rebbe, the Rebbe would often stress our duty to[5] "dedicate all the days of our lives to bring about the days of *Mashiach*."[6]

Ideally, we could hasten the arrival of *Mashiach* by merely engaging acts of kindness, by spreading light instead of having to directly confront darkness. However, the constant threat posed by our enemies necessitates quelling them to achieve lasting peace. For Jews in Israel, this means creating a society that prioritizes peace and the value of life, attained through realistic methods rather than mere dreams. Jews in the diaspora can contribute in various ways, such as defending Israel, participating in public discourse, or engaging in Torah study and education, which, as explored in Chapter 9, is crucial to winning the war and creating peace.

The Rebbe's fervent love for all humanity and his intense desire to usher in the Messianic era — a time of ultimate human flourishing — drove him to develop a realist, pragmatic approach to making peace. Our mission is to share and implement his vision, thereby realizing the Messianic era. Despite the challenging battle ahead, by staying the course with the guidance of the Rebbe's principles, we can help create a reality in which "no nation will raise up a sword to another, and they will no longer study warfare."[7] Maimonides describes this era as follows:[8]

> In the Messianic era, hunger, warfare, jealousy, and strife will cease to exist. Abundance and prosperity will be widespread, with all luxuries as readily available as dust. Humanity's sole focus will be knowing G-d. The Jewish people, as great sages, will gain [deep insight] into the profound mysteries [of the universe] and will attain the greatest possible understanding of their Creator, fulfilling the prophecy: "For the earth shall be full of the knowledge of G-d, as the waters cover the sea."

A Crash Course
In History

CENTRAL ELEMENTS of this book's discussion, particularly questions of Land for Peace and the topographic nature of security depend on a knowledge of geography. The following maps visually contextualize the Land of Israel's geographic location, its proximity to its various neighbors, and the strategic realities that emerge from this context.

MAP 1

The Land of Israel in a Larger Regional Context – a Bridge Between Continents

Google Maps

MAP 2

Israel with the Sinai in Context

Google Maps

M A P 3

Israel and Its Immediate Neighbors

Google Earth

MAP 4

Israel, from "The River" to "The Sea"

Google Earth

MAP 5

The United Kingdom of Ancient Israel Kingdom

Regno De Davide

MAP 6

The Divided Kingdom of Ancient Israel

Kingdoms of the Levant – revised by Tomas Pueyo

A Crash Course in History

TO CONTEXTUALIZE MANY of the questions we've explored in this book, it is helpful to look at a timeline to place everything in perspective.

Historical Overview of Jewish Presence in the Land of Israel

What is the Jewish people's relationship with the Land?
Let's explore the history.

The Biblical Period

circa 19th to 16th Century BCE

Era of the Patriarchs

Abraham, Isaac, and Jacob, the forefathers of today's Jewish people, lived in Canaan, the area that later came to be known as the Land of Israel. The Bible teaches that G-d promised this land to Abraham and his descendants as part of an eternal

291

covenant, establishing the Jewish people's connection to the land.

circa 15th – 14th Century BCE
Egyptian Exile and Exodus

The Children of Israel (Jacob along with his children and their families) moved to Egypt during the time of Joseph, who had risen to a high position in the Egyptian court. After Joseph's death, the Israelites were enslaved by the Egyptians for centuries. The Books of Exodus, Numbers, and Deuteronomy chronicle how Moses led the Israelites out of slavery in Egypt and back to the Land of Israel.

circa 13th Century BCE
Conquest and Settlement of the Land

After the Exodus from Egypt and the death of Moses, Joshua, Moses' successor, led the Israelites in conquering Canaan from the seven Canaanite nations mentioned in the Bible (Deuteronomy 7:1). The Book of Joshua teaches that the Israelites successfully conquered and settled in the land, which had been promised to them by G-d as part of His covenant with their ancestors.

circa 1228–879 BCE
Era of the Judges

Following Joshua's conquest and the initial settlement of the Israelite tribes in Canaan, there was a period of decentralized leadership known as the Era of the Judges, recorded in the Book of Judges. This marked the beginning of Israelite settlement in Canaan, laying the foundations for the establishment of a unified Israelite monarchy in later centuries.

circa 879–797 BCE
United Monarchy

The reigns of Kings Saul, David, and Solomon marked the transition from the decentralized rule of the judges to a centralized Israelite monarchy. Saul, chosen by the prophet

Samuel, was succeeded by David, who established Jerusalem as the capital. David's son, Solomon, further strengthened the kingdom and built the First Temple in Jerusalem. However, tensions between the northern and southern tribes led to the division of the kingdom after Solomon's death.

797-423 BCE
Divided Kingdom

After Solomon's death, the United Monarchy split into two separate kingdoms: Israel (Northern Kingdom) and Judah (Southern Kingdom). Israel was led by Jeroboam I, while Judah was ruled by Rehoboam, Solomon's son. The two kingdoms fought each other and faced external threats from neighboring empires, such as the Assyrians and Babylonians. After several waves of attacks, the Assyrians finally exiled the entire Kingdom of Israel by 556.

423 BCE
Babylonian Exile

The Babylonian Empire, led by King Nebuchadnezzar II, conquered the Kingdom of Judah, destroyed the First Temple in Jerusalem, and exiled a significant portion of the Jewish population to Babylon. This marked the beginning of the Babylonian Exile that lasted until the Persian Empire allowed the Jews to return to their homeland and rebuild the Temple.

The Second Temple Period

371-332 BCE
Persian Period

After the Persian Empire, led by Cyrus the Great, conquered Babylon, the exiled Jews were allowed to return to their homeland. Under Persian rule, the Jewish people rebuilt the Temple in Jerusalem (known as the Second Temple). The Persian Period lasted until Alexander the Great's conquests in 332 BCE.

293

332–63 BCE

Hellenistic and Hasmonean Period

After Alexander the Great's conquests, the Land of Israel was influenced by Hellenistic culture. Tensions arose as some Jews adopted Greek customs. In 167 BCE, the Seleucid ruler Antiochus IV banned Jewish practices and desecrated the Temple, triggering the Maccabean Revolt. The Maccabees successfully recaptured Jerusalem, rededicated the Temple (commemorated by Chanukah), and established the Hasmonean dynasty, which ruled an independent Jewish kingdom until the Roman conquest in 63 BCE.

Roman and Byzantine Period

63 BCE–324 CE

Roman Period

The Roman Empire conquered the Land of Israel in 63 BCE, ending Hasmonean rule. In 69 CE, following the First Jewish-Roman War, the Romans destroyed the Second Temple in Jerusalem. The Jews revolted again under the leadership of Bar Kokhba in 132-133 CE, but the Romans suppressed the rebellion, leading to widespread destruction and the exile of many Jews from their homeland.

After suppressing the Bar Kokhba revolt in 133 CE, the Roman Emperor Hadrian renamed the Land of Israel "Syria Palaestina." This name was derived from the Biblical Philistines and used to minimize Jewish connection to the Land following the revolt. Over time, the term "Palestine" became more widely used in English and other European languages to refer to the region.

Following the Bar Kokhba revolt, the Jewish population in the Land of Israel significantly declined due to Roman persecutions and expulsions. Hadrian killed over 500,000 Jews during the revolt.[1] He then sold many survivors into slavery across the empire. Many Jews fled the region to escape the aftermath of the failed rebellion. This led to an influx of Jewish refugees into existing diaspora communities across Europe, North Africa, and the Middle East. As Jews faced further persecution in those lands over the following centuries, they were dispersed even more widely across the world.

324–637 CE
Byzantine Period

Following the fall of the Roman Empire, the Christian Byzantine Empire controlled the Land of Israel. Christianity became the dominant force in the land, although Jewish communities persisted, particularly in the Galilee.[2]

Four Warring Caliphates (638-1099 CE)

637–661 CE
Rashidun Caliphate

Islamic rule began soon after the founding of Islam with the Arab conquests. The Rashidun Caliphate, an early Islamic empire based in contemporary Saudi Arabia, conquered the Land of Israel from the Byzantine Empire in 637 CE. Under Rashidun rule, the conditions for the Jewish population improved. They were allowed to return to Jerusalem and establish a yeshivah. This period marked a shift in the region's political and religious landscape, with Islam becoming the dominant power and providing a relatively tolerant environment for Jewish communities.

661–750
Umayyad Caliphate

The Umayyads, based in Damascus, overthrew the Rashidun Caliphate in the first Islamic Civil War (661 CE) and took control of its territories, including the Land of Israel. The Umayyads constructed the Dome of the Rock on the Temple Mount in Jerusalem.

750–969 CE

Abbasid Caliphate

The Abbasids, a new Islamic dynasty based in Baghdad overthrew the Umayyads and seized control of their vast empire, which included the Land of Israel.

969–1099 CE

Fatimid Caliphate

The Fatimid Caliphate, a Shi'ite Islamic dynasty from North Africa, took control of the Land of Israel in 969 CE, establishing their capital in Cairo. During their rule, the region faced internal strife, challenges from rival Islamic groups, and the First Crusades (1096-1099 CE), resulting in the capture of Jerusalem by European Christians in 1099 CE.

During this period, the Land of Israel was known to its Muslim rulers as part of "Al-Sham" meaning "the left" or "the north." This term was applied to the entire Levant (Syria, Lebanon, Jordan, and the Land of Israel) since the Levant is to the left or north of Arabia. The term Palestine only entered the Arab–Muslim lexicon with the advent of European colonial influence in the 1800s.

The Crusaders

1099–1291 CE

In 1099 CE, European Christian Crusaders captured Jerusalem from the Fatimid Caliphate and established the Kingdom of Jerusalem, controlling much of the Land of Israel. The Crusader period lasted until 1291 CE.[3]

The Mamluk Era

1291–1516 CE

The Mamluk Sultanate, a non-Arab Islamic dynasty, began to eradicate the Crusader states in 1260 CE. Under Mamluk rule, which lasted until 1516 CE, the Jewish population in the Land of Israel remained small but stable. During this period, some Jewish immigration from Europe occurred, primarily led by Ashkenazi Jewish leaders.[4]

Ottoman Period (1516–1917 CE)

The Ottoman Empire conquered the Land of Israel from the Mamluks in 1516 CE and ruled the region until 1917.[5]

During the Ottoman period, the Jewish population dramatically increased due to the immigration of Sephardic Jews expelled from Spain and Portugal, as well as Jews from other parts of the Ottoman Empire. The Four Holy Cities of Jerusalem, Hebron, Safed, and Tiberias emerged as major centers of Jewish population and religious life under Ottoman rule.

1777–1882

A significant number of Jewish students and followers of influential spiritual movements, particularly the chassidim and disciples of the Vilna Gaon, immigrated to the Land of Israel.

1882–1903

The First *Aliyah*[6] saw approximately 35,000 Jews, mainly from Eastern Europe and influenced by secular Zionism, immigrate to the Land of Israel.

1904–1914

The Second *Aliyah* brought approximately 40,000 Jewish immigrants, primarily from Eastern Europe, to the Land of Israel.

British Mandate (1917–1948 CE)

After World War I, the British took control of the Land of Israel from the Ottoman Empire. Under British rule, the region experienced significant Jewish immigration.

1919 – 1923

The Third *Aliyah* brought about 40,000 Jewish immigrants to the Land of Israel, mainly from Russia and Eastern Europe. This wave of immigration was driven by harsh post-World War I conditions, the Russian Revolution, and rising antisemitism in the region.

1924 – 1929

The Fourth *Aliyah* brought approximately 82,000 Jewish immigrants to the Land of Israel, primarily from Poland and other parts of Eastern Europe.

1932 – 1939

The Fifth *Aliyah* saw the arrival of approximately 250,000 Jewish immigrants to the Land of Israel, primarily from Germany and other parts of Central and Eastern Europe. This massive wave of immigration was largely driven by the rise of Nazism and the increasing persecution of Jews in Europe during the 1930s.

1939 – 1945

During World War II, the British government issued the White Paper of 1939, which severely restricted Jewish immigration to the Land of Israel. Despite these restrictions, covert immigration efforts, known as "Aliyah Bet," continued throughout the war years, as Jews sought to escape Nazi-occupied Europe and find refuge in their ancestral homeland.

1945 – 1948

Post-World War II, Holocaust survivors and other Jews from around the world sought to immigrate to the Land of Israel, driven by the desire to rebuild their lives and contribute to the establishment of a Jewish homeland. Despite ongoing British restrictions on immigration, the Jewish population in the region continued to grow through covert immigration efforts.

The Modern State of Israel

The State of Israel was established in 1948 following the United Kingdom's withdrawal from the region, resulting in significant Jewish population growth. Jews from around the world flocked to Israel, among them many Holocaust survivors who had been in Displaced Persons camps in Europe. Sephardic Jews fleeing persecution in newly formed Islamic states across the Middle East and North Africa due to the withdrawal of British and French colonial powers also came to Israel en masse. In this context, Operation Wings of Eagles (1949-1950) brought 50,000 Jews from Yemen to Israel while Operation Ezra and Nehemiah (1950-1951) brought 120,000 Jews from Iraq to Israel.

Ever since, Jewish people from around the world have streamed back to the Land of Israel, some fleeing persecution and others wishing to return to the biblical Land of their ancestors. Significant signposts along the way were the Soviet aliyah in the 1990s, with close to a million Soviets of Jewish ancestry moving to Israel following the collapse of the Soviet Union, and aliyah from countries such as France in the 2000s in response to elevated antisemitism and the desire for Jewish belonging.

Today, 7.2 million Jews, 47% of the global Jewish population, reside in the Land of Israel. The population has been buttressed by *aliyah*, but more by natural growth, given that across all demographics, Israel has the highest birth rate of any developed country in the world.[7]

A History of Violence Against the Jewish People in Israel

Having told the story of the Jewish connection to the Land from forefathers of the Jewish people to the present, it is important to understand the origins of the contemporary violence in the region. While the Babylonians, Romans, and Crusaders all treated the Jews violently in the past, those groups no longer exist. So, let's trace the roots of the current conflict.

Some narratives suggest that terrorism and violence against the Jewish people derives from resentment over contemporary Jewish settlement in Judea and Samaria. However, the historical record shows that Islamic violence towards Jews has been a constant since the seventh century, long before the invention of Palestinian national identity in the early 20th century and the development of contemporary nationalist narratives. The roots of the conflict predate the current political situation and are not primarily a result of recent events.

In what follows, we will explore the history of Islamic violence against Jews from the seventh century to the present day. This historical background will introduce us to the key characters and events that have contributed to the ongoing cycle of violence in the region.[8]

Anti-Jewish Violence Before the State's Founding

Byzantine period
Byzantine rulers engaged in violence against the Jewish population.

7th Century
Following the rise of Islam and the Arab conquests, Jews were considered "dhimmis," second-class citizens, resulting in

discrimination and sporadic violence.[9]

10th Century

Periods of violence against Jews occurred during the Fatimid Caliphate's rule.

1090s

The Crusaders often perpetrated violence against Jews, notably killing and expelling the Jews from Jerusalem.

1165

Maimonides visited Jerusalem and noted the oppression of Jews under local Islamic rule.

1260s

During their conquest, the Mamluks perpetrated violence against the Jews.

1516–1917

The Ottoman Empire ruled the Land of Israel. Jews faced discrimination and occasional violence from the local population.

1834

Hebron Massacre

Arab rioters attacked the Jewish community in Hebron.

1920

Nebi Musa riots

Arab rioters killed and wounded Jews in Jerusalem. From 1920 onwards, Arab riots began as a reaction to increased Jewish presence in the Land, and in opposition to the eventual establishment of a Jewish state.

1921

Jaffa riots

A major outbreak of violence in Jaffa and surrounding areas, where the local Arabs killed many Jews and perpetrated widespread property damage and looting.

1929

Hebron Massacre

A large-scale riot and massacre against the Jewish community in Hebron. The rioters killed 67 Jews, mutilating and raping many others. As a result of the brutal attack, the Jewish population evacuated the city until the 1970s, only partially returning in the following decades.

1936–1939

The Arab Revolt

A nationalist uprising against the British Mandate and Jewish immigration, marked by widespread violence against Jewish communities.

1947–1948

Arab violence escalated significantly following the U.N.'s partition plan for Palestine, leading to the 1948 War of Independence.

May 13, 1948

The Gush Etzion massacre
(1 day before the establishment of the State of Israel)

Gush Etzion, a cluster of Jewish towns south of Jerusalem, had been besieged for months by Arab forces. After intense fighting, the Arabs killed 120-130 Jewish defenders and some civilians who had surrendered. They took others as prisoners to Jordan.

Mapping The Cycle of Violence
Since the State of Israel's Founding

1948

Arab-Israeli War (War of Independence)

Following the U.N. Partition Plan and the dissolution of the British Mandate, Israel declared independence. As a result, five neighboring Arab states declared war on Israel. Israel miraculously won the war and expanded its territory beyond the U.N.-proposed borders.

1950s

Fedayeen Attacks

Palestinian fedayeen (terrorists) launched cross-border attacks into Israel, primarily from Egypt, Jordan, and Syria.

1956

Sinai War (also known as the Suez Crisis)

Israel, along with the United Kingdom and France, invaded Egypt in response to Egyptian President Nasser's nationalization of the Suez Canal, and to stop fedayeen raids. While they won the war, Israel and its allies ultimately withdrew under pressure from the United States.

1964

Establishment of Palestine Liberation Organization (PLO)

The PLO aimed for the "liberation of Palestine," namely, the entire State of Israel, which then did not include Judea, Samaria, or Gaza, through armed violence.

1965

First PLO Attack

A failed attempt to bomb Israel's National Water Carrier. Still celebrated in Palestinian memory as "the detonation of the Eilabun tunnel."[10]

1967

Six-Day War

Israel launched preemptive strikes against Egypt, Jordan, and Syria, leading to a rapid and decisive victory. Israel captured the Gaza Strip, Sinai Peninsula, Judea and Samaria (West Bank), East Jerusalem, and Golan Heights.

1967–1970

War of Attrition

A low intensity war along the Suez Canal broke out between Israel and Egypt, with some Russian involvement on the Egyptian side. The war ended under U.S. pressure for a ceasefire.

1970–1971

Jordanian Civil War and Black September

After the Six-Day war, the PLO moved their international terror operations' base to Jordan. The PLO's increased violence in Jordan (against Jordanians) and attempt to assassinate the Jordanian King Hussein provoked a civil war. Hussein expelled the PLO and thousands of Palestinians to Lebanon. The Black September organization, a breakaway faction of the PLO, emerged as a result.

1972

Munich Olympics Massacre

Palestinian terrorists from the Black September organization murdered 11 Israeli athletes at the Munich Olympic Games.

1973

Yom Kippur War

Egypt and Syria launched a surprise attack on Israel on Yom Kippur, initiating a costly war that ended with a military victory for Israel but high losses. Israel stopped short of conquering Cairo and Damascus, fearing international condemnations.

1975–1990

Lebanese Civil War

The PLO set up an autonomous region of control in Southern Lebanon, and clashed with the Lebanese government and Lebanese Christian clans. Syria entered the war, sometimes fighting against the PLO, and at others times fighting on the PLO's side against other factions. The civil war led to tremendous destruction and humanitarian crises in Lebanon.

1974

Ma'alot Massacre

The Democratic Front for the Liberation of Palestine (DFLP), a Palestinian terrorist group based in Lebanon, attacked Israelis in the northern city of Ma'alot, killing 25 people, including many children.

1976

Operation Entebbe

The Popular Front for the Liberation of Palestine – External Operations (PFLP-EO) hijacked an Air France plane en route to Israel and held it in Entebbe, Uganda. Israeli commandos successfully rescued the hostages.

1978

Coastal Road Massacre and Operation Litani

The massacre by a PLO faction invading Israel led to Israel's Operation Litani, aiming to push PLO forces away from its northern border. The operation ended indecisively given international pressure, and the U.N. sent a peacekeeping force UNIFIL to the region.

1978

Camp David Accords

Peace talks between Egypt and Israel, mediated by the United States, which led to the 1979 Egypt-Israel Peace Treaty wherein Israel conceded the Sinai peninsula and began to discuss Palestinian autonomy in return for Egypt's promise of no further wars. This led to Israel ceding important oil fields, military bases, and dismantling significant Jewish communities such as Yamit.

1982
First Lebanon War
Israel invaded Lebanon to expel the PLO. This war led to the establishment of the South Lebanon Security Zone. After three months of fighting and international involvement, the PLO finally departed for Tunisia.

1985
Founding of Hezbollah
In response to Israel's presence and the ongoing war, Hezbollah, a Shi'ite Islamist militant group, was founded in 1985. The organization emerged as a formidable force, posing an enduring challenge to Israel.

1985-2000
South Lebanon Security Zone
Israel maintained a security zone in Southern Lebanon to protect its northern borders from attacks by Hezbollah. In 2000, Israel unilaterally withdrew due to international pressure and domestic divisions.

1987-1991
First Intifada
A violent Palestinian uprising against Israel, marked by widespread protests and violence.

1987
Founding of Hamas
The Islamic Resistance Movement, known as Hamas, was founded during the First Intifada.

1991
Madrid Conference
Hosted under U.S. and Soviet guidance, this conference marked Israel's first open engagement in direct negotiations with Palestinians. The Madrid Conference laid the groundwork for the Oslo Accords.

1993
Oslo Accords
Signed in 1993, this treaty officially legitimized the PLO and its leader Yasser Arafat as the Palestinians' only representatives. The agreements facilitated autonomy in Palestinian majority cities, contributing to a spiral of terror and decades of suffering. These accords thus escalated instability and conflict, rather than advancing peace.

1994
Israel-Jordan Peace Treaty
Israel and Jordan signed a peace treaty. In return for Jordan agreeing to not initiate any further wars (Israel and Jordan had not fought since 1967), Israel gave approximately 380 square kilometers[11] of land to Jordan.

2000
Camp David Summit
A summit between Israel and the Palestinian Authority took place, brokered by President Bill Clinton of the United States, that failed to reach a final agreement, despite Israeli Prime Minister Ehud Barak offering 90% of Judea and Samaria for a Palestinian state.

2000–2005
Second Intifada
Another Palestinian uprising, more violent than the first, following the failure of the 2000 Camp David Summit. In this intifada, Hamas, PIJ, and several PLO groups introduced heavy use of suicide bombings.

2002

Operation Defensive Shield

An extensive Israeli military operation in Judea and Samaria in response to the Second Intifada, targeting terrorist infrastructure. This helped quell the Second Intifada.

2002

Construction of the West Bank Barrier

Israel began constructing a security barrier in the West Bank in 2002 to prevent terrorist attacks. Since this wall's construction, there have been markedly fewer attacks from the regions it covers.

2005

Israel's Unilateral Disengagement from Gaza

Israel dismantled the Gush Katif Jewish communities from Gaza. The IDF forcibly evicted all of Gaza's Jewish residents, and all IDF forces left the Gaza strip.

2006

Hamas' Victory in the Palestinian Elections After winning an election, Hamas took control of Gaza. Soon after, Hamas kidnapped Israeli soldier Gilad Shalit, leading to Israeli military responses.

2006

Israel-Hezbollah War (Second Lebanon War)

A conflict between Israel and Hezbollah in Lebanon arose, triggered by a Hezbollah cross-border raid.

2007

Battle of Gaza

Hamas seized full control of Gaza after several days of intense fighting with the PLO.

2008–2009

Operation Cast Lead

An Israeli military operation in the Gaza Strip, aimed at stopping rocket fire into Israel from Hamas and other militant groups. Israel withdrew after a ceasefire with Hamas.

2011

Itamar Massacre

Palestinian infiltrators brutally killed five members of an Israeli family in the town of Itamar.

2011

Gilad Shalit Exchange

The Israeli government and Hamas made a deal where Hamas released Gilad Shalit in exchange for 1,027 Palestinian prisoners, including convicted terrorists, among them Yahya Sinwar, architect of the October 7, 2023, massacres.

2012

Operation Pillar of Defense

An Israeli operation conducted in Gaza to stop rocket attacks and destroy Hamas' military infrastructure. The operation ended with a ceasefire.

2014

Three Boys Kidnapped, Operation Brother's Keeper, and Operation Protective Edge

Hamas militants kidnapped and murdered three Israeli teenagers. Israel responded with a large-scale operation in Judea and Samaria to look for the boys and clamp down on terrorism. This escalated into a full-scale conflict in Gaza. The operation ended with a ceasefire.

2015–2016

Knife Intifada

A wave of stabbing, shooting, and car-ramming attacks was perpetrated by Palestinians against Israelis. This took place across Israel, in Jerusalem, Tel Aviv, Haifa, Afula, Ra'anana, Hebron, Judea, and Samaria.

2018

U.S. Embassy Relocated to Jerusalem

The United States officially moved its embassy from Tel Aviv to Jerusalem, recognizing Jerusalem as the capital of Israel.

2020

Abraham Accords

Israel signed peace agreements with several Arab states (United Arab Emirates, Bahrain, Sudan, Morocco). Israel did not concede any land and instead promised economic cooperation.

2021

Israel-Gaza Conflict

An 11-day conflict between Israel and Hamas, sparked by tensions in Jerusalem and rocket fire from Gaza into Israel.

2021

Arab Riots in Israel

In response to tensions in Jerusalem and the Gaza conflict, Israeli Arabs[12] began widespread riots and attacks on Jewish communities and properties in the central and northern Israeli cities of Lod, Acre, Haifa, Jaffa, Bat Yam, and Ramat Gan.

2023

Simchas Torah Massacre and Subsequent Gaza War

On October 7, Hamas perpetrated the bloodiest attack on Israel in its entire history. So many Jews have not been killed in one day since the Holocaust. Israel responded with an air and ground incursion into Gaza, more serious than ever, with the stated goal of dismantling Hamas and ensuring that Gaza would cease to be a source of terror.

A Practical Statement of Policy

THE REBBE'S VISION for an Israel where peace reigns is deeply nuanced. Over the course of Make Peace's nearly 400 pages, one might begin to get lost in the history, Torah and strategic arguments, and careful analyses. In that light, the following statement of practical policy emerges from the Rebbe's teachings, covering the entire gamut of issues pertaining to creating a lasting peace in Israel.

However, it is important to note that if someone begins with different ideological assumptions than the Rebbe's, or is not sufficiently educated on the facts of the conflict, the Rebbe's practical advice might come across as jarring or foreign. The reader should carefully study the arguments that ground these policies before passing judgment. To fully understand and appreciate the conclusions, one must thoroughly examine the path that led to them.

The policy statement that follows is not a standalone document, but rather a culmination of the extensive research, historical context, and Torah-based principles presented throughout this book.[13]

1. **ASSERT ISRAEL'S G-D** given right to the entire Land of Israel, including Judea, Samaria, and Gaza, as promised in the Torah, and reject any pressure to compromise on this principle.

2. **REJECT SIMPLISTIC SOLUTIONS** for peace, such as unconditional ceasefires without achieving military objectives, relying on international community mediation, or engaging in "Land for Peace" negotiations, as these approaches have only led to greater loss of life and historically failed to bring lasting peace and security.

3. **ADOPT A TORAH-BASED** military strategy that emphasizes:

a. Credible deterrence: Demonstrate unwavering resolve to respond decisively to any aggression, making it clear that attacks on Israel will be met with overwhelming force.

b. Proactive neutralization of threats: Take preemptive action against enemies with hostile intentions, eliminating their capacity to harm Israel before they can strike.

c. Fully neutralizing threats: Wage comprehensive offensives to dismantle the enemy's capacity for warfare until they surrender unconditionally, ensuring that they cannot regroup and pose a future threat.

d. Low risk tolerance: Actively assess potential risks and do not tolerate minor risks that have the potential to turn into more serious security issues.

e. Respect for territory's strategic value: Land is not mere space that can be traded at will. Instead, land has has critical strategic value and serves to save lives. In contrast, giving up land to current or potential enemies increases the odds of war and loss of life.

4. **RECOGNIZE THE IDEOLOGICAL** motivation of Israel's enemies and counter their fervor with an equally strong commitment to Jewish values and the Torah's teachings.

5. **PRIORITIZE JEWISH EDUCATION** and the cultivation of a deep connection to the Land of Israel among Israeli youth and diaspora Jewry to foster the necessary resilience necessary to withstand the challenges posed by the Jewish people's enemies.

6. **ASSERT FULL JEWISH** sovereignty over Judea, Samaria, and Gaza, and reject Palestinian autonomy.

7. **ACTIVELY ENCOURAGE** and facilitate Jewish settlement throughout the entire Land of Israel, particularly in Judea, Samaria, and Gaza, to proudly assert Israel's claim to its ancestral Land and to prevent the establishment of a hostile Palestinian state.

8. **IMPLEMENT A ZERO-TOLERANCE** policy towards domestic terrorism, swiftly arresting and deporting all identified terrorists and maintaining strict rules of engagement that prioritize neutralizing threats.

9. **REJECT PRISONER EXCHANGES** that release convicted terrorists, as they incentivize further attacks and kidnappings.

10. **CULTIVATE JEWISH UNITY** as a crucial factor in Israel's security, addressing internal disputes through peaceful dialogue and a shared commitment to the Torah's values, while encouraging all Jews to educate themselves on Israel's security challenges and advocate for policies that align with the Torah's vision.

Appendix: The Rebbe's Correspondence With Rabbi Immanuel Jakobovits

RABBI IMMANUEL JAKOBOVITS (1921-1999) served as the Chief Rabbi of the United Kingdom from 1966-1991. He strongly advocated for the Camp David Accords with their attendant significant territorial compromises In October 1980, as controversy over Land for Peace raged across the Jewish world, Rabbi Jakobovits penned an article associating the Rebbe's opposition to ceding land for peace with the ideologies of Rabbi Meir Kahane and the Gush Emunim settlement movement. Mr. Peter Kalms, an associate of the Chief Rabbi and a follower of the Rebbe, wrote to Rabbi Jakobovits, taking umbrage with his characterization of the Rebbe. Rabbi Jakobovits responded with a letter defending his portrayal of the Rebbe's views.

Subsequently, Kalms shared the correspondence with the Rebbe. The Rebbe then wrote Kalms a detailed six-page letter dated 3rd Light of Chanukah 5741 (December 1980), clearly elucidating and arguing his position in English and in layman's terms. The Rebbe explored many facets of the question of Land for Peace, emphasizing that his opposition stemmed primarily from the paramount concern of saving Jewish lives (*pikuach nefesh*) as outlined in the *Shulchan Aruch*. He stressed that his position was not based on the sanctity of *Eretz Yisrael* or political considerations. He directed Kalms to share the letter with Rabbi Jakobovits.

Rabbi Jakobovits responded to the Rebbe's letter, still maintaining his position in favor of Land for Peace. In a second letter, written around seven weeks later (13 Shvat 5741 – February 1981), the Rebbe reiterated that his position was based purely on raw halachic principles and saving Jewish lives, not on a partisan political ideology. He further clarified that military expertise related to security, and not political considerations, should be the deciding factor in territorial matters.

Finally, in a third letter in Elul 5741 (Fall 1981), the Rebbe restated his opposition to the Camp David Accords and the grave error of surrendering the Sinai oil fields. He pointed out how recent events had vindicated his earlier warnings, particularly regarding the economic consequences for Israel. The Rebbe also touched on Israeli government policy being weak on terrorism and the need to strengthen policy to safeguard Jewish lives.

Throughout the correspondence, the Rebbe maintained that his position was consistently based on halachic considerations of *pikuach nefesh*, applicable universally and not limited to *Eretz Yisrael*.

Beyond these issues, in the letters, the Rebbe touched on a broad range of topics and arguments relating to Israel's security which we have explored throughout this work. The Rebbe's letters to Rabbi Jakobovits are presented here in the original for the first time, courtesy of Rabbi Elkanah Shmotkin and the JEM foundation.

RABBI MENACHEM M. SCHNEERSON
Lubavitch
770 Eastern Parkway
Brooklyn, N. Y. 11213

Hyacinth 3-9250

מנחם מענדל שניאורסאהן
ליובאוויטש

770 איסטערן פּאַרקוויי
ברוקלין, נ. י.

By the Grace of G-d
3rd Light of Chanukah, 5741
Brooklyn, N.Y.

Mr. Pinchus Meir Kalms (Mr. P. Kleeman)
45 Sheldon Avenue
Highgate, London, N. 16

Greeting and Blessing:

This is to acknowledge receipt of your letter and enclosure.

I am reluctant, on principle, to involve a layman, however knowledgeable, even if he possesses Smichah, in a matter that is the
subject of debate between Rabbis. However, after you received a
detailed letter from a Rabbi, and request a clarification, I have
no choice but to address myself to the issues at hand in reply,
though necessarily not in depth.

I must begin with a general but crucial point, namely, that the
arguments against my supposed stand are based on misinformation,
or on misconception of what my stand is. Indeed, I find it difficult
to understand how this could have happened, since I have repeatedly
explained my position. So I will recap it once again:

1.   I am completely and unequivocally opposed to the surrender of
any of the liberated areas currently under negotiation, such as
Yehuda and Shomron, the Golan, etc., for the simple reason, and only
reason, that surrendering any part of them would contravene a clear
Psak-Din in Shulchan Aruch (Orach Chayim, sec. 329, par. 6,7). I
have repeatedly emphasized that this Psak-Din has nothing to do with
the sanctity of Eretz Yisroel, or with "days of Moshiach," the Geula,
and similar considerations, but solely with the rule of Pikuach-Nefesh.
This is further emphasized by the fact that this Psak-Din has its
source in the Talmud (Eiruvin 45a), where the Gemora cites as an
illustration of a "border-town" under the terms of this Psak-Din -
the city of Neharde'a in Babylon (present-day Iraq) - clearly not in
Eretz Yisroel. I have emphasized time and time again that it is a
question of, and should be judged purely on the basis of, Pikuach-Nefesh,
not geography.

2.   The said Psak-Din deals with a situation where gentiles (the
term is גוים, not enemies) besieges a Jewish border-town, ostensibly
to obtain "straw and hay," and then leave. But because of the possible
danger, not only to the Jews of the town, but also to other cities,
the Shulchan Aruch rules that upon receiving news of the gentiles (even only -)
preparations, the Jews must mobilize immediately and take up arms even
on Shabbos - in accordance with the rule that "Pikuach-Nefesh supersedes Shabbos."

3.   Should there be a question whether the risk does in fact create
a situation of Pikuach-Nefesh, then - as in the case of illness, where

a medical authority is consulted - the authority to make a judgment
is vested in the military experts. If military experts decide that
there is a danger of Pikuach-Nefesh, there could be no other overriding considerations, since Pikuach-Nefesh overrides everything
else. Should the military experts declare that while there is such
a risk, yet it should be taken for some other reason, such as
political considerations (good will of the gentiles) - this would
clearly be contrary to the Psak-Din, for the Psak-Din requires that
Pikuach-Nefesh, not political expediency, should be the decisive
factor.

Now is regard to the liberated areas, all military experts, Jewish and
non-Jewish, agree that in the present situation giving up any part of
them would create serious security dangers. No one says that giving
up any part of them would enhance the defensibility of the borders.
But some military experts are prepared to take a chance in order not
to antagonize Washington and/or to improve the "international image,"
etc. To follow this line would not only go against the clear Psak-
Din, but would also ignore costly lessons of the past. One glaring
case in point is "the Yom-Kippur War." Days and hours before the
attack, there were urgent sessions of the government discussing the
situation with the military. Military intelligence pointed to
unmistakeable evidence that an Egyptian attack is imminent, and the
military experts advised a preemptive strike that would save many lives
and prevent an invasion. However, the politicians, with the acqui-
escence of some military experts, rejected this action on the ground
that such a step, or even a general mobilization, before the Egyptians
actually crossed the border, would mean being branded as the aggressor,
and would jeopardize relations with the USA. This decision was contrary
to the said Psak-Din of the Shulchan Aruch, as pointed out above. The
tragic results of that decision bore out the validity of the Shulchan
Aruch's position (as if it necessary(!) for many lives were needlessly
sacrificed, and the situation came close to total disaster, but for
G-d's mercies. Suffice it to mention that the then Prime Minister
later admitted that all her life she would be haunted by that tragic
decision.

4. I know, of course, that there are Rabbis who are of the opinion
that in the present situation, as they see it, it would be permissible
from the viewpoint of the Shulchan-Aruch to return areas from Eretz
Yisroel. But it is also known on what information they based this
view. One argument is that the present situation is not identical
with the hypothetical case of Neharde'a cited in the Talmud, because
Eretz Yisroel is not in a state of "being besieged by gentiles." A
second argument is that the present surrendering some areas would not
endanger lives.

That these arguments are based on misinformation is patently clear.
The Arab neighbors are prepared militarily; What is more; they do
demand these areas as theirs to keep, and openly declare that if not
surrendered voluntarily, they will take them by force, and eventually
everything else. A Rabbi who says that the said Psak-Din of the
Shulchan Aruch does not apply in the present situation, is completely
misinformed on what the situation actually is.

-3-

5.   A further example of how facts can be publicly distorted is in connection with the surrender of the oil wells in Sinai. Some warned at that time that it would be a terrible mistake to give them up, since oil, in this day and age, is an indispensable vital weapon, for without it planes and tanks are put out of action as surely as if they had been knocked out. Nevertheless, there were Rabbis that defended the surrender of the oil wells - again having received and accepted the "information" that the country has ample oil reserves that would last for months. When it was suggested to them to verify this information with anyone who has some idea about the physical limitations of storing oil to build up reserves, especially in a small country with limited storage space - the suggestion was ignored. Sure enough, before long the Government found it necessary to demand from the USA urgent oil deliveries, because the reserves would last only a few days. Moreover, prominent members of the Government publicly admitted that it was a serious mistake to have surrendered the oil wells.

Be it also noted that since the surrender of the oil wells in Sinai - according to the Government's figures - some 2-1/2 billion dollars was paid by it to Egypt for oil from the very same wells that had been surrendered. Not to mention the fact of having to buy oil also in the spot market, all at exorbitant prices.

6.   Parenthetically, it is known, who supplied the Rabbis with this "information." When one of the Rabbis was asked - after it had become all too obvious that their Psak-Din was based on false information - why he does not come out and openly reverse his position, the answer was that if he admitted publicly that he had been misled by a prominent Jew, with beard and Peos, who is active in Jewish affairs, it would create a Chilul Hashem. Queried further whether this consideration Halachically overrides correcting a Psak-Din affecting the Pikuach-Nefesh of many Jews -- there was no further response.

7.   I was taken to task (and this also in full public view) for placing so much emphasis on the security of Eretz Yisroel, the argument being that what has protected the Jewish people during the long Golus has been the study of Torah and the practice of Mitzvos; hence Torah-observant Jews should not make the inviolability of Eretz Yisroel as the overriding cause. I countered that they missed the point, for my position has nothing to do with Eretz Yisroel as such, but with the Pikuach-Nefesh of the Jews living there - which would apply to any part of the world. I have not yet received an answer to this point, either.

8.   I was similarly criticized for accusing the Government of Eretz Yisroel of reluctance to find and apprehend the perpetrators of the murderous attack in Hebron on that Friday night. I do not know what this has to do with the issue of returning liberated areas! At any rate, the facts are as follows. Before coming out to charge the Government publicly with not trying to apprehend the murderers, I tried to do what I could behind the scenes. It is known that there were two schools of thought in the Government on this issue. One held that it would be expedient not to press the hunt for the killers on the ground that to find and put them on trial, etc. would exacerbate tensions; therefore it would be better to put the matter at rest by procrasternation. The other held, that the Government should take all

possible action to apprehend the killers and punish them swiftly, not only because "the blood of our brethren cries out to us from the earth", but also, and just as importantly, for Pikuach-Nefesh reasons, to prevent further similar attacks. For, anyone who knows the mentality of those Arab circles from which the terrorists came, knows that failure to punish them would be interpreted as a sign of weakness and be an encouragement to repeat such attacks. This debate went on for weeks. When I saw that inaction was the Government's policy, and that it would be a serious blow to Pikuach-Nefesh, I made my public statement. Fortunately it had an impact, and finally the hunt began in earnest, resulting in the speedy apprehension of the leader of the gang.

Parenthetically the sad epilogue of this chapter, which is in itself a reflection of the state of affairs in Eretz Yisroel, is that although many weeks have passed since the murderer was caught, he has not as yet been put on trial, and there is still no word as to when this will come to pass. No further commentaries are necessary.

It should be noted, however, that the policy of playing down terrorist attacks and avoiding counter-action wherever possible is, unfortunately, one that goes back many years, evidently for the reasons indicated above, as is also borne out by enclosed newspaper clipping.

9.   A further criticism leveled against me is that my pronouncements on the issues are more political than Rabbinic. This, too, baffles me, for inasmuch as the matter has to do with Pikuach Nefesh, it is surely the duty of every Jew, be he Rabbi or layman, to do all permitted by the Shulchan Aruch to help forestall - or, at any rate, minimize - the danger. In a case of Pikuach-Nefesh, every possible effort must be made, even if there is a ספק (doubt) and many doubts whether the effort will succeed.

10.   As for the matter regarding the reception given to the person involved in this controversy on his arrival in New York, as if I, or my emissaries, instigated the demonstration against him, etc. - needless to say that this charge is totally not true. - Even in an oral discussion I am careful not to identify by name anyone who takes an opposing view, and limit myself to issues and not personalities. Especially when the person is known to me personally and I have a high regard for him, and - from my side - still regard as a friend.

In conclusion, I must also say that in general I find myself in an uncomfortable position in any situation where I find it necessary to disagree with an orhtodox Rabbi publicly in such a matter of Halachah. For when a layman sees that there are Rabbis who having been misled by misinformants, yet still do not retract their ruling even after the misinformation has been brought to light, it must necessarily affect his confidence in the credibility of Rabbinic authority in general. Especially this, obviously, runs counter to the basic policy and work of Lubavitch in disseminating Torah-true Yiddishkeit, with emphasis on the honor of the Torah, and the honor of the true bearers of the Torah, the Rabbis who dedicate all their life to the study of Torah and who live accordingly and exemplify Torah-true Yiddishkeit in the fullest measure.

Wishing you a bright and inspiring Chanukah,

                With esteem and blessing

-5-

P.S.
The following has been delayed as I was waiting for the enclosed
newspaper clippings before replying to the criticism against the group
of Rabbis who are alleged to have brought the controversy into the
limelight of the English press. Actually, the complaint should have
been addressed to the group of Rabbis, and, in any case, it has <u>no</u>
<u>relevance to my stand.</u> However, in view of the general confusion
regarding these issues, as already noted above, I will clarify this
point also.

The <u>fact</u> is that the subject matter had <u>at first</u> been publicized in
the same English press, giving expression to the <u>opposite</u> view, and
in a much sharper form, by a group of prominent Jews, as can be seen
from the enclosed clippings, as early as June 15, and there was also
a sequel to it. The declaration by the group of Rabbis (which
received less favorable coverage) appeared, around or on the 2nd of
July. I do not have this particular clipping at hand, but no doubt
critics have it and can verify it.

One point which I hesitated embodying in my letter, but decided to
add in this P.S., is this. Rabbis who, differing from my view,
declared their Torah - and Halachah - view on the question of returning liberated areas in Eretz Yisroel - also based it on the principle
of Pikuach-Nefesh, but in reverse to mine. Their opinion is based on
the belief that returning liberated areas would advance the cause of
peace with the Arabs and thus <u>save lives</u>. If this opinion is valid,
it inexorably follows from it that the thrust of the argument as it
is applied to the Golan, Yehuda and Shomron applies also the Old City
of Jerusalem; and in fact more forcefully, since the clamor for the
return of Old Jerusalem is more genuinely unanimous and stronger by
all the Arabs, including Egypt, Saudi Arabia, and the whole Islamic
world (while not all of them are so "enthusiastic" about creating a new
and independent Palestinian state on the West Bank). For the said
Rabbis to be consistent Halachically, the return of Old Jerusalem is
not only permissable, but imperative! Hence, in all conscience, they
are duty-bound to incorporate in their Psak-Din the return of the Old
City of Jerusalem!

PP.S.
Needless to say, this letter is personal and confidential, except, of
course, in regard to your correspondent on this matter. As for showing
it to others, I suggest you consult with your Lubavitch friends, to
ensure the honor of the Torah.

6

SUMMARY

1. The subject matter of the controversy centers on a Shaalah in Halachah, namely <u>Pikuach Nefesh</u>. Therefore, the position of both the Rabbis whose opinion differs from mine, as well as my position, must rest exclusively on the Halachah and treated purely as a Halachah-Shaalah.

2. The Shaalah is not a theoretical one, but a practical one that is high on the actual agenda, namely, whether - from the Halachah view - it is permitted, mandatory, or forbidden to return liberated areas in the so-called West Bank and Gaza, as well as in Sinai, including oil wells, military installations, etc. The Psak-Din on this Shaalah must, of course, be based on the actual and factual circumstances of the situation as they affect the security of Eretz Yisroel and of our brethren living there.

3. Both sides in the controversy, namely, the Rabbis who ruled that it is Halachically permissible to make territorial concessions and those (myself included) who oppose this view, based their decisions on the principle of Pikuach Nefesh; the difference being that the former concluded that territorial concessions would avert or minimize Pikuach Nefesh, while the latter hold that any territorial concessions would create or aggravate Pikuach Nefesh.

4. There can be no difference of opinion among Rabbis that in a case of Pikuach Nefesh it is the duty of a Rabbi not to remain silent and wait until approached to express his opinion. A rabbi who waits to be approached in such a situation is termed <u>meguneh</u> (reproachable, blameworthy). Similarly there can be no difference of opinion about the duty of every Jew, without exception, to do everything possible (consistent with the Shulchan Aruch) to avert the danger of Pikuach Nefesh. The Rabbi himself may not consider his duty done simply by pronouncing his Psak-Din, but must take every possible <u>action</u> in this direction. Indeed, there are many precedents of Gedolei Yisroel actually doing things on Shabbos and Yom Kippur which but for the fact of Pikuach Nefesh would be most serious transgressions.

5. Since, as noted, the sole deciding factor is Pikuach Nefesh, it is quite irrelevant what political orientation or party the Rabbi issuing the Psak-Din subscribes to, for his Psak-Din must not be influenced in the slightest by anything except the Halachah alone.

6. The evidence on which a Rabbi or Beth Din bases the Psak-Din must strictly conform to the principle of דין ו אמת לאמתו - that is to say, the judgment must be based on <u>true facts</u> and on <u>objective truth</u>. If there is any doubt about the veracity of the presented evidence, it is the duty of the Rabbi or Beth Din to investigate and verify the facts and ascertain the real and complete truth; and upon discovery that the Psak-Din was based on a misrepresentation of the Shaalah or of the facts submitted to them, they must, of course, promptly retract the erroneous Psak-Din and rectify it.

RABBI MENACHEM M. SCHNEERSON
Lubavitch
770 Eastern Parkway
Brooklyn, N. Y. 11213

Hyacinth 3-9250

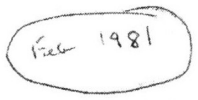

מנחם מענדל שניאורסאהן
ליובאוויטש

770 איסטערן פּאַרקוויי
ברוקלין, נ. י.

By the Grace of G-d
13th of Shevat, 5741
Brooklyn, N. Y.

Mr. Pinchas Meir Kalms
45 Sheldon Ave.
Highgate
London N. 6, England

Greeting and Blessing:

I am in receipt of your correspondence, enclosing copy of the letter of January 5th, pursuant to my letter of the 3rd of Chanuka.

I must confess that after reading the letter carefully, I still have to reiterate what I wrote in the beginning of my previous letter, namely, that I find it difficult to understand how my position can be misunderstood.

Before responding to the comments made in the January 5th letter, I must again emphasize the basic premise on which my stand rests, which is the only subject matter for discussion. Unless this basic premise and frame of reference is clearly understood and adhered to, a debate could go on indefinitely - at cross purposes. Any extraneous issue that does not bear directly on the basic premise, is irrelevant and confusing.

The only subject matter under discussion - at any rate, from my treatment of it - is the purely Halachic subject of Pikuach Nefesh as it affects the question of returning any part of the liberated areas. Be it also remembered that we are not dealing with an academic question, but one of actuality and urgency, since definite action has been taken in regard to some areas (in Sinai), and as regards others (Yehuda, Shomron, Golan, etc.), commitments have been made, and some of them would have probably been surrendered long ago, but for the fact that the other side refused to take them, demanding more.

Since the subject matter, as noted, is purely Halachic, namely the question of Pikuach Nefesh, the sanctity of the territories is irrelevant; so is irrelevant one's political affiliation or philosophy, or one's personal attitude to the Government, and the like. A Rabbi has to rule on the matter purely from the objective viewpoint of the Halacha, without allowing any other considerations or opinions, however strongly he may feel about them, to cloud his Halachic judgment.

With the above in mind, I will now respond to the comments point

- 2 -

Mr. Pinchas Meir Kalms

by point:

1. The reference to my stand on Zionism and the Jewish State as a factor in the Psak Din is, of course, quite irrelevant, as noted above, for, as has been emphatically emphasized also in my previous letter, the Halacha applies equally to Eretz Yisroel and everywhere else.

It is curious that I have been placed , in the same breath, in the category of Gush Emunim and Kahana, whose stand on Zionism and the Jewish State as such, is not questioned, though in actual facts their position on the return of the territories is not based on Zionism and the Jewish State, but on Bris-bein-ha'Bsorim. This only goes to show how, by bringing in extraneous issues, the central and real issue could be side-tracked and confused.

I have stated repeatedly, also in my previous letter, that my unequivo-cal stand against returning any part of Yehuda and Shomron, etc., is the same as on returning the Sinai oil wells, and any part of Sinai. Even those Rabbis who "reached the same conclusion on the territories precisely because of the sanctity of Eretz Yisroel" will admit that there is no question of sanctity in-volved in regard to Sinai and Sinai oil, but it is only a question of Pikuach Nefesh, plain and simple.

2. The contention that "the agreement among Rabbis... is not about (the rule of Pikuach Nefesh), but on what constitutes Pikuach Nefesh in the present situation," is true, of course. I already addressed that point in my previous letter, though I did not wish to overemphasize it, for obvious reasons. I pointed out that the other Rabbis based their evaluation of the present situa-tion on misinformation presented to them together with the Shaala. I cited one glaring example of the misinformation in that the Rabbis were told that the Government had ample oil reserves to last for months. Another item of misinformation was that the situation in Eretz Yisroel was described to them as not being comparable with the situation that the Gemoro in Eiruvin speaks of, where the enemy is actually besieging the Jews, and there is the danger of further penetration. This is obviously a misrepresentation, for everybody knows that the Golan, Shomron and Yehuda are the very borders with Syria and Jordan, which are under strong influence of the PLO, etc. These avowed enemies are not only besieging Eretz Yisroel, but have actually carried out bloody attacks, and openly declared their determined intention to take every-thing back by force. A further "distinction" between the existing situation and that of the Gemoro on which the opinion of those Rabbis was partially formulated was that in the case of the Gemoro situation the enemy came to take "hay and straw" that belonged to Jews, whereas in the present situation, the enemy is demanding the return of territories that had been taken from them. This argument, too, has been published, and not anonimously.

Of course, I can have no debate with those that believe that the Arabs have a legitimate claim for the return of territories that belong to them, be-cause there is no common ground on which to debate. But, they should surely

- 3 -

Mr. Pinchas Meir Kalms

keep in mind that if the Arabs have a legitimate claim to the pre-'67 territories, they have an equally legitimate claim to the Old City, ▓▓▓▓▓▓▓▓▓▓▓▓ ▓▓▓▓▓▓▓▓▓▓▓▓▓▓▓▓▓"   XX X XXX XX

To be sure, "a Dayan must rule on the basis of testimony before his eyes"; but the public is entitled to know precisely on what arguments and reasons he arrived at his decision, and this is something one is entitled to know even if the Psak-Din concerns one Pruta, not to mention the Pikuach Nefesh of three million Jews, and if there has been an error of facts, a Dayan should readily retract.

3. The Rabbis who declared that territories may be surrendered "for peace", based their opinion, among other things, on the information supplied to them (not by military experts) that territorial concessions would advance the cause of peace with the Arabs. Hence, they argued that the principle of Pikuach Nefesh that is at the root of the "straw and hay" rule is not relevant to the situation at hand, but to the contrary.

Actually, it is clear from the said Halacha that the deciding factor is not what the enemy demands or promises, but whether it is a case of מתח האדץ לפניהם - opening the land before the enemy; in other words, giving them an opportunity to breach the defenses. Whether or not the return of territories would indeed be such a case is, of course, for the military experts to decide, and not for politicians.

To argue that the fate of the country and the lives of the people depend also on factors beyond the competence of military experts, and that if political and economic factors will be ignored, it would lead to Pikuach Nefesh later on - does not affect the immediate decision relating to the return of territories. All the more so since it is certain that returning further territories will immediately weaken security, and would be an irreversible act, whereas the political and economic climate is unpredictable. So are, by and large, the other arguments that "territorial concessions under certain conditions might reduce the threat of war, or enhance Israel's ability to defend itself," etc. These are highly speculative conjectures, and I am certain that no military commander would bet on such chances. I repeat, the Halacha is clear - and it is, after all, the viewpoint of Halacha that is at the heart of the debate.

4. With regard to the "misinformation," it is surely astounding, and I regret it very much, that I am accused of charging "men like Dayan, Weizman, and countless other knowledgeable Israelies" with being "misinformed." I could not have been more explicit and specific in my letter of the 3rd of Chanuka that I was speaking of the misinformation supplied to the Rabbis by (known) interested parties. persons

It is true, of course, that all Rabbis have access to the same informa-

324

- 4 -

Mr. Pinchas Meir Kalms

tion on what the situation is, but unfortunately they did not make use of this access, and didn't bother to check it out, as in the case of the Sinai oil, etc.

5. I welcome the comment "I entirely agree on the Sinai oil," etc. It, of course, bears out my position, except that I see no difference between surrendering the Sinai oil or an inch of Sinai and surrendering an inch of Yehuda, Shomron, and Golan, and I cannot envision "a prolonged period of absolutely normal relations with all Arab neighbors", except in the Messianic Era when the wolf and the lamb will dwell together in peace.

6. With regard to the "Chilul HaShem" argument that I referred to, I clearly explained in my previous letter, and suggest a further perusal.

7. I do not understand what is so completely puzzling about this point. Of course, every G-d-fearing Jew must affirm that the security of Jews anywhere in the world, particularly in the Holy Land, lies with the study of the Torah and the practice of Mitzvoth. But, when it comes to a question of Pikuach Nefesh, as indeed in any situation, be it a matter of health or Parnosso, G-d Himself ordained that in addition to the strict observance of Torah and Mitzvoth an absolute Bitochon in Him, a Jew is required to do what is necessary in the natural order of things. This, too, is part of the teachings of Rabbis.

8. The "strange charge against the Israel Government of complicity (my emphasis) with terrorists," would indeed be puzzling, nay shocking, if any Jew made such a charge against any other Jew, let alone against the Government. I must admit, however, that though I have been accused of various strange things, this is the first time that such an accusation has been imputed to me. I stand by my statement that there is a school of thought in the Government that holds that "it would be expedient not to press the hunt for the killers on the ground that to find and put them on trial, etc., would exacerbate tensions; therefore, it would be better to put the matter at rest by procrastination," (point 8, letter of the 3rd of Chanuka). But this is a far cry from complicity (!) with the terrorists, not to mention all the other epithets attributed to the said school by the writer, which cannot be repeated, especially as the whole matter is irrelevant to the central issue.

I also stand by my charge of playing down terrorist attacks, etc., as stated in my previous letter. As for the question "would Israel's public opinion... really have tolerated such a policy?" - anyone who has been following the press in Eretz Yisroel over the past years knows that the subject has cropped up from time to time in various newspapers, from various directions and viewpoints, in articles and editorials. Be it remembered that it is not a case of "indifference" or negligence, for no one questions the deep concern of any Jew about the terrorist attacks. It is a question of well-intentioned, though in my opinion, ill-conceived

Mr. Pinchas Meir Kalms

policy. As a matter of fact (though I did not want to mention it in my previous letter), there are also Rabbis who agree with the said school, on the basis of the Maamar Chazal אל תתגרה בגוי קטן, especially when it is not "גוי קטן" אלא גויים וגדולים.

9. With reference to the policies pursued by Gush Emunim - I do not know what this has to do with the debate. I only responded to the charge against me of being "more political than Rabbinic" - with the obvious reply that in a matter of Pikuach Nefesh, every Jew, Rabbi or not, is obligated by Halacha to use every possible means to prevent it, including personal relationships and influence with any personage that can be helpful in the situation.

10. With regard to the matter of demonstrations, etc., I regret to note that it is again expressly implied in the letter that these were "Lubavitch inspired." It is clearly implied and taken for granted that I had been either consulted about it, or that I had foreknowledge that "Rabbis and men loyal to Lubavitch" are planning such action, and that a simple hint from me would have stopped it. I fail to understand, a priori, how a Rabbi can make such a categorical accusation on the basis of inference or assumption, and repeat it after I had emphatically denied any prior knowledge of the whole incident, and first became aware of it from the press. Whether some people involved in it were "Lubavitcher," and acting as such, as is alleged - I do not know to this day. I am inclined to think that the allegation is based on a misinformation. Especially that according to reliable information I received after learning of the demonstrations from the press and subsequently inquiring about them, these were organized by two groups (neither of them Lubavitch), with headquarters in Eretz Yisroel. I am therefore entitled to know, and would be obliged for, the names of the alleged Rabbis and men loyal to Lubavitch who participated in the incident. Besides, the term "loyal" to Lubavitch is rather vague, since "loyalty" is a term that can be stretched indefinitely. Also, the matter of the alleged "summons" is something that I first learned from this letter of January 5th. And since I have been dragged into this, I am surely entitled to specific information, including the names of the alleged perpertrators who are Lubavitcher or Lubavitch loyalists, so that I can investigate the matter further.

→ Lubavitch Beth-Din knows nothing about all this.

With the exception of the last paragraph, I think we can now put the whole debate at rest.

With esteem and
blessing, M. Schneerson

- 6 -

Mr. Pinchas Meir Kalms

P.S. What follows here pertains to your accompanying correspondence, and it is therefore written on a separate page, so that you have the option of passing it on along with the rest of the letter, or not.

     1. With regard to the opinion of Dyyan, Weizman and Rabin, I know that they stated clearly that from the viewpoint of military expertise, they would not advocate surrender of territory, but from the political view-point some territorial concessions may be justified.

     2. The people who misinformed the Rabbis on the matter of the Sinai oil are known by name in Eretz Yisroel. As you know, it is not my custom to mention names.

     3. With regard to the argument concerning the Old City to the effect that "one must draw the line somewhere" - the Halacha of Pikuach Nefesh does not recognize such an argument, which, in fact, would be a misinter-pretation of the Halacha and in complete contradiction to it. This has also been clearly indicated in my previous letter.

     Incidentally, the said argument also contradicts the opinion quoted in the letter of January 5th in the name of Rabbi Soloveichik that he would readily give up the Kotel Hamaaravi to save a Jewish life. This is also my opinion, with this qualification, that the Old City as it was after the Six Day War, was not in dispute and had no bearing then on the question of "opening the land before the enemy." But the position of the Old City now is in the same category as Golan, Yehuda and Shomron. In other words, and I believe Rabbi Soloveichik would agree, the sanctity of the Old City, including the sanctity of the Kotel, would not justify sacrificing a single Jewish soldier. But, when it is a case of "opening the land," as it is in the present situation, in relation to Jerusalem Beyond the Walls - the Old City (as any other place) falls under the rule of Pikuach Nefesh that man-dates the taking up of arms on Shabbos to defend it (and not because "one must draw the line somewhere").

- 7 -

Mr. P. Kalms

ADDENDUM

I see from the correspondence that certain points which I had taken for granted as self-evident, have not been given sufficient consideration. Hence this addendum, at the risk of some redundance.

1. The subject matter of the controversy centers on a Shaalah in Halachah, namely Pikuach Nefesh. Therefore, the position of both the Rabbis whose opinion differs from mine, as well as my position, must rest exclusively on the Halachah and treated purely as a Halachah-Shaalah.

2. The Shaalah is not a theoretical one, but a practical one that is high on the actual agenda, namely, whether - from the Halachah view - it is permitted, mandatory, or forbidden to return liberated areas in the so-called West Bank and Gaza, as well as in Sinai, including oil wells, military installations, etc. The Psak-Din on this Shaalah must, of course, be based on the actual and factual circumstances of the situation as they affect the security of Eretz Yisroel and of our brethren living there.

3. Both sides in the controversy, namely, the Rabbis who ruled that it is Halachically permissible to make territorial concessions and those (myself included) who oppose this view, based their decisions on the principle of Pikuach Nefesh; the difference being that the former concluded that territorial concessions would avert or minimze Pikuach Nefesh, while the latter hold that any territorial concessions would create or aggravate Pikuach Nefesh.

4. There can be no difference of opinion among Rabbis that in a case of Pikuach Nefesh it is the duty of a Rabbi not to remain silent and wait until approached to express his opinion. A rabbi who waits to be approached in such a situation is termed meguneh (reproachable, blameworthy). Similarly there can be no difference of opinion about the duty of every Jew, without exception, to do everything possible (consistent with the Shulchan Aruch) to avert the danger of Pikuach Nefesh. The Rabbi himself may not consider his duty done simply by pronouncing his Psak-Din, but must take every possible action in this direction. Indeed, there are many precedents of Gedolei Yisroel actually doing things on Shabbos and Yom Kippur which but for the fact of Pikuach Nefesh would be most serious transgressions.

5. Since, as noted, the sole deciding factor is Pikuach Nefesh, it is quite irrelevant what political orientation or party the Rabbi issuing the Psak-Din subscribes to, for his Psak-Din must not be influenced in the slightest by anything except the Halachah alone.

6. The evidence on which a Rabbi or Beth Din bases the Psak-Din must strictly conform to the principle of דן דין אמת לאמתו - that is to say, the judgment must be based on true facts and on objective truth. If there is any doubt about the veracity of the presented evidence, it is the

The portion of text from this point until the conclusion of the paragraph is absent from the photocopy. Peter Kalms provides the missing content in his Guidance from the Rebbe. (Shamir Publishing, 1994).

duty of the Rabbi or Beth Din to investigate and verify the facts and ascertain the real and complete truth; and upon discovery that the Psak-Din was based on a misrepresentation of the Shailoh or of the facts submitted to them, they must of course, promptly retract the erroneous Psak-Din and rectify it. I trust the above will finally clarify the issues and the points I made in my previous correspondence as well as this letter.

RABBI MENACHEM M. SCHNEERSON
Lubavitch
770 Eastern Parkway
Brooklyn. N. Y. 11213
493-9250

מנחם מענדיל שניאורסאהן
ליובאוויטש

770 איסטערן פּאַרקוויי
ברוקלין, נ. י.

P.S. This P.S. follows in English, consistent with our previous correspondence on the subject, which was conducted in English.

Now that we are in the month of Elul, the month of "stocktaking," I can no longer delay my response to some points in our correspondence, which are as yet unanswered. The reason for the delay being that I had hoped that there would be some positive developments that would have a bearing on them. Regrettably, these my hopes have not materialized; indeed, the situation has further deteriorated.

To begin with the basic point, namely, the question of returning the liberated areas of Yehuda, Shomron, etc. I maintain, as I have insisted from the beginning, that according to Halacha it is forbidden to return any of these territories. The same applies to the vital oil wells in Sinai, which should not have been surrendered. The claim that "for the sake of peace" it is Halachacally justifiable to surrender the territories and the oil wells, is hollow, for what was gained was not real lasting peace, but the promise of peace on paper, and from past and present experience, it is well known what such paper promises are worth.

Since the surrender of the oil wells is now a fait accompli and the consequences have already become quite evident, it can well serve as an illustration of the fallacious and misguided arguments that had been employed in regard also to the other points of the controversy. When I quoted that the war specialists warned that surrendering the oil wells meant giving up a most vital resource, both in time of peace and, even more so, in time of emergency, and that it would create a serious stranglehold both on the economy and security of the land, the answer was, firstly, that there was a three months' reserve of oil (a physical impossibility in the prevailing circumstances. Since oil cannot be compressed, a small (territorially) country like Eretz Yisroel cannot possibly provide storage space for such a large quantity of oil reserves, either underground or in surface tanks.) And, secondly, a promise from the other side to supply all the petroleum needs. Yet, soon after the surrender of the oil wells, emissaries had to be dispatched to Mexico and elsewhere in a frantic effort to obtain oil (at inflated prices and costly transportation). More recently, it was necessary to negotiate contracts for the importation of coal from distant countries (South Africa, Australia). This further emphasizes the seriousness of the energy situation in Eretz Yisroel.

Similarly, shortly before the current visit of the P.M. and his entourage to Washington, a personal friend of mine, who spoke to a personal friend of his, one who actively participated in all the Camp David negotiations, and will participate in the upcoming Washington discussions, and stated quite clearly that serious mistakes had been made in signing the treaty, since the same objective (normalization, etc.) could have been obtained without surrendering all that has been surrendered, the latter replied (verbatim): "Let's not go further into it," and added that ways and means are now being explored to move away from that policy, etc.

-2-

To refer to a further point of our discussion, namely, my criticism of the Government policy regarding terrorist attacks, in response to which I was taken to task for accusing the Government of collusion with the terrorists, which is, of course, entirely untrue. My criticism was only that the same policy of meekness and subservience pervades many departments of the Government. I could mention a few recent events to support my contention, but will cite only two. First, while it has long been common knowledge, though not discussed publicly, it was recently publicized in the media that in his time, B.G. gave a directive to stop the search for Dr. Mengele (Yimach Shmo) right when the search had become intensive.

Secondly, even more recently, the controversy in connection with the excavations in the City of David. There is no need to point out what the attitude and treatment shown by the police, with the backing of higher-ups, has been towards the demonstrators against this desecration. Yet, when there was an Arab demonstration in another place, but in a similar situation (the newly discovered tunnel under Temple Mount), further exploration was immediately stopped. No further commentary is necessary.

Another recent development bore out a view I expressed during the Yom Kippur War. I urged then, on the basis of Halacha, to pursue the enemy עד רדתה (Deut. 20:20; and see also Num. 33:55), namely, to take Damascus - not for occupation, but to ensure that it "never" again would pose a threat. It was then also common knowledge that Soviet advisors were present there, with headquarters, etc. Only a few hours of occupation would have been sufficient to accomplish the task. But for "strange" reasons, it was not done. The results of the failure are evident, and have been particularly underscored recently by the moving of the Soviet SAM's, and the military actions that were necessary to counter Soviet penetration, including the bombing of the nuclear reactor in Iraq (though the latter actions shows a salutary departure from the policy of appeasement and subservience).

Finally, a more personal point, hence it come to the last - in reference to the accusation that Lubavitch instigated, or participated in, the demonstration against the Chief Rabbi on his visit here. Be it noted that it is the accepted rule in all ████████ legal systems, not to mention the Halacha, that the burden of proof is on the accuser and not on the accused, and that everyone is deemed innocent until proven guilty, especially in regard to Jews who are all בחזקת כשרות . This elementary principle was ignored, and as yet no basis for the said charge has beeen submitted. Moreover, various Rabbinic Organizations came out publicly against the Chief Rabbi, while Lubavitch was the one that did not come out against him.

In light of the above, it is hardly right to consider that "the case is closed" because I said so and so. The proper conclusion should be that there should not have been a "case" in the first place, since the informer of the Chief Rabbi's office could not substantite the charge. Indeed, if a case is in order it is against the informer, also to prevent the repetition of such a mistake.

ומסיימים בטוב ובשלום ובאיחולים י"בצ
כתיבה וחתימה טובה

Key Resources for Further Study

The Rebbe's insights into Israel's security and his roadmap for achieving lasting peace are documented across many volumes of letters (many of which are collected in *Igros Kodesh*) and talks (largely compiled in *Sichos Kodesh* and *Toras Menachem*) spanning his entire leadership. However, even these do not capture the full volume of his commentary, as many relevant insights remain scattered in personal memoirs, or in unpublished letters and notes.

For those interested in exploring the primary source material, a good place to begin is the anthology titled *Karasi V'Ein Oneh*. This work, of over 700 pages, is a comprehensive, though not exhaustive,[14] collection of the Rebbe's talks, meetings, and letters concerning the Land of Israel. *Karasi V'Ein Oneh* also features concise historical contextualization notes, interspersed within the talks. That said, *Karasi V'Ein Oneh* is a Hebrew translation of the original Yiddish talks; therefore, to get the most accurate flavor of the original *sichah*, one should study the original transcripts, listen to the recordings or watch the videos of the talks where those are available.

For a more narrative approach, which sets the Rebbe's talks, audiences, and letters within a broader historical and thematic framework, *B'Rega HaEmet* is an excellent resource. This work draws on personal biographies and accounts, as well as provides transcriptions of many conversations the Rebbe had with influential figures in Israeli military and politics. *B'Rega HaEmet* is more a historical study of the Rebbe's rich relationship with Israel's leaders than it is an explicit statement or exploration of policy, and in that sense, significantly differs from the present work. Rabbi Shalom Dov Ber Wolpo's *Daas Torah* provides a thematic analysis of key issues in the Rebbe's thinking on the conflict, articulated in the language of contemporary rabbinic scholarship. Rabbi Wolpo's **Shalom Shalom V'Ein Shalom** presents the Rebbe's view through the lens of contemporary historical and political analysis. It is filled with Israeli newspaper clippings from the late 1970s and early 1980s as well as political and military commentary from the time.

Another invaluable resource is the JEM archive, which preserves video and audio recordings of many of the Rebbe's public addresses and private audiences. It also features interviews with individuals who consulted with the Rebbe on Israel-related matters. JEM also produces narrative films that skillfully integrate the Rebbe's teachings, providing a more extensive context. We have extensively utilized all of these resources in the preparation of the current book.

Selected Bibliography

Primary Sources:

Recordings of many of the Rebbe's original talks and audiences are available at ashreinu.app and indexed by date on the Hebrew calendar.

The Rebbe's original talks can be accessed in various formats and languages at Mafteiach.app.

—*Igros Kodesh,* 33 Vols. Brooklyn, Kehot Publication Society. 1987-2021.

  • A comprehensive collection of the Rebbe's letters, with extensive notes and essays providing historical context.

—*Sichos Kodesh 5710-5741*, 54 Vols. Brooklyn, *Vaad HaNachos HaTmimim*. 1985-1986.

  • Yiddish transcripts of the Rebbe's *sichos* from 1910-1980.

—*Sichos Kodesh 5742-5751*, 34 Vols. Brooklyn, *Vaad HaNachos HaTmimim*. 2016.

  • Yiddish transcripts of the Rebbe's *sichos* from 1981-1991.

—*Sefer HaSichos 5747-5752*, 11 Vols. Brooklyn, Kehot Publication Society. 1989-1998.

  • Edited Yiddish transcripts of the Rebbe's *sichos* from 1987-1992, along with extensive footnotes containing sources.

—*Toras Menachem – Hisvaaduyos 5710–5734*, 78 Vols. Brooklyn, *Lahak Hanochos*. 1992–2022.

  • Hebrew translation of the Rebbe's *sichos* from 1950-1973, edited for clarity, along with extensive footnotes offering sources and historical context.

—*Toras Menachem – Hisvaaduyos 5742–5752*, 43 Vols. Brooklyn, *Lahak Hanochos,* 1990–1994.
  - Hebrew translation of the Rebbe's *sichos* from 1981-1992, edited for clarity.

Collections and Analyses of the Rebbe's Teachings on the Land of Israel:

Groner, L.Y. ed. (2004). *Karasi V'Ein Oneh [I called and no one answered],* 2. Vols. Jerusalem.
  - A collection of many of the Rebbe's *sichos* (public talks) on Israel's security. Volume 1 spans 1969-1979, while Volume 2 covers 1980-1992. Volume 2 also contains a collection of the Rebbe's correspondence, as well as transcripts of *yechiduyos* (private audiences with the Rebbe), often with various dignitaries discussing Israel's security. Finally, Volume 2 contains an extensive topical index, indexing the Rebbe's commentary on Israel's security by topic. While comprehensive, the work is not exhaustive. All of the *sichos* were originally delivered in Yiddish. *Karasi V'Ein Oneh* translates them to Hebrew. Make Peace used the 2004 edition.

— (2013). *Karasi V'Ein Oneh*. Kiryat Malachi, *Malchut HaKeter.*
  - This one volume version of the work omits the extensive topical index.

Yerusalmi, S., Elitov, Y., & Ehrlich, A. (2017). *B'Rega HaEmet [The Moment of Truth].* Hevel Modi'in: Kineret, Zemorah-Bitan, Dvir.

Wolpo, S. D. (1982). *Daas Torah [Torah opinion on matters concerning the situation in the Holy Land] (3rd ed.).* Kiryat Gat.
— (1982). *Shalom Shalom V'Ein Shalom [Peace, Peace, and There Is No Peace].* Kiryat Gat.

JEM (Jewish Educational Media)

Jem.TV
JEM's Youtube Channel – @JewishMedia
JEM - The Lubavitcher Rebbe - YouTube [https://www.youtube.

com/@JewishMedia].

Resources on Military History and Strategy

The following websites offer articles, studies, podcasts, and full length monographs on strategic military insight on warfare in general and modern warfare in particular. Israel's wars are discussed extensively, but often as instances within larger military trends, such as counterinsurgency and urban warfare. Given that the Rebbe grounded his arguments extensively in facts on the ground and case studies, these resources are worth studying for those who want to gain a deeper understanding of the many dimensions of armed conflict.

Modern War Institute | United States Military Academy West Point
MWI Podcast Archives - Modern War Institute
The Spear Archives - Modern War Institute
Urban Warfare Project Archives - Modern War Institute
Irregular Warfare Podcast Archives - Modern War Institute
Wilson Center
International Centre for Counter-Terrorism
US Department of Defense: Defense Technical Information Center
- An extensive database of studies written by military officers from around the world analyzing conflicts and military strategy.

School of War Podcast [https://schoolofwar.substack.com/].
- A helpful podcast hosted by a former USMC officer, Aaron B. Maclean, who served in Afghanistan, analyzing all aspects of warfare from ancient time to the present day.

RAND Corporation

Books and Writings on Military Strategy

Clausewitz, C. von. (1989). *On War* (M. E. Howard & P. Paret, Trans.; Revised ed.). Princeton University Press. (Original work published 1832).

- Clausewitz's work is a classic on understanding the dynamics of warfare from a perspective which seeks to win wars. While the work is dense and written two centuries ago, it remains a classic in military academies across the world to this day. The Rebbe likely read this work, and many of the Rebbe's strategic insights align with it.

Trinquier, R. (1964). *Modern Warfare: a French View of Counterinsurgency*; A French View of Counterinsurgency [https://www.armyupress.army.mil/Portals/7/combat-studies-institute/csi-books/Modern-Warfare.pdf].

- Trinquier was an officer in France's counterinsurgency wars in Southeast Asia and Africa, most notably in Algeria. Trinquier analyzes the Algerian insurgency and compares terrorist groups' operations to those of gangs. He calls his book "modern warfare" as he predicts a shift in warfare from large conventional militaries facing one another to armed insurgencies undermining greater powers. He offers strategies for preventing and undermining insurgency.

Luttwak, E. N. (2001). *Strategy: The logic of war and peace* (Revised and enlarged edition). Belknap Press of Harvard University Press.

—Luttwak, E. N., & Richard, T. (2006). *Modern war: Counter-insurgency as malpractice.* Politique étrangère. p. 4, 849-861. I.F.R.I.; Modern War: Counter-Insurgency as Malpractice | Cairn International Edition [https://www.cairn-int.info/revue-politique-etrangere-2006-4-page-849.htm&wt.src=pdf].

- Edward Luttwak is a leading contemporary grand strategist. His writings deal with pursuing effective strategy and winning wars, something that has fallen out of style in contemporary Western discourse.
- For more of Luttwak's relevant writings see:
Israel's Intelligence Failure - Tablet Magazine
The NYT is wrong about Israeli intelligence - UnHerd

<u>Give War a Chance | Foreign Affairs</u>
<u>The middle of nowhere</u>

Military Strategy and History Specific to Israel
<u>Begin-Sadat Center for Strategic Studies</u>
- An influential Israeli military think-tank whose strategic views often align with those of the Rebbe's. More broadly, it offers valuable strategic insight.

<u>IDF: Israeli Defense Force Website</u>
- The Israel Defense Force's official website. A valuable repository of Israeli military history.

<u>The Institute for National Security Studies</u>
- An influential Israeli military think-tank whose views often **do not** align with those of the Rebbe's, given its ideological framework. Nonetheless, it offers valuable insight into many raw facts on Israel's military engagements and provides a contrasting perspective.

<u>Israel Defense And Security Forum</u>
- A think-tank developed by leading Israeli reservists dedicated to discussing Israel's security. The think-tank broadly expresses a secular Zionist orientation, yet it places a priority on realism about security, and in that sense strongly aligns with the Rebbe's views on military strategy, counterterrorism, and international relations.

Eidelberg, P. (1979). *Sadat's Strategy*. Dawn.
- A Detailed Strategic Analysis of Why the 1979 Israel-Egypt peace treaty was a mistake. This work offers extensive analysis which aligns with and enriches the Rebbe's teachings on the "peace" treaty.

Arnon-Ohana, Y. (2013). *Line of Furrow and Fire: The Conflict for the Land of Israel 1860-2010*. Achiasaf Ltd (Hebrew).
- Arnon-Ohana's work masterfully catalogs the historical, ideological, and social roots of the conflict from its inception to its evolved form circa 2010. Ohana's work demonstrates that the conflict has little to do with the State of Israel itself,

and far more to do with the large presence of Jews in the Land of Israel.

Glossary

Hebrew Terms

Achos Temimim – a division for young women in the Chabad movement.

ahavas Yisrael – love for [any and every] fellow Jew.

aliyah – [lit., "going up"] a term used to describe Jewish people moving to the Land of Israel since the biblical period [1800 BCE].

Alter Rebbe – The title given to Rabbi Shneur Zalman of Liadi (1745-1812), the founder of Chabad Chassidism. "Alter Rebbe" means "Old Rabbi" in Yiddish, signifying his status as the first leader of the Chabad movement. He is renowned for authoring the Tanya, the foundational text of Chabad philosophy, and the *Shulchan Aruch HaRav, a codification of Jewish law.

Alter Rebbe's *Shulchan Aruch* – the legal code authored by the *Alter Rebbe; also known as *Shulchan Aruch HaRav.*

Bar Kochba revolt – a rebellion of the Jews of the Roman province of Judea against the Roman Empire. The Romans brutally suppressed the revolt in 133 BCE, killing and enslaving hundreds of thousands of Jews.

beis din – Jewish Court of Law.

Beit Hadassah – a building in Hebron purchased by Jews in 1893. In 1929, after the Hebron riots, Jews were expelled from Hebron. In 1980, a group of Jewish women retook the building.

bitachon – trust, or taking security, in G-d. The attitude that G-d will orchestrate events with the greatest revealed good.

Bris Bein HaBesarim – Covenant Between the Parts, a biblical covenant between G-d and Abraham in Genesis Ch. 15. G-d promises Abraham that his descendants will inherit the Land of Israel.

bris milah – circumcision.

Chabad – an acronym for the Hebrew words *Chochmah, Binah,* and *Daas,* referring to the first three *Sefiros* (Divine emanations) and the corresponding stages of the intellectual process in the mind. Chabad signifies: (a) The intellectually-oriented branch of Chassidism

340

founded by the *Alter Rebbe, also known as Lubavitch. (b) The philosophy of this school of chassidic thought.

Chassidus – a movement in Orthodox Judaism founded by Rabbi Yisrael Baal Shem Tov (1698-1760), emphasizing prayer, serving G-d through the material, sincerity, mysticism, joy, music, love for all Jews, mutual responsibility, and attachment to a Rebbe. Also refers to the movement's philosophy and literature.

chassidic – pertaining to the chassidic movement in Judaism.

chassidim – adherents of the chassidic movement in Judaism.

Chayalei Beis David – Warriors of the House of David, an acronym for the Chabad-Lubavitch *yeshivah* students coined by Rabbi Sholom Dovber Schneerson, the Chabad-Lubavitch movement's fifth leader.

Daas Torah – Torah opinion on matters. Also the title of an important work presenting the Rebbe's views on Israel's security by Rabbi Shalom Dov Ber Wolpo.

emunah – faith in G-d.

Eretz Yisrael – the Land of Israel.

farbreng (verb), **farbrengen** (noun) (Yiddish) – (a) an assembly addressed by the Rebbe, often featuring a *maamar* or *sichah*. (b) an informal gathering of chassidim, with singing, refreshments, and a spontaneous exchange of Torah insights, chassidic oral traditions, personal challenges, and aspirations, aimed at mutual and brotherly edification.

Gemara (Aramaic) – (a) the part of the Talmud that discusses and explains the Mishnah. (b) loosely, the Talmud as a whole.

geulah – redemption.

Gush Katif – a group of Israeli communities in the Gaza Strip, dismantled in 2005 by the Ariel Sharon government.

Haganah – a Jewish paramilitary organization in the Land of Israel British Mandate period (1920-1948), key precursor of the IDF.

halachah – (lit.,"way" / "walking"/ "the path"): (a) the entire corpus of Jewish law. (b) a specific Jewish law.

halachic – pertaining to Jewish law.

Har Sinai – Mount Sinai.

heter – a Torah ruling or consideration that permits an action that is otherwise forbidden.

Igros Kodesh – the title of several dozen volumes containing much of the written correspondence of the seven Chabad Rebbeim.

Irgun – a Zionist paramilitary organization that operated in the Land of Israel during the British Mandate between 1931 and 1948.

Karasi V'Ein Oneh - "I called and no one answered" (from Isaiah 50:2). The Rebbe quoted this verse bemoaning the fact that he foresaw Israel's military policies bringing about great tragedy, but no one heeded his call. This refrain became the title of an important compendium of the Rebbe's teachings on Israel's security.

Kever Rachel – Rachel's Tomb in Bethlehem.

Kiryat Arba – an urban Israeli community on the outskirts of biblical Hebron and the Cave of the Patriarchs. The modern city of Kiryat Arba was founded in 1968, but Jews have lived in the region since biblical times.

Kosel – the Western Wall in Jerusalem.

lo techanem – "do not show them favor" (from Deuteronomy 7:2); an injunction not to sell land in the Land of Israel to non-Jews who do not agree to abide by the Seven Noahide Laws.

Lubavitcher Rebbe – Rabbi Menachem Mendel Schneerson, the seventh Rebbe of the Chabad-Lubavitch movement.

maamar (pl. *maamarim*): In Chabad usage, a formal chassidic discourse first delivered by a Rebbe, as distinct from a *sichah.

Maaras HaMachpelah – the biblical Cave of the Patriarchs in Hebron.

Mashiach – the Jewish Messiah. The prophesied descendant of King David who will reinstate the Torah-ordained monarchy (which he will head), rebuild the Holy Temple, and gather the exiled Jewish people to their homeland. This series of events (collectively called "the Redemption") will usher in an era of eternal, universal peace and true knowledge of G-d, called "the messianic era."

medina shel chessed – "a country of kindness." A term that the Rebbe applied to the United States.

Merkos L'Inyonei Chinuch – a Jewish educational organization founded by the *Rebbe Rayatz, and led by the Rebbe. Merkos L'Inyonei Chinuch is the umbrella organization responsible for Chabad's outreach institutions around the world, as well as for many of Chabad's programs aimed at particular demographics, such as youth, teens, campus students, young professionals, and seniors.

Midrash – biblical exegesis by ancient Rabbis. A corpus of classical *aggadic* works (2nd-8th cent. CE) containing the Sages' homiletical, non-literal teachings on the Torah's ethical and spiritual dimensions (*derush*). Includes the *Rabbah* series, *Tanchuma*, *Pirkei D'Rabbi Eliezer*, *Tanna D'vei Eliyahu*, and later collections like *Yalkut Shimoni*. Halachic Midrashim: *Mechilta*, *Sifra*, *Sifrei*.

Mikveh – A ritual bath in Judaism used for spiritual purification. It consists of a pool of natural water, typically rainwater or spring water, in which Jews immerse themselves. Women use the mikveh for purification following menstruation, childbirth, or before marriage, while men use it before *Shabbos and holidays, or as a general spiritual practice. Central to the laws of family purity, the mikveh plays a significant role in Jewish life. Immersion in mikveh is also a crucial part of the conversion process for both men and women becoming Jewish.

Mishnah – see Talmud.

Mishnaic – pertaining to the Mishnah.

mitzvah (lit., "commandment"; pl., *mitzvos*) – (a) one of the 613 commandments given by G-d to the Jewish people or the seven commandments given to the nations at Mt. Sinai. (b) One of the 7 rabbinic commandments. (3) Idiomatically, any good deed.

Motzaei Shabbos (lit., "the outgoings of the Sabbath") – the night after the termination of *Shabbos; Saturday night.

pikuach nefesh – the principle in Jewish law that the preservation of human life overrides virtually any other religious rule.

psak din – a legal ruling.

Rashi – a medieval French rabbi and author of a comprehensive commentary on the Talmud and *Tanach*. *Rashi* is viewed as the most fundamental commentator in traditional Judaism.

Rebbe Rashab – Rabbi Sholom Dovber Schneersohn, the fifth Chabad-Lubavitch Rebbe (1860-1920).

Rebbe Rayatz – Rabbi Yosef Yitzchak Schneersohn, the sixth Chabad-Lubavitch Rebbe (1880-1950).

Rebbe (pl., Rebbeim) – *tzaddik* who is the mentor and spiritual head of a community of *chassidim.

Rebbe, the: the seventh Chabad Rebbe, Rabbi Menachem Mendel Schneerson.

Shabbos – the Jewish Sabbath; the day of rest beginning sunset on Friday and ending at nightfall on Saturday.

shalom – peace.

shamir – in the Jewish tradition, a creature capable of cutting through the hardest of stones.

Shekel – Israeli currency, the term was used in biblical times, and contemporary Israeli currency also follows the Shekel system.

Shemini Atzeres – "the eighth day of Assembly," a Jewish holiday that immediately follows the seventh day of *Sukkos.

Shemiras Shabbos KeHilchasah – an authoritative contemporary guidebook on the laws of Shabbos observance by Rabbi Yehoshua Nuewirth.

Shulchan Aruch (lit., "the Set Table" [Ezekiel 23:41]) – Rabbi Yosef Karo (1488-1575). The Code of Jewish law. Cited by volume name (*Orach Chaim, Even HaEzer, Yoreh Deah*, and *Choshen Mishpat*), chapter, and paragraph. Venice, 1564.

sichah (pl. *sichos*) – in Chabad usage, a talk or public address by a Rebbe, as distinct from a *maamar*.

Simchas Torah – a Jewish holiday the day after Sukkos that celebrates the completion of the annual Torah reading cycle.

Sichos Kodesh: A fifty-volume set containing the unedited talks of the Rebbe delivered between 1950-1981.

Sefer HaMaamarim – collection of learned chassidic discourses first delivered by one of the Rebbeim, usually specified by the year of their teaching.

Sefer HaSichos – Toras Shalom – a collection of talks delivered by the Rebbe Rashab.

Sefer HaSichos – a volume of collected chassidic talks first delivered by one of the Rebbeim, usually specified by the year of their teaching.

Sukkos (lit., "huts," "booths") – the Jewish fall holiday celebrating the harvest and commemorating the clouds of glory that accompanied the Jewish people on their desert journey after the Exodus from Egypt.

Tanach – The Hebrew Bible; the written Torah, comprising twenty-four books divided into three sections:

> 1. Torah ("teaching") – the five books of Moses.
>
> 2. Prophets – eight books, with Samuel, Kings, and the twelve "minor" prophets each considered as one book.
>
> 3. Writings – eleven books, with Ezra-Nehemiah and Chronicles each considered as one book.
>
> The Hebrew acronym for these three sections is *Tanach*.

Talmud (lit., "learning") – the written version of the Jewish oral tradition of Torah, containing legal, homiletic, and mystical material. Comprises the **Mishnah** ("repetition"), a compendium of oral laws redacted by Rabbi Yehudah the Prince (2nd cent. CE), and the **Gemara** ("completion"), elaborations on the Mishnah from the academies of the Holy Land and Babylonia (3rd-6th cent. CE).

> There are two Talmuds: *Talmud Yerushalmi* (Jerusalem Talmud), completed in the 3rd century, and *Talmud Bavli* (Babylonian Talmud), completed in the 6th century. The Mishnah and Talmud are divided into tractates, with references citing the tractate, chapter, and mishnah/*halachah* number. *Talmud Yerushalmi* references are prefaced with "Y." to distinguish from Mishnah citations. *Talmud Bavli* references include the tractate, page, and column ("a" or "b"), following the pagination of the first complete edition (Venice, 1520-23).

temimim – students and graduates of Chabad's *Tomchei Temimim yeshivah* network.

teshuvah – (lit., "return [to G-d]") repentance.

Tikkun Olam – repairing the world, according to the Torah's teachings.

Torah – the first five books of the Hebrew Bible. More expansively, the Torah refers to the entire body of Jewish religious teachings, including the Written Torah (five books of Moses), Oral Torah (Mishnah, Talmud, *Midrash*), *halachah* (Jewish religious laws), and Jewish spiritual and ethical teachings. Encompasses the sacred texts and ongoing interpretations, teachings, and practices developed over centuries of Jewish scholarship and communal life.

Toras Chaim – the Torah of life; a term meaning that the Torah is the guide to a good wholesome life, and confers life upon those who live by it.

Toras Emes – the Torah of truth; a term meaning that the Torah is the ultimate source of truth.

Tzivos Hashem – "Army of G-d." A term from the book of Exodus. The Rebbe founded a Jewish youth movement in 1980 with the name, which continues to thrive to this day.

Utzu Eitzah – "Contrive a scheme" (from Isaiah 8:10). A Jewish song on the theme that G-d will save the Jewish people from those that plot against it. The Rebbe would sing this song together with children at children's rallies, and particularly emphasized it at times that Israel was in crisis.

Yamit – an Israeli community in the Sinai Peninsula, dismantled by the Israeli government as a result of the Camp David Accords.

Yechidus (plural: *yechiduyos*) – a private audience with the Rebbe (rather, an encounter of souls) at which an individual seeks guidance and enlightenment from his Rebbe.

yeshivah – a Jewish educational institution that focuses on the study of traditional religious texts.

yishuv – a Jewish community in Israel. The term is also used to refer to the Jewish community in Israel in the centuries before the modern State of Israel's establishment.

Yom Kippur – the Day of Atonement in Judaism. Marked by fasting and *teshuvah, particularly through confession of sin.

yom tov (lit., "good day" or "holiday") – a festive holiday on which, with certain exceptions, weekday work is prohibited just as on

*Shabbos.

yordim – Jews who leave Israel and settle elsewhere; a term used since the biblical period.

Arabic Terms

Dar al-Islam – "the domain of Islam." In fundamentalist iterations of Islam, the objective is to turn the entire world into Dar al-Islam, while the rest of the world is Dar *al-harb* ("the domain of the sword/war").

Fedayeen – militants or terrorists.

Hizb Allah (more commonly Hezbollah) – "Party of G-d," a Shi'ite Islamist political party and militant group based in Lebanon.

hudna – ceasefire or truce.

Intifada – an organized wave of Palestinian terrorism, as in the First and Second Intifadas.

Muqawwama – "resistance," at term associated with Hezbollah and Hamas and part of their ideological justification for terror.

Shabab – Arab youth.

Other Languages

Birobidzhan – a town in Russia designated as the Jewish Autonomous Oblast by the early Russian communist regime in 1931. Various antisemitic actors have begun to make the revisionist claim that Birobidzhan, not the Land of Israel, is the true Jewish homeland.

Osirak – an Iraqi nuclear reactor partially built by Saddam Hussein with French and Italian assistance. Saddam explicitly stated that he hoped to use the reactor against Israel. In 1981, Israel preemptively bombed the reactor, rendering it inoperational.

Thanks to Uri Kaploun, Rabbi Naftoli Hertz Pewzner, and Rabbi Moshe Wisnefsky for their insights in preparing this glossary. Some entries are based on Rabbi Pewzner's glossary in the Basics of Chassidus (Sichos in English, 2022) and Rabbi Wisnefsky's glossary in The Mystery of Marriage (Gal Einai Institute, 2005).

Acknowledgements

October 7, 2023, will remain a day that fundamentally shifted Jewish identity and the Land of Israel's security for a lifetime. We likely have still not seen the full extent of the day's reverberations. Much as those of us who remember September 11, 2001, recall where we were when we heard of it, and remember how the world fundamentally changed thereafter, October 7 marks a similar watershed moment for Jews everywhere.

I remember when I first heard of the carnage. The day after Yom Kippur, I had flown from the Land of Israel to New York to spend time with family and friends over the Sukkos holiday. On the afternoon of Shemini Atzeres, I stood on Kingston Avenue, a three-minute walk from 770, the famed study hall and synagogue where the Rebbe had taught (and guided Israel's leadership) for more than half a century. A friend from Jerusalem walked down the street, with a dark cloud over his head. "Hamas has invaded the south and has begun massacring people," he told me. We were in shock.

Only after the holiday ended did we get perspective. Soon thereafter, I took a trip to an American university, where I would spend several weeks studying with students and engaging in Jewish outreach. That weekend, portents of the madness that would grip campuses across America began to appear. In a well publicized rally, a professor praised Hamas' massacres, and anti-Israel graffiti began to fill prominent locations on campus.

In the coming days, ironically while walking over anti-Israel graffiti at said campus, I worked on essays and research pertaining to the Rebbe's views on Israel's security, and how they could be articulated to provide answers to the present predicament. On October 23, 2023, after writing an op-ed on the Rebbe's views, I had a call with **Rabbi Levi Avtzon**, Senior Rabbi of the Linksfield Shul and member of the **Yonah Press** board. He told me: "It's time for a comprehensive book on the Rebbe's views on Israel's security that will speak to contemporary reality – get to work on writing it." And thus, Make Peace was conceived. Rabbi Levi's commentary and support have been significant from beginning to end. This book would not have been written without him.

Rabbi Shmuel Avtzon, director of Sichos in English and Yonah Press, took charge of the project and enhanced every aspect of production, from assembling a stellar team to providing insight and critical feedback on the work's style and content. **Rabbi Naftoli Hertz Pewzner**, Professor of chassidic thought (*Mashpia*) at the Rabbinical College of America, has been a constant source of knowledge, support, and insight in framing the many issues discussed in this work. Additionally, he read the entire manuscript critically and deeply enriched the work.

Make Peace is immeasurably indebted to **Rabbi Elkanah Shmotkin,** director of **JEM** (Jewish Educational Media) and his entire team. Rabbi Shmotkin has made it his life's mission in the past three decades to collect, digitize, and organize the Rebbe's vast audiovisual oeuvre. Moreover, Rabbi Shmotkin has personally focused on the topic of Israel's security, compiling a vast wealth of data, oral history, and interviews with key players in Israel's story as they interacted with the Rebbe. Make Peace has been profoundly enriched by this wealth of information Rabbi Shmotkin has assembled. Rabbi Shmotkin served as a constant source of knowledge and inspiration throughout the project. He also outlined Chapters 11-12 of Make Peace, and many of the insights there are his. Rabbi Shmotkin's work also played a significant role in the book *B'Rega HaEmet*, an important resource for the present book.

Finally, thanks to Rabbi Shmotkin for convening the "Enduring Peace" think-tank, a group of Chabad scholars who engaged in helpful discussions regarding the Rebbe's views on Israel's security that enriched this book and numerous related projects. Many thanks to the think tank's members: **Rabbi Levi Greenberg, Rabbi Mendy Greenberg (Twinsburg, Ohio)**, **Rabbi Michoel**

Lipsker, **Rabbi Dovid Margolin**, **Rabbi Mendel Misholovin**, and **Rabbi Levik Korf**. Rabbi Korf deserves special mention for reviewing the manuscript, research collaboration, and offering his vast knowledge of Jewish history and the Rebbe's teachings. Thanks as well to **Chavi Bromberg** of the JEM foundation for her expert assistance in curating photos of the Rebbe for this work.

Make Peace builds upon **Rabbi Eli Touger's** "Eyes Upon the Land" (Sichos in English, 1997), which first presented the Rebbe's views on Israel's security in the English language nearly 30 years ago.

Rabbi Shimon Gansburg and **Rabbi Chaim Muss** of the **Rebbe Respona** project shared troves of original research enhancing this work. Rabbi Gansburg carefully reviewed the entire manuscript offering valuable conceptual and technical suggestions.

The stellar editorial team vastly improved Make Peace's accessibility. **Malki Barouchi** punctiliously weighed every sentence, comma and citation, with tremendous dedication and attention to detail. Her tireless commitment to all aspects of the project immeasurably enhanced its quality. **Noam Harris** worked to ensure a book that would be accessible to a broader audience. **Rabbi Matisyahu Wolf's** editorial skill markedly raised the book's caliber. **Moussia Lesches** meticoulously proofread the manuscript and suggested insightful improvements.

Zevi Slavin helped articulate the Rebbe's humanity and sensitivity on an issue so harsh as war. **Uri Kaploun** offered sage insights and important historical perspective. **Levi Shmotkin** offered careful analysis of the manuscript and pointed out several important sources and letters.

Rabbi Mendel Fogelman, **Rabbi Mendel Heller**, **Jochanan Mussel PhD,** and **Eliezer Weston** each read the manuscript and provided valuable feedback.

Meir Avtzon offered passionate dedication to the project, from high-level conceptual critique to proofreading and project management.

The space a work a is written in impacts its soul. While Make Peace was written in numerous locations, from an office in Crown Heights, Brooklyn, to an Ivy League College Campus, to Hebron, the overwhelming majority of the work was written in the Beis Medrash and corridors of **Yeshivat Har Etzion.** Thanks to **Rabbi Eliezer Shalom Weber,** *Menahel Ruchni* of the Yeshiva, for believing in this project, and providing a most ideal location for its creation. Thanks as well to **Rabbi Aharon Bejell, Rabbi David Aharonovsky** and the Har Etzion library staff for providing a wealth of scholarly resources, both of the Rebbe's works and of Israeli history. Finally, writing this book in the presence of the *yeshiva's* young Torah scholar-warriors, who risk their lives to protect *Am Yisrael* and *Eretz Yisrael* deeply impacted the work. May G-d bless them for their self-sacrifice, may He grant them safety, and put an end to war.

The Mishnah teaches: "Without flour, there is no Torah."[15] In that vein, thanks to **Rabbi Joseph Gutnick** for his significant sponsorship, and to **Benji Licht** for raising much of the funds, providing the proverbial "flour" that went towards the book's production.

Finally, thanks to the team at **Spotlight Design,** particularly Creative Director **Moishe Muchnik** and Designer **Aliza Chekroun,** for their cover, book design, and naming the book. Thanks to **Yosef Yitzchok Turner** of Yonah Press for speedily executing the book's layout.

Make Peace is a challenging work. It responds to a tragic reality, and comments on ongoing sorrow and loss of life. May this English articulation of the Rebbe's insights achieve its intended goal, and by inspiring and educating, contribute to lasting Peace in the Land of Israel, the Middle East, and the world at large.

Elisha Pearl
The Judean Hills
3 Tammuz, 5784

About the Author

Rabbi Elisha Pearl, a writer and researcher at the Sichos In English institute, has lectured and written extensively on Jewish Law, Philosophy, and Mysticism. He holds Rabbinic ordination from Rabbi Zalman Nechemia Goldberg and Yeshiva University, where he also did graduate studies in philosophy and psychology. He has studied at leading institutes of advanced Jewish study from Kollel Menachem to Yeshivat Har Etzion. Rabbi Pearl has taught Jewish texts and tradition to diverse groups of students, from the Himalayas to the Alps, and from the Judean Hills to the Texan Plains.

Notes

OPENING QUOTES

1 *Mishneh Torah, Hilchos Shabbos,* 2:3. See also *Likkutei Sichos,* Vol. 23, pp. 206-213.

2 Proverbs 3:17.

3 *Mishneh Torah, Hilchos Chanukah,* 4:14. See Likkutei Sichos Vol. 8, p. 349ff.

4 *Karasi V'Ein Oneh,* Vol. 1, p. 475, 20 Menachem Av 5739 (1979); Vol. 2, pp. 207-208, 24 Teves 5742 (1982); p. 321, 19 Kislev 5743 (1982); Video of Sichah [https://videos.jem.tv/video-player?clip=735]; Audio of Sichah [https://ashreinu.page.link/8ZXb]; pp. 348-349, *Mikeitz* 5744 (1983).

5 *Toras Menachem 5742,* Vol. 3, p. 1,724, 3 Tammuz (1982); *Karasi V'Ein Oneh,* Vol. 2, pp. 230, 234, 236, 247; Video of Sichah [https://jemtv.page.link/6AzU]; Audio of Sichah [https://ashreinu.page.link/3XKE]. See *Bava Basra* 11a, *Sanhedrin* 37a.

PREFACE

1 Almost all of these were delivered in Yiddish or Hebrew.

2 *Igros Kodesh,* Vol. 31, p. 244, Letter #11,848 to prominent Israeli journalist Yonah Cohen, dated Isru Chag HaShavuos 5736 (1976). In this letter, the Rebbe encourages Cohen to publicize his new book, "Jerusalem Under Siege," and to explain that the siege on Jerusalem was not just a singular crisis that took place in 1948, but that Jerusalem is still in pressing danger from its enemies. For Cohen's book in Hebrew, see Cohen, Y. (1976). *Yerushalayim bematzor* (Rabin, I., Foreword) (2nd ed.). Tel Aviv: Maluah. For the book in English, see Cohen, Y. (1982). *Jerusalem under siege: Pages from a 1948 diary* (D. Shefer-Vanson, Trans.). Los Angeles: Ridgefield Pub. Co.

3 See, for example, the Mitteler Rebbe's *Shaarei Teshuvah,* pp. 49ff.; *Sefer HaMaamarim 5659,* pp. 161-175 (Kehot, 2011); *Toras Menachem — Sefer HaMaamarim Melukat,* Vol. 2, p. 150; *Toras Menachem — Derushei Chassunah,* pp. 244-247; *Toras Menachem — Hisvaaduyos 5747,* Vol. 2, p. 78.

INTRODUCTION

1 One particularly outspoken anti-Israel advocate distilled this sentiment, describing the massacres as "exhilarating" and "energizing." See Hamas attack on Israel was 'exhilarating and energising', Ivy League professor told crowd [https://www.youtube.com/watch?v=_foZMY8xfD8].

2 See *Toras Menachem* 5729 Vol. 2, p. 359, Purim (1969) and *Sichos Kodesh* 5729, Vol. 1, pp. 437-438 where the Rebbe notes that those who attack Israel and the Jewish people have a tendency to then attack non-Jewish people and nations.

3 The IDF Approach to Protecting Civilians in Urban Warfare — Modern War Institute [https://mwi.westpoint.edu/the-idf-approach-to-protecting-civilians-in-urban-warfare/]; Urban Warfare | INSS [https://www.inss.org.il/wp-content/uploads/systemfiles/HirschUrbanWarfare.pdf]; Israel Has Created a New Standard for Urban Warfare. Why Will No One Admit It? | Opinion [https://www.newsweek.com/israel-has-created-new-standard-urban-warfare-why-will-no-one-admit-it-opinion-1883286].

4 World Report 2024: Myanmar | Human Rights Watch [https://www.hrw.org/world-report/2024/country-chapters/myanmar];

Situation of human rights in Myanmar — Report of the United Nations High Commissioner for Human Rights (A/HRC/54/59) (Advance unedited version) — Myanmar | ReliefWeb [https://reliefweb.int/report/myanmar/situation-human-rights-myanmar-report-united-nations-high-commissioner-human-rights-ahrc5459-advance-unedited-version].

5 World Report 2024: Haiti | Human Rights Watch [https://www.hrw.org/world-report/2024/country-chapters/haiti].

6 Syrian Arab Republic: WHO Health Emergency Appeal 2024 [https://www.who.int/publications/m/item/syria-who-health-emergency-appeal-2024].

7 World Report 2024: Ukraine | Human Rights Watch [https://www.hrw.org/world-report/2024/country-chapters/ukraine].

8 Yemen Humanitarian Needs Overview 2024 (January 2024) [https://yemen.un.org/en/259542-yemen-humanitarian-needs-overview-2024-january-2024].

9 Azerbaijan must let ethnic Armenians return to Nagorno-Karabakh: UN court | United Nations News | Al Jazeera [https://www.aljazeera.com/news/2023/11/17/azerbaijan-must-let-ethnic-armenians-return-to-nagorno-karabakh-un-court]; Ethnic Cleansing Is Happening in Nagorno-Karabakh. How Can the World Respond? | Council on Foreign Relations [https://www.cfr.org/article/ethnic-cleansing-happening-nagorno-karabakh-how-can-world-respond]; As an Azerbaijani, I have to speak out about my country's ethnic cleansing of Armenians | Ruslan Javadov | The Guardian [https://www.theguardian.com/commentisfree/2023/oct/09/azerbaijani-ethnic-cleansing-armenians-nagorno-karabakh-children].

10 Sudan: Ten months of conflict — Key Facts and Figures (15 February 2024) | OCHA [https://www.unocha.org/publications/report/sudan/sudan-ten-months-conflict-key-facts-and-figures-15-february-2024].

11 The 2023 Humanitarian Response Plan (HRP) for Somalia [https://somalia.un.org/en/219986-2023-humanitarian-response-plan-hrp-somalia].

12 A perusal of humanitarian aid websites demonstrates that the world is filled with many other humanitarian crises, most often precipitated by "liberation movements," organized crime syndicates, or militant Islamist groups. Some fit all these criteria. See International Rescue Committee [https://www.rescue.org/]; Humanitarian Crises to Know About Right Now | Save the Children [https://www.savethechildren.org/us/charity-stories/humanitarian-crises-you-need-to-know-about]; Humanitarian Emergencies Around the World | USA for UNHCR [https://www.unrefugees.org/emergencies/]; Humanitarian Emergencies [https://www.unfpa.org/emergencies].

13 As Edward Luttwak notes in a 2007 article:

The ease of filming and reporting out of safe and comfortable Israeli hotels inflates the media coverage of every minor affray. But humanitarians should note that the dead from Jewish-Palestinian fighting since 1921 amount to fewer than 100,000—about as many as are killed in a season of conflict in Darfur.

See The middle of nowhere [https://www.prospectmagazine.co.uk/essays/57794/the-middle-of-nowhere].

14 For a sober analysis of why it would seem that this conflict will last interminably, see Why Can't We Solve the Arab-Israeli Conflict? [https://fakenous.substack.com/p/the-arab-israeli-conflict].

15 For an excellent collection of these conversations contextualized historically, see *B'Rega HaEmet*.

Consider the following record of correspondence and meetings between the Rebbe and Israeli Prime Ministers:

For the Rebbe's correspondence with David Ben-Gurion, see *Igros Kodesh*, Vol. 18, pp. 209-215, Letters #6,714, #6,715; for Menachem Begin's audience with the Rebbe, see *Sichos Kodesh 5737* (1976-7), Vol. 2, pp. 669-673; Video of Sichah [https://videos.jem.tv/video-player?clip=694]; Audio of Sichah [https://ashreinu.app/player?parentEvent=2449&event=2450]; for Yitzchak Shamir's relationship with the Rebbe, see Faithful and Fortified: Israel's Prime Ministers [https://videos.jem.tv/video-player?clip=694] The film goes through the Rebbe's relationship with Yitzchak Rabin, Menachem Begin, Yitzchak Shamir, Ariel Sharon, and Benjamin Netanyahu.

for the Rebbe's correspondence with Sharon, see *Igros Kodesh*, Vol. 27, pp. 208f., Letter #10,201, 12 Elul 5728 (1968); Vol. 32, p. 314, Letter #12,213, 18 Av 5730 (1970); *Karasi V'Ein Oneh*, Vol. 2, pp. 431-434, 450-452; for Benjamin Netanyahu's reflections on the impact the Rebbe had on him, see *B'Rega HaEmet*, Ch. 14; The Essence of Things — Benjamin Netanyahu — Program One Hundred Twenty Eight — Living Torah [https://www.chabad.org/therebbe/livingtorah/player_cdo/aid/471241/jewish/The-Essence-of-Things.htm]; Truth vs. Darkness in the United Nations — Chabad.org [https://www.chabad.org/therebbe/article_cdo/aid/1394394/jewish/Truth-vs-Darkness-in-the-United-Nations.htm]; Don't Be Intimidated — Program Two Hundred Sixty Seven — Living Torah [https://www.chabad.org/therebbe/livingtorah/player_cdo/aid/1001699/jewish/Dont-Be-Intimidated.htm]. Records of some of the Rebbe's meetings and correspondences with Netanyahu are included in *Toras Menachem — Hisvaaduyos 5748* (1987-8), Vol. 2, p. 614, and *Likkut Maanos Kodesh 5748*, p. 88.

16 *Karasi V'Ein Oneh* is an excellent collection of primary sources.

17 On this point, see *Daas Torah*, p. 18:

Torah scholarship is the first pillar upon which discerning the Torah's perspective is built.... The second pillar in understanding the Torah's perspective is that in order to render a halachic opinion on a question, one must fully understand the dimensions of the question and the situation at hand.

Thus, for example, the Talmud (*Sanhedrin* 5a) teaches that Rav, an Amoraic sage, had an eight month internship by a herder in order to become an expert in areas of *halachah* relevant to animals. The Talmud continues to say that one can only receive ordination in a subject area if they have expertise in the real world applications of that subject area.

18 The Rebbe explicitly clarifies that while some erroneously conflated his positions with those of the religious Zionist Gush Emunim movement or Rabbi Meir Kahane, in fact, the Rebbe did not fully agree with either of their views. While he may have agreed with both on **certain** practical points, the Rebbe stresses that his holistic position and those of Gush Emunim and Kahane proceed from **different principles**. Therefore, to properly assess the approach, one must understand the principles upon which it is based. See Letter to Mr. Peter Kalms, 13 Shvat 5741 (1981) (see Appendix); *Karasi V'Ein Oneh*, Vol. 2, pp. 492, 496. For further exploration of the theoretical divergence between the Rebbe's views and those of Gush Emunim and Kahanism, see *Daas Torah*, Ch. 1. Moreover, the Rebbe explains that he does not unreservedly support any political party or political orientation. Instead, his sole allegiance is to policies in line with the Torah values of *pikuach nefesh* (saving lives) and the Land's sanctity. As he clarified in a letter to Rabbi Immanuel Jakobovits, 3rd Light of Chanukah 5741 (1980), p. 6 (see Appendix): "Since the sole deciding factor is *pikuach nefesh*, it is quite irrelevant what political orientation or party the rabbi issuing the *psak din* subscribes to." See *Petakim MiShulchano Shel HaRabbi*, Vol. 1, p. 274, where the Rebbe criticizes the Likud, an ostensibly "right-wing" party, for their territorial concessions.

19 See *Igros Kodesh*, Vol. 33, p. 49, Letter #12,266 to Israeli poet, journalist, and politician Uri Tzvi Greenberg, 22 Sivan 5738 (1978); *Karasi V'Ein Oneh*, Vol. 2, p. 465.

20 The Rebbe particularly stresses this point in his correspondence with Rabbi Immanuel Jakobovits, a former Chief Rabbi of the United Kingdom. We have reprinted the original letters in this book's Appendix, courtesy of JEM. Some of the letters are also available in English in Kalms, P. (2001). *Guidance from the Rebbe: Personal Recollections 1961-1993, 5721-5733.* Shamir Publishing House. pp. 103f., 131-138. This correspondence is also printed with explanatory notes in Rebbe Responsa, Issue 25. See *Karasi V'Ein Oneh*, Vol. 2, pp. 483-503, for a Hebrew translation. This point is also amply developed in the Rebbe's *sichos*. See, for example, *Karasi V'Ein Oneh*, Vol. 1, pp. 110-111, Simchas Torah 5736 (1975); pp. 182-184, Second Day of Shavuos 5737 (1977); pp. 214-216, Motzaei Shabbos *Vayeitzei* 5738 (1977); pp. 251-253, Purim 5738 (1978); pp. 271-274, Motzaei Shabbos *Tzav* 5738 (1978); Vol.

2, pp. 6-9, Erev Shabbos *Vayeitzei* 5740 (1979); pp. 23-24, 10 Shvat 5740; pp. 27-30, *Mishpatim* 5740 (1980); pp. 53-54, *Ki Sissa* 5740 (1980); pp. 60-61, *Vayakhel-Pekudei* 5740 (1980); pp. 122-126, *Tzav* 5741 (1981); pp. 162-165, Simchas Torah 5742 (1981); pp. 363, 367, *Chayei Sarah* 5746 (1985); pp. 409-410, *Yechidus* with Sadigura Rebbe; pp. 484-498, Letters to various recipients. See also *Daas Torah*, Ch. 6, p. 8, and throughout that work.

21 Meta-halachic principles are not the legal principles themselves, but rather underlying principles that frame how we observe *halachah*. Peace is one such key principle. The value of human life is another. See Rabbi Chaim Rapoport's Halachah and Meta-Halachic Considerations — Chabad.org [https://www.chabad.org/multimedia/video_cdo/aid/3894343/jewish/Halachah-and-Meta-Halachic-Considerations.htm].

22 See *Karasi V'Ein Oneh*, Vol. 1, p. 131, 19 Kislev 5736 (1975); p. 387, 19 Kislev 5739 (1978); Vol. 2, p. 85, *Shlach* 5740 (1980); p. 207, 24 Teves 5742 (1982).

23 See *Karasi V'Ein Oneh*, Vol. 2, p. 294, 13 Tishrei 5743 (1982): "This will also benefit the opposing side... when there is no need for war [as a result of the Jewish people standing strong], there will be no one killed or injured on the opposing side". See there, p. 298: "Behaving in this way [i.e., with military vigilance] will also bring blessing to our opponents and we will not injure them at all because 'they will flee on seven paths before us.'" See also *Toras Menachem 5743*, Vol. 1, pp. 136, 139; Audio of Sichah [https://ashreinu.page.link/nHGP].

24 Genesis 12:7. See *Karasi V'Ein Oneh*, Vol. 2, pp. 233, 240, 3 Tammuz 5742 (1982).

25 *Toras Menachem — Hisvaaduyos 5742*, Vol. 3, p. 1,727; *Karasi V'Ein Oneh*, Vol. 2, p. 240, 3 Tammuz 5742 (1982); Audio of Sichah [https://ashreinu.app/player?parentEvent=3885&event=3890] 42:17-42:50.

26 See *Berachos* 10a, based on the verse in Psalms 104:35.

27 *Toras Menachem Hisvaaduyos 5742*, Vol. 4, p. 2,171ff., 13 Elul (1982). For a similar application, see *Likkutei Sichos*, Vol. 7, p. 188ff.; Vol. 27, p. 191ff.

INTRODUCTION TO PART 1

1 See, for example, Laslovi, O. (2022). *Operation Protective Edge: From Tolerance to Resolution*. Ministry of Defense, for an analysis on Israel's response to the Second Intifada. Laslovi explains how Israel did not respond to incessant terror until there was sufficient international outrage over a Passover suicide bombing. See Passover massacre — Wikipedia [https://en.wikipedia.org/wiki/Passover_massacre]; Passover suicide bombing at Park Hotel in Netanya | Ministry of Foreign Affairs [https://www.gov.il/en/Departments/General/passover-suicide-bombing-at-park-hotel-in-netanya].

2 As we will see, while this is a very kind mode of thinking, it ultimately leads to more death. In the words of famed military theorist Claude von Clausewitz:

Kind-hearted people might of course think there was some ingenious way to disarm or defeat an enemy without too much bloodshed, and might imagine this is the true goal of the art of war. Pleasant as it sounds, it is a fallacy that must be exposed: war is such a dangerous business that the mistakes which come from kindness are the very worst.

Clausewitz, C. (1976). On War. (M. Howard & P. Paret, Eds. & Trans.). Princeton University Press. p. 75.

CHAPTER 1

1 Consider that Hamas has openly threatened to repeat attacks like October 7 in the future. See Hamas official vows to 'repeat' Oct 7 attack repeatedly to teach Israel a lesson — The Economic Times [https://economictimes.indiatimes.com/news/international/hamas-official-vows-to-repeat-oct-7-attack-repeatedly-to-teach-israel-a-lesson/articleshow/104903949]; Hamas Official: We Will Repeat October 7 Attacks Until Israel Is Annihilated [https://www.haaretz.com/israel-news/2023-11-01/ty-article/hamas-official-we-will-repeat-october-7-attacks-until-israel-is-annihilated/]; 'Oct. 7 was just a rehearsal,' warns Sinwar — JNS.org [https://www.jns.org/oct-7-was-just-a-rehearsal-warns-sinwar/].

2 Eitan, R., & Goldstein, D. (1985). *Raful: A Soldier's Story*. Maariv. p. 213; cited in *B'Rega HaEmet*, p. 303, footnote 12. See also *Shalom Shalom V'Ein Shalom*, pp. 266-268.

3 A note on the use of the word "Palestinian": Historically, there was no such thing as a "Palestinian people." After quelling the Bar Kochba revolt, the Roman Emperor Hadrian renamed Judea "Syria Palestina." The term "Palestine" seems to originally refer to the biblical Philistines, a non-indigenous people who settled the coast of ancient Israel. As such, the contemporary Palestinians are a fictitious construct in that they do not link to a historical "Palestinian people." Palestinian identity was first constructed by the antisemitic Islamist leader Haj Amin Al Husseini in the early 20th century. It took on greater traction with the emergence of the PLO in 1963 and then became progressively weaponized by various factions aiming to weaken or destroy Israel. That said, the Rebbe does explicitly use the term "Palestinian" in numerous instances. The term does not convey historical legitimacy. Rather, it indicates a contemporary group of people with common heritage and interests. Consider the following sources: Letter to Rabbi Immanuel Jakobovits, 3rd Light of Chanukah 5741 (1980) (see Appendix); *Karasi V'Ein Oneh*, Vol. 1, p. 46, *Yechidus* with Yonah Cohen; pp.

216-217, Motzaei Shabbos *Vayeitzei* 5738 (1977); Vol. 2, p. 414, *Yechidus* with Rav Efraim Yalles, Second Day of Chol HaMoed Pesach 5742 (1982); p. 427, *Yechidus* with Moshe Katzav, 10 Shvat 5752 (1992); *Sichos Kodesh 5739*, Vol. 1, p. 102, 13 Tishrei (1978). The Rebbe also explicitly uses the term "Palestine" in reference to a possible Palestinian state in a letter to Peter Kalms, 13 Shvat 5743 (1983). See also *Sichos Kodesh 5730*, Vol. 1, p. 629, Purim (1970); *Toras Menachem 5730*, Vol. 2, p. 396; Audio of Sichah [https://ashreinu.page.link/q63Y]. In the *sichah* there, the Rebbe says: "The Land of Israel which is called 'The Holy Land' in English, or 'Palestine,' as the Arabs call it."

4 On the PLO using ceasefires to regroup, see *Shalom Shalom V'Ein Shalom*, p. 171. In August 1981, Israel agreed to a ceasefire with the PLO. The PLO used the opportunity to enhance its fighting capabilities and violated the ceasefire agreement innumerable times. This allowed the PLO to strengthen itself for the First Lebanon War, which began in June 1982, where it again violated ceasefire agreements countless times, a point we will explore at greater length later in this work.

5 See *Sefer HaSichos 5746*, Vol. 1, p. 721; *Toras Menachem — Hisvaaduyos 5746*, Vol. 1, p. 613; *Karasi V'Ein Oneh*, Vol. 2, p. 363, *Chayei Sarah* 5746 (1985). In the Rebbe's words there:

Egypt made the strategic decision to receive everything it wanted—territory, oil wells—without sacrificing a single soldier! They know that achieving their ultimate ends will take time, but they realize that they should arm themselves with patience, and, ultimately, they will receive everything they want.

6 See *Karasi V'Ein Oneh*, Vol. 1, p. 38, *Matos-Maasei* 5730; p. 41, *Eikev* 5730 (1970).

7 Tamil Tigers used truce to rearm, says former commander | World news | The Guardian [https://www.theguardian.com/world/2007/apr/04/srilanka].

8 For an early articulation of terrorist strategy, much of which still holds true today, see

Trinquier, R. (1964). *Modern Warfare: A French View of Counterinsurgency*; A French View of Counterinsurgency [https://www.armyupress.army.mil/Portals/7/combat-studies-institute/csi-books/Modern-Warfare.pdf].

9 Consider also the Irish terrorist group, the Irish Republican Army (IRA), and the Colombian terrorist group, the Revolutionary Armed Forces of Colombia (FARC).

10 Interfaith Relations in the Quranic Tradition — Jewish Policy Center [https://www.jewishpolicycenter.org/2020/04/06/interfaith-relations-in-the-quranic-tradition/]. For further applications in our context, see MacEoin, D. (2008). *Tactical Hudna and Islamist Intolerance.* Middle East Quarterly, 39 [http://www.meforum.org/1925/tactical-hudna-and-islamist-intolerance]; From Yassin to Sinwar: Hamas' Leaders Sell Lies of Peace while they Prepare for War [https://mida.org.il/2018/10/07/בין-סינוואר-ליאסין-מנהיגי-חמאס-מוכרים/]. For a thesis arguing that the *hudna* doctrine can lead to a lasting peace, see Winning the Strategic Narrative in the Israeli-Palestinian Protracted Conflict [https://apps.dtic.mil/sti/tr/pdf/ADA574789.pdf]. While this work is optimistic, it does not align with the way in which Hamas has thus far applied the concept of *hudna*.

11 Hudna — Wikipedia [https://en.wikipedia.org/wiki/Hudna].

12 Treaty of al-Hudaybiya — Wikipedia [https://en.wikipedia.org/wiki/Treaty_of_al-Hudaybiya#].

13 Anwar Sadat was an Egyptian President who initiated the Yom Kippur War against Israel. He then exacted heavy concessions from Israel in the Camp David Accords, which dealt a serious blow to Israel's economy, national security, morale, and trust in the government. This will be discussed extensively in Part 2. On weaponizing ceasefires, see *Shalom Shalom V'Ein Shalom*, p. 208.

14 The Oslo Accords were an agreement between Israel and the PLO ostensibly intended to engender a lasting peace between Israel and the Palestinian population. In fact, the Oslo Accords contributed to greater tension, culminating in the Second Intifada.

15 See Karsh, E. (2016). *The Oslo Disaster.* Begin-Sadat Center for Strategic Studies, JSTOR [https://www.jstor.org/stable/resrep04764.5]. p. 12.

16 See Tepas, M. E. (2009). *A Look at Traditional Islam's General Discord with a Permanent System of Global Cooperation.* Indiana Journal of Global Legal Studies, 16(2), 698-700. See also Goodman, M. (2017). *Malkod 67.* pp. 141-142. There, Micah Goodman makes the incredible argument that given this cultural context, from a pragmatic perspective, Israel should accept that no agreement with the Palestinians will ever be final, but should instead be viewed as inherently temporary. He then draws the conclusion that this fact is a good thing and will ultimately allow for an ethical, realistic resolution to the conflict. For more on this point in Hamas and Hezbollah's logic, see A New Existential War — Part I: Israel's Perception of the Enemy's Goals [https://besacenter.org/a-new-existential-war-part-i-israels-perception-of-the-enemys-goals/]. There, we read:

To simplify the concept of Al-Muqawama [literally "resistance" a central tenet of Hamas and Hezbollah's ideology and strategy] somewhat, it can be viewed as the inverse of Clausewitz's well-known description of war as "the continuation of politics by other means." The Al-Muqawama idea sees politics as the continuation of war by other means. Thus, negotiation is viewed not as a means to bring about the end of a war, but simply as a pause that serves its continuation at a more opportune time under more favorable conditions.

17 However, Hamas leaders have frequently offered similar *hudnas* with similar conditions. For many examples, see Between Hudna and Crackdown: Assessing the Record of Hamas Ceasefires | The Washington Institute [https://www.washingtoninstitute.org/policy-analysis/between-hudna-and-crackdown-assessing-record-hamas-ceasefires].

18 See Article 2 of the Hamas Charter; Hamas in 2017: The document in full | Middle East Eye [https://www.middleeasteye.net/news/hamas-

2017-document-full].

19 For extensive analysis of *hudna* and the Treaty of Hudaybiyyah in the context of Hamas, see Hamas's Concept of a Long-term Ceasefire: A Viable Alternative to Full Peace? [https://www.files.ethz.ch/isn/144215/Hamas%20Concept%20of%20a%20Long-term%20Ceasefire,%20PRIO%20Paper%202010.pdf]. It's important to note that not all iterations of Islam understand the concept of *hudna* and the Treaty of Hudaybiyyah in this way. However, the PLO and Hamas, Israel's most constant adversaries, have used this reasoning in their conflict with Israel, and it is something that we must take seriously.

20 *Sichos Kodesh 5730*, Vol 2, pp. 480ff.; *Toras Menachem 5730*, Vol. 4, p. 160; *Karasi V'Ein Oneh*, Vol. 1, pp. 38-40, *Matos-Maasei* 5730 (1970); p. 272, *Tzav* 5738 (1978).

21 At different points in World War II, Germany and Japan asked for conditional ceasefires that would allow them to mainatin their governin structure. The Allies rejected all such offers, demanding unconditional surrender.

22 See *Sichos Kodesh 5734*, Vol. 1, *Noach*, p. 16; *Karasi V'Ein Oneh*, Vol. 1, p. 70, *Noach* 5734 (1973).

23 *Igros Kodesh*, Vol. 26, pp. 450-452, Letter #9,953, 18 Menachem Av 5730 (1970).

24 Isaiah 50:2. See *Sichos Kodesh 5730*, Vol. 2, p. 460-4; *Toras Menachem 5730*, Vol. 4, p. 155, footnote 98; *Karasi V'Ein Oneh*, Vol. 1, p. 44, *Eikev* 5730 (1970). Notably, this stark verse became the title of the most comprehensive and influential collection of the Rebbe's *sichos* on Israel's security, entitled *"Karasi V'Ein Oneh"* ("I have called out, but no one answers").

25 The Rebbe explained that failing to take a decisive stand would lead to a situation of *"bechiyah l'doros"*: literally, "crying for generations," or enduring suffering that weak decisions would bring on generations to come.

See *Karasi V'Ein Oneh*, Vol. 1, p. 245, Motzaei Shabbos *Mishpatim* 5738 (1978); p. 257, Purim 5738 (1978); Vol. 2, p. 134, *Metzora* 5741 (1981); pp. 373, 379, Motzaei Zos Chanukah 5746 (1985).

26 See *Karasi V'Ein Oneh*, Vol. 2, p. 221, 22 Sivan 5742 (1982). See also *Shalom Shalom V'Ein Shalom*, pp. 266-268.

CHAPTER 2

1 See discussion in *Toras Menachem 5725*, Vol. 3, pp. 35-38, Purim (1965).

2 *Sichos Kodesh 5729*, Vol. 1, pp. 436-441, Purim (1969); *Toras Menachem — Hisvaaduyos 5729*, Vol. 2, pp. 357-363. For an excerpt of the *sichah*, see The Lubavitcher Rebbe on the Way to Combat Terrorism [https://www.youtube.com/watch?v=IWOACDZHwwk&list=PLkXcDdOrqRird5k5aYocVFZ7NlZN39azU&index=6 or https://videos.jem.tv/video-player?clip=3574].

3 The Cossacks were Slavic warriors who lived in communities across Eastern Europe and were known for their military prowess and semi-nomadic lifestyle. Over time, they became synonymous with antisemitic violence due to their involvement in numerous pogroms and massacres against Jewish populations, particularly during events like the Khmelnytsky Uprising in the mid-17th century. This has left a lasting impact on their portrayal in Jewish memory. "Cossack," then, is a metaphor for a violent antisemite of any background.

4 For other instances of the Rebbe heaping scorn on the corrupt and inefficient International Court of Justice at the Hague, see *Sichos Kodesh 5728*, Vol. 1, p. 39, 6 Tishrei (1967); Audio of Sichah [https://ashreinu.app/player?parentEvent=1328&event=1333].

5 U.N. chief "shocked" at Hamas attack tunnels, condemns rocket fire — BICOM [https://www.bicom.org.uk/news/22692/].

6 U.N. chief rejects Israel accusations he justified Hamas attacks | Reuters [https://www.reuters.com/world/un-chief-says-false-accuse-him-justifying-hamas-attacks-2023-10-25/].

7 See *Karasi V'Ein Oneh*, Vol. 1, p. 88, *Naso* 5734 (1974).

8 Suez Crisis, 1956 [https://2001-2009.state.gov/r/pa/ho/time/lw/97179.htm].

9 President Eisenhower threatened to destroy the British economy, leading the United Kingdom to withdraw. See Katz, D. J. (2013). *Waging Financial War*. The US Army War College Quarterly: Parameters, 43(4), 77-85 [https://press.armywarcollege.edu/cgi/viewcontent.cgi?article=2956&context=parameters].

10 FIRST UNITED NATIONS EMERGENCY FORCE (UNEF I) [https://peacekeeping.un.org/en/mission/past/unefi.htm].

11 Similarly, after the Yom Kippur War, Egypt violated its ceasefire agreement with Israel by moving forces into Sinai. U.N. peacekeeping forces were present, but did not stop the Egyptian advance. See *Shalom Shalom V'Ein Shalom*, pp. 231-233. For the terms of the agreement, see Egyptian — Israeli Agreement on Disengagement of Forces in Pursuance of the Geneva Peace Conference (Sinai I) | UN Peacemaker [https://peacemaker.un.org/egyptisrael-disengagementforces74]. For more on UNEF's ineffectiveness, see Jones, R. D. (1996). *Israeli Air Superiority in the 1967 Arab-Israeli War: An Analysis of Operational Art*. Naval War College. p. 3.

12 See *Karasi V'Ein Oneh*,Vol. 1, p. 39, *Matos-Maasei* 5730 (1970).

13 Although Egypt and Israel are technically not at war, later in this work we will explore why the peace treaty is unstable and has very much hurt Israel in the past and the present.

14 For discussion of Lebanon's collapse, see Kanaaneh, A. (2021). *Hezbollah in Lebanon* (Hebrew). Jerusalem: Y.L. Magnes Press — The Hebrew University. pp. 59-95.

15 Operation Litani | IDF [https://www.idf.il/en/mini-sites/wars-and-operations/operation-litani/].

16 UNIFIL [https://unifil.unmissions.org/].

17 See *Sichos Kodesh 5738*, Vol. 2, pp. 288-289,

Pesach Sheini (1978).

18 After being evicted by the local Muslim leadership in response to Israeli bombardment, the PLO leadership fled to Tunisia. They did not return to Israel until Israel invited them back during the 1993 Oslo Accords.

19 U.N. Security Council Resolution 1701 [https://peacemaker.un.org/israellebanon-resolution1701].

20 The treaty included UNSC Resolution 1701 which stipulated that Hezbollah would not be allowed past the Litani River, which is 20 kilometers North of the Israel-Lebanon border. UNIFIL has failed to prevent this. Instead of stemming Hezbollah, UNIFIL has allowed terrorist groups including Hezbollah for nearly half a century.

21 Missiles and Rockets of Hezbollah [https://missilethreat.csis.org/country/hezbollahs-rocket-arsenal/]; List of military equipment of Hezbollah — Wikipedia [https://en.wikipedia.org/wiki/List_of_military_equipment_of_Hezbollah]. Consider also Hezbollah affiliated Al-Ahed News, see The Al-Aqsa Deluge: Has 'Israel' lost its job [https://alahednews.com.lb/article.php?id=62266&cid=185]: There, we read:

Over the 23 years since the Israeli army left Lebanon, the resistance has been accumulating its strength and adding to its experiences every day. The most important thing is that the entity [Israel] will turn into an area besieged by a belt of fire from all directions, which will destroy the origin of the idea on which it was founded, which is immigration to Palestine. In the eyes of many settlers, the "promised" land is no longer a promised land, nor a land of peace, nor a land of prosperity, so why do they continue living in it?

Note that in this context, the term "settlers" refers to all Jews living in the entire Land of Israel.

22 *The Third Lebanon War: Target Lebanon | INSS* [https://www.inss.org.il/publication/the-third-lebanon-war-target-lebanon/].

23 *Sichos Kodesh 5739*, Vol. 1, p. 112, 13 Tishrei (1978); Audio of Sichah [https://ashreinu.page.link/HDua].

24 1975-1990.

25 See *Daas Torah*, p. 116. The Rebbe further notes that under Israeli rule, Arabs can expect a better quality of life than they would receive in any of the surrounding countries. Relative to Syria, Jordan, Egypt, and Lebanon, Israel has the highest standard of living. It boasts a strong economy, advanced healthcare system, and high life expectancy. Arabs in Israel can also expect a higher yearly income than Arabs in other countries in the region. See *Karasi V'Ein Oneh*, Vol. 1, p. 62, *sichos* of *Bamidbar* and *Naso* 5733 (1973). Moreover, relative to other countries in the region, such as Lebanon, Syria, and Iraq, Arabs are less likely to die in war in Israel, especially civil war. It is also the only country in the area where Muslims have full freedom of religion, with the right to practice whichever version of Islam they like. For an especially crisp articulation of this point, see Alexander, S. (2013, March 3). *Reactionary philosophy*. Slate Star Codex [https://slatestarcodex.com/2013/03/03/reactionary-philosophy-in-an-enormous-planet-sized-nutshell/].

26 See *Karasi V'Ein Oneh*, Vol. 1, pp. 320-321, *Re'eh* 5738 (1978). More broadly, the Rebbe argues that such forces undermine Jewish sovereignty. See *Sichos Kodesh 5741*, Vol. 1, pp. 14-15, 19 Tishrei (1980); Video of Sichah [https://videos.jem.tv/video-player?clip=12530]; International Peacekeeping Force In Israel? Absolutely Not! | The Lubavitcher Rebbe [https://www.youtube.com/watch?v=GLqxT3G4z68].

27 U.N. peacekeeping forces are notoriously inept and corrupt. Consider:

An AK-47 should cost no more than $20 or a small goat. Other equipment to procure includes: ammo, RPGs, crew-served weapons, and the ubiquitous Toyota Hilux pickup truck with .50cal attachment

(aka a "technical"). If you have problems sourcing equipment, try the local United Nations mission, who spend months collecting weapons from former warring parties. For a little baksheesh, UN peacekeepers. are often willing to under-report a few tons of weapons.

How to Take Over a Small Country in 10 Easy Steps — War on the Rocks [https://warontherocks.com/2015/05/how-to-take-over-a-small-country-in-10-easy-steps/]. See also UN peacekeeping arms losses could equip an army: report | United Nations News | Al Jazeera [https://www.aljazeera.com/news/2017/11/13/un-peacekeeping-arms-losses-could-equip-an-army-report]; UN: Tackle Wrongdoing by Peacekeepers | Human Rights Watch [https://www.hrw.org/news/2008/04/30/un-tackle-wrongdoing-peacekeepers-0].

28 For a strategic analysis of why foreign cease-fires and international intervention often prolong suffering, see Luttwak, E. N. (1999). *Give War a Chance*. Foreign Affairs, 78(4), 36-44; [https://www.foreignaffairs.com/articles/1999-07-01/give-war-chance].

29 Leviticus 26:6.

30 See *Taanis* 22a.

31 See *Igros Kodesh*, Vol. 32, p. 190, Letter #12,105 to IDF Captain Shimon Vajim, dated 11 Nissan 5737 (1977); p. 191, Letter #12,106 to Shimon Peres, dated 13 Nissan 5737 (1977). Peres would go on to become interim Prime Minister of Israel the following week. See also *Sichos Kodesh 5727*, Vol. 1, p. 197, 19 Kislev (1966); *Sichos Kodesh 5730*, Vol. 1, p. 135, Simchas Torah (1969); *Karasi V'Ein Oneh*, Vol. 1, p. 473, *Devarim* 5739 (1979); Vol. 2, p. 225, 22 Sivan 5742 (1982); p. 245, 7 Tammuz 5742 (1982); p. 284, 18 Elul 5742 (1982).

CHAPTER 3

1 The "leech" represents a person or entity that constantly demands more, while its two "daughters" symbolize the unending nature of these demands. The phrase "Give! Give!" emphasizes the relentless and persistent nature of such cravings. See *Tanya*, Ch. 19. For the application of this verse in the context of "Land for Peace," see *Karasi V'Ein Oneh*, Vol. 2, p. 116, 10 *Shvat* 5741 (1981); *Sichos Kodesh*, 5741, Vol. 2, p. 170, 10 Shvat.

2 See *Sichos Kodesh 5740*, Vol. 1, p. 460, 10 Kislev (1979); p. 566, 19 Kislev (1979); Vol. 2, p. 30. There, the Rebbe uses this phrase from the Midrash to explain that those who seek concessions do so not for peace, but instead brazenly demand more. Tragically, the Rebbe notes that not only do Israel's enemies have this approach, but benighted Israeli politicians develop a taste for more and more concessions. See *Toras Menachem 5742*, Vol. 2, p. 371 (1981); *Sichos Kodesh 5740*, Vol. 3, p. 52.

3 Biden Says Two State Solution Is Needed for Peace in Israel [https://www.youtube.com/watch?v=-TVSePFCJ4Y]; Opinion | Joe Biden: U.S. won't back down from the challenge of Putin and Hamas — The Washington Post [https://www.washingtonpost.com/opinions/2023/11/18/joe-biden-gaza-hamas-putin/].

4 Blinken Says Two-State Solution Is Still Best Option for Peace [https://www.wsj.com/livecoverage/israel-hamas-war-gaza-hostages-2023-11-28/card/blinken-says-two-state-solution-is-still-best-option-for-peace-T0X54jEylG2khrbopIQ0].

5 Guterres: It is long past time to move in a determined, irreversible way towards a two-State solution | United Nations in Türkiye [https://turkiye.un.org/en/254149-guterres-it-long-past-time-move-determined-irreversible-way-towards-two-state-solution].

6 Vladimir Putin stresses two-state solution to Israeli-Palestinian conflict [https://www.business-standard.com/article/international/vladimir-putin-stresses-two-state-solution-to-israeli-palestinian-conflict-121112400061_1.html].

7 Israel-Gaza war: only a two-state solution can bring real peace, China president says in first public speech on conflict [https://www.scmp.com/news/china/diplomacy/article/3242369/israel-gaza-war-only-two-state-solution-can-bring-real-peace-china-president-says-first-public]. In his words:

The fundamental way out of the recurring Palestinian-Israeli conflicts is to implement the two-state solution, establish an independent State of Palestine, and achieve peaceful coexistence between Palestine and Israel.

8 The less influential socialist Popular Front for the Liberation of Palestine (PFLP), as well as the affiliated Jihad Jibril Brigades, also feature an image of the entire landmass of the State of Israel in their emblems. The hostile Palestinian Land Authority (PLA), a subsidiary of the PA, the Palestinian organization that administers the West Bank, also features Israel's entire landmass in its emblem. See Palestinian Land Authority [https://www.facebook.com/PalLandAuth].

9 See Goodman, M. (2017). *Malkod 67.* p. 194, footnote 64.

10 Hamas in 2017: The document in full | Middle East Eye [https://www.middleeasteye.net/news/hamas-2017-document-full].

11 As Tomas Pueyo, an influential contemporary analyst, explains, this refers to Mandatory Palestine, Israel, Gaza, and the West Bank.

12 See *Sichos Kodesh 5730*, Vol. 2, p. 460-3; *Karasi V'Ein Oneh*, Vol. 1, p. 42, *Eikev* 5730 (1970); pp. 50-51, *Noach* 5731 (1970); p. 158, *Nasso* 5736 (1976).

13 *Karasi V'Ein Oneh*, Vol. 1, pp. 50-51, *Noach* 5731 (1970).

14 Sheikh Muhammad Ali Ja'abari. The Rebbe explicitly mentions Jabari by name in *Sichos Kodesh 5736*, Vol. 2, p. 325, *Naso* (1976).

15 I Kings 21:19. The phrase "you have killed and also taken possession" originates from the story of King Ahab and Naboth's vineyard. Ahab desired Naboth's vineyard, but Naboth refused to sell it. Ahab's wife, Jezebel, had Naboth falsely accused and stoned to death. After Naboth was murdered, Ahab took possession of the vineyard. The Prophet Elijah rebuked Ahab, saying, "You have killed and also taken possession," meaning, he had not only murdered an innocent man, but also wrongfully seized his property. The phrase is used to condemn someone who commits a wrongdoing and then exploits its consequences for their own benefit. In this case, the Arab population of Hebron literally killed the Jews in the 1929 massacre and then "inherited" the city as a result.

16 In a disturbing video, Sneineh proudly recounts the attack's details to a group of Palestinians, mainly youth. The video, filmed in Arabic, features Abu Sneineh offering a tour of the site where the attack took place. See https://www.youtube.com/watch?v=VUY1ScAWghE&list=PLYYBIsai7GRh5BRbDnWpsQTHyJhIcvftc\.

17 Antisemitic remarks by Palestinian Authority President Mahmoud Abbas | E-002606/2023 | European Parliament [https://www.europarl.europa.eu/doceo/document/E-9-2023-002606_EN.html].

18 Abbas: Palestinian people have the right to defend themselves | Reuters [https://www.reuters.com/article/idUSS8N3AU0AU/]; Abbas stresses Palestinian right to defence after Hamas op [https://www.newarab.com/news/abbas-stresses-palestinian-right-defence-after-hamas-op].

19 Battle of Gaza (2007) — Wikipedia [https://en.wikipedia.org/wiki/Battle_of_Gaza_(2007)]; Fatah—Hamas conflict — Wikipedia [https://en.wikipedia.org/wiki/Fatah%E2%80%93Hamas_conflict]. Elections were held in both Gaza and Judea and Samaria. In Judea and Samaria, Hamas initially had less support and could not take control, in part due to Israeli military backing for the PA. This support, along with Israel's capacity to intervene in these territories, played a role in maintaining the PA's rule there.

20 Henry Kissinger's (Maybe) Last Interview: Drop the Two-State Solution — POLITICO [https://www.politico.com/news/magazine/2023/12/02/henry-kissinger-interview-israel-hamas-war-00129374]. Even Henry Kissinger, a one-time proponent of the two-state solution, said that by 2023, Hamas' conduct in Gaza has proven that this is practically untenable.

21 Al Ahed (Lebanon newspaper) — Wikipedia [https://ar.wikipedia.org/wiki/العهد (جريدة لبنانية)].

22 Enemy Entity — Al-Manar Channel Website — Lebanon [https://www.almanar.com.lb/tag/%D9%83%D9%8A%D8%A7%D9%86%D8%A7%D9%84%D8%B9%D8%AF%D9%88/page/3].

23 Al-Aqsa Storm — Between Their North and Our South.... [https://alahednews.com.lb/article.php?id=62024&cid=185]

24 Iran's 'verbal' war against Israel continues — analysis — The Jerusalem Post [https://www.jpost.com/middle-east/iran-news/article-697050].

25 Iranian press review: Pro-government media celebrates Hamas rocket strikes | Middle East Eye [https://www.middleeasteye.net/news/iranian-press-review-farsi-media-divide-over-israels-bombardment-gaza].

26 Osama bin Laden, Letter to the American People, p. 3.

27 Consider the 1517 Hebron and Safed Attacks, the 1834 Safed Plunder, and the 1840 Damascus affair. See History of the Jews under Muslim rule — Wikipedia [https://en.wikipedia.org/wiki/History_of_the_Jews_under_Muslim_rule].

28 Jaffa riots — Wikipedia [https://en.wikipedia.org/wiki/Jaffa_riots]; Palestine. Disturbances in May, 1921. Reports of the Commission of Inquiry with Correspondence Relating Thereto [https://archive.org/details/palestinedisturb00grearich/page/10/mode/2up].

29 1929 Riots | the Jewish Community of Hebron [http://en.hebron.org.il/history/topic/3]; The Hebron Massacre of 1929 [https://www.jewishvirtuallibrary.org/the-hebron-massacre-of-1929]

30 This indicates that the sexual violence perpetrated on October 7 was not an exception in Arab violence towards Jews.

31 The pogroms continued. Consider the notable 1936 Jaffa Riots Pre-State Israel: Photographs from 1936 Arab Riots [https://www.jewishvirtuallibrary.org/photographs-from-1936-arab-riots]; The Palestine Post, 17 April 1936; [https://www.nli.org.il/en/newspapers/?a=d&d=pls19360417-01.1.1&e=-------en-20--1--img-txIN%7ctxTI-------------1].

32 War of Independence | IDF [https://www.idf.il/en/mini-sites/wars-and-operations/war-of-independence/].

33 In neither case did Israel conquer the land

from "Palestinians," but rather from hostile neighboring states who did not intend to turn these tracts of land into Palestine. Palestinian national identity became a major Arab weapon against Israel following the Yom Kippur War in 1973.

34 The term "Intifada," derived from the Arabic word meaning "shaking off," describes two periods of heightened Palestinian terrorism, the First Intifada (1987-1993), the Second Intifada (2000-2005), and the "Knife Intifada" (circa 2015).

35 Fatah's Tanzim and Al-Aqsa Martyrs Brigades' divisions.

36 See *Karasi V'Ein Oneh,* Vol. 1, pp. 315-316, Motzaei Shabbos *Pinchas* 5738 (1978); p. 387, 19 Kislev 5739 (1978); p. 401, Motzaei Shabbos *Mikeitz* 5739 (1978); Vol. 2, p. 355, *Purim* 5745 (1985); p. 410, *Yechidus* with Sadigura Rebbe; p. 446, Letter to Rechavam Ze'evi, Rosh Chodesh Adar I 5730 (1970) (also printed in *Igros Kodesh*, Vol. 26, pp. 308-309, Letter #9,833); pp. 466-467, Teves 5738 (1978); p. 474, Chanukah 5740 (1979).

37 Operation Defensive Shield | IDF [https://www.idf.il/en/mini-sites/wars-and-operations/operation-defensive-shield/].

38 Part of the Oslo agreement was that if the Palestinian authorities did not contain terror threats against Israel, Israel could intervene and reassert security control. See the Oslo Accords, Article VIII and XIII, available at knesset.gov [https://web.archive.org/web/20021115183950/http://knesset.gov.il/process/docs/oslo_eng.htm].

39 This was a surprising reversal for Sharon who, throughout his long military and political career, had been a staunch advocate of settlement policy. See:

תוכנית חמש האצבעות של אריאל שרון | מכון התורה והארץ '-למעשה' אקטואליה הלכתית Ariel Sharon's Five-Point Plan | Torah VeHa'aretz Institute — 'LeMa'aseh' Current Halachic Issues [https://www.toraland.org.il/מאמרים/הארץ-ומצוותיה/ארץ-ישראל/קדושת-הארץ/תוכנית-חמש-האצבעות-של-אריאל-שרון/];

מדיניות ממשלות ישראל כלפי ההתיישבות היהודית בחבל עזה בשנים 1967—2005 The Policy of Israeli Governments Towards Jewish Settlement in the Gaza Strip from 1967-2005 [http://www.ariel.ac.il/wp/judea-and-samaria-research-studies/wp-content/uploads/sites/144/2019/12/06_BiligHuberman_JSRS28-2.pdf];

תוכנית חמש האצבעות – ויקיפדיה The Five-Point Plan — Wikipedia/ [https://he.wikipedia.org/wiki/תוכנית_חמש_האצבעות/].

40 How the Palestinian Authority Failed Its People — The Atlantic [https://www.theatlantic.com/international/archive/2023/10/palestinian-authority-gaza-hamas/675695/];

Corrupt, discredited: could a reformed Palestinian Authority run Gaza? [https://www.theguardian.com/world/2023/nov/27/corrupt-discredited-could-a-reformed-palestinian-authority-run-gaza]; The Palestinian Authority's corruption and its impact on the peace process [https://jcpa.org/article/the-palestinian-authoritys-corruption-and-its-impact-on-the-peace-process/].

41 The leaders financially benefit from cooperating with Israel. This monetary support comes partly from Israel, but mainly from international aid; since they are not labeled as terrorists, they are able to receive funds from countries such as the U.S.

42 Strikingly, the PA has committed to paying the families of slain October 7 terrorists. See PA to immediately reward families of Oct. 7 terrorists with nearly $3 million — JNS. org [https://www.jns.org/pa-to-immediately-reward-families-of-oct-7-terrorists-with-nearly-3m/].

Consider also a representative excerpt from the PA anthem:

Chorus:

I sacrifice, I sacrifice, I sacrifice, O my land, O land of my ancestors

Verse 1:

With determination, fire, and volcano of revenge

And the yearning of my blood for my land and my home

I climbed the mountains and took up the struggle

A peaceful anthem indeed.

43 The Resurgence of Armed Groups in the West Bank and Their Connections to Gaza [https://acleddata.com/2023/12/14/the-resurgence-of-armed-groups-in-the-west-bank-and-their-connections-to-gaza/].

Note that most of these brigade names are just the names of the Palestinian cities in Northern Samaria. Each major city or town has its own terror brigade.

44 See *Igros Kodesh*, Vol. 26, pp. 44-47, Letter #9,613 to Rabbi Shlomo Yosef Zevin, dated Kislev 5729 (1968); also printed in *Karasi V'Ein Oneh*, Vol. 2, pp. 437-439; *Sichos Kodesh 5740*, Vol. 3, p. 1,157, *Yechidus* with Sadigura Rebbe (1980); *Karasi V'Ein Oneh*, Vol. 1, p. 24, *Matos-Maasei* 5729 (1969). For a comprehensive list of terrorist attacks across Israel's history, see Johnston's Archive [https://www.johnstonsarchive.net/].

45 In the Hamas-Fatah civil war, over 600 Palestinians killed one another. The tensions have been ongoing since then. See Over 600 Palestinians killed in internal clashes since 2006 [https://www.ynetnews.com/articles/0,7340,L-3409548,00.html]. Moreover, since taking control of Gaza, Hamas has sentenced 180 Palestinians to death and killed many others extrajudicially.

46 Between 1967 and 2005, Israeli security forces killed Palestinians in the low thousands. These killings were aimed at terrorists, but came with collateral damage. Between 2005 and 2024, Israel has killed many times that number, as a result of its being forced to retaliate in order to quell Hamas attacks.

47 *Sichos Kodesh 5740*, Vol. 3, pp. 1,157, *Yechidus* with Sadigura Rebbe (1980); *Sichos Kodesh 5746*, Vol. 2, pp. 261, 266, Motzaei Zos Chanukah (1985).

48 See the Hamas Charter which says:

1) "Hamas" is a Palestinian Islamic national liberation and resistance movement. Its goal is to liberate Palestine and confront the Zionist project. Its frame of reference is Islam.

2) Palestine extends from the River Jordan in the east to the Mediterranean in the west, and from Ras al-Naqurah in the north to Umm al-Rashrash in the south. [This is basically present-day Israel, Gaza, and the West Bank, excluding the Golan Heights — thanks to Tomas Pueyo for this observation.]

3) Palestine is an Arab-Islamic land.

10) Jerusalem is the capital of Palestine. Its Islamic and Christian holy places belong exclusively to the Palestinian people and to the Arab and Islamic Ummah. Not one stone of Jerusalem can be surrendered or relinquished. The measures undertaken by the occupiers in Jerusalem, such as Judaisation, settlement building, and establishing facts on the ground, are fundamentally null and void.

Hamas in 2017: The document in full | Middle East Eye [https://www.middleeasteye.net/news/hamas-2017-document-full].

49 See *Karasi V'Ein Oneh*, Vol. 2, p. 298, 13 Tishrei 5743 (1982); p. 365, *Chayei Sarah* 5746 (1985).

50 See *Sichos Kodesh 5746*, Vol, 2, pp. 261, 266, Motzaei Zos Chanukah (1985); Video of Sichah [https://www.youtube.com/watch?v=NB97MScOOaI; https://videos.jem.tv/video-player?produced=2860]. As the Rebbe put it there:

Every concession and every appeasement strengthens and encourages them [the Palestinians] and, as a result, they [the Palestinians] increase the terrorist attacks throughout the Land of Israel!

In recent times, there have been numerous terror attacks in which several Israelis, civilians or soldiers, were killed — in the Old City of Jerusalem, in Hebron, in Shechem (Nablus) and in Ramallah!

See also *Karasi V'Ein Oneh*, Vol. 2, p. 355, Purim 5745 (1985); p. 389, *Haazinu* 5749 (1988); *Toras Menachem — Hisvaaduyos 5749*, p. 95.

51 See *Yechidus* with Israeli Air Force pilot Ran Ronen-Pekker, 5735 (1975); cited in *Karasi V'Ein Oneh*, Vol. 1, p. 135.

52 Islamist Influencer Suggests Birobidzhan is the Jewish Homeland [https://twitter.com/mohammed_hijab/status/1731281034124095746]. Birobidzhan is a remote province in Russia which the early Soviet government designated for Jewish settlement. Part of the goal of this settlement was to isolate Jews from central Russia. The settlement failed, yet various antisemitic individuals and influencers have made the claim that Birobidzhan is the true Jewish homeland, and that the Jewish people have no right to be in the Land of Israel. UNRWA'S TEACHERS OF HATE [https://unwatch.org/wp-content/uploads/2022/06/2022-Report-UNRWAs-Teachers-of-Hate.pdf], p. 29.

53 See, for example, Trinquier, R. (1964). *Modern Warfare: a French View of Counterinsurgency*; A French View of Counterinsurgency [https://www.armyupress.army.mil/Portals/7/combat-studies-institute/csi-books/Modern-Warfare.pdf]. See also Luttwak, E. N., & Richard, T. (2006). *Modern war: Counter-insurgency as malpractice.* Politique étrangère. p. 4, 849-861. I.F.R.I.; Modern War: Counter-Insurgency as Malpractice | Cairn International Edition [https://www.cairn-int.info/revue-politique-etrangere-2006-4-page-849.htm&wt.src=pdf].

INTRODUCTION TO PART 2

1 See *Sichos Kodesh 5738,* Vol. 3, p. 493, 9 Elul (1978).

2 See *Toras Menachem 5743,* Vol. 2, p. 772, 10 Teves (1982).

3 See Luttwak, E.N., & Richard, T. (2006). *Modern War: Counter-insurgency as malpractice.* Politique étrangère. p. 4, 849-861. I.F.R.I.; Modern War: Counter-Insurgency as Malpractice | Cairn International Edition [https://www.cairn-int.info/revue-politique-etrangere-2006-4-page-849.htm&wt.src=pdf].

4 See *Karasi V'Ein Oneh,* Vol. 1, p. 124, 19 Kislev 5736 (1975).

5 See *Karasi V'Ein Oneh,* Vol. 2, p. 319, 19 Kislev 5743 (1982).

6 See *Shulchan Aruch, Orach Chaim,* 328:10; *Levush* 328:10; *Magen Avraham* 328:7.

7 See *Karasi V'Ein Oneh,* Vol. 2, pp. 363-364, *Chayei Sarah* 5746 (1985). See also *Daas Torah,* p. 85, which extends the metaphor: A physician will make decisions that are in a patient's best interest, while a hospital director, who takes broader operational considerations into account, may choose to sacrifice a patient's optimal care for the sake of the hospital's bottom line.

8 See *Karasi V'Ein Oneh,* Vol. 1, pp. 110-111, Simchas Torah 5736 (1975); p. 124, 19 Kislev 5736 (1975); pp. 160-161, 20 Menachem Av 5736 (1976); pp. 214-215, *Vayeitzei* 5738 (1977); pp. 238-239, 10 Shvat 5738 (1978); pp. 264-267, Purim 5738 (1978); p. 324, *Re'eh* 5738 (1978). Here, the Rebbe notes that having once been in the army is insufficient. Instead, the relevant opinion must come from an active military expert who is offering a purely military perspective without taking politics into account at all. The Rebbe also notes that soldiers-turned-politicians often present political assessments rather than strategic ones. See also *Daas Torah,* pp. 84-85, including footnote 16 there, which explains that (a) King David made all of his military decisions only upon consulting experts, and (b) the Talmud lends credence even to a non-Jewish area expert.

9 See *Talmud Yerushalmi, Yoma,* 8:5; *Mishneh Torah, Hilchos Shabbos,* 2:2; *Shulchan Aruch, Orach Chaim,* 328:2; *Shemiras Shabbos KeHilchasah,* 40:1. See also *Karasi V'Ein Oneh,* Vol. 1, p. 239, 10 Shvat 5738 (1978); p. 253, Purim 5738 (1978). See also *Daas Torah,* p. 159.

10 See *Karasi V'Ein Oneh,* Vol 1, pp. 111-112, Simchas Torah 5736 (1975); p. 118, *Chayei Sarah* 5736 (1975); pp. 124-125, 19 Kislev 5736 (1975); p. 182, 2nd Day of Shavuos 5737 (1977); Vol. 2, p. 240, 3 Tammuz 5742 (1982); Audio of Sichah [https://ashreinu.page.link/3VyN]; p. 311, 6th Night of Sukkos 5743 (1982); p. 313, *Chayei Sarah* 5743 (1982); p. 356, Purim 5745 (1985). See also *Daas*

Torah, pp. 84-85.

11 See *Karasi V'Ein Oneh,* Vol 1, pp. 112-113, Simchas Torah 5736 (1975); pp. 118-112, *Chayei Sarah* 5736 (1975). See also *B'Rega HaEmet,* p. 434, citing a conversation between the Rebbe and Benjamin Netanyahu at *Hakkafos.*

12 See *Karasi V'Ein Oneh,* Vol. 1, p. 44, *Eikev* 5730 (1970); Vol. 2, p. 313, *Chayei Sarah* 5743 (1972).

13 See *Karasi V'Ein Oneh,* Vol. 1, p. 265, Purim 5738 (1978); p. 336, Motzaei Shabbos *Haazinu* 5739 (1978); Vol. 2, p. 464, Letter to Rabbi Moshe

Buchko, dated 25 Tammuz 5737 (1977); also printed in *Igros Kodesh,* Vol. 32, pp. 267-268, Letter #12,176.

14 See Trinquier, R. (1964). *Modern Warfare: a French View of Counterinsurgency*; A French View of Counterinsurgency [https://www.armyupress.army.mil/Portals/7/combat-studies-institute/csi-books/Modern-Warfare.pdf]. See also Clausewitz, C. (1976). *On War*; On War by Carl von Clausewitz [https://www.icct.nl/sites/default/files/import/publication/On-War.pdf].

CHAPTER 4

1 *Sanhedrin* 72a, 102a; *Berachos* 58a; *Tanchuma, Pinchas,* 3; *Zohar,* Vol. 1, 138a. *Rashi* on Exodus 22:21 demonstrates how this principle is derived from a Torah verse. For the Rebbe's application of this source to the conflict, see *Toras Menachem — Hisvaaduyos 5729,* Vol. 1, p. 242; *Toras Menachem — Hisvaaduyos 5729,* Vol. 2, pp. 357-363; pp. 388-389, *Ki Sissa; Sichos Kodesh 5729,* Vol. 1, p. 95, *Bereishis;* pp. 438-441, Purim; p. 459, *Ki Sissa;* also printed in *Karasi V'Ein Oneh,* Vol. 1, pp. 2-4, *Bereishis* 5729 (1968); *Sichos Kodesh 5734,* Vol. 1, pp. 145-146, 19 Kislev (1973); *Sichos Kodesh 5736,* Vol. 2, p. 231, *Bamidbar* (1976); *Sichos Kodesh 5738,* Vol. 1, p. 227, Motzaei Shabbos *Vayeitzei* (1977); also printed in *Karasi V'Ein Oneh,* Vol. 1. p. 213; *Sichos Kodesh 5739,* Vol. 3, p. 311, 13 Tammuz (1979); also printed in *Karasi V'Ein Oneh,* Vol. 1. p. 456; *Sichos Kodesh 5740,* Vol. 3. p. 1,154, *Yechidus* with Sadigura Rebbe (1980); *Karasi V'Ein Oneh,* Vol. 2, p. 415, *Yechidus* with Rabbi Efraim Eliezer Yalles, Av Beis Din of Philadelphia, Chol HaMoed Pesach 5743 (1983). For a more theoretical discussion of the principle, see *Sichos Kodesh 5725,* Vol. 2, p. 252, *Balak* (1965); also printed in *Likkutei Sichos,* Vol. 8, pp. 139, 151. See also *Likkutei Sichos,* Vol. 14, p. 83.

2 The Rebbe uses the term "preventative" since, although Israel would be attacking first in the war, their objective would not be to wage an offensive war of conquest, but rather to launch a preliminary attack to prevent almost certain future aggression. See *Sichos Kodesh*

5738, Vol. 1, p. 226-228 (1977); *Karasi V'Ein Oneh,* p. 213, Motzaei Shabbos *Vayeitzei* 5738 (1977). The concept of a "preventive war" is well documented in military strategy. Consider Gentile, G. P. (2000). *Planning for Preventive War, 1945-1950.* National Defense University, Institute for National Strategic Studies. Consider also Jones, J. R., Hammond, I., Ramos, S., Williams, C., Schade, S., & Taylor, D. C. (2007). *Preemptive and Preventive Operations.* United States Sergeants Major Academy Class 58. See also Jones, R. D. (1996). *Israeli Air Superiority in the 1967 Arab-Israeli War: An Analysis of Operational Art.* Naval War College. pp. 4-5; For a contemporary Israeli General's writing on the necessity of introducing preventative war, see Finkel, M. (2024, March 26). The Preventive War Doctrine: Its Disappearance from the Security Toolbox and the Need for Its Return. The Begin-Sadat Center for Strategic Studies. https://besacenter.org/he/-מסל-היעלמותה-מנע-מלחמת/הכלים-הביטחוני/.

3 See Will Hamas and Hezbollah Try Again to Tear the Israeli Spiderweb? [https://besacenter.org/will-hamas-and-hezbollah-try-again-to-tear-the-israeli-spiderweb/]. There, it reads:

After several failed attempts, Hezbollah attacked an IDF patrol along the border fence on July 12, 2006, killing several Israeli soldiers and abducting two more. In response, Israel embarked on the Second Lebanon War, which came as a complete surprise to Hezbollah. Nasrallah even publicly

conceded that had he known Israel would react the way it did, he would not have ordered the abductions.

4 See Psalms 20:8.

5 See *Karasi V'Ein Oneh,* Vol 1, pp. 1-3, *Bereishis* 5729 (1968); pp. 10-12, *Vayeitzei* 5729 (1968); p. 224, 10 Teves 5738 (1977); p. 243, 15 Shvat 5738 (1978); p. 262, Purim 5738 (1978); *Karasi V'Ein Oneh,* Vol. 2, pp. 224-225, 22 Sivan 5742 (1982).

6 *Sichos Kodesh 5736,* Vol. 2, p. 231, *Bamidbar* (1976).

7 See *Sichos Kodesh 5738,* Vol. 1, p. 542, *Vayeitzei* (1977).

8 *Toras Menachem 5743,* Vol. 2, p. 772; *Karasi V'Ein Oneh,* Vol. 2, p. 330, 10 Teves 5743 (1984); Audio of Sichah [https://ashreinu.app/player?parentEvent=4075&event=4075].

9 Deuteronomy 28:10.

10 Deuteronomy 28:7.

11 See *Sichos Kodesh 5729,* Vol. 1, pp. 436, 456, Purim (1969); *Toras Menachem — Hisvaaduyos 5729,* Vol. 2, pp. 331-332, 357.

12 See *Sichos Kodesh 5729,* Vol. 1, p. 441, Purim (1969); *Toras Menachem — Hisvaaduyos 5729,* Vol. 2, pp. 357-358.

13 Shukeiri at a press conference held on PLO Radio in Cairo, November 25, 1967.

14 *Karasi V'Ein Oneh,* Vol. 2, p. 460, Letter dated 3 Elul 5731 (1971); also printed in *Igros Kodesh,* Vol. 27, p. 205, Letter #10,200. See also *Karasi V'Ein Oneh,* Vol. 1, p. 57, citing an interview with General Ariel Sharon; also printed in *Kfar Chabad,* Issue 684, and The Bar Lev Line — Living Torah [https://www.chabad.org/therebbe/livingtorah/player_cdo/aid/2222314/jewish/The-Bar-Lev-Line.htm].

15 The Maginot Line was a series of fortifications built by France along its borders with Germany and Italy after World War I. During World War II, the Germans invaded via the Ardennes Forest, which the Allies thought to be impassable. This allowed the Germans to bypass the Maginot Line, leading to the fall of France in 1940. The Maginot Line failed due to the German's unexpected strategy and the Allies' over-reliance on the fortifications, leaving them unprepared for an attack from a different direction. On the fallacy of over-reliance on fortification systems such as the Maginot Line, see Brodie, B. (1984). *A guide to the reading of On War;* M. Howard & P. Paret (Eds.). *On War.* Princeton University Press. p. 683. For an analysis comparing Israel's Iron Dome system and the Maginot Line, see Israel's Iron Maginot Line System — War on the Rocks [https://warontherocks.com/2014/08/israels-iron-maginot-line-system/]. Similarly, consider the following reflection from a U.S. Army Corps of Engineers study: "a fixed and static barrier system can be viewed as a puzzle contrived for the prospective attacker to solve." See Seguin, P. B. (1988). *The Strategic Performance of Defensive Barriers.* Engineer Studies Center, U.S. Army Corps of Engineers; https://apps.dtic.mil/sti/tr/pdf/ADA197303.pdf. That study critically compares and analyzes the failures of the Bar-Lev and Maginot lines. See also The Wall is the Wall: Why Fortresses Fail [https://warontherocks.com/2018/02/wall-wall-fortresses-fail/]. Taking a broad historical view, the author suggests that over-reliance on fortifications is a persistent tendency throughout history, and that security strategies should not depend solely on the hope that a fortification will not fail.

16 Such as Jeeps or pickup trucks. For example, in the October 7, 2023, massacre, Hamas primarily overran Israel in Jeeps and pickup trucks. Similarly, the Toyota War (1978-1987) demonstrated the superiority of highly mobile forces over conventional fortifications in modern warfare. In the Toyota War, Chadian forces using light pickup trucks outmaneuvered heavily armored Libyan forces, exploiting their weaknesses in the desert terrain. Highly mobile forces can exploit weaknesses, launch surprise attacks, and rapidly redeploy as needed, making them more formidable than static defenses in modern warfare. For more on this point, see The Pickup Truck Era of Warfare — War on the Rocks [https://warontherocks.com/2014/02/the-pickup-truck-era-of-warfare/].

17 By keeping them occupied with building the fortifications.

18 See *B'Rega HaEmet*, pp. 156-161.

19 Similarly, in the October 7 massacres, Hamas had planned to penetrate much farther into Israel than it in fact did. Among Hamas' bold plans were to raid a prison in Ashkelon, launch an attack in Be'er Sheva, and even strike as far as Judea and Samaria, in cooperation with Hamas operatives in those regions. Their failure to execute these plans can also be described as miraculous. See Hamas planned 'second phase' of October 7 attack deeper into Israel, report says; [https://www.ynetnews.com/article/sjzdlb1va]; Hamas planned Ashkelon jail raid to free Palestinian Prisoners [https://www.timesofisrael.com/hamas-planned-ashkelon-jail-raid-to-free-palestinian-prisoners-on-october-7-report/]; Hamas sought to reach West Bank with Oct. 7 onslaught, spark wider war | The Times of Israel [https://www.timesofisrael.com/hamas-sought-to-reach-west-bank-with-oct-7-onslaught-spark-wider-war-report/].

20 *Karasi V'Ein Oneh*, Vol. 1, pp. 72-73, *Toldos* 5734 (1973). For further analysis, see *Karasi V'Ein Oneh*, Vol. 1, p. 213, *Vayeitzei* 5738 (1977).

21 For another letter, written in 1973, see Egyptians' Sudden Stop — Chabad.org [https://www.chabad.org/therebbe/letters/default_cdo/aid/397866/jewish/Egyptians-Sudden-Stop.htm].

22 Chassidic thought teaches that "exile" is primarily a psychological and spiritual state of alienation from one's true self and Divine mission. Thus, by giving into international pressures and diplomatic considerations, politicians demonstrate that they are psychologically and spiritually "in exile," misaligned with the Torah's values and G-d's Will which favors saving Jewish lives over political exigencies.

23 See *Karasi V'Ein Oneh*, Vol. 1, p. 111, *Simchas Torah* 5736 (1975); p. 118, *Chayei Sarah* 5736 (1975); Vol. 2, p. 315, *Chayei Sarah* 5743 (1982); p. 319, 19 Kislev 5743 (1982).

24 See *Karasi V'Ein Oneh*, Vol. 1, p. 213, 9 Kislev 5738 (1977).

25 See *B'Rega HaEmet*, pp. 157-159. See also Weitz, Y., Kalman, O., & Di-Nur, M. (2013). *From the archives: A summary of the consultation with the Prime Minister on the eve of the Yom Kippur War — Morning of October 6, 1973. Yisraelim: The Ben-Gurion Research Institute for the Study of Israel and Zionism.* Vol. 5, pp. 214-230; [https://in.bgu.ac.il/bgi/israelis/DocLib/Pages/2013/ישראלים%02%-02%שלם.pdf.

26 See *Karasi V'Ein Oneh*, Vol. 1, p. 213, *Vayeitzei* 5738 (1977).

27 Golda's decision not to attack preemptively haunted her for the rest of her life. As she wrote in her autobiography:

On that Friday morning [the day before the Yom Kippur War started, at a meeting discussing the situation in Israel], I had to listen to my heart and call for a mobilization [of reserves]. For me, this incident cannot fade. I cannot be comforted no matter what others say, no matter what excuses others tried comforting me with. I knew I had to do it, and this awful knowledge will accompany me for the rest of my life. I will never be the person I was before the Yom Kippur War.

Golda Meir. (1975). *Golda Meir: Chayai. Sifriyat Maariv.* pp. 308-309.

28 Much of the barrier was also concrete, underground, and designed to prevent tunneling. See Israel Completes Vast, Billion-dollar Gaza Barrier Haaretz.com [https://www.haaretz.com/israel-news/2021-12-07/ty-article/.premium/israel-completes-vast-billion-dollar-gaza-barrier/0000017f-ee2c-d4cd-af7f-ef7c25d40000#:~:text=Dec%207%2C%202021%20A%20barrier,11%20billion%29%20-to%20build]; How Israel's NIS 4 billion fence failed — Globes [https://en.globes.co.il/en/article-how-israels-nis-4-billion-fence-failed-1001459742].

29 Years of subterfuge, high-tech barrier paralyzed: How Hamas busted Israel's defenses [https://www.kan.org.il/content/kan/kan-11/p-12043/s7/582554/].

30 The Lookouts saw and reported everything — but no one listened | Kan News [https://www.kan.org.il/content/kan/kan-11/p-12043/

s7/582554/].

31 Jericho Wall: The Hamas Plan to Conquer Settlements and Bases Presented on 5.22.2023 [https://www.kan.org.il/content/kan-actual/p-591147/628830/]; Israel Knew Hamas's Attack Plan Over a Year Ago — The New York Times [https://www.nytimes.com/2023/11/30/world/middleeast/israel-hamas-attack-intelligence.html]. For Edward Luttwak's counteranalysis, see The NYT is wrong about Israeli intelligence — UnHerd [https://unherd.com/2023/12/the-nyt-is-wrong-about-israeli-intelligence/]. A further challenge that Israel faced was that due to the Simchas Torah holiday, many soldiers were on leave at the time and the bases were thus understaffed. See Where Was the Israeli Military When Hamas Attacked? [https://nytimes.com/2023/12/30/world/middleeast/israeli-military-hamas-failures.html].

32 For extensive data and analysis on the failure to address hostile actors at the border in the years leading up to the October 7 attacks, see The Path to Failure: This is How the Red Lines Were Crushed at the Gaza Border [https://mida.org.il/2023/10/24/הדרך-כך-נשחק-הקו-האדום-בגבול/].

33 For a comprehensive compilation of statistics and resources on this point, see Chronology of terrorist attacks in Israel, introduction [https://www.johnstonsarchive.net/terrorism/terrisrael.html]; קטגוריה: פיגועי טרור בישראל לפי שנה – ויקיפדיה.

34 For more on the development of *Chomat Magen*, see Laslovi, O. (2022). *Operation Protective Edge: From Tolerance to Resolution.* Ministry of Defense.

35 Elisha Yered, the Silver Platter: For the Jews or the Arabs? [https://olam-katan.co.il/archives/12129].

36 Personal communication between the author and an intelligence officer.

37 2011 Itamar attack — Wikipedia [https://en.wikipedia.org/wiki/2011_Itamar_attack].

38 Referring to the Jewish towns surrounding Gaza, which were brutally massacred on October 7.

39 In some periods, Judea and Samaria have been less prone to lethal terror attacks than Jerusalem or Central Israel.

40 In the case of the Fogel family, for instance, the army eventually apprehended the terrorists. However, it did not address the core issues in Judea and Samaria, which include rampant possession of weaponry by Palestinians and a general educational climate that incites violence against Jews.

41 See, for example, *Sichos Kodesh 5734,* Vol. 2, p. 106, *Emor* (1974); also printed in *Karasi V'Ein Oneh Vol. 1,* p. 85; *Sichos Kodesh 5738,* Vol. 2, pp. 37-38, Purim (1978); also printed in *Karasi V'Ein Oneh,* p. 260.

42 Based on reports by the Israel Security Agency (*Shabak*), Israel's equivalent of the FBI. See Shabak January 2024 — Significant Terror Attacks [http://shabak.gov.il/media/arjj514v/ינואר-4202-דוח.pdf]; Shabak February 2024 — Significant Terror Attacks [https://shabak.gov.il/media/faipe43w/פברואר-4202-דוח.pdf]. Although numerous terrorist attacks were actually executed, *Shabak* routinely undermines hundreds of terrorist attacks before they can be actualized. For a brief insight into *Shabak's* operations, see their Youtube channel: Israeli Security Agency — YouTube [https://www.youtube.com/@israelsecurityagency]. Hebrew Wikipedia contains detailed lists and statistics on terrorist attacks in Israel from year to year. The best way, however, to obtain up-to-date information on the details is from local Jewish and Arab social media which extensively document attacks.

43 A major intersection in southern Israel.

44 Terrorist Attacks Against Israelis in Israel and Judea and Samaria in 2023 [https://he.wikipedia.org/wiki/ פיגועי טרור נגד ישראלים בישראל ובשטחים ב-2023].

45 Personal communication with the author.

CHAPTER 5

1 *Shulchan Aruch, Orach Chaim,* 329:6. For commentary, see the Rebbe's extensive correspondence with Rabbi Immanuel Jakobovits, then Chief Rabbi of the United Kingdom, included in the Appendix of this book and printed in Hebrew translation in *Karasi V'Ein Oneh,* Vol. 2, pp. 483-503. This is a very prevalent theme in *sichos* from 1978 onwards. Consider *Karasi V'Ein Oneh,* Vol. 1, pp. 230-232, 24 Teves 5738 (1978); pp. 236-237, Motzaei Shabbos *Va'eira* 5738 (1978); pp. 254-255, Purim 5738 (1978); pp. 301-307, *Naso* 5738 (1978); p. 327, 18 Elul 5738 (1978); pp. 335-338, *Haazinu* 5739 (1978); pp. 386-387, 19 Kislev 5739 (1978); pp. 303-304, 10 Teves 5739 (1979); pp. 494-495, Motzaei Shabbos *Bereishis* 5740 (1979); Vol. 2, pp. 19-20, 23 Kislev 5740 (1979); pp. 23-24, 10 Shvat 5740 (1980); pp. 61-62, *Vayakhel-Pekudei* 5740 (1980); pp. 96-103, 29 Elul 5740 (1980); p. 112, *Bo* 5741 (1981); p. 121, *Tzav* 5741 (1981); p. 136, *Kedoshim* 5741 (1981); pp. 210-211, *Beshalach* 5742 (1982); p. 246, *likkut* of *sichos* for 22 Sivan, 3 Tammuz, 7 Tammuz 5742 (1982); pp. 286-287, 29 Elul 5742 (1982); p. 293, 13 Tishrei 5743 (1982); p. 314, *Chayei Sarah* 5743 (1982); pp. 329-330, 10 Teves 5743 (1982); p. 395, *Bereishis* 5752 (1991); *Sichos Kodesh 5738,* Vol. 3, p. 493-494, *Yechidus* with the *Gerrer Rebbe,* 9 Elul (1978); Audio of Yechidus [https://ashreinu.app/player?parentEvent=2765&event=2766] 6:01-9:43.

2 *Eiruvin* 45a.

3 This is based on the principle that in cases where lives **might** be in danger, *halachah* dictates doing anything necessary to save them. Applying this to battle for the Land of Israel, the Rebbe noted:

We can be certain that they are coming to kill us. We know where they received their education, what they did yesterday, and what they are doing today. Thus, we can be certain, without a doubt, that they are coming to kill us.

Karasi V'Ein Oneh, Vol. 1, p. 2, *Bereishis* 5729 (1968).

Elsewhere, the Rebbe taught:

Saving lives supersedes Shabbos. [Consider the scenario of] a Jew leading hundreds of Jews in prayer on Shabbos. He is told that if he interrupts his prayers and goes outside, there is a **remote possibility** *that he might be able to temporarily extend a small child's life. [Even if, based on medical assessments, the child will ultimately die in the near future,] he must interrupt his prayers and leave the synagogue, given the* **possibility** *that he might save the child's life.*

Karasi V'Ein Oneh, Vol. 1, pp. 265-266, Purim 5738 (1978).

Similarly:

In cases where lives may be at risk ([and it is thus a case of] pikuach nefesh), we do not need definite information [in order to act]. If there is even a **very remote possibility, or even one hundred doubts,** *as to whether lives are in danger, the halachic status of pikuach nefesh still applies. How much more so in our situation, where there is no doubt and we know they are coming. Moreover, we have seen more than three times who we are dealing with.*

Karasi V'Ein Oneh, Vol. 1, pp. 282-283, Motzaei Shabbos *Acharei* 5738 (1978).

See also *Karasi V'Ein Oneh,* Vol. 1, p. 271, *Tzav* 5738 (1978); p. 299, *Bechukosai* 5738 (1978); pp. 335-336, *Haazinu* 5739 (1978); pp. 386-387, 19 Kislev 5739 (1978); Vol. 2, p. 23, 10 Shvat 5740 (1980); p. 76, Motzaei Lag BaOmer 5740 (1980); pp. 99-100, 29 Elul 5740 (1980); p. 106, 18 Tishrei 5741 (1980), pp. 125-126, *Tzav* 5741 (1981); p. 286, 29 Elul 5742 (1982); p. 502, Letter to Rabbi Immanuel Jakobovits, 11 Shvat 5742 (1982) (see Appendix); *Daas Torah,* p. 79

4 In situations where military action is necessary on Shabbos, several Shabbos laws will need to be breached. These include traveling beyond the permitted Shabbos boundary, carrying weapons in public spaces, and engaging in activities that can harm or kill, all of which are generally prohibited on Shabbos. However, Jewish law permits these actions if they are necessary to save lives.

5 Letter to Rabbi Immanuel Jakobovits, 3rd Light

of Chanukah 5741 (1980), p. 1 (see Appendix).

6 A town located next to Hebron. For the full story, see I Samuel, Ch. 23. See analysis in *Daas Torah*, p. 79. See also Rabbi Yechezkel Sofer's *Shorashim BeHalachah* in the essay entitled *Territorial Concessions for a Peace Treaty*, p. 12; *Maayanei Rashi*, Vol. 2, p. 202ff. Contemporary Ke'ilah is inhabited by hostile ideological descendants of the biblical Philistines.

7 See Letter to Rabbi Immanuel Jakobovits, 3rd Light of Chanukah 5741 (1980), p. 1 (see Appendix); also printed in *Karasi V'Ein Oneh*, Vol. 2, p. 484; *Karasi V'Ein Oneh*, Vol. 1, p. 326, Motzaei Shabbos *Re'eh* 5738 (1978); pp. 440-442, *Bamidbar* 5739 (1979); Vol. 2, p. 9, *Vayeitzei* 5740 (1980); p. 210, *Beshalach* 5742 (1982); p. 246, *likkut of sichos* for 22 Sivan, 3 Tammuz, 7 Tammuz 5742 (1982); p. 298, 13 Tishrei 5743 (1982); pp. 404-413, *Yechidus* with Sadigura Rebbe. See also *Sichos Kodesh 5740*, Vol. 3, pp. 1,157-1,164 (1980); *Daas Torah*, p. 87, footnote 19.

8 Letter to Rabbi Immanuel Jakobovits, 3rd Light of Chanukah 5741 (1980), p. 1 (see Appendix).

9 329:6.

10 *Rama* on *Shulchan Aruch* 329:6. See also *Mishnah Berurah* 329:15, citing *Ohr Zarua Shabbos* 84:13. See also See *Igros Kodesh*, Vol. 33, p. 102, Letter #12,313 to Rabbi Aizik Schwei, dated 3 Teves 5738 (1977); also printed in *Karasi V'Ein Oneh*, Vol. 2, p. 466.

11 41:29-39.

12 In fact, Israel's enemies often choose to attack it on Shabbos and holidays given that the Jewish people are more likely to be celebrating on those days and are thus more vulnerable to attack. Rabbi Yoel Bin-Nun* has observed that many of Israel's wars can be referred to by the names of holidays. For example: the Rosh HaShanah War commemorates the outbreak of the Second Intifada; the Yom Kippur War commemorates Israel's war in 1973; the Simchas Torah War commemorates the 2023 Hamas Massacre; Operation Defensive Shield was sparked by a terrorist attack on the Seder Night in 2002. *(Rabbi Yoel Bin-Nun is an influential Israeli rabbi, educator, and scholar who fought in the Six-Day War and the Yom Kippur War. He played a significant role in the religious Zionist movement and the establishment of Jewish communities in Judea and Samaria. He shared these observations in lectures after the onset of the Simchas Torah War and in conversation with the author.)

13 See *Karasi V'Ein Oneh*, Vol. 1, p. 223, 10 Teves 5738 (1977); p. 304, *Naso* 5738 (1978); p. 319, 20 Menachem Av 5738 (1978).

14 See Alter Rebbe's *Shulchan Aruch* 329:14; *Rashi* on *Eiruvin* 45a, s.v. *LaSfar*. See also *Karasi V'Ein Oneh*, Vol. 1, p. 223-224, 10 Teves 5738 (1977); 18 Elul 5738 (1978).

15 See *Karasi V'Ein Oneh*, Vol. 1, pp. 224-225, 10 Teves 5738 (1977); p. 278, Motzaei Shabbos *Shemini* 5738 (1978).

16 See *Sichos Kodesh 5740*, Vol. 2, p. 197, *Mishpatim* (1980).

17 See *Karasi V'Ein Oneh*, Vol. 1, p. 301, Motzaei Shabbos *Naso* 5738 (1978); p. 318, 20 Menachem Av 5738 (1978).

18 See *Sichos Kodesh 5740*, Vol. 3, pp. 1,157-1,158, *Yechidus* with Sadigura Rebbe (1980).

19 *Sichos Kodesh 5740*, Vol. 3, p. 1,158, *Yechidus* with Sadigura Rebbe (1980).

20 See also *Karasi V'Ein Oneh*, Vol. 1, p. 224, 10 Teves 5738 (1977); pp. 231-232, 24 Teves 5738 (1978).

21 See *Talmud Yerushalmi Yoma* 8:5; *Mishneh Torah, Hilchos Shabbos*, 2:3; *Tur, Shulchan Aruch*, and Alter Rebbe's *Shulchan Aruch* 328:2. The principle derived from the *Yerushalmi* and codified in later halachic works is that one who promptly acts to save a life is praiseworthy — even if doing so demands violating Shabbos — while hesitating or asking if a certain act is permissible is disgraceful and tantamount to shedding blood. Extending this principle, in any case where there is a possibility that lives may be at risk, one is obligated to take action without hesitating.

22 *Karasi V'Ein Oneh*, Vol. 1, pp. 230-231, 24 Teves 5738 (1978).

23 *Karasi V'Ein Oneh*, Vol. 1, pp. 225-226, 10 Teves 5738 (1977).

24 *Karasi V'Ein Oneh*, Vol. 1, p. 230, 24 Teves 5738 (1978). Here, the Rebbe is responding to the claim that since we are in exile, we cannot engage in self defense. The Rebbe notes that the *halachah* clearly teaches that we may defend ourselves in exile, clearly demonstrating that this claim has no basis.

25 Genesis 27:22. This verse indicates that Jews engage in battle through prayer, using their "voices," rather than wielding weapons using their hands.

26 See *Sefer HaSichos 5752*, Vol.1, p. 56, *Bereishis* (1991).

27 Letter to Rabbi Immanuel Jakobovits, 3rd Light of Chanukah 5741 (1980) (see Back Matter).

28 See *Igros Kodesh*, Vol. 33, p. 102, Letter #12,313 to Rabbi Aizik Schwei, dated 3 Teves 5738 (1977); also printed in *Karasi V'Ein Oneh*, Vol. 2, p. 466.

29 The Golan Heights had been part of biblical Israel, given to the Jewish people by G-d. See, for example, Numbers 21:33-35, which describes the Jewish people defeating and taking the land of Og, King of Bashan. "Bashan" is in the Golan. In fact, in the contemporary Golan, one of the closest Israeli towns to the Syrian border is called "Alonei HaBashan." See the verse in Deuteronomy 4:43: "Golan in Bashan for the tribe of Menashe." See also Joshua 20:8; Chronicles I, 6:56.

30 There have been several U.N. resolutions calling for Israel to return the Golan Heights to Syria. Consider:

1. UN Security Council Resolution 242 (1967): Passed in the aftermath of the Six-Day War, it called for the "withdrawal of Israeli armed forces from territories occupied in the recent conflict," which included the Golan Heights.

2. UN Security Council Resolution 497 (1981): Declared Israel's annexation of the Golan Heights "null and void and without international legal effect" and called on Israel to rescind its decision.

3. UN General Assembly Resolution 63/99 (2008): Titled "The Occupied Syrian Golan," reaffirmed the illegality of Israel's annexation of the Golan Heights and called on Israel to withdraw from the territory.

4. UN General Assembly Resolution 73/23 (2018): Also titled "The Occupied Syrian Golan," once again reaffirmed the illegality of Israel's annexation and called for Israel's withdrawal from the Golan Heights.

31 See *Karasi V'Ein Oneh*, Vol. 1, p. 43, *Eikev* 5730 (1970). There, the Rebbe notes that when Poland signed a treaty with Germany, withdrawing from strategic territory, it ultimately led to Poland's conquest by Nazi Germany. Similarly, reasons the Rebbe, withdrawal from the Golan Heights invites Syrian aggression. See *Karasi V'Ein Oneh*, Vol. 1, p. 326, Motzaei Shabbos *Re'eh* 5738 (1978); Vol. 2, pp. 193-200, 24 Teves 5742 (1982); *Igros Kodesh*, Vol. 27, pp. 18-19, Letter #10,012 to Rabbi Shlomo Yosef Zevin, Mar Cheshvan 5731 (1970); also printed in *Karasi V'Ein Oneh*, Vol. 2, p. 455. See also Letter to Rabbi Immanuel Jakobovits, 3rd Light of Chanukah 5741 (1980) (see Back Matter); 13 Shvat 5741 (1981) (see Appendix). Consider also that Syria's proposed peace treaty in return for Israel's withdrawal did not include an offer for an Israeli embassy in Syria and allowed for Syria to remain in partnership with Hamas and Hezbollah. See Withdrawal from the Golan Heights in Stages | INSS [https://www.inss.org.il/publication/withdrawal-from-the-golan-heights-in-stages/].

32 Will Israel Be at War? — by Tomas Pueyo [https://unchartedterritories.tomaspueyo.com/p/will-israel-be-at-war]. The analysis of the map presented here is a slightly modified version of Pueyo's.

33 Syria would need to capture both because the mountains offer a strategic vantage point for observation and artillery. Control of the high ground enables an attacking force to observe enemy movements, direct fire onto enemy positions, and defend against counterattacks. If it would only attack the valley, then it would be exposed from the high ground, so it must attack both the valley and the highgrounds simultaneously. For more on the strategic importance of the Golan Heights, see Israeli Control of the Golan Heights: High Strategic and Moral Ground for Israel [https://besacenter. org/israeli-control-of-the-golan-heights-high-strategic-and-moral-ground-for-israel-3-2/].

34 The war pits Bashar al-Assad's Syrian Arab Republic (supported by Russia, Iran, and Hezbollah) against various rebel groups, including the Free Syrian Army (supported by Western nations and Gulf states), and separately against the Islamic State (ISIS) and Al-Qaeda-affiliated organizations. In addition, Kurdish forces, primarily the Syrian Democratic Forces (SDF), are fighting against ISIS and Turkish-backed forces in Northern Syria.

35 On the possibility of the Golan Heights being a new battlefront, see The Golan Heights: Another Front in the Campaign? | INSS [https://www.inss.org.il/social_media/the-golan-heights-another-front-in-the-campaign/]; The Rise of the Non-State Actors in Syria: Regional and Global Perspectives [https://www.inss.org.il/wp-content/uploads/2017/03/memo156.1Chapter1.pdf].

36 Strategic depth — Wikipedia [https://en.wikipedia.org/wiki/Strategic_depth]; The Attack in the Golan Heights: Is an Israel-"Axis" Conflict Expected? | INSS [https://www.inss.org.il/publication/the-attack-in-the-golan-heights-is-an-israel-axis-conflict-expected/].

37 Consider:

Even in 1973, the Arab objectives in the war were limited, while from Israel's perspective, the Sinai and the Golan Heights provided strategic depth that enabled it to halt the surprise attack. If such an attack had been carried out from the 1967 border, it could have destroyed Israel.

War and Peace: Thoughts on Israel's Security Concept from a Perspective of Fifty Years | INSS [https://www.inss.org.il/publication/war-peace-thoughts-israels-security-concept-perspective-fifty-years/].

38 Iran's Proxy War [https://besacenter.org/irans-proxy-war/].

39 See *Karasi V'Ein Oneh*, Vol. 1, p. 324, *Re'eh*

5738 (1978); pp. 329-331, 18 Elul 5738 (1978); pp. 335, 343, Motzaei Shabbos *Haazinu* 5739 (1978); p. 376, Motzaei Shabbos *Chayei Sarah* 5739 (1978); pp 390-391, 19 Kislev 5739 (1978); p. 412, Motzaei Shabbos *Ki Sissa* 5739 (1979); Vol. 2, pp. 37-38, Purim 5740 (1980).

40 Doctrine of Hamas | The Iran Primer [https://iranprimer.usip.org/blog/2023/oct/19/doctrine-hamas].

41 Both from Tomas Pueyo. See Will Israel Be at War? — by Tomas Pueyo [https://unchartedterritories.tomaspueyo.com/p/will-israel-be-at-war]; The Problem of West Bank Settlements. — by Tomas Pueyo [https://unchartedterritories.tomaspueyo.com/p/the-problem-of-west-bank-settlements].

42 See *Karasi V'Ein Oneh*, Vol. 2, p. 337, Taanis Esther 5743 (1983); p. 464, Letter to Rabbi Moshe Buchko; also printed in *Igros Kodesh*, Vol. 32, pp. 267-268, Letter #12,176.

43 See *Sichos Kodesh 5746*, Vol. 2, pp. 261, 266, Motzaei Zos Chanukah (1985). See also *Shalom Shalom V'Ein Shalom*, Ch. 6. For an excellent contemporary analysis of the threat Egypt poses to Israel and the dangerous gamble of the Camp David Accords, see Dekel: Grounded Strategic Intelligence [https://www.dekelegypt.co.il/] (an active website run by retired IDF Lt. Col. Eli Dekel). See also Dekel-Dolitzky, E. (2010). מודיעין תלוש מהקרקע: הצלחה וכשלון בעבודת המודיעין הגיאוגרפי בצה"ל [*Groundless intelligence: Success and failure in the IDF's Field Intelligence*] (D. Baum, Ed.). For Dekel's English language lecture on the topic, see Is Egypt threatening Israel? Why is the Egyptian army intensifying [https://www.youtube.com/watch?v=GVpVbJyoRSw&t=5s]. More broadly, see his YouTube Channel dedicated to the topic; Strategic Analysis Of Egypt [https://www.youtube.com/@strategicanalysisofegypt7786/videos].

44 See *Sichos Kodesh 5730*, Vol. 2, pp. 460-462, *Re'eh* (1970).

45 See *Karasi V'Ein Oneh*, Vol. 2, p. 15, 19 Kislev 5740 (1979); p. 152, 4th Night of Sukkos 5742 (1981); p. 168, *Noach* 5742 (1981); p. 221, 22 Sivan

5742 (1982); pp. 326f., *Vayeishev* 5743 (1983). Sadat violated the terms of the treaty by stationing soldiers in the Sinai's demilitarized zones. For reports of this, see *Shalom Shalom V'Ein Shalom*, p. 227.

46 Consider the following analysis:

If Egypt cancels the 1979 peace agreement over an incident on the Gaza border, Israel's border with Egypt could, overnight, turn into its most dangerous problem zone. El-Sisi has transformed his country's military into one of the region's most powerful armies — and Israel hasn't been preparing itself for a showdown with it for decades. The Egyptian armed forces, already one of the region's largest militaries, are in the middle of an enormous acquisition spree and an accompanying buildup of infrastructure such as bases, highways, and bridges, all pointing east toward Israel.

Israeli retired Lt.-Col. Eli Dekel has been warning against this growing threat for years. He served in the IDF Military Intelligence's Research Department, specializing in recognizing military and civilian infrastructure and its implications. According to Dekel, Egypt's military has added some 60,000 soldiers since el-Sisi came to power, with its alignment being against only one enemy: Israel. Egypt has volatile borders with Libya, Sudan, and a potentially life-threatening dispute over the Nile's water rights with Ethiopia in the south. Despite this, Dekel's research shows that only three out of the Egyptian army's 16 divisions are stationed west or south of Cairo. The rest are based east of the capital, toward the Sinai and the Israeli border.

Moreover, Israel enabled a large build-up of forces near its border when Egypt was fighting the ISIS forces in Sinai, allowing more Egyptian troops into the Sinai than was originally agreed upon in the peace treaty of 1979. In addition, Egypt has built a massive network of roads and bridges, created dozens of opportunities to cross the Suez Canal, and acquired hundreds of tank transporters, enabling it to rapidly reinforce troops in the Sinai Peninsula.

In the event that Egypt's leadership sees itself forced to cancel the peace treaty, it could leverage its newly hostile position against Israel to lower the domestic pressures from Islamist forces and attempt to reassert itself as the leading Arab power in the region, Dekel warns.

Further complicating the situation for Israel and the United States, Egypt could choose to deepen its incremental alignment with the anti-Western Axis currently forming under Russian and Chinese leadership.

It already joined the explicitly anti-Western economic alliance BRICS, together with Russia, China, Iran, and South Africa; it is becoming reliant on the import of tons of Russian wheat; and part of its military buildup has been sourced from Russia, instead of its main military supplier in recent decades, the United States. If Israel should learn one lesson from recent disasters, it is this: Israel cannot be blinded by peace treaties, international accords, and false notions of deterrence, even on borders that have been quiet in recent years.

Headed into another crisis? Relations between Egypt and Israel are being tested like never before   [https://allisrael.com/headed-into-another-crisis-relations-between-egypt-and-israel-are-being-tested-like-never-before].

47 See *Karasi V'Ein Oneh*, Vol. 2, pp. 362-363, *Chayei Sarah* 5746 (1985).

48 For a book-length treatment on how Sadat exploited the Israel-Egypt peace deal as a strategy to weaken Israel and prepare for war, see Eidelberg, P. (1979). *Sadat's strategy*. Dawn. This approach also emerges from Sadat's interview in Encyclopedia Britannica. See Anwar Sadat on international affairs — Egypt, Peace, Diplomacy [https://www.britannica.com/topic/Anwar-Sadat-on-international-affairs-1960770/Egypts-role-in-the-world].

49 Armed Forces Day [https://www.britannica.com/topic/Armed-Forces-Day-Egyptian-holiday]. See there:

Armed Forces Day, [a] public holiday observed in Egypt on October 6, celebrating the day in 1973 when combined Egyptian and Syrian military forces launched a surprise attack on Israel and crossed into the Sinai Peninsula, which marked the beginning of the October (Yom Kippur) War.

50 The Plight of Egyptians Living in Israel [https://besacenter.org/egyptians-living-in-israel/].

51 *Karasi V'Ein Oneh,* Vol. 2, pp. 168-169, *Noach* 5742 (1981).

52 Cited in *Karasi V'Ein Oneh,* Vol. 1, p. 433. See there for the *sichah* of *Bamidbar* 5739 (1979). See also *Shalom Shalom V'Ein Shalom,* p. 386.

53 "Ya" is the Arabic version of "Hey!" in English.

54 Sooner than expected: The Palestinians set the Synagogues Aflame [https://www.ynet.co.il/articles/0,7340,L-3140761,00.html].

55 See *Sichos Kodesh 5739,* Vol. 2, p. 334 (1979); *Karasi V'Ein Oneh,* Vol. 1, pp. 418-422, *Ki Sissa* 5739 (1979); Vol. 2, pp. 146-147, 18 Elul 5741 (1981); *B'Rega HaEmet,* pp. 340-344. In Iran, the Shah Reza Pahlavi's pro-Western regime was overthrown in 1979 by an extreme Islamist regime that seriously threatens Israel and the West today.

56 The Muslim Brotherhood in Egypt and Its True Intentions Towards Israel [https://besacenter.org/the-muslim-brotherhood-in-egypt-and-its-true-intentions-towards-israel/].

57 See *Karasi V'Ein Oneh,* Vol. 1, p. 422, *Ki Sissa* 5739 (1979).

58 Consider the civil wars that have wracked Jordan (1970-1971), Lebanon (1975-1990), and Syria (2011-present). While Jordan quickly recovered, Syria and Lebanon have not. Consider also the Arab Spring (2010-2012), which undermined several authoritarian regimes, including those in Tunisia (Zine El Abidine Ben Ali, ousted in 2011), Egypt (Hosni Mubarak, ousted in 2011), Libya (Muammar Gaddafi, overthrown in 2011), Yemen (Ali Abdullah Saleh, ousted in 2012), and Syria (Bashar al-Assad, contending with an ongoing civil war since 2011). Bahrain and other countries also faced significant protests in 2011. The outcomes varied: Tunisia achieved a fragile democracy; Egypt (2013), Libya (2014), and Yemen (2014) faced instability and renewed authoritarianism; Syria descended into a devastating civil war; and Bahrain's uprising was quashed by the monarchy in 2011.

59 The Sinai terrorist group formed in 2011 in response to Egyptian stability. It first aligned with Al-Qaeda, but switched allegiance to ISIS in 2014. See The Muslim Brotherhood and Egypt-Israel Peace [https://besacenter.org/the-muslim-brotherhood-and-egypt-israel-peace/]; Egypt's Constitutional Crisis [https://besacenter.org/egypts-constitutional-crisisthe-military-versus-the-islamists/].

60 Islamic State — Sinai Province — Wikipedia [https://en.wikipedia.org/wiki/Islamic_State_%E2%80%93_Sinai_Province]; Islamic State Province in Sinai Changes its Strategy: Are Israel and the Suez Canal in the Crosshairs? | INSS [https://www.inss.org.il/publication/sinai-isis/]; 2011 southern Israel cross-border attacks — Wikipedia [https://en.wikipedia.org/wiki/2011_southern_Israel_cross-border_attacks]; Egypt and the Threat of Islamic Terror [https://besacenter.org/egypt-threat-islamic-terror/]; The Muslim Brotherhood and Egypt-Israel Peace [https://besacenter.org/the-muslim-brotherhood-and-egypt-israel-peace/]; ISIS-Sinai flag [https://www.dni.gov/nctc/ftos/isis_sinai_fto.html].

61 Occasionally firing rockets. See Islamic State claims responsibility for Sinai rocket attack on Israel [https://www.timesofisrael.com/islamic-state-claims-responsibility-for-sinai-rocket-attack-on-israel/].

62 Hamas Tunnels to Egypt Played Key Role in Arming Hamas [https://www.fdd.org/analysis/2023/10/28/hamas-tunnels-to-egypt-played-key-role-in-arming-hamas/].

63 See *Karasi V'Ein Oneh,* Vol. 2, p. 323, 19 Kislev 5743 (1982); pp. 326-327, *Vayeishev* 5743 (1983); p. 337, Taanis Esther 5743 (1983). There, the Rebbe notes the troubling phenomenon of a state using non-state entities to undermine its enemies. The blame devolves to the terrorists, even though their actions are encouraged by the state. The Rebbe observes that Egypt indirectly supported the PLO, welcoming them into their country and providing them with both financial aid and weapons. See *Karasi V'Ein Oneh,* Vol. 2, p. 351, *Bo* 5744 (1984).

64 The Long Record of Terror on the Sinai Peninsula [https://www.dw.com/en/the-long-record-of-terror-on-the-sinai-peninsula/a-41538401].

65 The Rebbe frequently used this term in bemoaning negotiations with Egypt that were punctuated by one-sided Israeli concessions. He used the metaphor as early as 1975 in repudiating "Sinai II," the interim agreement between Egypt and Israel facilitated by U.S. Secretary of State Henry Kissinger, in which Israel agreed to withdraw from strategic areas in the Sinai Peninsula in exchange for Egyptian pledges of non-belligerency. For more on this agreement, see Egypt-Israel Interim Peace Agreement (Sinai II) (September 1975) [https://www.jewishvirtuallibrary.org/egypt-israel-interim-peace-agreement-sinai-ii-september-1975]. See *Sichos Kodesh 5736*, Vol. 1, p. 239, 19 Kislev 5736 (1975); also printed in *Karasi V'Ein Oneh*, Vol. 1, p. 127. Using the Talmudic metaphor (see *Bava Basra* 76b and Alter Rebbe's *Shulchan Aruch, Orach Chaim*, 307:26), the Rebbe states that the agreement has absolutely no value. It is akin to a contract which one cannot even use as a bottle stopper. For further use of this metaphor regarding peace treaties with Egypt (and other Arab countries under the paradigm at the time), see *Karasi V'Ein Oneh*, Vol. 1, p. 74, 19 Kislev 5734 (1973); p. 322, Motzaei Shabbos *Re'eh* 5738 (1978); p. 426, Motzaei Shabbos *Vayakhel-Pekudei* 5739 (1979); pp. 482-486, 13 Tishrei 5740 (1979); p. 500, Motzaei Shabbos *Chayei Sarah* 5740 (1979); Audio of Sichah [https://ashreinu.app/player?parentEvent=3166&event=3173]; Vol. 2, pp. 87-88, *Shlach* 5740 (1980); p. 116, 10 Shvat 5741 (1981); p. 167, *Noach* 5742 (1981); pp. 343-344, 347, *Mikeitz* 5744 (1983); pp. 357, 364, *Chayei Sarah* 5746 (1985); p. 372, Motzaei Zos Chanukah 5746 (1985); Video of Sichah [https://videos.jem.tv/video-player?clip=12888]. See also *Daas Torah*, pp. 100, 104-105, 147, 257. There, the author cites the Rebbe's analysis that Israel's enemies had long been opposed to peace. However, once they realized that they could use "peace" agreements as a tool to extract concessions from Israel, some chose to do so.

66 Israel Gives Up an Oilfield to Egypt In Biggest Sacrifice for Treaty Yet — The New York Times [https://www.nytimes.com/1979/11/26/archives/israel-gives-up-an-oilfield-to-egypt-in-biggest-sacrifice-for.html];

Israel Losing Crucial Oil Source to Egyptians [https://washingtonpost.com/archive/politics/1979/11/25/israel-losing-crucial-oil-source-to-egyptians/].

67 See *Karasi V'Ein Oneh*, Vol. 1, pp. 112-113, Simchas Torah 5736 (1975); pp. 124-126, 19 Kislev 5736 (1975); p. 259, Purim 5738 (1978); pp. 417-422, Motzaei Shabbos *Ki Sissa* 5739 (1979); pp. 433-435, *Bamidbar* 5739 (1979); p. 469, *Matos-Maasei* 5739 (1979); p. 471, *Devarim* 5739 (1979); p. 503, Motzaei Shabbos *Chayei Sarah* 5739 (1978); Vol. 2, pp. 14-15, 19 Kislev 5740 (1979); p. 24, 10 Shvat 5740 (1980); p. 37, Purim 5740 (1980); p. 88, *Shlach* 5740 (1980); p. 96, 29 Elul 5740 (1980); p. 116, 10 Shvat 5740 (1980); p. 146, 18 Elul 5741 (1981); p. 164, Simchas Torah 5742 (1981); p. 233, 3 Tammuz 5742 (1982); p. 373, Motzaei Zos Chanukah 5746 (1985); pp. 476-477, Letter to an anonymous resident of Los Angeles, 5740; p. 486, Letter to Rabbi Immanuel Jakobovits, 3rd Light of Chanukah 5741 (1980) (see Appendix); p. 500, Letter to Rabbi Immanuel Jakobovits, Elul 5741 (1981) (see Appendix). See also *Sefer HaSichos 5746*, Vol. 2, p. 260 (1986). The Rebbe explicitly mentions that Israel had to go as far as South America to procure oil. As of 2023, Israel primarily buys its oil from Kazakhstan and Azerbaijan, but it also sources oil from the U.S. and Brazil. For the Rebbe's explanation on the fallacy of relying on the U.S. for oil, see *Sichos Kodesh 5740*, Vol. 1, pp. 426-427, 28 Mar Cheshvan 5740 (1979); Audio of Sichah [https://ashreinu.app/player?parentEvent=3166&event=3173]; Where Does Israel Get Its Oil From? [https://www.youtube.com/watch?v=Xi4fuiEYZNk]; Crude Petroleum in Israel | The Observatory of Economic Complexity [https://oec.world/en/profile/bilateral-product/crude-petroleum/reporter/isr].

See also the following: :

The Alma oil field, discovered and developed by Israel, was the country's largest single source of energy, supplying half the country's energy needs. Israel, which estimated the value of untapped reserves in the Alma field at $100 billion, had projected that continued development there would make the country self-sufficient in energy by 1990. Instead of becoming independent, Israel *became dependent on other countries. As part of the peace negotiations, Egypt agreed to supply oil to Israel. This was critical because Israel's main oil supplier, Iran, broke relations with Israel following the Islamic revolution in 1979. Due to poor regional relations with its neighbors, Israel does not share any international oil pipelines.*

Oil & Natural Gas in Israel [https://www.jewishvirtuallibrary.org/oil-and-natural-gas-in-israel#gaza].

68 See *Karasi V'Ein Oneh*, Vol. 1, pp. 112-113, Simchas Torah 5736 (1975); pp. 124, 126, 19 Kislev 5736 (1975).

69 El Molla: Sinai's Oil & Gas Infrastructure Remain Vital [https://egyptoil-gas.com/news/el-molla-sinais-oil-gas-infrastructure-remain-vital/].

70 Letter to Rabbi Immanuel Jakobovits, 3rd Light of Chanukah 5741 (1980) (see Appendix). For corroboration of the Rebbe's view that liquid fuel is a decisive factor in the outcome of modern wars, see Brodie, B. (1984). *A guide to the reading of On War*; Howard, M., & Paret, P. (Eds.), *On War*. Princeton University Press. pp. 690, 699, 704. There, on p. 690, it reads:

Motor-driven tanks, guns, and vehicles of all kinds have of course made an enormous difference, especially in the speed of penetration of an invading force, so have aircraft and radio communications. But there are compensating costs in the huge requirements of supply, especially of the liquid fuel by which all things move.

See also p. 699:

Eisenhower has often been criticized for halting his headlong rush to the east in the late summer of 1944 largely for fear that his tanks would run out of fuel, and the pause did permit the retreating and disorganized Germans to regroup and restore their battle line. But when the Germans counterattacked in the Ardennes in December of that year their tanks did run out of fuel and became sitting ducks to Allied air power. Eisenhower played it safe and paid a price for doing so, but the price was an insurance against catastrophe.

71 In the words of some contemporary military writers:

Liquid fuel logistics is both the lifeblood of modern military operations and its tether. Without it, strategy is mere fantasy, as it enables everything a military force does. If a command of logistics is what separates professionals from amateurs, then liquid fuel logistics is where the battlefield most ruthlessly enforces this axiom.

The Greatest Risk in Mobile Nuclear Power? Failing to Take Advantage of the Decisive Edge it Offers the US Military [https://mwi.westpoint.edu/the-greatest-risk-in-mobile-nuclear-power-failing-to-take-advantage-of-the-decisive-edge-it-offers-the-us-military/].

Further highlighting oil's crucial role in warfare, Hezbollah's military capacity to attack Israel is heavily blunted by Lebanon's lack of oil. See How Energy Considerations Affect Hezbollah's Involvement in the War in Gaza [https://besacenter.org/how-energy-considerations-affect-hezbollahs-involvement-in-the-war-in-gaza/].

To provide further perspective on fuel's critical role in counterterrorism, consider RAND Corporation. (2021). *The Role of U.S. Airpower in Defeating ISIS*. Technical Report. There we learn that in bombing missions against ISIS, "Tankers offloaded 3,500 million pounds of fuel to coalition combat, cargo, and reconnaissance aircraft." Israel needs a vast quantity of fuel to sustain the Israeli Air Force, particularly in the event that the IAF will need to engage in a multi-front war. As we have seen thus far in the 2023 war, the IAF has been simultaneously dealing with Gaza, Lebanon, Syria, and even Samaria; moreover, given regional volatility, it may even need to expand these operations and possibly operate in more areas.

72 Consider Anwar Sadat's assessment of his victory over Israel in taking Sinai's oil wells through the Camp David Accords:

We have the new oil that has been discovered. In 1975 we still imported oil. We are now exporters rather than importers. We now have an income of $2 billion a year from our oil sales. By 1985, we *hope this figure will be $12 billion.*

Anwar Sadat on international affairs — Egypt, Peace, Diplomacy [https://www.britannica. com/topic/Anwar-Sadat-on-international-affairs-1960770/Egypts-role-in-the-world].

73 Israel Air Force History — Orbats [https:// www.scramble.nl/planning/orbats/israel/israel-air-force-history]. Israel abandoned the Ofir, Eitam, Etzion, and Refidim air bases, all critical for its security and deterrence.

74 See *Shalom Shalom V'Ein Shalom*, p. 246. For more on the pivotal role of the Sinai airfields, see Air Superiority and Airfield Attack — Lessons from History [https://apps.dtic.mil/ sti/tr/pdf/ADA166210.pdf]; The Israeli Defense Force's Operational Synchronization During the Six Day War of 1967 [https://apps.dtic.mil/ sti/tr/pdf/ADA325045.pdf]; Evaluating Possible Airfield Deployment Options. Middle East Contingencies [https://apps.dtic.mil/sti/tr/pdf/ ADA393155.pdf], p. 56.

75 This was the Ofir Air Force Base, which served as Israel's southernmost air force base. See Entebbe | Air & Space Forces Magazine [https://www.airandspaceforces.com/ article/1210entebbe/]. In addition to defending against potential attacks by African countries such as Egypt or Libya, the base also served to defend Israeli passenger planes flying over hostile African countries.

76 See *Shalom Shalom V'Ein Shalom*, pp. 400-401, 507. In addition, tens of thousands of Israelis regularly visited the Sinai until the onset of the current conflict, pumping money into the Egyptian economy which could otherwise have helped develop the Israeli economy. Consider that on October 7, 2023, over 10,000 Israelis vacationing in the Sinai returned to Israel. "מכה קשה לתיירות": הישראלים עזבו את סיני ב-7 באוקטובר – ולא ברור אם יחזרו – תיירות — TheMarker [https://www.themarker.com/consumer/ tourism/2023-11-02/ty-article/0000018b-8b4b-db71-a7df-ffcf9a8f0000].

77 See *Karasi V'Ein Oneh*, Vol, 2, p. 344, *Mikeitz* 5744 (1984); p. 355, *Purim* 5745 (1985). See also *Daas Torah*, pp. 193-194, for a letter of the Rebbe,

dated 15 Kislev 5741 (1980). The letter, addressed to the residents of the Sinai, attempted to encourage them as the specter of expulsion hung over their heads. The expulsion was ultimately carried out in April 1982.

78 See *Karasi V'Ein Oneh*, Vol, 2, p. 355, *Purim* 5745 (1985); p. 358, *Chayei Sarah* 5746 (1985).

79 See *Karasi V'Ein Oneh*, Vol, 2, p. 358, *Chayei Sarah* 5746 (1985). See also *Petakim MiShulchano Shel HaRabbi*, Vol. 3, pp. 250-251. There, the Rebbe notes that even though the Sinai settlements are not part of the original biblical Israel (though the Sinai is part of greater Israel promised to the Jewish people in the Messianic era), since the Sinai settlements enhanced Israel's security, it was forbidden to relinquish them. See *Karasi V'Ein Oneh*, Vol. 2, p. 414, *Yechidus* with Rav Efraim Yalles, 2nd Day of Chol HaMoed Pesach 5742 (1982).

80 The Rebbe conceded that non-strategically important regions of the Sinai were open for negotiation. See *Karasi V'Ein Oneh*, Vol. 1, p. 217, *Vayeitzei* 5738 (1977).

81 The *B'nai B'rith Messenger* was a weekly Jewish newspaper published in Los Angeles, California, from 1897 until the late 20th century. It was one of the oldest and most influential Jewish newspapers in the Western United States.

82 The Outcome of the Camp David Accords — Chabad.org [https://www.chabad.org/therebbe/ letters/default_cdo/aid/2387552/jewish/The-Outcome-of-the-Camp-David-Accords.htm].

83 See *Karasi V'Ein Oneh*, Vol. 1, p. 65, 13 Tishrei 5734 (1973); Vol. 2, p. 76, Lag BaOmer 5740 (1980). As the Rebbe expressed it there:

G-d instructs us that when He gives a gift, we must show appreciation, and not treat it as trivial or disposable. Every inch of the Land of Israel is precious. We received the Land directly from G-d, so ingratitude is absolutely forbidden — that was Adam's sin with the Tree of Knowledge. The mitzvah of Bikkurim [first fruits], where we express thanks to G-d for this gift and commit to bringing more first fruits each year, living by the Torah, is the antithesis of such ingratitude.

The Rebbe frequently referred to Israel's return to Jewish possession in the 20th century as a "gift from G-d." See *Karasi V'Ein Oneh*, Vol. 1, p. 57, 20 Menachem Av 5731 (1971); p. 311, Motzaei Shabbos *Balak* 5738 (1978); p. 329, 18 Elul 5738 (1978); p. 383, Motzaei Shabbos *Vayeitzei* 5739 (1978); Vol. 2, p. 36, Purim 5740 (1980); p. 87, *Shlach* 5740 (1980); pp. 121, 127, *Tzav* 5741 (1981); p. 189, 10 Teves 5742 (1982); p. 473, 13 Menachem Av 5739 (1979); also printed in *Likkutei Sichos*, Vol. 18, p. 489. This contemporary gift is a continuation of the gift that G-d originally bestowed upon the Jewish people 3,000 years ago. See *Karasi V'Ein Oneh*, Vol. 1, p. 17, 13 Tammuz 5729 (1969); Vol. 2, p. 143, 18 Elul 5741 (1981); pp. 174-176, *Vayishlach* 5742 (1981).

84 *Karasi V'Ein Oneh*, Vol. 2, pp. 501-502, Letter to Rabbi Immanuel Jakobovits, dated 11 Shvat 5742 (1982)).

85 Here, the Rebbe is referring to Israel's military victories in 1948, 1967, and 1973, despite very steep odds against Israel.

CHAPTER 6

1 Deuteronomy 20:20.

2 *Shabbos* 19a. The broader context of Shammai's teachings is that sieges should not be initiated less than three days before Shabbos in order to minimize the risk of Shabbos violation. However, if a siege has already begun, it should not be halted, even for Shabbos.

3 *Mishneh Torah, Hilchos Shabbos*, 2:25.

4 See *Rashi* on Deuteronomy 20:20.

5 See *Karasi V'Ein Oneh*, Vol. 2, p. 136, *Kedoshim* 5741 (1981); pp. 260-262, *Chukas-Balak* 5742 (1982).

6 See *Daas Torah*, p. 225.

7 Leviticus 26:6. See *Karasi V'Ein Oneh*, Vol. 1, p. 51, *Noach* 5734 (1973); p. 194f., 20 Menachem Av 5737 (1977); p. 274f., *Tzav* 5738 (1978); p. 347, Night of *Shemini Atzeres* 5739 (1978); p. 401f., Motzaei Shabbos *Mikeitz* 5739 (1978); Vol 2, p. 104f., 18 Tishrei 5741 (1980); p. 245, 7 Tammuz 5742 (1982). See also *Likkutei Sichos*, Vol. 20, p. 424, 17 Kislev 5741 (1980).

8 Numbers 33:55. See Letter to Rabbi Immanuel Jakobovits, Elul 5741 (1981), p. 2 (Appendix). *Karasi V'Ein Oneh*, Vol. 2, p. 230, 3 Tammuz 5742 (1982); p. 246, *likkut* of *sichos* for 22 Sivan, 3 Tammuz, 7 Tammuz 5742 (1982); Video of Sichah [https://videos.jem.tv/video-player?clip=11958]. For further analysis of this verse, see the essay by Rabbi Yechezkel Sofer entitled "Stings in your eyes and thorns in your sides: Territorial Compromise and Minority Rights in Israel — Then and Now" in *Maayanei Rashi*, Vol. 2, pp. 197-210.

9 Iran: The Flaws of Containment [https://besacenter.org/iran-the-flaws-of-containment/]; PA Weakness and Israel's Policy of Containment Propel Sinwar and Hamas toward Palestinian National Leadership | INSS [https://www.inss.org.il/strategic_assessment/pa-weakness/]; Hamas Must Be Comprehensively Routed [https://besacenter.org/hamas-must-be-routed/]; Asking Big Questions: Containment and Rollback Ride Again — Modern War Institute [https://mwi.westpoint.edu/2014810asking-big-questions-containment-and-rollback-ride-again/].

10 Mowing the Grass: Israel's Strategy for Protracted Intractable Conflict [https://doi.org/10.1080/01402390.2013.830972]; The IDF even officially referred to the policy as such — See We joined the "Lawn Mowers" of Etzion 36 hours before their Deployment [https://www.idf.il/אתרי-יחידות/חטיבת-כפיר/כל-הכתבות/1202/גדוד-שמשון-מסכם-תעם-תעסוקה-מבצעית-עציון-מג-ד-סהר-פוגל/]; Israel and the Demise of "Mowing the Grass" — War on the Rocks [https://warontherocks.com/2014/08/israel-and-the-demise-of-mowing-the-grass/].

11 *Karasi V'Ein Oneh*, Vol. 2, pp. 251-252, *likkut* of *sichos* for 22 Sivan, 3 Tammuz, 7 Tammuz 5742 (1982). See also *Karasi V'Ein Oneh*, Vol. 1, p. 39, *Matos-Maasei* 5730 (1970); p. 45, *Yechidus* with Yonah Cohen, Summer 5730 (1970); Vol. 2, p. 222, 22 Sivan 5742 (1982); p. 236, 3 Tammuz 5742 (1982); p. 276, 13 Tammuz 5742 (1982).

12 The End of Mowing the Grass: If Israel Wants to Continue to Exist, It Must Uproot Hamas from Gaza [https://besacenter.org/the-end-of-mowing-the-grass-if-israel-wants-to-continue-to-exist-it-must-uproot-hamas-from-gaza/].

13 For the Rebbe's account of this narrative and its application, see *Karasi V'Ein Oneh,* Vol. 1, p. 21, 13 Tammuz 5729 (1969); pp. 23-24, *Matos-Maasei* 5729 (1969); pp. 53-54, 19 Kislev 5731 (1970); pp. 181-182, 2nd day of Shavuos 5737 (1977); Vol. 2, p. 147, 18 Elul 5741 (1981); p. 153, 4th Night of Sukkos 5742 (1981); p. 414, *Yechidus* with Rabbi Efraim Eliezer Yalles, Av Beis Din of Philadelphia, 2nd Day of Chol HaMoed Pesach 5742 (1982); *Sichos Kodesh 5734,* Vol. 1, p. 401, *Terumah* (1974); *Sichos Kodesh 5736,* Vol. 1, p. 252, 19 Kislev (1975); *Sichos Kodesh 5738,* Vol. 1, p. 400, 24 Teves (1978); *Likkutei Sichos,* Vol. 21, p. 288. See also *Daas Torah,* pp. 59- 60; *Toras Menachem 5742,* Vol. 2, p. 278, Simchas Torah (1981); *Shemen Sasson MeiChaveirecha,* Vol. 2, pp. 75-76, Letter to Rabbi Shlomo Yosef Zevin, dated 13 Iyar 5735 (1975). See the same letter and analysis in *Menachem Meishiv Nafshi,* Vol. 1, p. 364.

14 I Kings Ch. 20.

15 Aram consisted of ancient city-states in Syria. Ben-Hadad was king of Damascus and the surrounding region.

16 See *Rashi* on I Kings 20:13, s.v. *Navi Echad.* There, we learn that the prophet is Michiyahu, the son of Yimlah. See also *Seder Olam Rabbah,* Ch. 20.

17 Sackcloth was traditionally worn as a sign of mourning. See Esther 4:1.

18 This is a major theme throughout the Rebbe's thought. See *Karasi V'Ein Oneh,* Vol. 1, p. 21: "The Torah's stories are not mere tales. Instead, they are meant to offer practical lessons"; Vol. 2, p. 243, 7 Tammuz 5743. See also *Maamarei Admur HaZakein HaKetzarim,* p. 171; *Chanah Ariel,* Vol. 1, p. 38; *Sefer HaMaamarim 5716,* p. 385; *Toras Menachem 5729,* Vol. 4, p. 107, 13 Tammuz (1969).

19 See *Karasi V'Ein Oneh,* Vol. 1, p. 23, *Matos-Maasei* 5729 (1969); *Toras Menachem 5729,* Vol. 4, p. 107, 13 Tammuz (1969).

20 *Sichos Kodesh 5734,* Vol. 2, p. 106, *Emor* (1974).

21 See *Yechidus* with Israeli Air Force General Ran Ronen-Pekker, 5735 (1975); cited in *Karasi V'Ein Oneh,* Vol. 1, p. 100.

22 See Bergman, R., & Meltzer, G. (2003). *Milchemet Yom Kippur — Zman Emet, Tel Aviv: Miskal.* p. 134; (2012, March 15). *Lamah lo takafnu kodem?* [*Why didn't we attack earlier?*]. *Yisrael HaYom;* https://www.israelhayom.co.il/article/33452, updated December 4, 2012; cited in *B'Rega HaEmet,* p. 178. See the Rebbe's comments in *Sichos Kodesh 5734,* Vol. 1, pp. 118-119; *Karasi V'Ein Oneh,* Vol. 1, pp. 69-70, *Noach* 5734 (1933).

23 See *B'Rega HaEmet,* p. 177.

24 Operation Mole Cricket 19.

25 For arguments framing the Yom Kippur War as an Arab victory, see The 1973 Ramadan War — A Clausewitzian Victory [https://apps.dtic.mil/sti/tr/pdf/ADA196037.pdf]; Anwar Al-Sadat's Grand Strategy in the Yom Kippur War James W. Bean and Craig [https://apps.dtic.mil/sti/pdfs/ADA442407.pdf]; Illusion Of Defeat: Egyptian Strategic Thinking And The 1973 Yom Kippur War [https://apps.dtic.mil/sti/tr/pdf/AD1022141.pdf], p. 45, where we learn:

Sadat went to war not for territorial gain but to create a crisis that would disrupt the status quo, open the way for negotiations, and increase Egypt's diplomatic flexibility. Golda Meir acknowledged as much in her memoirs, where she conceded that Sadat's conduct of the war and overtures to the United States put Egypt in a far stronger position diplomatically than Israel. While Egypt had lost tactically, they won politically. Negotiations for the return of at least some of the territories Israel had captured in 1967 were inevitable.

26 *Karasi V'Ein Oneh,* Vol. 2, p. 501, Letter to Rabbi Immanuel Jakobovits, Elul 5741 (1981) (see Appendix).

27 For the Rebbe's extended analysis on the First Lebanon War and the application of various halachic principles, see *Karasi V'Ein Oneh,* Vol. 2, pp. 217-225, 22 Sivan 5742 (1982) [the Rebbe delivered this *sichah* just one week after the war's

outbreak, already expressing frustration over the fact that the Israeli army did not decisively end the war]; pp. 230-259, *likkut* of *sichos* for 22 Sivan, 3 Tammuz, 7 Tammuz 5742 (1982); pp. 263-278, 13 Tammuz 5742 (1982); p. 281, 17 Tammuz 5742 (1982); pp. 305-312, 6th Night of Sukkos 5743 (1982); pp. 317-325, 19 Kislev 5743 (1982); pp. 343-349, *Mikeitz* 5744 (1983); pp. 355-356, Purim 5745 (1985). The presentation in this section relies heavily on *B'Rega HaEmet,* Ch. 10. For a book-length treatment of that conflict, see Schiff, Z., & Ya'ari, E. (1984). *Milkhemet Sholel* [*The 1982 Lebanon-Israel War*]. Jerusalem: Schocken. p. 91.

28 In the Dawson's Field Hijackings. See The PFLP Hijacking of Five Planes [https://www.jewishvirtuallibrary.org/the-pflp-hijacking-of-five-planes].

29 Black September — Wikipedia [https://en.wikipedia.org/wiki/Black_September].

30 In the 1991 Battle of Sidon.

31 Palestinian insurgency in South Lebanon — Wikipedia [https://en.wikipedia.org/wiki/Palestinian_insurgency_in_South_Lebanon]. Highlights of Lebanon-based PLO terrorism include: Kiryat Shmonah Massacre, Ma'alot Massacre, 1974 Nahariya Attack, Savoy Hotel Attack, Kfar Yuval Hostage Crisis, Coastal Road Massacre, 1978 South Lebanon Conflict, 1979 Ma'alot Attack, 1979 Nahariya Attack, and the Misgav Am Hostage Crisis.

32 See *Karasi V'Ein Oneh,* Vol. 1, p. 288, *Emor* 5738 (1978), where the Rebbe cites a military expert who attributes the United States' loss in Vietnam to their failure to employ a decisive military strategy. Consider also Israel's Vietnam? | Office of Justice Programs [https://www.ojp.gov/ncjrs/virtual-library/abstracts/israels-vietnam]. For an analysis of the U.S. failure in Vietnam and its relevance to Israel's wars with terrorist organizations, see Wheat, T. (2023, December 20). *Israel, Hamas, & "Winning" Asymmetric Wars.* LinkedIn; https://www.linkedin.com/pulse/israel-hamas-winning-asymmetric-wars-treston-wheat-phd-ouade/.

33 See *B'Rega HaEmet,* p. 303.

34 *Karasi V'Ein Oneh,* Vol. 2, pp. 246ff. See

historical discussion in *B'Rega HaEmet,* pp. 304-307.

35 *Karasi V'Ein Oneh,* Vol. 2, p. 248, *likkut* of *sichos* for 22 Sivan, 3 Tammuz, 7 Tammuz 5742 (1982). See also *Sichos Kodesh 5742,* Vol. 3, 22 Sivan, p. 21, 22 Sivan; *Toras Menachem — Hisvaaduyos 5742,* Vol. 3, pp. 1,738-1,739; *Karasi V'ein Oneh,* Vol. 2, p. 220, 22 Sivan 5742 (1982) [*sichah* to graduating class of Beis Rivkah; Video of Sichah [https://videos.jem.tv/video-player?clip=8465], 45:00; Audio of Sichah [https://ashreinu.page.link/CBGN].

36 The Rebbe's logic here is that in geopolitical terms, the United States is the only global superpower. However, as we will explore in Chapter 11, the Rebbe advocates Israel decoupling itself from absolute reliance on the United States by creating alliances with other states. See *Shalom Shalom V'Ein Shalom,* p. 482.

37 For corroboration of the Rebbe's view, see Schiff, Z., & Ya'ari, E. (1984). *Milkhemet Sholel* [*The 1982 Lebanon-Israel War*]. Jerusalem: Schocken. p. 91; cited in *B'Rega HaEmet,* p. 307, footnote 15.

38 See *B'Rega HaEmet,* pp. 309-310.

39 *Karasi V'Ein Oneh,* Vol. 2, p. 230, 3 Tammuz 5730 (1970).

40 *Karasi V'Ein Oneh,* Vol. 2, p. 263, *Chukas-Balak* 5742 (1982).

41 *Toras Menachem — Hivaaduyos 5742,* Vol. 4, p. 1,851; *Karasi V'Ein Oneh,* Vol. 2, p. 273, *Chukas-Balak* 5742 (1982).

42 See *Targum Yonasan* on Deuteronomy 13:17. The Rebbe called on the Israeli army to turn the area into a "mound of ruins" through airstrikes, artillery fire, and tanks, without risking infantry soldiers.

43 For the perils of urban combat, see The Eight Rules of Urban Warfare and Why We Must Work to Change Them — Modern War Institute [https://mwi.westpoint.edu/the-eight-rules-of-urban-warfare-and-why-we-must-work-to-change-them/]; The City Is Not Neutral: Why Urban Warfare Is So Hard — Modern War Institute [https://mwi.westpoint.edu/city-not-neutral-urban-warfare-hard/]; Urban Warfare Project — Modern War Institute [https://mwi.westpoint.edu/urban-warfare-project/]; IDF Deaths Highlight Perils of Urban Warfare — JINSA [https://jinsa.org/jinsa_report/idf-deaths-highlight-urban-warfare-perils/].

44 *Toras Menachem 5742*, Vol. 4, pp. 1,853-1,854, 13 Tammuz 5742 (1982); *Karasi V'Ein Oneh*, Vol. 2, p. 276; Video of Sichah [https://videos.jem.tv/video-player?clip=11958]. See similar comments in *Karasi V'Ein Oneh*, Vol. 1, pp. 325-326, *Re'eh* 5738 (1978); Vol. 2, pp. 313-316, *Chayei Sarah* 5743 (1982).

45 The Sinai Campaign | IDF [https://www.idf.il/en/mini-sites/wars-and-operations/the-sinai-campaign/].

46 Namely, this is a cavalier, unhelpful approach.

47 Numbers 23:9.

48 For similar comments on the perverse desire for global approval, see *Sichos Kodesh 5738*, Vol. 3, p. 171, Motzaei Shabbos *Balak* (1978).

49 See Schiff, Z., & Ya'ari, E. (1984). *Milkhemet Sholel* [*The 1982 Lebanon-Israel War*]. Jerusalem: Schocken. p. 140; cited in *B'Rega HaEmet*, p. 320, footnote 31.

50 See *B'Rega HaEmet*, pp. 320-321.

51 See *B'Rega HaEmet*, p. 321.

52 Tyre, known as *Tzor* in the Bible (see, for example, Isaiah Ch. 23), is an ancient city in Southern Lebanon. It is crucial given its strategic position near Israel, only 27 miles north of Safed. It is 51 miles south of Beirut. Tyre is just south of the Litani River, a vital strategic point in Lebanon. Capturing Tyre would have enhanced Israel's control and operational capabilities in Lebanon, as the Litani serves as a natural barrier to hold back hostile forces who threaten Israel's north.

53 *Sichos Kodesh 5738*, Vol. 2, pp. 291-292; *Karasi V'Ein Oneh*, Vol. 1, pp. 288-289, *Emor* 5738 (1978).

54 An 8,500-mile journey (a 17-hour flight).

55 Expert: Hezbollah has built a vast tunnel network far more sophisticated than Hamas's | The Times of Israel [https://www.timesofisrael.com/expert-hezbollah-has-built-a-vast-tunnel-network-far-more-sophisticated-than-hamass/].

56 2006 Hezbollah cross-border raid [https://en.wikipedia.org/wiki/2006_Hezbollah_cross-border_raid].

57 The infrastructural damage in Lebanon was far more severe than the damage in Israel, highlighting the suicidality of Hezbollah's wars and their lack of concern for Lebanon's citizens.

58 "Divine Victory" and Earthly Failures: Was the War Really a Victory for Hizbollah? [https://www.inss.org.il/wp-content/uploads/2017/08/The-Second-Lebanon-War-123-134.pdf].

59 For more on the lead-up to and the strategy employed in the Second Lebanon war, see Golan, S. (2022). *Fire in Lebanon, 2006: Strategic level decision making in the Second Lebanon War*. Modan Publishing House; Ministry of Defense Publishing House. For an updated view of Hezbollah, see Hezbollah [https://hezbollah.org/].

60 Six months after Oct. 7, Israel's north and south are frozen in time — and fear — The Washington Post [https://www.washingtonpost.com/world/2024/04/06/israel-six-months-october-7/]; Displaced Israelis: An Update on the Evacuees from the North and the South — American Zionist Movement [https://azm.org/displaced-israelis/]; How Hezbollah attacks displace 60,000 Israelis, six months on | Reuters [https://www.reuters.com/world/middle-east/six-months-hezbollah-fire-keeps-uprooted-israelis-limbo-2024-04-04/].

61 Fatah is the most dominant faction in the PLO and the current ruling party in Palestinian cities in Judea and Samaria.

62 Operation Cast Lead | IDF [https://www.idf.il/en/mini-sites/wars-and-operations/operation-cast-lead/].

63 Over 6 billion in 2024's U.S. Dollars.

64 Operation Pillar of Defense | IDF [https://www.idf.il/en/mini-sites/wars-and-operations/

operation-pillar-of-defence/operation-pillar-of-defense/].

65 Operation Brother's Keeper | IDF [https://www.idf.il/en/mini-sites/wars-and-operations/operation-brother-s-keeper/operation-brother-s-keeper/].

66 During the May 2021 Gaza war, the IDF reportedly destroyed over 62 miles of Hamas' underground network. After the war, Yahya Sinwar, Hamas' leader in the Gaza Strip, claimed that the group possessed over 500 kilometers (approximately 310 miles) of tunnels and that at best, Israel had "only destroyed 20 percent of the tunnels." See Hamas Tunnels to Egypt Played Key Role in Arming Hamas [https://www.fdd.org/analysis/2023/10/28/hamas-tunnels-to-egypt-played-key-role-in-arming-hamas/]. For more on the war, see Operation Guardian of the Walls | IDF [https://www.idf.il/en/mini-sites/wars-and-operations/operation-guardian-of-the-walls/operation-guardian-of-the-walls-1/].

67 On the importance of citing case studies from the general/non-Jewish world to reinforce teachings from the Torah, see *Sichos Kodesh 5736*, Vol. 1, p. 126, Simchas Torah; *Karasi V'Ein Oneh*, Vol. 1, p. 106, Simchas Torah 5736 (1975).

68 From 1987-2008, the Black Tiger suicide bombers carried out over 378 suicide attacks, with females making up over 25% of the attackers. Through suicide attacks they assassinated a Sri Lankan president and the former prime minister of India. See Premaratne, N. P. (2015). *Impact of Changing External Conditions on Counterinsurgency: The Sri Lankan Experience*. Naval Postgraduate School, Monterey, California. On p. 25 there, it specifies:

Apart from the death of thousands of civilians, LTTE [the Tigers official name — Liberation Tigers of Tamil Eelam] was also responsible for the killings of two heads of states, 104 politicians, 1,555 Indian Peace Keeping Forces (IPKF) personnel, 23,387 Sri Lankan security forces personnel, and 2,825 missing in action (MIA).

69 For perspective, see De Silva, A. I. P. (2013). *International intervention in intra-state conflicts: The case in Sri Lanka*. Naval Postgraduate

School. On p. 92, it reads:

By that time, the LTTE controlled one-third of the country with full-fledged military forces, a policing system, and an administrative system. It was a separate state with all the basic necessities, even though it did not have legal recognition as such.

P. 93 continues to explain:

At the beginning of the war, India did not believe that Sri Lankan forces would win the war in Sri Lanka militarily, since the LTTE— at that time — was a strong force that could overrun army camps, killing thousands of soldiers in a day. For instance, on July 18, 1996, the LTTE killed 1,200 soldiers and acquired U.S. $70 million worth of military equipment from the Mulativu army base.

70 See Premaratne, N. P. (2015). *Impact of Changing External Conditions on Counterinsurgency: The Sri Lankan Experience*. Naval Postgraduate School, Monterey, California. On p. 64, it explains:

At one point, the LTTE had collected 80 percent of its annual operating budget through the Tamil diaspora. By 2007, this fund had reached 'an output of 200—300 million USD.' Other than through the diaspora, the LTTE raised funds through both legal and illegal businesses like 'international shipping, arms smuggling, human trafficking and other businesses.

For more on the Tigers' funding sources, see Financial Fodder — External Sources of LTTE Funds | IPCS [https://www.ipcs.org/comm_select.php?articleNo=1530]. The Tigers even exploited international aid earmarked for hurricane relief to fund their terror organization. See Treasury Targets Charity Covertly Supporting Violence in Sri Lanka [https://home.treasury.gov/news/press-releases/hp683].

71 Sri Lanka rejects Tamil Tigers truce offer [https://www.theguardian.com/world/2009/feb/05/sri-lanka-ceasefire-tamil-tigers]. Following the ceasefire in 2002, which the Tigers utilized as an opportunity to rearm, the Sri Lankans wisely chose to end the cycle.

72 For more on applying the Sri Lankan

technique in the current conflict, see To Defeat Hamas, Emulate the Destruction of the Tamil Tigers [https://www.meforum.org/65192/to-defeat-hamas-emulate-the-destruction-of]; Defeat of LTTE: A Lesson in COIN Operations [https://apps.dtic.mil/sti/tr/pdf/AD1019061.pdf]. The Tamil government's defeat of the Tigers has been the subject of numerous studies and is widely regarded as a paradigmatic example of how to overcome insurgencies. For further reading on this point, see Khan, A. S. (2013). *Sri Lankan counterinsurgency operations during Eelam War IV: Comparative analysis of Galula and Rajapaksa models to determine future applicability*. School of Advanced Military Studies, United States Army Command and General Staff College, Fort Leavenworth, Kansas. The study discusses the Rajapaksa COIN (counterinsurgency) model used by Sri Lanka against the LTTE insurgency during the Eelam War IV (2005-2009). The Rajapaksa model had eight key principles: political will, ignoring criticism, no negotiations, regulating media, no ceasefires, operational freedom, young commanders, and keeping neighbors informed. It defeated the LTTE insurgency. See also Manage, N. (2012). *Counterinsurgency principles for contemporary internal conflict*. Naval Postgraduate School, Monterey, CA; Chandradasa, E. M. (2012). *Adaptive COIN in Sri Lanka: What contributed to the demise of the LTTE?*. Naval Postgraduate School, Monterey, CA; Blaha, C. (2013). *Defeating insurgencies with minimal force ratios*. Master's thesis, U.S. Army Command and General Staff College, Fort Leavenworth, Kansas.

73 MS13 [https://insightcrime.org/el-salvador-organized-crime-news/mara-salvatrucha-ms-13-profile/].

74 Barrio 18 [https://insightcrime.org/el-salvador-organized-crime-news/barrio-18-profile-2/].

75 Negotiating With Gangs: Lessons From the 2012 Truce in El Salvador — The SAIS Review of International Affairs [https://saisreview.sais.jhu.edu/negotiating-gangs-el-salvador-truce/].

76 Salvadoran gang crackdown — Wikipedia [https://en.wikipedia.org/wiki/Salvadoran_gang_crackdown].

77 For an analysis of the justice of Bukele's policies, see The Justice of Bukele? — by Bryan Caplan [https://www.betonit.ai/p/the-justice-of-bukele]; The Invisible Graveyard of Crime [https://www.richardhanania.com/p/the-invisible-graveyard-of-crime]; The Midwit Meme and the Denial of Tradeoffs [https://www.richardhanania.com/p/the-midwit-meme-and-the-denial-of].

78 For U.N. and human rights organizations' criticism of Sri Lanka, see Accountability key to Sri Lanka's future: UN rights chief | UN News [https://news.un.org/en/story/2023/09/1140422]; UN passes resolution on collecting evidence for Sri Lankan war crimes trials | Tamil Guardian [https://www.tamilguardian.com/content/un-passes-resolution-collecting-evidence-sri-lankan-war-crimes-trials]; Sri Lanka: How UN failed during Sri Lanka's armed conflict — Amnesty International [https://www.amnesty.org/en/latest/press-release/2012/11/sri-lanka-how-un-failed-during-sri-lanka-s-armed-conflict/]. For criticism of El Salvador by human rights organizations, including calls for sanctions, see Human Rights Abuses in Bukele's El Salvador Demand Sanctions [https://humanrightsfirst.org/library/human-rights-abuses-in-bukeles-el-salvador-demand-sanctions/]; El Salvador: President Bukele engulfs the country in a human rights crisis after three years in government — Amnesty International [https://www.amnesty.org/en/latest/news/2022/06/el-salvador-president-bukele-human-rights-crisis/]. Consider Bukele's unapologetic response to these critics in the U.N. on September 19, 2023 which in many respects can be aptly applied to Israel's situation:

[Foreign powers] made us sign false peace agreements, which had nothing to do with peace, and which only enabled the two warring factions to share the spoils.

We tried every formula they gave us and nothing worked. Then, under the protection of foreign powers, we handed the country over to the right. Then, again under the protection of foreign actors, we gave power to the left. This is how they kept us for 30 years post-war, where there were more deaths than in the civil war, more poverty, and more violence. Nobody did anything to change the root of the [problematic] system, neither the institutions nor the laws.

Everything that happened during those years was done with the backing, financing, consent, and imposition of those who have always called themselves great defenders of human rights and democratic institutionality. Instead of giving us medicine to heal, they were giving us poison....

But this time we said no! We rejected the poison and, for the first time, we tasted our own medicine. Thank G-d, it worked!

The first thing we did was to make sure we were on the side of G-d and the people, because no worthwhile transformation can be accomplished by obeying external powers. Secondly, we created our own method, a method designed for our own reality, created by those who live in that reality. If we had listened to [foreign powers and human rights organizations], we would still be losing thousands of Salvadorans to terrorists. Thank G-d we did not listen to them!

El Salvador | General Assembly [https://gadebate. un.org/en/78/el-salvador].

79 Explainer: What the UNHRC resolution means for Sri Lanka | United Nations News | Al Jazeera [https://www.aljazeera.com/ news/2021/3/25/what-does-un-human-rights-

resolution-mean-for-sri-lanka]. 'Unwaveringly loyal': Why El Salvador's Bukele is poised for re-election [https://www.aljazeera.com/ news/2024/1/31/unwaveringly-loyal-why-el-salvadors-bukele-is-poised-for-reelection].

80 See Trinquier, R. (1964). *Modern Warfare: a French View of Counterinsurgency.* p. 8. One of Trinquier's key arguments is that terrorist groups can only thrive when they have the support of the local population. Thus, a key aim of counterterrorism is to erode the terrorist group's capabilities and diminish their backing within the population.

81 Understanding Sri Lanka's Defeat of the Tamil Tigers [https://sangam.org/understanding-sri-lankas-defeat-tamil-tigers/]; Defeating Terrorism — Why the Tamil Tigers Lost Eelam... And How Sri Lanka Won the War — JINSA [https://jinsa. org/archive_post/defeating-terrorism-why-the-tamil-tigers-lost-eelam-and-how-sri-lanka-won-the-war/]; The Taming of the Tigers [https://mwi. usma.edu/wp-content/uploads/2020/04/The-Taming-of-the-Tigers_April-2020.pdf].

82 Warfare Through Misuse of International Law [https://besacenter.org/warfare-through-misuse-of-international-law/].

83 See Deuteronomy 8:17. See also *Karasi V'Ein Oneh,* Vol. 1, p. 34, *Naso* 5730 (1970).

CHAPTER 7

1 Genesis Ch. 12.

2 Genesis 12:7.

3 Genesis 13:14-15.

4 Genesis 15:18-12.

5 Genesis 17:7-8.

6 Genesis 26:3.

7 Genesis 28:13-14.

8 Deuteronomy 1:8. See also Deuteronomy 5:31; 7:1-2.

9 The story of this conquest is the primary

subject of the Book of Joshua.

10 11:23.

11 21:43-45.

12 Credit: Tomas Pueyo.

13 Byzantine Empire — World History Encyclopedia [https://www.worldhistory.org/ Byzantine_Empire/]; Muslim conquest of the Levant — Wikipedia [https://en.wikipedia. org/wiki/Muslim_conquest_of_the_Levant]; Byzantine Empire [https://en.wikipedia.org/ wiki/Muslim_conquest_of_the_Levant].

14 For an excellent historical survey of the

people who lived in the Land and different claimants, see Who Can Claim Palestine — Tomas Pueyo [https://unchartedterritories. tomaspueyo.com/p/who-can-claim-palestine]. The graphic cited in the text is from Pueyo. The term "Levant" refers to the eastern coast of the Mediterranean Sea. It includes countries such as Syria, Lebanon, Israel, Jordan, parts of Turkey, and parts of Iraq.

15 The prevailing philosophy among the aggressors at the time was Pan-Arabism, the belief that all countries inhabited by ethnic Arabs should form a contiguous unit. This philosophy is distinct from Islamism, which has become more prevalent in recent decades.

16 Cited by Pueyo. See Who Can Claim Palestine? [https://unchartedterritories.tomas pueyo.com/p/who-can-claim-palestine].

17 For an articulation and rejection of this claim, see *Likkutei Sichos*, Vol. 21, p. 411; *Sichos Kodesh 5728*, Vol. 1, pp. 36-38, 6 Tishrei (1967); Audio of Sichah [https://ashreinu.app/player? parentEvent=1328&event=1333]; *Sichos Kodesh 5734*, Vol. 2, p. 212, *Shlach* (1974); *Toras Menachem 5730*, Vol. 2, p. 391; *Karasi V'Ein Oneh*, Vol. 1, p. 32, Purim 5730 (1970).

18 Consider *Karasi V'Ein Oneh*, Vol. 2, p. 369, *Chayei Sarah* 5746 (1986), where the Rebbe explains:

All the nations of the world know that according to both the Bible and secular histories, Jerusalem belonged to the Jesubite nation. In due time, it was captured by the Jewish people and had continuous Jewish presence and influence for nearly a millennium. Subsequently, it was conquered by the Romans, Persians, and Muslims, experiencing a short period of Christian rule in the interim. Given that no Jesubites remain, only the Jewish people retain the primary right to the city.

19 Note that there was a continuous Jewish presence throughout.

20 See *Sotah* 34b; *Mechilta D'Rabbi Yishmael, Mesechte D'Amalek Parshah* 2, s.v. *VaYomer Hashem*; *Zohar*, Vol. 3, 71a. See also *Rashi* on Numbers 13:12, s.v. *VaYavo*. For a brief exploration of the site's history, see The Machpela Tomb: Historical Background, Facts and Justice | the Jewish Community of Hebron [http://en.hebron.org.il/history/669]. For an extensive scholarly exploration of the Jewish connection to the Cave of the Patriarchs and the different forces that sought to lay claim to it over time, see Arnon, N. (2021). *The Tomb of the Patriarchs — From Origins to Late Antiquity, Vol. 1*, Ph.D. thesis. Bar-Ilan University [https:// www.academia.edu/104852333/The_Tomb_ of_the_Patriarchs_From_Origins_to_Late_ Antiquity_Vol_1_Ph_D_Thesis_Noam_Arnon_ Bar_Ilan_University_2021]; Arnon, N. (2021). *The Tomb of the Patriarchs — From Origins to Late Antiquity Ph.D. Thesis Volume 2: Appendices and Illustrations* [https://www.academia. edu/104855139/The_Tomb_of_the_Patriarchs_ From_Origins_to_Late_Antiquity_Ph_D_Thesis_ Volume_2_Appendices_and_Illustrations].

21 The Seventh Step — Restriction on Jewish Prayer in Hebron [http://en.hebron.org.il/history/ 843]. This occurred in 1267, under the Mamluk Sultanate. Both Chrisitans and Jews were banned. The Jewish right to pray at the site was restored 700 years later in 1967.

22 Hand Grenade Hurled by Arab Terrorists, Explodes at Tomb, Injuring 39 Israelis — Jewish Telegraphic Agency [https://www.jta. org/archive/hand-grenade-hurled-by-arab- terrorists-explodes-at-tomb-injuring-39- israelis]; Tension in Cave of the Patriarchs in Hebron After a Hand Grenade Explodes [https:// jfc.org.il/en/news_journal/60918-2/105689-2/]; 48 Israelis Hurt by a Grenade at Hebron Shrine; Throng Was Worshiping at the Tomb of the Patriarchs Site Also Holy to Moslems — Arab Mayor Deplores Attack — The New York Times [https://www.nytimes.com/1968/10/10/ archives/48-israelis-hurt-by-a-grenade-at- hebron-shrine-throng-was.html]; Rabin in Hebron / Yom Kippur Riot in Machpela Cave [http://en.hebron.org.il/history/963]; Chronology of Terrorist Attacks in Israel Part II: 1968-1977 [https://www.johnstonsarchive.net/terrorism/ terrisrael-2.html].

23 For a particularly horrific attack, consider Murder of Shalhevet Pass [http://en.hebron.

org.il/fallen/214]. For a very recent attack, see Terrorist imam shot dead while firing at Hebron Jewish community — JNS.org [https://www.jns.org/terrorist-imam-shot-dead-while-firing-at-hebron-jewish-community/].

24 *Karasi V'Ein Oneh*, Vol. 1, pp. 174-176, Erev Shabbos *Noach* 5736 (1975).

25 Since multiple books have been written arguing for each narrative, by necessity we will be unable to explore each one in exhaustive detail.

26 There is no monopoly on the Islamist narrative. This presentation tries to capture key points of various anti-Israel groups and nations who ground their opposition in Islamism.

27 Notably, however, according to the Koran (5:21), Israel is called the "Holy Land" and described as destined for the Jewish people: "O, my people, enter the Holy Land which Allah has assigned to you and do not turn back [from fighting in Allah's cause] and [thus] become losers." On the halachic permissibility of citing the Koran in this context, see *Shabbos* 75a; *Shulchan Aruch, Yoreh De'ah*, 141:4.

28 For fuller articulation of this view, see Tepas, M. E. (2009). *A Look at Traditional Islam's General Discord with a Permanent System of Global Cooperation*. Indiana Journal of Global Legal Studies, 16(2), 681-701. Indiana University Press; https://www.jstor.org/stable/10.2979/gls.2009.16.2.681.

29 Fundamentalist Islamists view *Dar al-Islam* (the domain of Islam) as territories under Islamic rule, where Sharia is the supreme law of the land. They believe that it is an obligation for Muslims to establish and expand *Dar al-Islam* through various means, including political control and military conquests. This contrasts with *Dar al-Harb* (the domain of War). In the fundamentalist interpretation, *Dar al-Harb* consists of all regions not under Islamic rule. They view these territories as targets for conquest and believe that Muslims have a duty to wage jihad (holy war) against non-Muslim states to bring them under Islamic control.

30 Letter to the American People | Osama Bin Laden [https://www.dni.gov/files/documents/ubl2016/english/To%20the%20American%20people.pdf]. See this narrative as well in Bin Laden's Letter to America [https://www.dni.gov/files/documents/ubl/english/Letter%20to%20the%20American%20people.pdf]:

Justice is the strongest army, and security is the best way of life, but it slipped out of your grasp the day you made the Jews victorious in occupying our land and killing our brothers in Palestine. The path to security is for you to lift your oppression from us.

31 "The river" in this context refers to the Jordan river, while "the sea" refers to the Mediterranean Sea. This of course means that there is no room for a Jewish state. The slogan has become popular at Pro-Palestinian rallies across the world, and has particularly burst into the Western consciousness in the wake of the Pro-Palestinian protests after the onset of the October 7 War.

32 Hamas Is a Jihadist Organization Committed to Israel's Total Destruction [https://besacenter.org/hamas-is-a-jihadist-organization-committed-to-israels-total-destruction/]. See also The Hamas Charter [https://www.terrorism-info.org.il/Data/pdf/PDF_06_032_2.pdf];

May 2017 Revised Hamas Charter [https://web.archive.org/web/20170510123932/http://hamas.ps/en/post/678/].

33 See Hezbollah's "Open Letter":

Our primary assumption in our fight against Israel states that the Zionist entity is aggressive from its inception, and built on lands wrested from their owners, at the expense of the rights of the Muslim people. Therefore our struggle will end only when this entity is obliterated. We recognize no treaty with it, no cease fire, and no peace agreements, whether separate or consolidated. We vigorously condemn all plans for negotiation with Israel, and regard all negotiators as enemies, for the reason that such negotiation is nothing but the recognition of the legitimacy of the Zionist occupation of Palestine. Therefore we oppose and reject the Camp David Agreements, the proposals of King Fahd, the Fez and Reagan plan, Brezhnev's and the French Egyptian proposals, and all other programs that include the recognition (even the implied recognition) of the Zionist entity.

The Hizballah Program: An Open Letter [https://www.ict.org.il/UserFiles/The%20Hizballah%20Program%20-%20An%20Open%20Letter.pdf].

34 The Real Reason Iran Hates Israel — WSJ [https://www.wsj.com/articles/the-real-reason-iran-hates-israel-anti-semitism-gaza-4f7ad96e?mod=opinion_major_pos4].

35 For a critique of this general narrative, see *Sichos Kodesh 5729*, Vol. 1, pp. 437f.; *Toras Menachem 5729*, Vol. 2, p. 359. The Rebbe commonly invokes various versions and predecessors of this narrative, dismissing them as false or naive claims of "uprightness" and "justice." See *Karasi V'Ein Oneh*, Vol. 1, p. 182, 2nd Day of Shavuos 5737 (1977); p. 186, *Shlach* 5737 (1977); pp. 292, 294, Lag BaOmer 5738 (1978); p. 304, *Naso* 5738 (1978;) p. 320, Motzaei Shabbos *Re'eh* 5738 (1978); p. 420, Motzaei Shabbos *Ki Sissa* 5739 (1979); *Karasi V'Ein Oneh*, Vol. 2, pp. 85-89, *Shlach* 5740 (1980); p. 93, 4 Menachem Av 5740 (1980); also printed in *Sichos Kodesh 5740*, Vol. 3, pp. 705-706; Video of Sichah (Before You Preach Morality, Let's Look at History [https://www.youtube.com/watch?v=HXJ7Ty1fBqM]); *Karasi V'Ein Oneh*, Vol. 2, p. 144, 18 Elul 5741 (1981); p. 185, 19 Kislev 5742 (1981); p. 204, 24 Teves 5742 (1982); p. 232, 3 Tammuz 5742 (1982); pp. 267, 277, 13 Tammuz 5742 (1982); p. 282, *Devarim* 5742 (1982); p. 315, *Chayei Sarah* 5743 (1982); pp. 345, 347, *Mikeitz* 5744 (1983); p. 454, Letter to Eliezer Livneh, dated 13 Cheshvan 5731 (1970); also printed in *Igros Kodesh*, Vol. 27, p. 12, Letter #10,005. See also *Sichos Kodesh 5727*, Vol. 1, p. 430, Purim (1967); *Sichos Kodesh 5739*, Vol. 1, p. 230, *Bereishis* (1978); *Sichos Kodesh 5739*, Vol. 2, p. 212, *Noach* (1978); pp. 323, 326, *Ki Sissa* (1979); *Sichos Kodesh 5740*, Vol. 1, p. 436, 10 Shvat (1980); *Sichos Kodesh 5740*, Vol. 3, pp. 419-424, *Shlach* (1980); *Toras Menachem 5730*, Vol. 2, p. 112, 10 Shvat (1970).

36 In more radical forms, this conforms to Marxist narratives, which the Rebbe observes sometimes underlie these arguments. See *Karasi V'Ein Oneh*, Vol. 1, p. 90, *Shlach* 5734 (1974); p. 121, *Chayei Sarah* 5736 (1975). See also *Sichos*

Kodesh 5736, Vol. 1, p. 412, *Bo*; *Toras Menachem 5746*, Vol. 2, p. 234, Motzaei Zos Chanukah (1985).

37 *Sichos Kodesh 5739*, Vol. 2, pp. 330-331, *Ki Sissa*; *Karasi V'Ein Oneh*, Vol. 1, p. 420, Motzaei Shabbos *Ki Sissa* 5739 (1979); Audio of Sichah [https://ashreinu.page.link/grzQ].

38 The Western Social Justice and Islamist narratives contradict one another because they hold fundamentally different values. The Western Social Justice narrative champions principles such as equality, inclusion, and the protection of marginalized groups. It promotes secularism and the separation of religion and state. In contrast, Islamist groups seek to establish Islamic law (Sharia) as the basis for governing society, which restricts rights of women and religious minorities. Islamist narratives also reject secularism, insisting on the integration of religion and state. Despite these contradictions, some aspects of the Western Social Justice narrative can be exploited to serve Islamist interests against Israel. For example, the Social Justice narrative's emphasis on supporting oppressed and marginalized groups can be used to paint Israel as an oppressive force against Palestinians, while ignoring the oppressive elements within Palestinian society and Islamist groups. This selective application of Social Justice principles allows Islamist groups to gain support from Western audiences who are often unaware of the full context and the contradictions between the two narratives.

39 A point we explored at length in Chapters 3 and 5.

40 The jump from questioning Israel's ownership of Judea and Samaria to applying this criticism to all of Israel is based on the logical extension of the arguments used by the Western Social Justice narrative. If Israel's presence in Judea and Samaria is illegitimate due to the perception that Israel is a powerful, oppressive force against Palestinians, then the same logic can be applied to Israel's existence within the pre-1967 borders. This is because the creation of the State of Israel in 1948 also involved the displacement of Palestinians and gave Jews control of the Land. Moreover, if Israel is a colonial project, the logical conclusion of this perspective is that the Jewish people's ownership of the entire State is illegitimate, not just its presence in Judea and Samaria.

41 For more on this point, see If Anything Sustains the Arab-Israeli Conflict, It Will Be Progressives' Antisemitism [https://besacenter. org/progressives-antisemitism-israel/]. For many Arabs in the Middle East, pragmatic concerns override idealistic and ideological narratives of oppressor versus oppressed. However, in the West, Social Justice progressives often do not understand the situation's nuances or view it through a simplistic lens, which leads them to not let the argument die.

42 As well as Australia, Canada, New Zealand, and others.

43 *Sichos Kodesh 5730*, Vol. 1, p. 627; *Toras Menachem 5730*, Vol. 2, p. 391; *Karasi V'Ein Oneh*, Vol. 1, p. 32, Purim 5730 (1970); Audio of Sichah [https://ashreinu.page.link/j89G].

44 *Sichos Kodesh 5736*, Vol. 2, p. 54; *Karasi V'Ein Oneh*, Vol. 1, p. 149, 11 Nissan 5736 (1976); Audio of Sichah [https://ashreinu.page.link/LyNJ].

45 A reference to the representatives in the U.N. General Assembly.

46 *Sichos Kodesh 5740*, Vol. 3, p. 1,161, *Yechidus* with Sadigura Rebbe (1980); also printed in *Karasi V'Ein Oneh*, Vol. 2, p. 408.

47 For the Rebbe's commentary, see *Karasi V'Ein Oneh*, pp. 189-190, 12 Tammuz 5737 (1977); pp. 245, 257, Purim 5738 (1978); p. 276, Motzaei Shabbos *Shemini* 5738 (1978).

48 Richard Hanania: Israel Must Crush Palestinian Hopes [https://www.richardhanania. com/p/israel-must-crush-palestinian-hopes].

49 *Karasi V'Ein Oneh*, Vol. 1, p. 193, *Matos-Maasei* 5737 (1977).

50 Saudi Arabia intercepted Houthi missile headed toward Israel — report [https://www. timesofisrael.com/liveblog_entry/saudi-arabia-intercepted-houthi-missile-headed-toward-israel-report/].

51 For an articulation of this narrative, see *Sichos Kodesh 5734*, Vol. 2, pp. 102-107; *Toras Menachem 5734*, Vol. 3, p. 143; *Karasi V'Ein Oneh*, Vol. 1, p. 86, *Emor* 5734 (1974); p. 220, 19 Kislev 5738 (1977). See *Sichos Kodesh 5736*, Vol. 1, p. 127, Simchas Torah; *Karasi V'Ein Oneh*, Vol. 1, p. 107, Simchas Torah 5736 (1975). There, the Rebbe argues that this self-interested perspective can lead the international community to actively defend Israel. See similar comments in *Sichos Kodesh 5730*, Vol. 2, p. 68, Acharon Shel Pesach (1970); *Sichos Kodesh 5731*, Vol. 1, p. 303, *Shlach* (1971); *Sichos Kodesh 5732*, Vol. 1, p. 86, Simchas Torah (1971).

52 Although the Western Social Justice Narrative is often espoused by self-professed secular humanists, its assumptions and values are quasi-religious in nature often descending in some form from Biblical axioms rooted in Jewish or Christian sources. Moreover, it is held with religious zeal.

53 *Karasi V'Ein Oneh*, Vol. 1, p. 90, *Shlach* 5734 (1974); pp. 148-152, 11 Nissan 5736 (1976); p. 156, *Naso* 5734 (1974).

54 *Karasi V'Ein Oneh*, Vol. 1, p. 32, Purim 5730.

55 See *Rashi* on Genesis 1:1, s.v. *Bereishis*. For the Rebbe's commentary, see *Karasi V'Ein Oneh*, Vol. 1, pp. 28-29, *Bereishis* 5730 (1969) p. 32, Purim 5730 (1970); pp. 48-49, *Bereishis* 5731 (1970); p. 170, Simchas Torah 5736 (1975); p. 189, 12 Tammuz 5737 (1977); p. 203, Motzaei Shabbos *Bereishis* 5738 (1977); pp. 290-291, Lag BaOmer 5738 (1978); pp. 489-493, *Bereishis* 5740 (1979).

56 Psalms 111:6.

57 *Sichos Kodesh 5738*, Vol. 2, pp. 339-343; *Karasi V'Ein Oneh*, Vol. 1, p. 291, Lag Ba'Omer 5738 (1978); Video of Sichah [https://videos.jem.tv/video-player?clip=12158]. See also *Sichos Kodesh 5741*, Vol. 1, pp. 267-269 (1981), where the Rebbe notes:

Rashi lived in exile in France, where there were ghettos, and the children with whom Rashi studied came from families who were affected by the Crusades.... Given the dire circumstances in his times, one might think that Rashi would write that G-d gave the Land back to the non-Jews. But Rashi does not write this! So Heaven forbid that someone would even make the suggestion! Instead, Rashi writes that G-d gave the Land of Israel to the Jewish people as an eternal inheritance. And the five-year-old student will learn this point at greater length upon reaching the portion of Lech Lecha [Genesis Chs. 12-17].

For similar comments on *Rashi* being unfettered by the Crusades, see *Sichos Kodesh 5740,* Vol. 3, pp. 646-647 (1980).

58 The Crusades were a series of religious wars initiated by the Catholic Church and European Christian rulers between the 11th and 13th centuries, with the primary goal of reclaiming the Holy Land from Muslim control. During this period, Jewish communities in Europe and the Holy Land faced significant hardships, including massacres, forced conversions, and expulsions, such as the Rhineland massacres of 1096 during the First Crusade. The Crusaders, fueled by religious fervor and antisemitism, engaged in widespread looting, destruction of property, and mass murder. They stormed into Jewish quarters, setting fire to homes and synagogues. They ruthlessly slaughtered, mutilated, and raped many Jews. They burned some Jews alive and drowned others in rivers. Despite these challenges, the Jewish people remained resilient, drawing strength from their faith and the teachings of the Torah, often sacrificing their lives instead of converting to Christianity.

59 See *Klalei Rashi,* Ch. 3, pp. 94-108, which states that one of the principles for reading *Rashi* is that his commentary is meant to be accessible for a five year old beginning the study of Scripture (on this age, see Ethics of the Fathers 5:21). In his commentary on Genesis 3:8, *Rashi* declares: "I have come only to explain the simple meaning of the text," indicating that his commentary serves as a study aid for the novice student. For further elaboration of this point, see Rabbi Eliyahu Mizrachi's commentary on *Rashi* on Genesis 1:14, s.v. *Aval BeShivas;* Genesis 9:4, s.v. *B'Nafsho;* Genesis 33:17, s.v. *Nasa.* There, he uses *Rashi's* comment on Genesis 3:8 as a key principle for understanding *Rashi's* overall approach to his commentary. This concept is also discussed extensively in the Rebbe's *sichos.* See, for example, *Toras Menachem 5728,* Vol. 2, p. 213 (1968).

60 The Rebbe repeatedly emphasized that the tremendous miracles and upheavals involved in the Jewish people's return to Israel in the 20th century, as well as their attendant victories despite overwhelming odds, are a clear indication of G-d's hand in history, returning the Land to the Jewish people.

61 *Karasi V'Ein Oneh,* Vol. 1, p. 65, 13 Tishrei 5734 (1973).

62 *Karasi V'Ein Oneh,* Vol. 2, pp. 75-76, Lag BaOmer 5730 (1970).

63 Isaiah 41:20; Job 12:9.

64 *Karasi V'Ein Oneh,* Vol. 1, pp. 17-20, 13 Tammuz 5729 (1969).

65 Genesis Ch. 15.

66 Genesis 26:1-5.

67 Genesis 28:13. See the Rebbe's analysis in *Karasi V'Ein Oneh,* Vol. 1, pp. 145-146, *Tzav 5736* (1976).

68 See I Samuel 13:19; II Kings 5:2, 6:23; Ezekiel 27:17.

69 See *Karasi V'Ein Oneh,* Vol. 1, p. 18, 13 Tammuz 5729 (1969).

70 See *Karasi V'Ein Oneh,* Vol. 1, p. 141, 10 Shvat 5736 (1976).

71 Printed in *Igros Kodesh,* Vol. 26, pp. 143-145, Letter # 9,698. Geulah Cohen (1925-2019) was an Israeli political figure and former member of the Lehi, a Jewish paramilitary group. She played a significant role in Israel's pre-state struggle against British rule. After transitioning to politics, Cohen was a founding member of the Tehiya party, advocating for the expansion of Israeli settlements. Her work significantly influenced Israeli politics and ideologies. For Cohen's reflections on her relationship with the Rebbe, see Faithful And Fortified Israel's Journalists | After Me! 1964 [https://videos.jem.tv/video-player?clip=682]; Keep Your Eyes on Jerusalem 1967 [https://videos. jem.tv/video-player?clip=683].

72 See *Karasi V'Ein Oneh,* Vol. 1, pp. 115-116, *Chayei Sarah 5736* (1975). There, the Rebbe notes that many Muslims also accept the Bible's veracity. See also *Karasi V'Ein Oneh,* Vol. 1, p. 193,

Matos-Maasei 5737 (1977).

73 Moreover, the Rebbe adds that the biblical prophecy (see Numbers Ch. 24; Ezekiel 38:16) teaches that in the "End of Days," the Land of Israel shall belong to the Jewish people. Thus, all Bible believers should hold that since Israel has returned to Jewish hands, we are in the era of the "End of Days." As the Rebbe put it:

Since the prophecy of Balaam, the nations of the world have known that in the 'End of Days,' the Land of Israel will belong to the Jews. Now, they see without any doubt that we are already in the 'End of Days' — which is expressed through the revealed miracles that the Holy One, blessed be He, performs in our Holy Land.

Sichos Kodesh 5738, Vol. 3, p. 166; *Karasi V'Ein Oneh*, Vol. 1, p. 311, Motzaei Shabbos *Balak* 5738 (1978).

74 See *Igros Kodesh*, Vol. 29, p. 135, Letter #11,108; Vol. 31, p. 48, Letter #11,691; p. 283, Letter #11,901; *Sichos Kodesh 5730*, Vol. 1, p. 404, 10 Shvat (1970); *Karasi V'Ein Oneh*, Vol. 1, pp. 59-60, 20 Menachem Av 5731 (1971).

75 Deuteronomy 11:12. See *Sichos Kodesh 5729*, Vol. 2, p. 291, 13 Tammuz (1969); *Toras Menachem 5729*, Vol. 4, p. 104 (1969).

76 See *Sichos Kodesh 5735*, Vol. 1, p. 333, 10 Shvat (1975). For more on this association, see *Igros Kodesh*, Vol. 29, p. 35, Letter #11,007 to the soldiers of the IDF, dated Winter 5734 (1973); *Igros Kodesh*, Vol. 30, p. 125, Letter #11,436 to the 7th grade students of Degania's Joint Education School, located in Israel's Jordan Valley; *Igros Kodesh*, Vol. 32, p. 101, Letter #12,026 to Major Naftali Mendelovich, Deputy Commander of the IDF's Spokesperson's Unit; p. 190, Letter #12,105 to IDF Captain Shimon Vajim, dated 11 Nissan 5737 (1977); *Igros Kodesh*, Vol. 33, p. 270, Letter #12,493 to the Chabad Shluchim in Safed, dated 22 Iyar 5738 (1978).

77 See *Sichos Kodesh 5740*, Vol. 3, p. 1,165; *Karasi V'Ein Oneh*, Vol. 2, p. 410 (1980). Carter taught Sunday School from 1942-2019.

78 This is a popular justification for the State of Israel's necessity. The Rebbe acknowledges this argument. See, for example:

The year 5708 [1948] was a deliverance for many of the Children of Israel who went from bondage to freedom (that is, in relation to the situation that prevailed previously), and there were even those who were saved, going from death to life.

Sichos Kodesh 5736, Vol. 2, p. 53, 11 Nissan; *Karasi V'Ein Oneh*, Vol. 1, p. 147, 11 Nissan 5736 (1976); Audio of Sichah [https://ashreinu.page.link/bVHL]. The Rebbe also references the claim that the Jewish people have a right to Israel due to the Holocaust in *Sefer HaSichos 5752*, Vol. 1, p. 55, *Bereishis* (1991).

79 *Sanhedrin* 91a; *Megillas Taanis*, Ch. 3; *Bereishis Rabbah*, Ch. 61. For the Rebbe's retelling of this story and commentary, see *Sichos Kodesh 5734*, Vol. 2, pp. 212-213, *Shlach* (1974); *Sichos Kodesh 5737*, Vol. 2, pp. 142-144 (1977); *Sichos Kodesh 5739*, Vol. 1, p. 215, Motzaei Shabbos *Bereishis* (1979); *Karasi V'Ein Oneh*, Vol. 1, pp. 89-90, *Shlach* 5734 (1974); pp. 185-186, *Shlach* 5737 (1977); Vol. 2, pp. 140-141, *Korach* 5741 (1981); pp. 226-229, *Shlach* 5742 (1982). See also *Toras Menachem 5747*, Vol. 3, pp. 162-164 (1987), where the Rebbe depicts Geviha ben Pesisa as responding to "people of Hamas" who contested the Jewish people's claim to Israel. (In context, the word "Hamas" means violence or robbery.) The Rebbe would retell this story in the weeks in which the portions of *Shlach* and *Korach* are read from the Torah, since these correspond to the date 25 Sivan, when the encounter between Geviha and the foreign nations occurred.

80 *Karasi V'Ein Oneh*, Vol. 1, p. 90, *Shlach* 5734 (1974).

81 From a purely logical perspective, the effectiveness of a refutation depends on the framework within which an argument is made. The Rebbe contends that most claims supporting the Jewish people's right to the Land of Israel can be refuted within their respective frameworks. However, the Torah's claim stands apart as internally consistent. So, if someone declares, "My claim is based on the Torah," and their primary commitment is to the Torah, then their claim cannot be undermined from within that framework.

The Torah's assertions form a self-contained, coherent system. Attempting to refute such a claim using external arguments would be futile, as the claim's validity rests on the acceptance of the Torah's authority, which the claimant already accepts as their foundational premise. As the Rebbe put it:

All the different formulas [narratives and arguments] have been attempted, yet this remains the sole formula that has not been put to the test! This approach is also the only one acknowledged by the non-Jews, as they study Scripture (which they refer to as the "Bible").

Karasi V'Ein Oneh, Vol. 1, p. 150, 11 Nissan 5736 (1976); see also *Daas Torah,* p. 57.

Additionally:

When telling a gentile that the Land of Israel belongs to the Jews, one should not say that this is because Kissinger or Marx said so, or because Israel has weapons — a gentile is not at all impressed by these reasons. Only when he is told that the Land of Israel belongs to the Jews because it is written in the Torah is he impacted by it, to the point that [if he is belligerent] he flees.

Karasi V'Ein Oneh, Vol. 1, p. 90, *Shlach* 5734 (1974); see also *Sichos Kodesh 5734,* Vol. 2, p. 213.

As we will see, this approach causes enemies to "flee," as an opponent committed to a religious narrative is far more formidable.

82 See *Karasi V'Ein Oneh,* Vol. 1, p. 92, *Bereishis* 5735 (1974).

83 Deuteronomy, 14:1.

84 See *Karasi V'Ein Oneh,* Vol. 1, p. 19, 13 Tammuz 5729 (1969).

85 See *Karasi V'Ein Oneh,* Vol. 1, p. 20, Tammuz 5729 (1969); p. 30, Purim 5730 (1970).

86 Printed in *The Letter and the Spirit,* Vol. 5, pp. 408ff.; printed in Hebrew translation in *Karasi V'Ein Oneh,* Vol. 2, pp. 475-476; for the English letter online, see The Outcome of the Camp David Accords — Chabad.org [https://www.chabad.org/therebbe/letters/default_cdo/aid/2387552/jewish/The-Outcome-of-the-Camp-David-Accords.htm].

87 Genesis 15:18.

88 Genesis 17:18.

89 In the Gregorian calendar, this corresponds to the years 1272 BCE to 68 CE. This covers the period between Joshua's conquest and the destruction of the Second Temple.

90 Part of the *Avodah* blessing (*Retzei*), the 17th blessing of the *Amidah* (*Shemoneh Esreh*).

91 Printed in Igros Kodesh, Vol. 26, pp. 166-170, Letter # 9,716, dated "the Day Following the Days of Liberation [12-13 Tammuz] 5729" (1969). This is a point which we will address in greater detail in Chapter 9.

92 The Rebbe means to say that infusing the youth with the idea of the "Biblical Land of Israel," as opposed to the nationalist "State of Israel," will lead to improved morale. For more on this, see Chapter 9.

93 See *Shalom Shalom V'Ein Shalom* p. 77, where Rabbi Shalom Wolpo expands on this point as follows:

Today, some pundits try to explain the Prime Minister's capitulation to the Camp David debacle by claiming that IDF soldiers had low morale and were resentful, wondering, "What are we even fighting for?" They argue that this left Mr. Begin with no choice but to pursue a peace agreement.

This low morale is hardly surprising. From the moment children enter kindergarten, we fill their heads with the notion that Israel's entire history started on Yom Ha'Atzma'ut [Independence Day 1948], and that the possibility of an Independent State only arose thanks to the U.N. Partition Plan on November 29th, 1947. Since the world's nations gave their stamp of approval, we had the right to declare our new state. Children hear this over and over in school from first grade on.

After years of such rhetoric, they grow up, and learn that Arabs have rights as well. The partition plan obligates us to give them their rightful state in Judea and Samaria. Suddenly, we have no right to play conqueror and grab land by force. So the Israeli soldier becomes depressed and frustrated, questioning what he's sacrificing his best years for and why he should battle the "sons of Ishmael" [an archetypal name for Arab people] who are our equals.

Wouldn't it be better, he thinks, for Israel to embrace justice and integrity? To return what we stole from the Palestinians, the poor man's lone sheep [see II Samuel Ch. 12], and the holy Egyptian lands we seized in the Sinai? Then, at last, we could live beside our neighbors in

harmony and tranquility.

Rabbi Wolpo argues that the secular Zionist narrative, taken to its logical conclusion, leads to Israeli soldiers questioning the justice of their cause and losing motivation to fight for their country. In contrast, grounding Jewish youth in the Torah's account of G-d's promise of the Land to the Jewish people instills a sense of moral clarity, purpose, and strong morale.

CHAPTER 8

1 In the years since, such organizations have begun to proliferate, each with a different angle and sometimes different sources of funding. Other organizations founded in the same spirit and advocating for similar policies include: B'Tselem (founded 1989); Jewish Voice for Peace (JVP) (founded 1996); Shovrim Shtika (Breaking the Silence) (founded 2004); Yesh Din (founded 2005); J Street (founded 2008); +972 Magazine (founded 2010); IfNotNow (founded 2014); Looking the Occupation in the Eye (active on social media since 2021). These groups directly or indirectly work with full-fledged anti-Israel advocacy groups, such as Students for Justice in Palestine (SJP) (founded 1993) and Within Our Lifetime (founded 2019).

2 Notably, the Rebbe himself appreciated the value of demanding positive outcomes **now** — as demonstrated by his *"Mashiach Now"* campaign. He simply held that Peace Now activists were chasing a chimeric delusion.

3 *Karasi V'Ein Oneh*, p. 303, Motzaei Shabbos Naso 5738 (1978).

4 Adelist's 1978 Article in Maariv entitled 'Peace Now' [https://www.nli.org.il/he/newspapers/mar/1978/02/21/01/article/42].

5 *Karasi V'Ein Oneh*, Vol. 2, p. 426, 22 Kislev 5751 (1990). See "Will They Ever Make Peace With Us?" [https://www.youtube.com/watch?v=DIqAj66F7r4]; Territorial Compromise — A Problem, Not A Solution [https://videos.jem.tv/video-player?clip=3836].

6 For more on the deep rooted nature of antisemitism, see *Sichos Kodesh 5725*, Vol. 1, pp. 444-454 (1965); *Toras Menachem 5725*, Vol. 3, pp. 34-46 (1965); Audio of Sichah [https://ashreinu.app/player?event=7263&parentEvent=1097]. For a lecture on the *sichah* by Rabbi Elkanah Shmotkin, see 7 Rules for Combating Antisemitism | The Lubavitcher Rebbe (Presentation) [https://www.youtube.com/watch?v=IcWwkkQ7Dro]. For an article by Rabbi Shmotkin, see The Rebbe on How (Not) to Combat Antisemitism — Chabad.org [https://www.chabad.org/therebbe/article_cdo/aid/5992855/jewish/The-Rebbe-on-How-Not-to-Combat-Antisemitism.htm].

7 This shift has become more pronounced as these organizations move away from pragmatism and head towards moralism, a point which can be observed when looking at more recent iterations of these organizations, as well as their social media presence and activism.

8 *Karasi V'Ein Oneh*, Vol. 2, p. 85, *Shlach* 5740 (1980).

9 *Mishneh Torah, Hilchos Shabbos,* 2:3; *Hilchos Chanukah,* 4:14.

10 Psalms 125:8, 128:6.

11 *Karasi V'Ein Oneh*, Vol. 2, p. 86, *Shlach* 5740 (1980).

12 Isaiah 49:17.

13 *Sichos Kodesh 5740*, Vol. 3, p. 421; *Karasi V'Ein Oneh*, Vol. 2, pp. 86-88, *Shlach* 5740 (1980).

14 Isaiah 48:57.

15 Here, the Rebbe references the murder of Yehoshua Salome in Hebron on 13 Shvat 5740 (1980). Yehoshua had been a student at the *Hesder yeshivah, Yeshivat Nir* in Kiryat Arba. One Shabbos, while walking in the streets of Hebron, a terrorist murdered him at point blank range. The Rebbe discussed Salome's murder at length, seeing it as an indication of Israel's poor security for its citizens. See *Sichos Kodesh 5740,* Vol. 2, pp. 357-385; also printed in *Karasi V'Ein Oneh,* Vol. 2, p. 41, Purim 5740 (1980); Audio of Sichah [https://ashreinu.page.link/pFMw]; *Sichos Kodesh 5740,* Vol. 3, p. 50; also printed in *Karasi V'Ein Oneh,* Vol. 2, pp. 78-79, Motzaei Lag BaOmer 5740 (1980); Audio of Sichah [https://ashreinu.page.link/n6ss]; *Karasi V'Ein Oneh,* Vol. 2, p. 87, *Shlach* 5740 (1980); p. 409, *Yechidus* with Sadigura Rebbe, 5740 (1980). For historical discussion, see Private Yehoshua Salome | the Jewish Community of Hebron [http://en.hebron.org.il/fallen/250]; In Memoriam: Hebron Terrorist Victims [http://en.hebron.org.il/history/527]. For a record of the murder in the New York Times, see The Hebron Hurdle — The New York Times [https://www.nytimes.com/1996/08/25/magazine/the-hebron-hurdle.html]. In a twist of tragic irony, one of Yehoshua's kidneys was posthumously given to an Arab girl from Shechem (Nablus) who made anti-Jewish remarks and advocated violent terrorism.

16 *Karasi V'Ein Oneh,* Vol. 1, p. 303, *Naso* 5738 (1978).

17 *Karasi V'Ein Oneh,* Vol. 2, pp. 89-90, *Shlach* 5740 (1980).

18 Numbers 13:28.

19 See *Tanya, Shaar HaYichud Veha'Emunah,* Ch. 4.

20 *Karasi V'Ein Oneh,* Vol. 1, p. 304, *Naso* 5738 (1978).

21 In conversation with the author, Edward Luttwak observed that the present Jewish pacifist movements are reminiscent of Hellenistic Judaism, where the Hellenizers ultimately converted to paganism or Christianity, and North African Judaism, where

the local populations converted to Islam. Luttwak then noted that a perennial historical pattern is now playing out. Jews the world over are at a crossroads: Will they stay true to Jewish values, or will they assimilate?

22 *Sichos Kodesh 5731,* Vol. 1, p. 308; *Toras Menachem 5731,* Vol. 1, pp. 367ff.; *Karasi V'Ein Oneh,* Vol. 1, p. 53, 19 Kislev 5731 (1970); Audio of Sichah [https://ashreinu.page.link/yHpF].

23 Referred to in Rabbinic literature as *misyavnim.*

24 *Sichos Kodesh 5735,* Vol. 2, p. 66; *Karasi V'Ein Oneh,* Vol. 1, pp. 99-100, Rosh Chodesh Iyar 5735 (1975); Audio of Sichah [https://ashreinu.page.link/yrn4].

25 Ezekiel 20:32.

26 *Sichos Kodesh 5736,* Vol. 1, p. 683; *Karasi V'Ein Oneh,* Vol. 1, pp. 145-146, *Tzav* 5736 (1976).

27 Genesis 28:14.

28 *Kesubos* 111a. The broader context of the passage is a dispute over the status of making *aliyah* (i.e., moving to Israel from Babylon, or from other places where the Jewish people have been exiled to). The consensus favors *aliyah.* Yet the Talmud cites the Three Oaths as a teaching of Rabbi Yosi the son of Rabbi Chanina. It concludes that so long as Jews do not return to Israel using force, they may return — and indeed, the overwhelming consensus in the Talmud encourages moving to the Land of Israel even before the Messianic era. See also *Shir HaShirim Rabbah,* Ch. 2; *Shulchan Aruch, Even HaEzer,* sec. 75.

29 The "oaths" are mentioned in Songs of Songs 2:7, 3:5, 8:4.

30 See *Rashi* there, s.v. *shelo ya'alu bachomah* — "That they shall not ascend as a wall — together and forcefully."

31 See *Pesachim* 113a, cf. *Berachos* 7b; *Megillah* 6b; *Tikkunei Zohar* 7b.

32 In these discussions, the Rebbe primarily disputes the ideas expressed in the work *VaYoel Moshe.* For further presentation of these views,

see Rabbi Aharon Rosenberg's work *Hishbati Eschem*; Rabbi Moshe Dovid Katz's *Efes Biltecha Go'alenu*; and the anonymous *Kuntres Toras HaGalus.*

33 As the Rebbe responded to the Sadigura Rebbe in a 1980 exchange:

The question of the Three Oaths has no practical relevance today, since for those living in the Land of Israel, "it is forbidden to leave the Land of Israel for the Diaspora," regardless of any connection to the Three Oaths.

Karasi V'Ein Oneh, Vol. 2, p. 408, *Yechidus* with Sadigura Rebbe, 5740 (1980). See also *Daas Torah,* p. 144, Ch. 13, note 2.

34 *Karasi V'Ein Oneh,* Vol. 1, p. 469, Motzaei Shabbos *Matos-Maasei* 5739 (1979). The Rebbe reiterated this argument numerous times. See *Karasi V'Ein Oneh,* Vol. 1, p. 306, *Naso* 5738 (1978); p. 318, 20 Menachem Av 5738 (1978); pp. 360-362, *Bereishis* 5739 (1978); Vol. 2, p. 61, *Vayakhel-Pekudei* 5740 (1980); p. 112, *Bo* 5741; p. 407, *Yechidus* with Sadigura Rebbe, 5740 (1980).

35 This prohibition derives from Deuteronomy 7:1-2, which reads:

When the L-rd, your G-d, brings you into the land which you are entering to possess, and has cleared away many nations before you — the Hittites, the Girgashites, the Amorites, the Canaanites, the Perizzites, the Hivites, and the Jebusites, seven nations more numerous and mightier than you — and when the L-rd, your God, delivers them over to you, you shall conquer them and utterly destroy them. You shall make no covenant with them and show no favor to them.

The verse's last clause, "and you shall show them no favor," (in Hebrew, "*v'lo techanem*") has many layers of interpretation. See *Rashi* there, s.v. *v'lo techanem,* which, based on the Talmud (*Avodah Zarah* 20a) reads "*v'lo techanem*" as "Do not give them a resting place (*chanayah*) in the land." The Rebbe is asserting that while this verse dictates that one should not make territorial concessions, and thus could be brought to counter the point of the Three Oaths, it is nonetheless irrelevant to the discussion since *pikuach nefesh* overrides other Torah

principles.

36 *Karasi V'Ein Oneh,* Vol. 1, p. 498, Motzaei Shabbos *Bereishis* 5740 (1979).

37 *Sichos Kodesh 5738,* pp. 390-391, Motzaei Shabbos *Bechukosai; Karasi V'Ein Oneh,* Vol. 1, pp. 298-299 (1978); Audio of Sichah [https://ashreinu.page.link/hhbT].

38 The term "small gentile" used here does not refer to the size or power of the U.S. government, which was undoubtedly a great power. Rather, it echoes a Talmudic phrase found in *Pesachim* 113a and is employed by the Rebbe to emphasize the folly of refraining from advocating for Jews in distress out of fear of provoking any earthly authority, regardless of its perceived might. The Rebbe's point is that when Jewish lives are at stake, no government should deter one from speaking out forcefully.

39 In Jewish tradition, fasting is a practice often used for penitence. See Jonah 3:5-9; Joel 2:12-13; *Berachos* 17a, 32b; *Mishneh Torah, Hilchos Taanis,* 5:9; *Shulchan Aruch, Orach Chaim,* sec. 662. Cf. *Tanya, Iggeres HaTeshuvah,* Chs. 1-3.

40 Isaiah 49:17. Namely, that these Jews are contributing to the Jewish people's destruction.

41 Rabbi Wolpo, a prolific Israeli Chabad author and scholar, wrote two critical works explicating the Rebbe's perspective on Israel's security: *Daas Torah* (1979) and *Shalom Shalom V'Ein Shalom* (1982). *Daas Torah* offers a more systematic, theoretical perspective aimed at a rabbinic audience, while *Shalom Shalom V'Ein Shalom* focuses on constructing a more popular presentation of the Rebbe's perspective, supporting it with copious citations of current events and political analyses at the time of the book's publication. For the Rebbe's approving letters on Wolpo's works, see the introduction to *Shalom Shalom V'Ein Shalom.* See also *Teshurah,* 22 Shvat 5760, pp. 321-322 (2000); *Teshurah (Halperin),* 24 Sivan 5778 (2018).

42 *Daas Torah,* p. 229.

43 *Mishneh Torah, Hilchos Melachim,* 5:9, based on *Kesubos* 111a. See also *Tosafos, Gittin* 2a, s.v. *V'Ashkelon K'Darom; Levush Orach Chaim,* 531:5. The Rebbe explicitly invokes this argument in numerous cases to show that the argument of the oaths is not relevant in contemporary reality. See *Sichos Kodesh 5740*, Vol. 3, p. 1,161, *Yechidus* with Sadigura Rebbe (1980); also printed in *Karasi V'Ein Oneh*, Vol. 2, p. 407. The Rebbe also invoked the relevance of this halachic principle in a variety of contexts as early as 1950. See *Toras Menachem 5711*, Vol. 1, p. 92, *Chayei Sarah* (1950); *Toras Menachem 5713*, Vol. 2, p. 4, *Tetzaveh* (1953); *Toras Menachem 5730*, Vol. 4, p. 193, *Re'eh* (1970); *Sichos Kodesh 5737*, Vol. 1, p. 181, Simchas Torah (1976); *Likkutei Sichos*, Vol. 18, pp. 399-410; *Likkutei Sichos*, Vol. 25, p. 152.

See the Rebbe's extensive comments on this topic systematically collected in *Shaarei Eretz Yisrael*, pp. 285-313; *Shulchan Menachem, Choshen Mishpat*, sec. 44, pp. 147-149.

44 See, for example, the Rebbe Rayatz's Hebrew introduction to the Rebbe Rashab's *Kuntres U'Maayan*, pp. 45-53. This is also a prevalent theme in the Rebbe Rashab's letters. See, for example, *Igros Kodesh*, Vol. 1, pp. 206-210, 290-298.

45 Approximately eight months.

46 *Sefer HaSichos 5706-5170*, p. 162, 2nd Day of Rosh HaShanah Meal 5708 (1947).

47 The term "*yishuv*" was the colloquial name for the Jewish community in the Land of Israel in the centuries prior to the State's founding.

48 *Karasi V'Ein Oneh*, Vol. 2, p. 173, *Vayishlach* 5742 (1981).

49 *Toras Menachem Hisvaaduyos 5742*, pp. 662-663; *Karasi V'Ein Oneh*, Vol. 2, p. 189 (1982).

50 *Daas Torah*, Ch. 13, p. 144, note 2.

51 I.e., the portion of Jerusalem that had been under Israeli control.

52 At the outset of the Six-Day War, Israel preemptively attacked Egypt. Jordan subsequently joined the war, attacking Israel, given that it had signed a defense pact with Egypt.

53 Printed in *Igros Kodesh*, Vol. 26, pp. 166-170, Letter #9,716, dated "the Day Following the Days of Liberation [12-13 Tammuz] 5729" (1969). Shazar and the Rebbe had a particularly voluminous correspondence.

54 Meaning, the Soviet Union supported the partition of British Mandatory Palestine into "Israel" for the Jews and "Palestine" for the Arabs. At the time, the only major states that did not support Israel's bid for statehood were the Arab countries.

55 By this, the Rebbe means that parts of the modern-day State of Israel were included in the Divine promise to Abraham but were not historically part of the ancient Israelite kingdoms of Judah and Israel, nor the united monarchy under David and Solomon. Therefore, these territories are considered as having been "added" to the biblical Land of Israel in the contemporary era.

56 See the continuation of the Talmudic passage there, and *Rashi* and *Rashbam*, s.v. *D'Malchusayhu*, who write, "they will [ultimately] exact revenge from you."

57 See *Karasi V'Ein Oneh*, Vol. 1, pp. 247-248, Motzaei Shabbos *Mishpatim* 5738 (1978).

CHAPTER 9

1 See Ryan, M. W. S. (2018). *Defeating ISIS and Al-Qaeda on the Ideological Battlefield: The Case for the Corporation Against Ideological Violence.* CIWAG Case Studies (No. 16), Center on Irregular Warfare & Armed Groups (CIWAG), U.S. Naval War College, Newport, RI; retrieved from https://digital-commons.usnwc.edu/ciwag-case-studies/16.

Ryan argues that the battle against Islamist terrorist groups consists of two elements. The first is the "close battle," which involves direct military action against these groups with the aim of dismantling them. Ryan shows that the West is generally effective at prosecuting the "close battle" against terrorist groups. However, when it comes to executing the second element, the "deep battle" — the ideological war — the West is far less adept. For this reason, even after a terrorist group has been bled dry or dismantled, it can either be resurrected or its vision will inspire others, forming an even more radical strain. The resurgence of al-Qaeda and the emergence of ISIS are the most obvious instances of this phenomenon, but it also manifests in the Palestinian arena. For example: Through a combination of military action and manipulative diplomacy, Israel largely neutered the PLO. However, it was replaced by even more virulent ideological strands. Hamas, PIJ, and various other militias emerged in Gaza, Judea, and Samaria, while Hezbollah established its presence in Lebanon. While Ryan pushes for early identification and neutralization of radicalization, we will see that the Rebbe argues that dangerous ideology can only be countered by a correspondingly strong positive ideology.

2 The phrase "party of G-d" is mentioned three times in the Koran (5:56; 58:19; 58:22). The party of Allah is contrasted with the party of Satan. These verses do not inherently have an anti-Israel bias.

3 The Sunni-Shi'ite divide, dating back to the 7th century, is the largest and oldest in Islam. It originated from a dispute over the succession of leadership after Muhammad's death in 632 CE. Sunnis believe Abu Bakr, Muhammad's close companion and son-in-law, was the rightful successor, while Shi'ites maintain it was another son-in-law, Ali, Muhammad's cousin. Sunnis follow the Koran and Sunnah, while Shi'ites believe in the authority of the Twelve Imams. Sunnis are the larger demographic (Sunnis 85-90% vs. Shi'ites 10-15%). The divisions have led to significant political and social tensions throughout history.

4 For reflections on the connection between Islam and terrorism, see Ben Ari, M. (2024). *Vision and Dagger: Islam and its War Against Heretics*. Alim Press. See also Arnon-Ohana, Y. (2013). *Line of Furrow and Fire: The Conflict for the Land of Israel 1860-2010*. Achiasaf Ltd. pp. 271-318.

5 There are numerous terrorist groups named Hezbollah across Asia, including: Afghanistan,

Hezbollah Afghanistan — Wikipedia [https://en.wikipedia.org/wiki/Hezbollah_Afghanistan]; Iraq, Kata'ib Hezbollah — Wikipedia [https://en.wikipedia.org/wiki/Kata%27ib_Hezbollah]; Saudi Arabia, Hezbollah Al-Hejaz — Wikipedia [https://en.wikipedia.org/wiki/Hezbollah_Al-Hejaz]; and Azerbaijan, Islamic Resistance Movement of Azerbaijan — Wikipedia [https://en.wikipedia.org/wiki/Islamic_Resistance_Movement_of_Azerbaijan].

6 The "Axis of Resistance" is an alliance of states, political parties, and armed groups in the Middle East that oppose the policies and influence of Israel, the United States, and their allies in the region, the Gulf States. The main members of this alliance are Iran, Syria, and the Lebanese militant group Hezbollah.

7 See Hezbollah's websites: moqawama.org; moqawama.news. For more on the ideology of *muqawwama*, see Kanaaneh, A. (2021). *Hezbollah in Lebanon* (Hebrew). Jerusalem: Y.L. Magnes Press — The Hebrew University. pp. 39-58, 142-151, 181-154.

8 Notably, Hezbollah and ISIS are at odds with one another as ISIS, a fundamentalist Sunni group, views Hezbollah's Shi'ite beliefs as heretical. Hezbollah has fought ISIS in Syria and ISIS has sent terrorists to attack civilians in Hezbollah neighborhoods in Lebanon.

9 For extensive detail on Lebanese Hezbollah as a social and educational movement, see Kanaaneh, A. (2021). *Hezbollah in Lebanon* (Hebrew). Jerusalem: Y.L. Magnes Press — The Hebrew University. Ch. 6, pp. 172-222. For the English translation, see Kanaaneh, A. (2021). *Understanding Hezbollah: The hegemony of resistance*. Syracuse University Press.

10 1983 Beirut barracks bombings. The US Marine Corps had not experienced such a deadly attack since the battle of Iwo Jima in World War II.

11 See *Sefer HaSichos 5702*, pp. 138-153, s.v. *Maamar Kol HaYotzei LeMilchemes Beis David* (1942); *Sefer HaSichos 5752*, pp. 103, 165, 202 (1992). See also *Toras Menachem — Hisvaaduyos 5742*, Vol. 1, pp. 218, 221, Shemini Atzeres (1981); Vol. 2,

p. 1,151, *Tzav* (1982), where the Rebbe explicitly connects the Warriors of the House of David with *Tzivos Hashem; Toras Menachem — Hisvaaduyos 5743*, Vol. 1, pp. 251-253, Hoshana Rabbah (1982); *Toras Menachem — Hisvaaduyos 5745*, Vol. 5, p. 2,669 (1985); *Toras Menachem — Hisvaaduyos 5746*, Vol. 4, pp. 170-172, *Devarim* (1986); pp. 358-359, 15 Elul 5746 (1986); *Toras Menachem — Hisvaaduyos 5747*, Vol. 1, pp. 490-491, 20 Mar Cheshvan (1986). See *Karasi V'Ein Oneh*, Vol. 2, p. 68, Pesach Sheini 5740 (1980), where the Rebbe applies the term *Chayalei Beis David*, Warriors of the House of David, to all Jewish children who receive a passionate Jewish education.

12 Notably, the acronym Chabad traditionally stands for the three intellectual qualities of *Chochmah, Binah,* and *Daas.* It indicates that the movement offers a contemplative spiritual path. *Chayalei Beis David* is an innovative spin on the same Hebrew letters, but deciphering them as an activist acronym, thus formally expanding the role of Chabad students.

13 For lists of King David's most notable warriors, see II Samuel 23:8-39; I Chronicles 11:10-47.

14 The *yeshivah* students were not a classical military movement in that they did not engage in combat training. Nonetheless, they would be called upon to risk their lives in spreading and preserving Judaism. Many did in fact lay down their lives while disseminating Judaism under the USSR's communist regime which would execute religious leaders and teachers as a matter of course.

15 See *Igros Kodesh, Rebbe Rayatz,* Vol. 4, pp. 10-13, 171, 362-363; Vol. 5, pp. 13-14, 19, 21, 171, 463; Vol. 12, pp. 33, 56, 143; *Sefer HaSichos 5696*, pp. 357-358 (1936).

16 For an overview and analysis of the Rebbe's involvement in childhood education, from his start at *Merkos L'Inyonei Chinuch* through his innovation of the Twelve *Pesukim* and children's rallies, see Kraus, Y. (2007). *HaShvi'i. Miskal.* pp. 183-223.

17 Exodus 12:41: "On that very day, the entire army of G-d left the Land of Egypt." The *Psikta*

Zutrasa, an 11th-century midrashic text, notes, "How fortunate are the Jewish people to be called G-d's army." See also Exodus 7:4: "I shall take My armies, the Children of Israel, out of Egypt." Throughout *Tanach*, G-d is referred to as the "G-d of armies." See I Samuel 1:3, 11; II Samuel 5:10; Isaiah 1:9.

18 See *Sefer HaMaamarim Basi LeGani,* Vol. 1, pp. 15-17, *Basi LeGani* 5710 (1950). See also *HaYom Yom* for 12 Nissan; *Sefer HaMaamarim 5683*, pp. 168, 182-185, 194-196 (1923); *Sefer HaMaamarim 5701*, pp. 81-82, 87 (1941). For an earlier exploration of these themes by the Rebbe Rashab, see *Sefer HaMaamarim 5680*, pp. 241-249 (1920).

19 This is a significant theme in *Basi LeGani maamarim.* Consider *Sefer HaMaamarim Basi LeGani,* Vol. 1, pp. 126-155, 572. The term *Tzivos Hashem* is used extensively throughout the *Basi LeGani maamarim* up to and including the final such *maamar* in 5748 (1988).

20 For *sichos* directed towards women which discuss their responsibility to raise *Tzivos Hashem,* see *Sichos Kodesh 5723*, p. 187 (1963); *Sichos Kodesh 5731*, Vol. 1, p. 459 (1971); *Sichos Kodesh 5732*, Vol. 1, p. 284 (1972); *Sichos Kodesh 5739*, Vol. 3, p. 11, Rosh Chodesh Sivan (1979). The Rebbe also uses the term *Tzivos Hashem* with respect to education as early as 5730 (1969). See *Toras Menachem 5730*, Vol. 1, p. 406 (1970); *Sichos Kodesh 5732*, Vol. 1, pp. 18, 95 (1972). In 5739 (1979), the Rebbe frequently used the term *Tzivos Hashem* in reference to children. Consider *Sichos Kodesh 5739*, Vol. 2, p. 317; Vol. 3, pp. 47, 83, 298 (1979). This trend continued throughout 5740 (1979-1980). See *Sichos Kodesh 5740*, Vol. 1, pp. 111-112, 115 (1980).

21 Psalms 8:3.

22 For background and discussion, see Dubov, N. D., & Pewzner, N. H. (2024). *The Life of a Jewish Child: An Exposition of the Rebbe's Messages for Children, Volume 1: The 12 Pesukim: Conversations that Shape Our Children's World.* Sichos in English.

23 *Sichos Kodesh 5740*, Vol 3, p. 133, Erev Rosh Chodesh Sivan (1980); p. 660, *Matos-Maasei* (1980); p. 693, Rosh Chodesh Menachem Av

(1980); *Likkutei Sichos,* Vol. 24, p. 268. The Rebbe had called for similar prayer gatherings as early as 1967, just four months after these holy sites were liberated and made accessible to Jews for the first time in two decades. See *Sichos Kodesh 5728,* Vol. 1, p. 499, 26 Tishrei (1968).

24 See *Yoman Shnas Hakhel 5741,* p. 13 (1980-1981).

25 On the 19th of Tishrei, the third day of Chol HaMoed Sukkos.

26 Isaiah 8:10.

27 See, for example, *Likkutei Sichos,* Vol. 21, p. 325; *Sichos Kodesh 5739,* Vol. 2, p. 262, *sichah* addressed to elementary school students, 12 Adar (1979); *Yoman 5738, Motzaei Shabbos Mevarchim Sivan; Kovetz LeChizzuk HaHiskashrus,* Vol. 37, p. 34, recounting the events of Simchas Torah 5731 (1970). See also Utzu Eitzah at a Rebbe's Farbrengen Purim 5732 — 1972 [https://videos. jem.tv/video-player?clip=4517]; Utzu Eitzah at Rebbe's Farbrengen, 12 Tammuz 5737 [https:// videos.jem.tv/video-player?clip=4103]; Utzu Eitzah at a Tzivos Hashem Rally, 14 Adar I 5741 [https://videos.jem.tv/video-player?clip=3110].

28 See *Sichos Kodesh 5726,* pp. 243-251, Purim (1966).

29 *Yoman Shnas Hakhel 5741,* pp. 23-24 (1980-1981). For a vivid description of the first *Tzivos Hashem* rally and more background on *Tzivos Hashem,* see (2017, March). *On the Front Line: The Founding of Tzivos Hashem, A Chassidisher Derher.* Issue (54)131. pp. 39-53. For the Rebbe's speech at the inaugural rally, see Tzivos Hashem — G-d's Army — An Inaugural Speech [https:// videos.jem.tv/video-player?clip=3788].

30 Many events relating to *Tzivos Hashem* pervade the diary for the year, including the Rebbe speaking with individual children and asking if they were involved in *Tzivos Hashem,* various *Tzivos Hashem* parades, and the Rebbe taking particular interest in ranks and symbols for the movement. For some examples, see *Yoman Shnas Hakhel 5741,* pp. 28, 38, 40, 48, 53-55, 64, 68, 71, 84 (1980-1981).

31 Tzivos Hashem [https://www.tzivoshashem. org/].

32 See Audio of the Interview [https://ashreinu. app/player?parentEvent=11272&event=11272], 16 Tammuz 5740 (1980). See citation and discussion in *B'Rega HaEmet,* pp. 344-346. For Eden's reflections on the meeting, see The Rebbe's interview with Israeli radio: Islam and the Arab world [https:// videos.jem.tv/video-player?clip=684]. For a video lecture by Rabbi Elkanah Shmotkin analyzing the interview, see JEM Presents — Motti Eden — Motivating The Youth [https://videos.jem.tv/ video-player?produced=2587]; "I'm Speaking of This for the First Time" | Private Recording of the Rebbe (Motivating the Youth) [https://www. youtube.com/watch?v=C6olYW1f2RE].

33 See *B'Rega HaEmet,* p. 151.

All the quotes from the Rebbe in this section are from the Motti Eden interview.

34 To corroborate the Rebbe's account, consider Kanaaneh, A. (2021). *Hezbollah in Lebanon* (Hebrew). Jerusalem: Y.L. Magnes Press — The Hebrew University. pp. 103-130. Kanaaneh describes how earlier Shi'ite scholars tended to be apolitical and in many countries were subservient to the financial elites. By the 1950s, a new generation of young scholars and religious activists were vocal about creating religious opposition movements. The local state establishments found these developments alarming as they threatened to undermine state authority. These scholars ultimately fomented the Iranian revolution and formed terrorist groups such as the Iranian revolutionary guard, Hezbollah, and others.

35 For a historical overview of this shift, see *B'Rega HaEmet,* pp. 336-344. For a historical retrospective, see Islamism at 50 in Politics, Power and War | Wilson Center [https:// www.wilsoncenter.org/article/islamism-50], which tracks the Iranian revolution and the development of Islamic fundamentalism and terrorism to the recent decade. For an application of this shift to understanding the recent war, see A New Existential War — Part I: Israel's Perception of the Enemy's Goals [https:// besacenter.org/a-new-existential-war-part-i-israels-perception-of-the-enemys-goals/]. There, Maj. Gen. (res.) Gershon Hacohen writes:

In the spiritual-cultural dimension as well, a new narrative is required. For years, it has been argued that economic development and prosperity for the Palestinians and the countries in the region are the key to achieving stability and order. But Hamas's leadership has taught us that its conduct is guided not by the Palestinians' economic situation but by a deep religious rationale. Western cultural observers, who for centuries have separated religious motives from the political, diplomatic, and military considerations of state leaders, have no tools with which to understand the leadership of Iran, Hezbollah, and Hamas, which are driven by religious conviction and carry out their daily work guided by faith.

The leadership of Hamas in Gaza, as an affiliate of the Muslim Brotherhood, embodies the new Islamic integration of religious, political, civic, and military interests. The fractures and divisions within Israeli society over the past year were seen as a divine omen that this was the time when the gates of heaven would open to herald their redemption. Muslim religious leaders and military strategists predicted years ago that this period would mark the beginning of the end for Israel.

Two years ago, a conference called "The End of Days" was held in Gaza where an approach was designed to advance the "end of the occupation." At the end of 2022, Palestinian writer Bassam Jarrar declared it the "year of reversal." Religious dreams and prophecies among Muslims led to a belief that the time had come for the revelation, and that what was required of them was military action. Mohammad Deif, head of Hamas's military wing, named the current war "Tufan al-Aqsa" [al-Aqssa flood] in the belief that through this battle, a great cosmic salvation would unfold.

36 See Westernization and the Decline of Collective Culture | The Jewish Agency [https://archive.jewishagency.org/israeli-culture/content/35871/].

37 Presumably, the Rebbe refers to the fact that "by the 20th century, the population of the Levant [the area including Israel, Lebanon, Jordan, and Syria] was lower than in Roman times." See https://unchartedterritories.tomaspueyo.com/p/who-can-claim-palestine. See also Demographic history of Palestine (region) — Wikipedia

[https://en.wikipedia.org/wiki/Demographic_history_of_Palestine_(region)]. The Land of Israel's population dropped precipitously after the Romans crushed the Bar Kochba rebellion in 133 CE, and did not recover until around 1930. Meaning to say, Israel has only had a large population during Jewish majority periods. In fact, since 1900, the Palestinian population has grown by a multiple of 12.5, increasing from 500,000 in 1900 to close to 7 million today.

38 Psalms 8:3.

39 Edward Luttwak explains that Israel's vulnerability to the October 7 attacks derived from Israel's government mistakenly believing that Hamas favored economic prosperity for the residents of Gaza over the commitment of violence against Israel. See Israel's Intelligence Failure — Tablet Magazine [https://www.tabletmag.com/sections/israel-middle-east/articles/israel-intelligence-failure-hamas-edward-luttwak].

40 Psalms 8:3.

41 See *Karasi V'ein Oneh*, Vol. 1, p. 76, *Vayeishev* 5734 (1973).

42 See *Karasi V'Ein Oneh*, Vol. 1, p. 92, *Bereishis* 5735 (1974).

43 *Karasi V'ein Oneh*, Vol. 1, pp. 166-167, 13 Tishrei 5737 (1976).

44 Rabin in Hebron / Yom Kippur Riot in Machpela Cave [http://en.hebron.org.il/history/963].

45 Psalms 29:11.

46 See *Karasi V'Ein Oneh*, Vol. 1, p. 154, Rosh Chodesh Iyar 5736 (1976).

47 Notably, this thinking was another dominant theme in the Rebbe's forming *Tzivos Hashem*. The Rebbe argued that Western hedonism and individualism were undermining society writ large. Thus, the militaristic imagery, with ranks and responsibilities, was calculated to raise a generation of children with a sense of responsibility and loyalty to G-d, their families, and the Jewish people at large. See Creating a Children's "Army" of G-d — Chabad.org [https://www.chabad.org/therebbe/letters/default_cdo/

aid/1237192/jewish/Creating-a-Childrens-Army-of-G-d.htm]. Nonetheless, the Rebbe noted that he had no intention to undermine individuality, but rather to ensure that individualism should not be antagonistic to responsibility. See *Igros Kodesh*, Vol. 23, pp. 263-268, Letter #8,885 [https://www.chabad.org/therebbe/article_cdo/aid/5413637/jewish/page.htm]. See also Kraus, Y. (2007). *HaShvi'i*. Miskal. pp. 193-196; *Sichos Kodesh 5741*, Vol. 4, p. 152, 12 Tammuz (1981).

48 *Karasi V'Ein Oneh*, Vol. 1, p. 420, Motzaei Shabbos *Ki Sissa* 5739 (1979).

49 Curtis Yarvin; see UR's advice for President Musharraf | Unqualified Reservations [https://www.unqualified-reservations.org/2007/11/urs-advice-for-president-musharraf/]. This suggestion is not just a theory articulated by Yarvin, but reflects the present practice in the United Arab Emirates (UAE), where Islam is the state religion. Alarmed by the spread of radical Islam and the resulting destabilization, the UAE has chosen to strictly regulate religious practice in the country. The Islamic Affairs and Charitable Activities Department (IACAD) in Dubai provides a range of services related to Islamic religious matters, including licensing and approving the publication and distribution of Islamic materials, issuing official *fatwas* (Islamic legal rulings), providing religious scholars and preachers, offering consultations, and facilitating educational programs. See, for example, approval to publish and print Islamic materials [https://www.iacad.gov.ae/en/services/new-request-issuance-of-permit-for-publication-or-printing-of-islamic-materials]. The purpose is to promote religious awareness and guidance in accordance with Islamic principles, with some restrictions on content that instigate conflicts or undermine state security. Administrative Resolution No. (9) of 2020 sets out the rules and procedures for licensing religious activities in Dubai (Laws & Legislations Islamic Affairs [https://www.iacad.gov.ae/en/about-us/laws-and-legistlations]). The UAE has been a leader in attempting to find solutions to Islamic extremism, with initiatives such as Hedayah [http://Hedayah.com], an organization that identifies and offers counter-narratives for extremism. Israel could institute a similar system, which would allow for thriving religious freedom but cancel terrorist incitement. For the previous Israeli government's policies of censoring antisemitic and hostile material in Arab textbooks used within Israel, see https://www.davar1.co.il/94764/. There, we read of a meeting that took place in 1967:

At the cabinet meeting on August 7, 1967, the ministers deliberated on what to do with the existing [Arab] textbooks, which contained harsh anti-Israeli content, and which curriculum to teach. It was decided to examine the existing books with the aim of allowing their use after censoring particularly problematic passages.

50 *Sichos Kodesh 5734*, Vol. 1, pp. 148-152, 19 Kislev (1973). See How war tactics have changed — and what it means for YOU [https://www.youtube.com/watch?v=BHOlvgOQ-J4&list=PLkXcDdOrqRird5k5aYocVFZ7NlZN39azU&index=10]. See also *Igros Kodesh*, Vol. 29, pp. 69-70, Letter #11,035 to Brigadier General Pinchas Lahav, Chief IDF Spokesperson, dated 15 Teves 5734 (1973).

51 Joel 4:10. See also *Igros Kodesh, Rebbe Rayatz*, Vol. 11, pp. 27, 38; *Sefer HaMaamarim 5682*, p. 129 (1922); *Sefer HaMaamarim 5706*, p. 99 (1946); *Sefer HaMaamarim 5714*, p. 132 (1954). See *Sefer HaMaamarim 5718*, p. 492 (1958). There, the Rebbe teaches:

When a person declares, "I am mighty," and this declaration truly touches him to the core, this then awakens his inner potential such that he will access powers thus far hidden to him. For example, the ability to lift things that he thought he could not, or to traverse distances that he thought were beyond him.

See *Toras Menachem 5726*, p. 190. There, the Rebbe explains the verse as follows:

This is the meaning of [the verse,] "the weak will say I am mighty." At first glance, what good is the mere statement if, in fact, the person is physically weaker? The answer is that a weak person does not tap into their latent potential, while a strong person does. Therefore, someone who is physically weak, but nonetheless declares that they are strong, truly becomes strong, since by virtue of this declaration, one accesses their latent potential.

52 Psalms 127:1.

53 Psalms 127:1.

54 Psalms 20:6.

55 Strategic theory stresses morale's importance. In Claude Von Clausewitz's classic work, *On War*, he discusses morale in every chapter. He examines the concept of morale from a theoretical perspective, and also evaluates the morale of various armies in the numerous case studies he conducts. As he put it: "The courage and morale of an army have always increased its physical strength, and always will." See Clausewitz, C. (1976). *On War*. p. 282. The importance of devoting special attention to morale and it being a key factor in winning wars and aiding soldiers has been a prevalent theme in the thinking of many officers in the U.S. military. Consider Vaughn, T. B., Lieutenant Colonel (P), U.S. Army. (1982). *Morale — The Tenth Principle of War?*. U.S. Army War College, Carlisle Barracks; Kisner, F. J., Lieutenant Colonel, USAF. (2000). *Morale—The 10th Principle of War: Returning the Art to the Science of War*. Naval War College; Michaelis, K. A., Lieutenant Commander, U.S. Navy. (2000). *Considering Morale as the Tenth Principle of War*. Naval War College; Kulifay, B. E., Jr., Colonel, United States Army. (2000). *The Missing Principle of War*. Naval War College; Cain, M. C., MAJ, U.S. Army. (2019). *Morale — Sustaining the Cognitive Weapon of War: Insights from the World War II Special Services Division*. Monograph, U.S. Army School of Advanced Military Studies, U.S. Army Command and General Staff College, Fort Leavenworth, KS.

56 On the difference between *emunah* and *bitachon*, see *Shaarei Emunah*, pp. 115-116. The Rebbe explains that *emunah* (faith) is a constant attitude, while *bitachon* (security) is an attitude one should have in times of crisis. Despite the crisis, one remains "secure" in their faith and belief that G-d will rescue them. See Faith and Trust — Chabad.org [https://www.chabad.org/therebbe/article_cdo/aid/2296503/jewish/Faith-and-Trust.htm].

57 As the Rebbe put it in a different context, in order to lift the soldier's spirits, the military leadership "brings them singers from New York and London to distract them." See *Sichos Kodesh 5734*, Vol. 1, p. 119, *Noach*; *Karasi V'Ein Oneh*, Vol. 1, p. 70, *Noach 5734* (1973).

58 See *Igros Kodesh*, Vol. 29, pp. 128-131; *Likkutei Sichos*, Vol. 1, p. 112; *Likkutei Sichos*, Vol. 6, p. 379; *Karasi V'Ein Oneh*, Vol. 1, p. 152, 11 Nissan 5731 (1971). The Rebbe explains that every generation has its own unique "idolatry," prevailing cultural trends that seem to be "reality" and seduce a person to not follow G-d's Will.

59 See also *Likkutei Sichos*, Vol. 9, p. 421.

60 Following the verse from Deuteronomy 23:15: "and your camp shall be holy."

61 Deuteronomy 23:15.

62 Exodus 15:16.

63 For example, we see that when soldiers are religiously motivated, they are more inspired to fight for the Land of Israel.

64 *Sichos Kodesh 5736*, Vol. 2, p. 231, Rosh Chodesh Sivan (1976).

65 Ran Ronen-Pekker — Wikipedia [https://en.wikipedia.org/wiki/Ran_Ronen-Pekker].

66 *Pegishot Im HaRabbi*, p. 104; cited in *B'Rega HaEmet*, pp. 165-166. For a further dimension of the encounter and Pekker's relationship with the Rebbe, see The View from 50,000 Feet — JEM [https://jemedia.org/email/newsletter/My_Encounter/3-Tammuz-74-v2.pdf].

67 Torahs Being Written in Merit of IDF Soldiers, Hostages [https://collive.com/torahs-being-written-in-merit-of-idf-soldiers-hostages/]; A Letter in the Sefer Torah Brings Protection — Chabad.org [https://www.chabad.org/multimedia/video_cdo/aid/4424364/jewish/A-Letter-in-the-Sefer-Torah-Brings-Protection.htm].

68 *Toras Menachem — Hisvaaduyos 5742*, p. 606, 2nd Night of Chanukah (1981).

69 See *Karasi V'Ein Oneh*, Vol. 1, p. 91, Simchas Torah 5735 (1974). There, the Rebbe explains the importance of Torah study and particularly of establishing *yeshivos* that are solely dedicated to Torah study, without delving into foreign ideologies. He notes that this will create an ideological climate where giving away land is not an option. Similarly, on 27 Tishrei 5734 (1973), the Rebbe told Rabbi Tuvyah Blau in a *yechidus* that encouraging Jews to put on *tefillin* would likewise have this effect. The Rebbe focused on the fact that *tefillin* call Jews to submit their

hearts and minds to G-d, and thus to His Will, which is that the Jewish people not give away land. For a record of this encounter, see *Heichal Menachem,* Vol. 1, p. 228; Riterman, Z. (2008). *HaTefillin.* p. 228. Kiryat Malakhi.

CHAPTER 10

1 See *Karasi V'Ein Oneh,* Vol. 1, pp. 227-228, 24 Teves 5738 (1978).

2 *Karasi V'Ein Oneh,* Vol. 1, p. 191, 12 Tammuz 5737 (1977).

3 See Ezekiel 20:32.

4 The Rebbe offers the example of disseminating the Seven Noahide Laws (see *Sandhedrin* 57a; *Mishneh Torah, Hilchos Melachim,* Ch. 9) as a means of fulfilling the Jewish people's role as a light unto the nations. Being a light unto the nations demands Jews to stand firmly in their own values and share them with the world, rather than adopting the dominant culture's values and presenting them as Jewish ones. However, the Rebbe's project of being a light unto the nations was more expansive than just disseminating the Seven Noahide Laws. His approach included far-reaching campaigns, such as introducing a nationwide moment of silence in public schools to encourage American students to reflect on the presence and importance of G-d in their lives.

5 *Karasi V'Ein Oneh,* Vol. 2, p. 309, 6th Night of Sukkos 5743 (1982); Audio of Sichah [https://ashreinu.app/player?parentEvent=4022&event=4022].

6 See Psalms 81:10. In this context, "the foreign g-d within" is a metaphor referring to internalizing non-Jewish values, which leads one to lack confidence in their claim to the Land.

7 Psalms 103:20.

8 I.e., ultimately G-d rules the world. See *Bereishis Rabbah* 39:1 for the source of this metaphor.

9 Proverbs 21:1.

10 *Karasi V'Ein Oneh,* Vol. 2, p. 353, *Bo* 5744 (1984).

11 *Karasi V'Ein Oneh,* Vol. 2, p. 330, 10 Teves 5743 (1982).

12 The tragic story of the spies is the subject of Numbers Chs. 13-14.

13 Numbers 13:33.

14 See *Karasi V'Ein Oneh,* Vol. 1, p. 60, 20 Menachem Av 5731 (1971); Audio of Sichah [https://ashreinu.app/player?parentEvent=5949&event=5957]; p. 181, 2nd Day of Shavuos 5737 (1977); pp. 412-414, 421, Motzaei Shabbos *Ki Sissa* 5739 (1979); Audio of Sichah [https://ashreinu.app/player?parentEvent=2947&event=2952]; pp. 423-424, Motzaei Shabbos *Vayakhel-Pekudei* 5739 (1979); Audio of Sichah [https://ashreinu.app/player?parentEvent=5949&event=5957]; pp. 456-458, 13 Tammuz 5739 (1979).

15 Numbers 14:9.

16 *Karasi V'Ein Oneh,* Vol. 1, p. 60, 20 Menachem Av 5731 (1971).

17 Numbers 14:9.

18 *Karasi V'Ein Oneh,* Vol. 1, p. 423, Motzaei Shabbos *Vayakhel-Pekudei* 5739 (1979).

19 See *Karasi V'Ein Oneh,* Vol. 2, p. 90, *Shlach* 5740 (1980); pp. 91-92, *Korach* 5740 (1980).

20 Leviticus 26:36.

21 *Karasi V'Ein Oneh,* Vol. 1, p. 247, Motzaei Shabbos *Mishpatim* 5738 (1978).

22 See Judges 9:36 and Psalms 80:11 for the source of the metaphor "shadow of the mountains." For a similar application of the phrase, see *Karasi V'Ein Oneh*, Vol. 1, p. 421, Motzaei Shabbos *Ki Sissa* 5739 (1979); *Sichos Kodesh 5741*, Vol. 1, p. 767, *Vayechi* (1981). The term appears in Talmudic discourse, and is used in the letters of the Rebbe Rayatz and of the Rebbe to describe the specter of a seemingly imposing phenomenon. See *Igros Kodesh, Rebbe Rayatz*, Vol. 17, p. 281, Letter #6,561; *Igros Kodesh*, Vol. 4, p. 128, Letter #869; Vol. 25, p. 84, Letter #9,445.

23 *Karasi V'Ein Oneh*, Vol. 2, pp. 21-22, 5th Night of Chanukah 5740 (1979).

24 Genesis 42:18.

25 See, for example, *Tanya, Iggeres HaKodesh*, Epistle 4. The theme is pervasive in Tanya, referenced in Chs. 6, 19, 32, and 35, among others.

26 *Karasi V'Ein Oneh*, Vol. 2, p. 330, 10 Teves 5743 (1982).

27 Isaiah 32:15.

28 Genesis 47:30.

29 This is a pervasive theme in chassidic thought. See, for example, *Sichos Kodesh 5710-5711*, p. 60, 9 Kislev 5711 (1950); p. 78, 19 Kislev 5711 (1950). See also *Tzavaas HaRivash*, pp. 122-123 (Kehot, 1998); *Sefer HaSichos— Toras Shalom*, pp. 12, 22, 229, 250; *HaKeriah VehaKedushah 5701*, p. 111; *Kuntres Ha'Ashirus*, p. 63.

30 Ethics of the Fathers 5:2.

31 See *Beis Yosef, Orach Chaim*, 1:1; Alter Rebbe's *Shulchan Aruch, Mahadura Tinyana, Orach Chaim*, 1:1; *Kitzur Shulchan Aruch, Orach Chaim*, 1:3, 29:8; *Aruch HaShulchan, Orach Chaim*, 1:16.

32 For more on Nachshon's work, see F. Brod. (2006). *Sipur ishi* [Personal story], Vol. 1. (Hebrew). *Kfar Chabad.* pp. 33-39. In this source, Miriam Levinger recalls that Nachshon's efforts for the burial empowered the women to have faith in the plan to reclaim Beit Hadassah. Devorah Attia observed to the author that her mother acted in the tradition of the biblical hero Nachshon, who had faith and jumped into the Red Sea before it split, namely, before it was clear that G-d would in fact save the Jewish people (see *Sotah* 37a). See also

Yechiduyos, Vol. 5. pp. 141-160; *Teshurah*, Karlstein, 5783 (2023). Many of the details discussed in this book's presentation are based on interviews the author conducted with Sarah Nachshon, as well as with her daughter Devorah Attia, in April 2024. For oral histories of Nachshon, see Mothers of the Motherland, available at https://jemcentral. org/wp-content/uploads/2023/11/565.-Chayei-Sarah-5784.pdf; Motherhood, Loss and Life: Sarah Nachshon and the Rebirth of Beit Hadassah [https://www.youtube.com/watch?v=Un_yM-l9ML24]; "זכרונות מרת שרה נחשון תי', אלמנת הצייר ר' ברוך ע"ה" [Memories of Mrs. Sarah Nachshon, wife of the artist Baruch], available at https://www.youtube.com/watch?v=Z5wrexC8gNA; "שרה נחשון במערת המכפלה בחברון" [Sarah Nachshon speaks in the Cave of the Patriarchs], available at https://www.youtube.com/watch?v=Z5wrexC8g-NA; Taking Back Hebron — Chabad.org [https://www.chabad.org/library/article_cdo/aid/1104048/jewish/Taking-Back-Hebron.htm]; 1994 Newspaper Clipping with Nachshon's Recollections [https://ranaz.co.il/articles/bigImg.asp?u=https://ranaz.co.il/Images/articles/newsp2/n19940901_1.jpg].

33 22 Adar 5735.

34 22 Tammuz 5735 — July 1, 1975.

35 This account is based on Nachshon's recollections documented in the article "I just wanted to bury my son in the Hebron cemetery." — Sarah Nachshon [https://hebronfund.org/bury-my-son-in-the-hebron-cemetery/], as well as on an April 2024 interview with the author.

36 Rabbi Gedaliah Koenig, a student of Chabad's *Yeshivas Toras Emes* in Jerusalem, became a renowned Breslov teacher and spiritual guide in Jerusalem.

37 Years later, towards the end of his life, Peres ruefully reflected that Nachson's actions had led to the reestablishment of a Jewish settlement in Hebron. The burial cemented Jewish presence in Hebron since, in the aftermath of the burial, residents of Kiryat Arba, most prominently Professor Ben-Tzion Tavger, organized to protect the Jewish cemetery from Arab vandalism. This ultimately pushed the Israeli government to station soldiers near the

Jewish cemetery in the city to make sure that local Arabs would not desecrate the new grave, as they had desecrated the graves of the Jews murdered in the 1929 massacre.

38 Beit Hadassah — From Historic Hospital to Symbol of Rebirth | the Jewish Community of Hebron [http://en.hebron.org.il/history/217].

39 In Memorium: Rabbanit Miriam Levinger | הישוב היהודי בחברון [http://www.hebron.org.il/node/1211].

40 In an April 2024 interview with the author.

41 This community was known as Shalhevet.

42 *Karasi V'Ein Oneh,* Vol. 1, p. 458, 13 Tammuz 5738 (1978).

43 This is a reference to the biblical daughters of Tzelafchad. See Numbers 27:1-7 with *Rashi's* commentary. In contrast to the spies, who spurned G-d's gift of the Land of Israel, the daughters of Tzelafchad demonstrated a tenacious love for the Land and demanded that they receive their rightful portion of it.

44 In an interview with the author, Sarah Nachshon confirmed that this *sichah* was said during her time in Beit Hadassah and that the conquest the Rebbe references is the women settling Beit Hadassah.

45 6 Tishrei 5740. See Audio of Sichah [https://

ashreinu.page.link/bSqV].

46 See Numbers 27:1-11.

47 For an account of the struggle for Beit Hadassah and, more broadly, Hebron, with interviews of Miriam Levinger and Sarah Nachshon, see JEM's film "Pride of Ownership," available at https://videos.jem.tv/video-player?clip=9379.

48 Esther 3:2.

49 *Karasi V'Ein Oneh,* Vol. 2, p. 45, Purim 5740 (1980).

50 *Karasi V'Ein Oneh,* Vol. 2, pp. 48-50, Purim 5740 (1980).

51 *Toras Menachem 5742,* Vol. 2, p. 926; *Karasi V'Ein Oneh,* Vol. 2, p. 212, 12 Adar 5742 (1982); Audio of Sichah [https://ashreinu.app/player?parentEvent=3772&event=3775].

52 Isaiah 8:10.

53 Esther 8:17.

54 Psalms 29:11.

55 See *Mechilta D'Rabbi Shimon Bar Yochai* 19:16; *Shir HaShirim Rabbah,* 1, s.v. *Mashcheini.*

56 *Karasi V'Ein Oneh,* Vol. 1, p. 123, 19 Kislev 5736 (1975).

CHAPTER 11

1 See commentary in *Toras Menachem 5725,* Vol. 3, pp. 35-38 (1965).

2 For a comprehensive analysis of the Israeli-American relationship and its evolution over time, particularly through the lens of the politics of self-interest, see Bar-Siman-Tov, Y. (1998). *The United States and Israel since 1948: A "Special Relationship"?* Diplomatic History, Oxford University Press, 22(2), 231-262. Bar-Siman-Tov examines the ebbs and flows of the relationship between the two nations, highlighting the role of strategic interests in shaping their interactions and the development of the "special relationship"

that has come to define their alliance.

3 For example, the global perception that the United States and Israel are allies is likely partially responsible for the Houthi chant: "Death to America! Death to Israel! Death to the Jews!"

4 As of 2020. See Jeremy M. Sharp, *"Foreign Aid to Israel,"* Congressional Research Service, updated November 16, 2020 [https://crsreports.congress.gov/product/pdf/RL/RL33222/41#:~:text=To%20date%2C%20the%20United%20States,also%20received%20significant%20economic%20assistance].

5 U.S. Navy Office of Information, *"Ike Carrier Strike Group Arrives in Middle East Region,"* Navy News Service, November 4, 2023. See https://www.navy.mil/Press-Office/News-Stories/Article/3580122/ike-carrier-strike-group-arrives-in-middle-east-region/; https://edition.cnn.com/2023/11/03/politics/us-military-buildup-middle-east-dg/index.html.

6 https://edition.cnn.com/2023/12/03/politics/uss-carney-shoots-down-houthi-drones-red-sea/index.html.

7 The United States has pressured Israel to make concessions in order to serve perceived U.S. geopolitical interests since before the 1967 Six-Day War. For example, during the 1956 Suez Crisis, the United States pressured Israel to withdraw from the Sinai Peninsula, citing concerns about the balance of power in the region. This hampered Israel's victory and considerably weakened Israel's position in the lead-up to the Six-Day War.

8 During the Cold War, U.S. and Soviet diplomats orchestrated Middle Eastern geopolitics, aiming to achieve a balance of power that would serve their respective interests. U.S. Secretary of State Henry Kissinger worked particularly hard to prevent Israel from decisively defeating the Arab states during the 1973 Yom Kippur War. See *"Kissinger Told Soviet Envoy during 1973 Arab-Israeli War: 'My Nightmare is a Victory for Either Side,'"* National Security Archive, August 9, 2019 [https://nsarchive.gwu.edu/briefing-book/henry-kissinger/2019-08-09/kissinger-told-soviet-envoy-during-1973-arab-israeli-war-my-nightmare-victory-either-side-soviet].

9 See *"Battle of the Letters, 1963: John F. Kennedy, David Ben-Gurion, Levi Eshkol, and the U.S. Inspections of Dimona,"* National Security Archive, May 2, 2019 [https://nsarchive.gwu.edu/briefing-book/nuclear-vault/2019-05-02/battle-letters-1963-john-f-kennedy-david-ben-gurion-levi-eshkol-us-inspections-dimona].

10 See *Karasi V'Ein Oneh,* Vol. 1, pp. 82-84, *Emor* 5734 (1974).

11 See *Sichos Kodesh 5737,* Vol. 1, p. 537 (1977); *Sichos Kodesh 5740,* Vol. 1, p. 56 (1980). See also *Sichos Kodesh 5735,* Vol. 1, p. 333 (1975), where the Rebbe explicitly raises this point in discussing U.S. military aid to Israel. See *Karasi V'Ein Oneh,* Vol. 1, p. 352, Simchas Torah 5739 (1978), where the Rebbe suggests that this should motivate the United States not to adopt policies which harm Israel. For the Rebbe's extended analysis of America's virtues, see *Toras Menachem Hisvaaduyos 5747,* Vol. 2, pp. 53-57 (1987).

12 See *Yechidus* with Israeli Air Force pilot Ran Ronen-Pekker, 5735 (1975); cited in *Karasi V'Ein Oneh,* Vol. 1, p. 135. See also *Yom Yom Im HaRabbi, Chodesh Mar Cheshvan,* p. 301. Records of this *yechidus* are also contained in JEM's *My Story,* Vol. 1, pp. 77-100.

13 Henry Kissinger, the famed U.S. Secretary of State from 1973 to 1977, played a key role in shaping State Department decisions during the Yom Kippur War and the Camp David Accords.

14 See *Yechidus* with Israeli Air Force pilot Ran Ronen-Pekker, 5735 (1975); cited in *Karasi V'Ein Oneh,* Vol. 1, p. 135. See also *Yom Yom Im HaRabbi, Chodesh Mar Cheshvan,* p. 301.

15 *Karasi V'Ein Oneh,* Vol. 2, p. 130, *Shemini* 5741 (1981).

16 Roughly Israel's population at the time.

17 *Yom Yom Im HaRabbi, Chodesh Mar Cheshvan,* p. 301.

18 *Karasi V'Ein Oneh,* Vol. 2, pp. 186-188, 19 Kislev 5742 (1982).

19 The Rebbe analyzed the political dynamics at play during the Camp David Accords, likening it to a game of chess between the United States, Israel, and Egypt. He asserted that Israel held the strongest position and could have been more resolute in its demands as, compared to the other parties involved, it had the least need for a deal. President Jimmy Carter was eager to secure a peace agreement in the Middle East, hoping to establish it as a defining legacy of his presidency. On the other hand, Egyptian President Anwar Sadat found himself in a precarious position, having isolated Egypt from both the Soviet Union and the Arab world. Sadat was in dire need of American aid and support to bolster his country's economy and standing in the region.

Recognizing the desperation of both Carter and Sadat to reach an agreement, the Rebbe argued that Israel had a unique opportunity to negotiate from a position of strength. By being more resolute in its demands and leveraging the other parties' need for a deal, Israel could have secured an outcome that better served its own interests.

The Rebbe's insights highlight the importance of understanding the motivations and constraints of all parties involved in a negotiation. By accurately assessing the political landscape and the relative bargaining power of each side, a nation can make strategic decisions that maximize its own benefits and safeguard its long-term security and prosperity.

20 19 Tishrei 5741 (1981). See *Sichos Kodesh 5741*, Vol. 1, p. 17 (1981); Video of Sichah [https://videos.jem.tv/video-player?position=326127.662&clip=730].

21 Deuteronomy 8:18.

22 Audience with the mayor of Ariel, 28 Tishrei 5752 (Oct. 6, 1991). For the video of this encounter, see Syria and Iran — JEM [https://videos.jem.tv/video-player?clip=7410https://videos.jem.tv/video-player?clip=7410]; The Rebbe to Israeli politician: How to talk to Americans about Israel [https://www.youtube.com/watch?v=7hObtm7wQ7c]; transcript printed in *Karasi V'Ein Oneh*, Vol. 2, p. 425.

23 The delivery of advanced U.S. fighter aircraft to Israel in 1972, notably the F-4 Phantom II and A-4 Skyhawk, was the first significant game-changing technology offered by the United States to Israel. This development marked a significant upgrade in Israel's air combat capabilities. See U.S. SAID TO AGREE TO SUPPLY ISRAEL 42 PHANTOM JETS — The New York Times [https://www.nytimes.com/1972/02/06/archives/us-said-to-agree-to-supply-israel-42-phantom-jets-90-skyhawks.html].

The United States had previously refused to sell these warplanes to Israel in 1965, highlighting the significance of this policy shift. See McDonnell Douglas F-4 Phantom (Hebrew

nickname: 'Kurnas' ('Sledgehammer')) [https://www.iaf.org.il/184-18176-en/IAF.aspx?indx=1].

The decision to provide Israel with these advanced fighter jets marked a turning point in U.S.-Israeli relations and had far-reaching implications for Israel's military capabilities and regional security. For an extended analysis of this development, see Bar-Siman-Tov, Y. (1998). *The United States and Israel since 1948: A "Special Relationship"?* Diplomatic History, Oxford University Press, 22(2), 231-262.

24 For more on this, see Bar-Siman-Tov, Y. (1998).

25 See *Sichos Kodesh 5730*, Vol. 2, p. 460-3; *Toras Menachem 5730*, Vol. 4, pp. 159-160, 188 (1970). In these *sichos*, the Rebbe discusses that although the United States gave Israel advanced fighter technology, such as the Phantom fighter jet, Israel lost this military advantage once it withdrew from the Sinai. Following the withdrawal, Egypt began to build fortifications that could withstand the Phantom. This led to a strengthened Egyptian position and resultant Israeli casualties during the Yom Kippur War.

26 See *Igros Kodesh*, Vol. 26, pp. 75-78, Letter #9,638.

27 For more on the role of NGOs (non-governmental organizations), see Arnon-Ohana, Y. (2013). *Line of Furrow and Fire: The Conflict for the Land of Israel 1860-2010.* Achiasaf Ltd. p. 75. To illustrate just how lucrative the conflict is for NGOs, consider the following from Ohana:

From June 2005 to January 2010, the European Union transferred 177 Million Shekel to NGOs in Israel and the Palestinian territories. The NGOs proceed to use this money to engage in lawfare, boycott campaigns, and other activities to isolate Israel on the international stage.

For more on the lucrative character of NGOs, see NGO Monitor [https://www.ngo-monitor.org/].

28 For an analysis of this point, see Do Arab States Support Palestine? — by Tomas Pueyo [https://unchartedterritories.tomaspueyo.com/p/do-arab-states-support-palestine].

In Pueyo's words:

Whereas all these countries kept Palestinian refugees in the past to pressure for a Palestinian state or the elimination of Israel, now they keep them as a bargaining chip. Keeping the problem festering gives an excuse to get more money and weapons from the U.S., and if there's ever a resolution, resettling them in Arab countries would be a huge negotiation tool they would lose if they simply made them citizens today.

Moreover, the Palestinian leadership benefits heavily from perpetuating the conflict. Consider Pueyo's commentary on Yasser Arafat in The Struggle for the Soul of Israel — by Tomas Pueyo [https://unchartedterritories. tomaspueyo.com/p/the-struggle-for-the-soul-of-israel]:

Why did Arafat walk away from Camp David without even a counter-offer? Why was he so wary of the negotiations to begin with? One of the hypotheses is that he didn't want peace. Maybe it's linked to the billions of dollars he controlled in personal accounts, or the arms deals he might have been involved with, or the Palestinian preference for violence at that time.

Consider also Yarvin, C. (2008, May 15). *The shortest way to world peace.* Unqualified Reservations; https://www.unqualified-reservations. org/2008/05/ol5-shortest-way-to-world-peace/. In Yarvin's words:

Hating Israel is the national industry of Palestine. That is, via American and European aid, it generates more or less the entire Palestinian GDP. If Palestinians stop attacking Israel, if they just settle down and live their lives like the normal people they are, there will be no reason for anyone to give them money. And the money will stop.

29 Earlier in this chapter, we saw that Henry Kissinger explicitly stated that he intended to maintain "a balance of power" with the aim of protecting perceived American interests. While the Rebbe offered his commentary in the context of Cold War dynamics, a very similar dynamic holds in the contemporary geopolitical situation

30 For extensive exploration of this point and geopolitical analysis, see Will Israel Be at War? — by Tomas Pueyo [https://unchartedterritories. tomaspueyo.com/p/will-israel-be-at-war].

31 Deuteronomy 11:12.

32 Psalms 121:4.

33 II Samuel 7:23.

34 Leviticus 26:6.

35 The Suez Canal was a man-made waterway connecting the Mediterranean Sea to the Red Sea. The canal, opened in 1869, serves as a crucial shipping route, greatly reducing the distance between Europe and Asia. Its strategic location and economic importance have made it a focal point of international politics for over a century. In 1956, Egyptian President Gamal Abdel Nasser nationalized the Suez Canal, which had previously been controlled by the British and French-owned Suez Canal Company. This action, coupled with rising tensions between Egypt and Israel, led to the Suez Crisis. Israel, with the support of France and the United Kingdom, launched a military offensive against Egypt, occupying the Sinai Peninsula and the Gaza Strip. However, under intense international pressure, particularly from the United States, Israel, France, and the United Kingdom were forced to withdraw their troops. Israel reluctantly agreed to pull back from the Sinai Peninsula and the Gaza Strip in early 1957. See The Sinai Campaign | IDF [https://www.idf.il/en/mini-sites/wars-and-operations/the-sinai-campaign/].

36 *Sichos Kodesh 5739*, Vol. 2, p. 730; *Karasi V'Ein Oneh*, Vol. 1, pp. 434-435, *Bamidbar 5739* (1979); Audio of Sichah [https://ashreinu.page. link/xcVy].

37 *Sichos Kodesh 5738*, Vol. 1, pp. 230-231; *Karasi V'Ein Oneh*, Vol. 1, pp. 216-217, Motzaei Shabbos *Vayeitzei 5738* (1977); Audio of Sichah [https://ashreinu.app/player?parentEvent= 2511&event=2514].

38 *Karasi V'Ein Oneh*, Vol. 1, pp. 462-463, 15 Tammuz 5739 (1979).

39 The United States relies heavily on oil

imports from the Middle East, and political leaders feared that supporting Israel could jeopardize relationships with oil-producing Arab nations.

40 See Deuteronomy 4:6, where the phrase "wise and understanding nation" is used to describe the Jewish people.

41 For example, a president might push for a peace agreement to improve their standing in upcoming elections. See *Karasi V'Ein Oneh*, Vol. 1, p. 340, Motzaei Shabbos *Haazinu* 5739 (1978); Vol. 2, p. 116, 10 Shvat 5741 (1981); p. 343, *Mikeitz* 5744 (1983). Alternatively, they might not have a personal stake in the deal, but cave to pressure from the State Department. See *Karasi V'Ein Oneh*, Vol. 2, p. 373, Motzaei Zos Chanukah 5746 (1985).

42 *Toras Menachem* 5742, Vol. 3, pp. 1,723-1,724; *Karasi V'Ein Oneh*, Vol. 2, p. 235, 3 Tammuz 5742 (1982); Audio of Sichah [https://ashreinu.page.link/w5eP].

43 *Sefer HaSichos* 5744, Vol. 2, p. 38, *Mikeitz*; *Karasi V'Ein Oneh*, Vol. 2, p. 343, *Mikeitz* 5744 (1983).

44 *Sichos Kodesh* 5739, Vol. 1, pp. 101-103; *Karasi V'Ein Oneh*, Vol. 1, p. 339, Motzaei Shabbos *Haazinu* 5739 (1978); Audio of Sichah [https://ashreinu.page.link/zrCh].

45 *Karasi V'Ein Oneh*, Vol. 2, p. 373, Motzaei Zos Chanukah 5746 (1985).

46 Menachem Begin and his cabinet.

47 Israel's Gaza Ground Invasion and the Return of "Strategic Depth" — War on the Rocks [https://warontherocks.com/2023/12/israels-gaza-ground-invasion-and-the-return-of-strategic-depth/].

48 See *Sichos Kodesh* 5730, Vol. 2, p. 460-1; *Toras Menachem* 5730, Vol. 4, pp. 155-156; *Karasi V'Ein Oneh*, Vol. 1, p. 41, *Eikev* 5730 (1970).

49 United States announces that it will recognize communist China | December 15, 1978 | HISTORY [https://www.history.com/this-day-in-history/united-states-announces-that-it-will-recognize-communist-china]. Note that although China and Russia were both communist, after the Sino-Soviet split, the two countries moved apart ideologically and in terms of policy. The State Department made the bet that it could develop a relationship with China and isolate Russia.

50 See *Sichos Kodesh* 5739, Vol. 1, pp. 447-448; *Karasi V'Ein Oneh*, Vol. 1, p. 394 (1979). See also *Shalom Shalom V'Ein Shalom*, p. 138; *Daas Torah*, pp. 105-106.

51 See *Sichos Kodesh* 5740, Vol. 3, pp. 1,139-1,140 (1980); Video of Sichah [https://videos.jem.tv/video-player?clip=729] 0.28-0.55.

52 For more on the Rebbe's analysis of the Iranian Revolution, regional instability, and why relying on American promises is unwise, see *Karasi V'Ein Oneh*, Vol. 1, pp. 418-422. See also *Sichos Kodesh* 5739, Vol. 2, p. 248 (1979); *Daas Torah*, p. 116. The Rebbe also suggests that the general American policy of capitulation and concession, showcased by America's behavior at Camp David, led to the fall of the Shah's government and the installation of an anti-American government. For this analysis, see *Sichos Kodesh* 5740, Vol. 1, pp. 567-569, 19 Kislev (1979); Audio of Sichah [https://ashreinu.app/player?parentEvent=3182&event=3185]. Many commentators suggest that similar instability during the Arab Spring resulted from an American display of weakness, which undermined regimes who were broadly more favorable for regional stability and American geopolitical interests.

53 Leading them directly into the arms of America's enemies. See Syrian Kurds request help from Assad regime after US abandons them [https://www.telegraph.co.uk/news/2018/12/28/abandoned-us-syrian-kurds-request-help-assad-regime/].

54 See *Sichos Kodesh* 5739, Vol. 1, p. 446, 19 Kislev (1979); Audio of Sichah [https://ashreinu.app/player?event=2843&parentEvent=2838&share=1].

55 *Karasi V'Ein Oneh*, Vol. 1, pp. 82-84, *Emor* 5734 (1974).

56 *Karasi V'Ein Oneh*, Vol. 1, p. 84, 86, *Emor* 5734 (1974).

57 See *Karasi V'Ein Oneh*, Vol. 1, p. 83, *Emor 5734* (1984). See also *Daas Torah*, p. 76.

58 See *Karasi V'Ein Oneh*, Vol. 1, pp. 53-54, Chanukah 5731 (1970). The Rebbe offered these examples in 1970. While geopolitics have since changed, the essential point remains the same.

59 See *B'Rega HaEmet*, pp. 111-112. See also Halperin, A. D. (2019). *Yechiduyos, Vol. 1.* Kfar Chabad. p. 42. There, Halperin cites Israeli politician Aharon Becker's recollection of his 1970 conversation with the Rebbe (also printed in Becker's autobiography: Becker, A. (1982). *Im hazman ubnei hador* [Of the era and the people of the generation]. *Am Oved*). As he writes:

As the conversation progressed, the Rebbe painted a broader picture of the international landscape, stating that the notion of "the nations of the world" is a misnomer. In reality, there are only three nations that truly matter: the United States, the Soviet Union, and China. He emphasized the importance of maintaining cordial relations with all three. However, given that China is currently alienated, it is crucial to uphold relations with at least the remaining two powers.

See also *Shalom Shalom V'Ein Shalom*, p. 482. This observation still holds true in more recent years. As Curtis Yarvin puts it:

The world of 2008 has one major sovereign state, the U.S. There are two smaller ones, Russia and China. By avoiding dependency on American aid, the oil kingdoms of the Gulf also retained a certain level of sovereignty.

See Yarvin, C. (2008, May 15). *The shortest way to world peace.* Unqualified Reservations; https://www.unqualified-reservations.org/2008/05/ol5-shortest-way-to-world-peace/.

60 However, consider the Rebbe's comments on the structural instability of these regimes. See *Karasi V'Ein Oneh*, Vol. 1, pp. 419-422, *Ki Sissa* 5739 (1979); *Karasi V'Ein Oneh*, Vol. 2, p. 235, 3 Tammuz 5742 (1982). Briefly, the Rebbe argues that since, in these regimes, vast sums of wealth are concentrated in the hands of a small elite, this could create resentment among the general populace, leading to a revolution which would install a hostile government.

61 *Petakim MiShulchano Shel HaRabbi*, Vol. 3, p. 272.

62 IAI Lavi — Wikipedia [https://en.wikipedia.org/wiki/IAI_Lavi]; Killing the Lavi: A Tale of Unintended Consequences — Tablet Magazine]. For a book length study, see Golan, J. W. (2016). *Lavi: The United States, Israel, and a controversial fighter jet.* Naval Institute Press; [https://www.nebraskapress.unl.edu/potomac-books/9781612347226/].

63 Personal communication from Rabbi Elkanah Shmotkin, based on the JEM archive.

64 *Karasi V'Ein Oneh*, Vol. 1, pp. 188-189, 12 Tammuz 5737 (1977).

65 See *Karasi V'Ein Oneh*, Vol. 1, p. 208, *Lech Lecha 5738* (1977); *Petakim MiShulchano Shel HaRabbi*, Vol. 2, p. 256; *Daas Torah*, p. 126.

66 *Igros Kodesh*, Vol. 33, p. 38, Letter #12,259, 11 Mar Cheshvan 5738 (1977).

67 For an excellent overview of the story, see Nakdimon, S. (1987). *First strike: The exclusive story of how Israel foiled Iraq's attempt to get the bomb.* Summit Books. Nakdimon presented the English version of his book to the Rebbe at a meeting on 7 Menachem Av 5750 (1990). The Rebbe encouraged Nakdimon's work.

68 Introduction: GENOCIDE IN IRAQ: The Anfal Campaign Against the Kurds (Human Rights Watch Report, 1993) [https://www.hrw.org/reports/1993/iraqanfal/ANFALINT.htm].

69 Brands, H. & Palkki, D. (Summer 2011). *Saddam, Israel, and the Bomb: Nuclear Alarmism Justified?* International Security, Vol. 36, No. 1, pp. 133-166 [https://doi.org/10.1162/ISEC_a_00047].

70 Baram served in Israeli military intelligence at the beginning of the Iran-Iraq War in 1980. He has served as an expert commentator on Iraq for more than five decades. See Saddam Hussein's Dreams of an End to the Zionist Nightmare [https://web.archive.org/web/20230530124420/https://www.haaretz.com/2012-01-06/ty-article/saddam-husseins-dreams-of-an-end-to-the-zionist-nightmare/0000017f-e8f1-dc91-a17f-fcfdd08c0000]. For the primary source, see The

Saddam tapes: the inner workings of a tyrant's regime, 1978-2001 [https://archive.org/details/isbn_9781107693487].

71 Chardell, D. (2023). *The origins of the Iraqi invasion of Kuwait reconsidered.* Texas National Security Review, 6(3), 51-78 [http://dx.doi.org/10.26153/tsw/47415].

72 The Ba'ath Party was a secular Arab nationalist political party that ruled Iraq from 1968 to 2003 and Syria from 1963 to the present day, promoting socialism, anti-imperialism, and pan-Arab unity.

73 Saddam Hussein's Dreams of an End to the Zionist Nightmare [https://web.archive.org/web/20230530124420/https://www.haaretz.com/2012-01-06/ty-article/saddam-husseins-dreams-of-an-end-to-the-zionist-nightmare/0000017f-e8f1-dc91-a17f-fcfdd08c0000]. For the primary source, see The Saddam tapes: the inner workings of a tyrant's regime, 1978-2001 [https://archive.org/details/isbn_9781107693487].

74 "The Protocols of the Learned Elders of Zion" presents a malicious, fictional portrayal of Jews supposedly engaging in a multi-faceted conspiracy to dominate the world. According to the text, Jews manipulate the media to control public discourse, censor opposing views, and shape political narratives to their advantage. They exploit economic systems, causing financial upheavals, and wield control over global financial institutions to secure economic dominance. The protocols allege that through corruption and infiltration, Jews aim to destabilize political systems and replace them with a totalitarian regime that they control. Furthermore, the text accuses Jews of exacerbating social, ethnic, and racial tensions to weaken societies internally, making them easier to manipulate. It also claims that they undermine traditional cultural values and corrupt educational systems to erode resistance to their influence. The text was taught to Nazi school children and is very popular in the Arab world. Saddam took it at face value.

75 Brands, H., & Palkki, D. (Summer 2011). *Saddam, Israel, and the Bomb: Nuclear Alarmism Justified?* International Security, Vol. 36, No. 1, pp. 133-166.

76 *Sichos Kodesh 5741,* Vol. 3, pp. 476-477, *Bechukosai* (1981). In the *sichah,* the Rebbe refers broadly to the concern of nuclear weapons in the hands of madmen. He continues to say that contemporary madmen brag about their destructive intentions, seemingly a reference to Saddam's bragging about his plans for his nuclear reactor. The Rebbe continues to discuss "a madman in Africa," referring to Muammar Gaddafi, the anti-Israel Islamist leader of Libya with nuclear ambitions. Indeed, in a 1979 letter, Menachem Begin, who would order the destruction of Iraq's reactor, wrote to British Prime Minister Margaret Thatcher, warning her of the dangers of Pakistan's nuclear program and the likelihood that it would offer nuclear capacity to the Gaddafi regime. As Begin put it, Thatcher should consider:

What could happen in the Middle East, and particularly to the men, women, and children in Israel, should the lethal weapons of mass killing and destruction fall, at any time, into the hands of an absolute ruler like Colonel Gaddafi.

For the full letter, see Letter from Israeli PM Menachem Begin to British PM Margaret Thatcher on Pakistan's Nuclear Program [https://digitalarchive.wilsoncenter.org/document/letter-israeli-pm-menachem-begin-british-pm-margaret-thatcher-pakistans-nuclear-program?_gl=1%2Af0z5g4%2A_gcl_au%2AMjUzODYwMDQ0LjE3MTYxNjc0NTg.%2A_ga%2AMzc1MDU5MTgyLjE3MTYxNjc0NTg.%2A_ga_6MDYB7KP94%2AMTcxNjUzMTQ1NC43LjEuMTcxNjUzMTYxNi42MC4wLjA].

77 Mueller, K. P., Castillo, J. J., Morgan, F. E., Pegahi, N., & Rosen, B. (2006). *Striking first: Preemptive and preventive attack in U.S. national security policy.* RAND Corporation. p. 215 [https://www.jstor.org/stable/10.7249/mg403af].

78 Israel conceded this airbase to Egypt in the Camp David Accords. Notably, two of Israel's most storied operations, Operation Entebbe and Operation Opera, were made possible by the Sinai airbases. This further shows how the Camp David Accords injured Israel's national security by depriving it of resources that greatly enhanced its defensive capabilities.

79 Three pilots, however, had died in training for the attack.

80 For detailed descriptions of the operation, see The Israeli Air Force: Operation "Opera" [https://www.iaf.org.il/4694-33056-en/IAF.aspx]; Operation Opera: An Inside Look into one of the Most Famous IDF Operations [https://www.idf.il/en/articles/2023/operation-opera-an-inside-look-into-one-of-the-most-infamous-idf-operations/]; Air Strike at Osirak [https://www.airandspaceforces.com/PDF/MagazineArchive/Documents/2012/April%202012/0412osirak.pdf].

81 ISRAELI AND IRAQI STATEMENTS ON RAID ON NUCLEAR PLANT — The New York Times [https://www.nytimes.com/1981/06/09/world/israeli-and-iraqi-statements-on-raid-on-nuclear-plant.html].

82 See *Daas Torah*, p. 493.

83 Air Strike at Osirak [https://www.airandspaceforces.com/PDF/MagazineArchive/Documents/2012/April%202012/0412osirak.pdf]. See also The Israeli Raid Against the Iraqi Reactor — 40 Years Later: New Insights from the Archives | Wilson Center [https://www.wilsoncenter.org/blog-post/israeli-raid-against-iraqi-reactor-40-years-later-new-insights-archives].

84 Opinion | Israel's Illusion — The New York Times [https://www.nytimes.com/1981/06/09/opinion/israel-s-illusion.html].

85 See the text of the condemnation here: Resolution 487 (1981) [https://digitallibrary.un.org/record/22225].

The resolution contains gems such as:

Deeply concerned about the danger to international peace and security created by the premeditated Israeli air attack on Iraqi nuclear installations on 7 June 1981, which could at any time explode the situation in the area, with grave consequences for the vital interests of all States, 1. Strongly condemns the military attack by Israel in clear violation of the Charter of the United Nations and the norms of international conduct 4. Fully recognizes the inalienable sovereign right of Iraq, and all other States, especially the developing countries, to establish programmes of technological and nuclear development to develop their economy and industry for peaceful purposes in accordance with their present and future needs and consistent with the internationally accepted objectives of preventing nuclear-weapons proliferation.

86 Pulcini, G., & Rabinowitz, O. *An Ounce of Prevention—A Pound of Cure? The Reagan Administration's Nonproliferation Policy and the Osirak Raid*. Journal of Cold War Studies 2021, 23 (2): 4—40. doi: https://doi.org/10.1162/jcws_a_01007 .

87 Three days after the attack. Similarly, on June 16, Reagan wrote a second diary entry in which he approved of the Israeli attack.

88 Reagan, R. (2009). *The Reagan diaries.* Harper Perennial. p. 24 [https://books.google.gr/books?id=MhR5a-2nrhoC&printsec=frontcover&dq=reagan+diaries&hl=en&sa=X&redir_esc=y#v=onepage&q=armegeddon&f=false].

89 Armageddon refers to a final battle that will result in the end of the world.

90 A Lesson from the 1981 Raid on Osirak | Wilson Center [https://www.wilsoncenter.org/blog-post/lesson-the-1981-raid-osirak].

91 See Giordana Pulcini, Or Rabinowitz. An Ounce of Prevention—A Pound of Cure? The Reagan Administration's Nonproliferation Policy and the Osirak Raid [https://doi.org/10.1162/jcws_a_01007]; *Journal of Cold War Studies* 2021; 23 (2): 4—40.

92 *Kovetz Pninei Ha'Asor 5740-5750*, p. 15, 9 Sivan 5741 (1981); *Yechidus* with Rabbi Shlomo Noach Karol, rabbi of the Israeli town Hemed.

93 *Karasi V'Ein Oneh*, Vol. 2, p. 501, Letter to Rabbi Immanuel Jakobovits, Elul 5741 (1981), p. 2 (see Appendix).

94 For extensive analysis of the Rebbe's pronouncements on the Gulf War, see *B'Rega HaEmet*, Ch. 13, pp. 382-407.

95 See the Rebbe's comments on the Gulf war in *Toras Menachem — Hisvaaduyos 5751,* Vol. 1, p. 203, *Bereishis* (1990); *Maayanei HaYeshuah* p. 137 (1990); p. 319, *Chayei Sarah* (1990); *Toras Menachem — Hisvaaduyos 5752,* Vol. 1, p. 297, *Chayei Sarah* (1991). For similar comments regarding global instability, Cold War dynamics, and their implications for Israel, see *Toras Menachem — Hisvaaduyos 5744,* Vol. 3, p. 1,463, *Shabbos HaGadol* (1984); *Toras Menachem — Hisvaaduyos 5747,* Vol. 2, p. 408, 10 Shvat (1987); Vol. 3, p. 58, *Shabbos HaGadol* (1987).

96 Cited in *B'Rega HaEmet,* p. 400.

97 *Toras Menachem — Hisvaaduyos 5751,* Vol. 2, p. 363 (1991).

98 See interview with Shamir's reflections on his relationship with the Rebbe: *A Singular Visionary Gifted With Profound Foresight* [https://he.chabad.org/library/article_cdo/aid/395917]; printed also in Marton, M., & Dickstein, A. (2013). *Lavo BeTzava* [To serve in the army]. Kfar Chabad, p. 102, as well as in *B'Rega HaEmet,* p. 400. On the Rebbe's general relationship with Shamir, see Faithful And Fortified: Israel's Prime Ministers — Yitzchak Shamir [https://videos.jem.tv/video-player?clip=692]; "The Rebbe Told Me Not to Fear" — The Lubavitcher Rebbe and Prime Minister Yitzchak Shamir — Chabad.org [https://www.chabad.org/multimedia/video_ cdo/aid/1897999/jewish/The-Rebbe-Told-Me-Not-to-Fear.htm].

99 Giordana Pulcini, Or Rabinowitz. An Ounce of Prevention—A Pound of Cure? The Reagan Administration's Nonproliferation Policy and the Osirak [https://doi.org/10.1162/jcws_a_01007]; Journal of Cold War Studies 2021; 23 (2): 4—40.

100 Opinion | The Osirak Option — The New York Times [https://www.nytimes.com/2002/11/15/opinion/the-osirak-option.html]. See also Mueller, K. P., Castillo, J. J., Morgan, F. E., Pegahi, N., & Rosen, B. (2006). *Striking first: Preemptive and preventive attack in U.S. national security policy.* RAND Corporation. p. 217 [https://www.jstor.org/stable/10.7249/mg403af].

101 Air Strike at Osirak [https://www.airandspaceforces.com/PDF/MagazineArchive/Documents/2012/April%202012/0412osirak.pdf].

102 The Rebbe on how to handle a US Secretary of State [https://youtu.be/pjVJE3i41Wo?feature=shared; https://videos.jem.tv/video-player?clip=4208].

103 *Karasi V'Ein Oneh,* Vol. 1, p. 397, 19 Kislev 5739 (1978).

CHAPTER 12

1 The difference in policy between presidents has been a matter of how much land in Judea and Samaria they maintained Israel should relinquish, and how forcefully they pushed the agenda.

2 For a video of the Rebbe encouraging settlement in Samaria, see Settling the Land [https://videos.jem.tv/video-player?clip=1169].

3 *Igros Kodesh,* Vol. 33, p. 49, Letter #12,266, dated 22 Sivan 5738 (1978); *Karasi V'Ein Oneh,* Vol. 2, p. 465.

Greenberg was an Israeli poet, journalist, and politician. He fought in the War of Independence, served in the Knesset, and after the Six-Day War played an active role in the Movement for Greater Israel (*HaTenu'a Lema'an Eretz Yisrael HaSheleima*).

4 *Karasi V'Ein Oneh,* Vol. 1, pp. 205-209, Motzaei Shabbos *Lech Lecha* 5738 (1977); Audio of Sichah [https://ashreinu.app/player?parentEvent=2506&event=2507].

5 Genesis 15:18.

6 *Rashi* on Genesis 1:1.

7 Genesis 13:17.

8 *Tanchuma, Lecha Lecha,* 12.

9 Genesis 12:7.

10 Ethics of the Fathers 1:17. See *Kiddushin* 40b; *Tikkunei Zohar* 93b.

11 *Sanhedrin* 11a.

12 Psalms 117:2.

13 *Igros Kodesh,* Vol. 33, pp. 37-38, Letter #12, 259, dated 11 Mar Cheshvan 5738 (1977).

14 *Karasi V'Ein Oneh,* Vol. 1, p. 260, Purim 5738 (1978); Audio of Sichah [https://ashreinu.app/player?parentEvent=2607&event=2610].

15 See *Rashi* on Genesis 33:4, s.v. *VaYishakayhu.* See also *Sifrei Bamidbar* Ch. 69; *Tanchuma, Shmos* Ch. 27; *Midrash Tehillim* Ch. 120, s.v. *Rabas Shachna.* The *Midrash* there comments on the verse in Psalms:

"My soul has long dwelt with those who hate peace." Is there a person who hates peace? Esau hates peace, as it is said, "And I will give peace in the land" (Leviticus 26:6). When will this be? "And I will make dangerous animals rest [so that they will not cause harm] in the land" (ibid.). And "dangerous animal" refers to Esau the wicked.

For the Rebbe's commentary on this theme, see *Sichos Kodesh 5732,* Vol. 2, p. 320 (1972). For an optimistic view, see *Sichos Kodesh 5725,* Vol. 1, p. 183, *Vayishlach* (1964); *Sichos Kodesh 5740,* Vol. 1, pp. 541-542 (1980); *Sichos Kodesh 5741,* Vol. 1, pp. 522-523, *Vayishlach* (1980). For an application of this principle with respect to the world's tendency to selectively criticize Israel and blow its misdeeds out of proportion, see *Daas Torah,* p. 116. For an application of this principle to Anwar Sadat and the peace treaty with Egypt, see *Shalom Shalom V'Ein Shalom,* p. 567.

16 Tower and Stockade [http://www.zionistarchives.org.il/en/Pages/TowerStockade.aspx]. See also *Daas Torah,* p. 137; *Shalom Shalom V'Ein Shalom,* p. 123. For arguments similar to the Rebbe's invoking the example of Tower and Stockade, see Practical Zionism Today [https://besacenter.org/practical-zionism/]; The PA Is Winning in Area C [https://besacenter.org/palestinian-authority-area-c/]; Israel's Self-Imposed "White Paper" [https://besacenter.org/israel-white-paper/].

17 Proverbs 21:1.

18 For unfortunate confirmation of this point, see The War of Attrition: the Palestinian Authority's Program for Establishing an Arab State in Area C [https://www.regavim.org.il/wp-content/uploads/2019/12/Fayyad-Report-2020.pdf].

19 *Karasi V'Ein Oneh,* Vol. 1, pp. 357-359, Motzaei Shabbos *Bereishis* 5739 (1978).

20 As we have seen, the government did not allow Jews to settle in Hebron until the summer of 1980, after Miriam Levinger, Sarah Nachshon, and their colleagues had courageously taken over Beit Hadassah. Tragically, that same summer, Palestinian terrorists, including Tayseer Abu Sneineh, the current Palestinian mayor of Hebron, brutally murdered six innocent *yeshivah* students in Hebron. In response to this horrific attack and the resultant public outcry, the government finally permitted limited Jewish settlement in Hebron.

21 This sweetens the bitter pill since, in the Bible, Hebron is identified with *Kiryat Arba.* See Genesis 23:2.

22 *Karasi V'Ein Oneh,* Vol. 1, p. 248, *Mishpatim* 5738 (1978).

23 A central theme in the Rebbe's social philosophy for the Jewish community and society at large is encouraging couples to have large families, a policy formally known as pronatalism. The Rebbe viewed population decline, which he saw as a result of secularizing values in the West, as a profound tragedy. He actively encouraged Jewish families to have more children, believing that birth rates are significantly influenced by social norms and policies. The Rebbe maintained that individuals and communal leaders have a responsibility to promote the birth of more children and the growth of the Jewish community. For further exploration of this point, see *Toras Menachem 5724,* Vol. 2, pp. 358-359 (1964); *Toras Menachem 5726,* Vol. 2, pp. 358-360 (1966); *Sichos Kodesh 5740,* Vol. 3, p. 1,153, *Yechidus with* Sadigura

Rebbe (1980); *Sichos Kodesh 5741*, Vol. 3, p. 426, Rosh Chodesh Iyar (1981). An extended collection of sources can be found in Weintraub, S. (2022). *Actualya BeZavit Chabadit* [Actuality from a Chabad perspective]. *Machon B'Oholei Tzaddikim*. pp. 163-167. Additionally, for video recordings of the Rebbe discussing this topic, see Planning for a Family [https://videos.jem.tv/video-player?clip=5012]; The Greatest Blessing [https://videos.jem.tv/video-player?clip=2911].

For an english essay elucidating the Rebbe's views see SIE – Family Planning - Chabad.org [https://www.chabad.org/therebbe/article_cdo/aid/2540403/jewish/Family-Planning.htm]

24 *Karasi V'Ein Oneh*, Vol. 2, p. 398, *Yechidus* with Avner Shaki.

CHAPTER 13

1 As we will see, this campaign continued until weeks before the Rebbe suffered a severe stroke in 1992. But even after that stroke robbed the Rebbe of his ability to publicly lecture, he continued to express strong opposition. This campaign is continued by the Rebbe's disciples until this day.

2 Consider the assessment of one Arab commentator:

Today, a staggering 87 percent of Palestinians in the West Bank and Gaza believe that the PA is corrupt, 78 percent want Abbas to resign, and 62 percent believe that the PA is a liability. This loss of popular legitimacy has had real-life implications. Even before the current war in Gaza, areas of the West Bank were practically ungoverned. The international community, appalled by the PA's corruption and dealing with competing crises elsewhere, reduced aid. Diplomatically, outside powers continued to treat the PA as the legitimate representative of the Palestinians. But in reality, world leaders have largely given up on it.

How the Palestinian Authority Failed Its People | The Washington Institute [https://www.washingtoninstitute.org/policy-analysis/how-palestinian-authority-failed-its-people]. See also There can be no partnering with the Palestinian Authority — opinion — The Jerusalem Post [https://www.jpost.com/opinion/article-776277]; /The State of Corruption and Anti-Corruption in Palestine | Aman [https://www.aman-palestine.org/cached_uploads/download/2021/12/14/1639488394.pdf-استطلاع-الرأي-السنوي-انجليزي].

3 In Resolution 242.

4 Pan-Arabism, an ideology advocating Arab unity, has declined since the 1970s, largely replaced by Islamism, which emphasizes Islamic identity over Arab nationalism. Pan-Arabism motivated many of the talks for Palestinian autonomy at their outset. Today, the discourse is often motivated by Islamism fused with post-colonialist discourse.

5 For a historical perspective on the dangers of autonomy, see *Shalom Shalom V'Ein Shalom*, Ch. 7: Autonomy — A Green Light to Arafat's State, pp. 273-300.

6 Madrid Conference of 1991 — Wikipedia [https://en.wikipedia.org/wiki/Madrid_Conference_of_1991]; The Madrid Framework [https://www.jewishvirtuallibrary.org/the-madrid-framework].

7 Absorbing over a million immigrants in a short period of time placed a massive strain on Israel's economy. For elaboration on the scope of this challenge, see the 1994 congressional report on U.S. aid to Israel: Mark, C. R. (1994, July 26). Israel: U.S. Foreign Assistance (Updated) [Congressional Research Service Report]. Foreign Affairs and National Defense Division [https://pdf.usaid.gov/pdf_docs/pcaaa469.pdf].

8 Areas A, B, and C [https://tbtnisrael.com/areas-a-b-and-c/]; Do You Know Your Area A, B and C? | HonestReporting [https://honestreporting.com/area-a-b-c-west-bank-palestinian-territories/].

9 Backgrounder: Tanzim | CAMERA [https://www.camera.org/article/backgrounder-tanzim/].

10 Al-Aqsa Martyrs Brigades (AMB) — Fatah | ECFR [https://ecfr.eu/special/mapping_palestinian_politics/al_aqsa_martyrs_brigades_amb_fatah/].

11 *Karasi V'Ein Oneh*, Vol. 1, p. 352, Simchas Torah 5739 (1978).

12 The Rebbe frequently referred to the United States as a "kingdom of kindness." For examples of this, see *Sefer HaSichos 5752*, pp. 151, 224 (1992); *Sichos Kodesh 5730*, Vol. 2, p. 450, *Eikev* (1970). Additionally, see *Toras Menachem 5749*, Vol. 1, p. 95, 13 Tishrei (1989), for a statement of the Rebbe near the end of the Reagan administration:

Washington, the kingdom of kindness, decided long ago that these territories must remain under Jewish control. The Arabs themselves have long since abandoned hope of ever gaining possession of these lands. [Tragically,] it is only certain Jews who relentlessly persist in their [misguided] efforts to relinquish portions of the Land of Israel, thereby [needlessly] provoking the Arabs [and undermining our own security].

13 Jeremiah 29:7.

14 This is a reference to Education and Sharing Day, U.S.A.: An annual proclamation issued by the U.S. president on the 11th of Nissan, the Lubavitcher Rebbe's birthday, honoring his commitment to education and morality. Initiated by President Carter in 1978.

15 Statement on Diplomatic Talks With the Palestine Liberation Organization | Ronald Reagan [https://www.reaganlibrary.gov/archives/speech/statement-diplomatic-talks-palestine-liberation-organization].

16 *Karasi V'Ein Oneh*, Vol. 2, pp. 427-430, *Yechidus* with Moshe Katzav, 10 Shvat 5752 (1991). See also *Toras Menachem — Hisvaaduyos 5752*, Vol. 2, pp. 376-379 (1992). At the time of this meeting, Katzav was a Cabinet Minister in the ruling Likud Government. Katzav would go on to serve as Israel's 8th president from 2000-2007. See JEM: Living Torah Program 638 Month of Miracles [https://videos.jem.tv/video-player?clip=3237], where the Rebbe reiterates these points 11 days later in a meeting with Likud politician Eliezer Kulas. For Katzav's reflection on the meeting, see The Rebbe and the Holy Land: Moshe Katzav [https://videos.jem.tv/video-player?clip=9549].

17 The Irgun, also known as Etzel, was a Zionist paramilitary organization that operated in the decades preceding Israel's statehood. Along with other groups such as the Haganah (the main precursor of the Israel Defense Forces) and the Lehi, the Irgun defended the Jewish community in the Land of Israel before the establishment of the State. Unlike the Haganah, which took a defensive posture, the Irgun took an offensive posture. Moreover, the Irgun was known for advocating bringing the entire biblical Land of Israel under Jewish control.

18 The Rebbe had played an influential role in maintaining the Shamir government. In a scandal known as *HaTargil HaMasriach* (the Dirty Trick), Shimon Peres, a politician known for his concessionary policies and a naive commitment to "peace," brought down the Shamir government with a vote of no confidence. Peres had cobbled together a narrow majority of parliamentary members to form a new government. The night before the new government was sworn in, two members of the Knesset disappeared just as the Rebbe expressed his strong condemnation of Peres' concessionary policies. When Peres and his allies tried to contact the missing Knesset members, they were unable to reach them. So, the Peres government could not be ratified. Thus, the Rebbe was directly responsible for the dissolution of the Peres government and the maintenance of Shamir as prime minister. For more on this affair, see *B'Rega HaEmet*, Ch. 12. See also the New York Times' contemporary description: One Brooklyn Rabbi's Long Shadow — The New York Times [https://www.nytimes.com/1990/04/13/world/one-brooklyn-rabbi-s-long-shadow.html]. In this conversation with Moshe Katzav, a year and a half after the Rebbe had worked to uphold the Shamir government, the Rebbe expressed disappointment that Shamir would consider concessions.

19 *Karasi V'Ein Oneh*, Vol. 1, p. 324, Motzaei Shabbos *Re'eh* 5738 (1978).

20 *Karasi V'Ein Oneh*, Vol. 1, p. 391, 19 Kislev 5739

(1978).

21 *Karasi V'Ein Oneh*, Vol. 1, p. 413, Motzaei Shabbos *Ki Sissa* 5739 (1979).

22 Gaza is a coastal enclave, which the Sharon government saw as a small area it could afford to sacrifice to quiet international criticism. In contrast, Judea and Samaria are much larger, contain significant natural resources and Jewish heritage sites, and include mountain ranges overlooking Israel's coastal plain. Additionally, while Israel fully withdrew its military from Gaza, it has never done so from the West Bank.

23 In Bad Company: Yasser Arafat and Saddam Hussein | The Washington Institute [https://www.washingtoninstitute.org/policy-analysis/bad-company-yasser-arafat-and-saddam-hussein]. This article is from 2002, but the story of Nizar Banat, a Palestinian dissident brutally beaten to death by PASF forces on June 24, 2021, for criticizing the corruption of the Palestinian Authority and, more particularly, Mahmoud Abbas and Mohammad Dahlan, provides a more recent example. While Banat may have been no friend of Israel, his death illustrates the brutality of rule under Palestinian autonomy. Ironically, Banat attempted to escape to Israeli controlled territory in order to save his life from the murderous Palestinian Authority. For more on Banat, see Palestine: Justice remains elusive two years after the killing of Nizar Banat — Amnesty International [https://www.amnesty.org/en/latest/news/2023/06/justice-remains-elusive-two-years-after-the-killing-of-palestinian-dissident-nizar-banat/].

24 A Window of Opportunity for Israel? | The Washington Institute [https://www.washingtoninstitute.org/policy-analysis/window-opportunity-israel].

25 Note that Rabin did not experience autonomy's bitter fruits as he was assassinated before he could see the Oslo Accords' disastrous consequences.

26 *Karasi V'Ein Oneh*, Vol. 1, p. 412, Motzaei Shabbos *Ki Sissa* 5739 (1979).

27 In an April 2024 interview conducted by the author.

28 *Karasi V'Ein Oneh*, Vol. 2, p. 202, 24 Teves 5742 (1982); Audio of Sichah [https://ashreinu.app/player?parentEvent=3727&event=3729].

29 *Sichos Kodesh 5739*, Vol. 1, p. 290; *Karasi V'Ein Oneh*, Vol. 1, p. 376, Motzaei Shabbos *Chayei Sarah* 5739 (1978); Audio of Sichah [https://ashreinu.app/player?parentEvent=2812&event=2816].

30 For a comprehensive overview of the Palestinian Authority's official security forces, see Security Forces | ECFR [https://ecfr.eu/special/mapping_palestinian_politics/introduction_security_forces/].

31 Palestinian Cop Murders Two Israelis in West Bank [https://www.fdd.org/analysis/2024/02/29/palestinian-cop-murders-two-israelis-in-west-bank/]. For an Arab perspective describing the terrorist attack as a "military operation" and the terrorist as a "martyr," see Fatal Shooting at Ayli Settlement: Palestinian Police Officer Identified as Perpetrator [https://www.watanserb.com/en/2024/02/29/fatal-shooting-at-ayli-settlement-palestinian-police-officer-identified-as-perpetrator/]; פיגוע הירי בתחנת הדלק בעלי (4202) – ויקיפדיה; Rabbi, teen hitchhiker killed in terror shooting at West Bank gas station | The Times of Israel [https://www.timesofisrael.com/two-killed-in-terror-shooting-at-gas-station-near-west-bank-settlement-of-eli/].

32 For more on this phenomenon, see Terrorists Connected to Palestinian Security Forces Carry Out Third Attack Within a Month [https://www.fdd.org/analysis/2024/03/31/terrorists-connected-to-palestinian-security-forces-carry-out-third-attack-within-a-month/]; Palestinian Authority Forces Attacks Against Israel | MEMRI [https://www.memri.org/reports/palestinian-authority-forces-attacks-against-israel]; Worrying Report: Police Officers in the Palestinian Authority by Day, Terrorists by Night [https://www.srugim.co.il/907915--דוח-הרשפ-שוטרים-ביום-מחבלים-בלילה].

33 This scenario has become a major topic of discussion in Israeli government, military, and media since October 7, 2023. See MK Edelstein,

Chairman of the Foreign Affairs and Defense Committee: "The 'flipping guns' scenario is not an imaginary threat, and the State of Israel must be prepared for it." [https://main.knesset. gov.il/news/pressreleases/pages/press02.01.24i. aspx]; Leaning on A Flipping Gun: When the PA Forces Join the Ranks of the Terrorists [https:// www.israelhayom.co.il/magazine/hashavua/ article/15382260]; The Concern of "Flipping Guns" | Preparing for War Against the PA [https://www.inn.co.il/news/622863]; Dr. Yigal Vardi: A Flipping Guns Scenario Would Mean a Holocaust [https://tovnews.co.il/156973].

34 Flipping Guns on the Way? [https://www. hakolhayehudi.co.il/item/security/ היפוך קנים בדרך]; A Serious Incident: PA Security Block IDF Forces [https://www.now14.co.il/-אירוע-חמור /שוטרי-הרשפ-חסמו-כוח-צהל-שנכ].

35 For reports on the Palestinian Authority training for full scale war, see Under Our Noses: This is How the Palestinian Authority's Brigades are Training for Battle | Israel Today [https:// www.israelhayom.co.il/magazine/hashavua/ article/14949730]; Israeli MK: Palestinians building a professional army under our nose — JNS.org [https://www.jns.org/israeli-mk-palestinians-building-a-professional-army-under-our-nose/]. Social media channels associated with both Jewish and Palestinian communities in Judea and Samaria are awash with videos of PA training in a variety of advanced military techniques.

36 How Will the Swords of Iron War Change Israel's National Security Strategy and Doctrine? [https://besacenter.org/how-will-the-swords-of-iron-war-change-israels-national-security-strategy-and-doctrine/].

37 Pinchas Peli (1930-1989) was an influential Israeli philosopher, rabbi, and professor. He authored several books on Jewish philosophy, ethics, and spirituality, but is best known for transcribing and editing Rabbi Joseph B. Soloveitchik's lectures into the book *"On Repentance,"* which has become a modern Jewish classic.

38 *Karasi V'Ein Oneh*, Vol. 1, p. 234, *Yechidus* with Pinchas Peli. Peli wrote an essay on this

visit to the Rebbe entitled "In the Presence of the Man of Faith," in which he records these reflections of the Rebbe. For the full essay, see במחיצתו של איש האמונה — BeitChabad.com — בית חבד [https://he.chabad.org/library/article_ cdo/aid/395255]. The essay was first printed in *Panim El Panim*, 3 Av 5729 (1969).

39 *Karasi V'Ein Oneh*, Vol. 1, p. 334, *Yechidus* with Shmuel Katz. Katz (1914-2008) was a prominent Revisionist Zionist activist, member of the Irgun, member of Knesset, and prolific writer who authored biographies of Ze'ev Jabotinsky and works on the Israel-Arab conflict. His best known book, *"Battleground,"* provides a narrative history of the origins of the Israeli-Palestinian conflict from a Revisionist Zionist perspective. Katz served as an adviser to Prime Minister Menachem Begin after the 1977 elections, but later broke with him over Begin's concessions at Camp David.

40 *Karasi V'Ein Oneh*, Vol. 1, pp. 321-322, Motzaei Shabbos Re'eh 5738 (1978).

41 Case in point, many attacks against Jews in Jerusalem originate in Hebron. For example: the 2005 Gush Etzion Junction shooting — Deadly Hebron cell caught [https://www.ynetnews. com/articles/0,7340,L-3211836,00.html]; the 2014 kidnapping of the three Jewish boys — Hamas funded killing of 3 teens, says ringleader | The Times of Israel [https://www.timesofisrael. com/hamas-funded-kidnapping-of-3-boys-says-ringleader/]; the attempted Passover Eve Massacre — Passover Eve Massacre in Jerusalem Averted [https://www.fdd.org/analysis/2024/04/ 22/passover-eve-massacre-in-jerusalem-averted/].

42 The editors of *Karasi V'Ein Oneh* observe that the Rebbe is referring to the Hilarion Capucci affair. Capucci, a Syrian Catholic Bishop, had smuggled weapons into Palestinian cities in 1974.

43 Additionally, the longstanding mayor of Hebron Tayseer Abu Sneineh is an unrepentant convicted murderer.

44 The term "West Bank" refers to Judea and Samaria as merely being the west bank of the Jordan river, erasing their connection to the historical Land of Israel.

45 The "Green Line" refers to the armistice lines established after the 1948 Arab-Israeli war, which distributed Judea and Samaria, the West Bank, East Jerusalem, the Gaza Strip, the Golan Heights, and the Sinai Peninsula among Syria, Jordan, and Egypt. In the Six-Day War, Israel miraculously conquered these territories. The "Green line" is often used by international leaders, perhaps most vocally in recent memory by Barack Obama, to refer to the demand that Israel must withdraw from all the conquered territories past the Green line; hence the term is used in attempts to partition the Land of Israel.

46 The "Red Line" metaphor is employed by foreign actors to circumscribe Israel's sovereignty. These red lines take the form of ultimatums declaring certain geographic areas or military actions surrounding them as unacceptable, with threats of punitive consequences if the red lines are crossed. For example, the Biden administration issued "red line" warnings stating that the United States would withhold offensive arms' transfers to Israel if it entered Rafah in the course of its military operations.

47 A technocrat is an area expert, appointed to government in light of their expertise. However, in Abbas' government, so-called area experts are often appointed based on their loyalty to Abbas. Abbas' administration is plagued by corruption and embezzlement, and in the event of his death, it is a reasonable possibility that a member of his circle will perpetuate the PA's unelected government.

48 For this characterization, see 'The most popular Palestinian leader alive': Releasing Marwan Barghouti could transform territories' politics | Israel-Gaza war | The Guardian [https://

www.theguardian.com/world/2024/feb/17/the-most-popular-palestinian-leader-alive-releasing-marwan-barghouti-could-transform-territories-politics]; Can Marwan Barghouti, the 'Palestinian Mandela', bring peace to Gaza? [https://www.theguardian.com/world/2024/feb/17/the-most-popular-palestinian-leader-alive-releasing-marwan-barghouti-could-transform-territories-politics].

49 See, for example, Jailed Palestinian Leader Marwan Barghouti Calls for Third Intifada Against Israel | IBTimes UK [https://www.ibtimes.co.uk/jailed-palestinian-leader-marwan-barghouti-calls-third-intifada-against-israel-1474273].

50 For more on Barghouti's terrorist pedigree, see Backgrounder Tanzim | Camera; Marwan Barghouti, Fatah-Tanzim, and the Escalation of the Intifada [https://jcpa.org/article/marwan-barghouti-fatah-tanzim-and-the-escalation-of-the-intifada/]; Will Marwan Barghouti be the Next Palestinian President? [https://jstribune.com/svetlova-will-marwan-barghouti-be-the-next-palestinian-president/].

51 This career has been marked by orchestrating international crime and violence.

52 Their rationale is simplistic. If they hear that a particular candidate, such as Barghouti, polls highly, they naively assume he would make a good leader, without considering the potential consequences. It is a similar mentality to the notion that if a problematic figure like corrupt South African Jacob Zuma is popular, he should be president, even if it risks plunging the nation into chaos.

53 "Full Security Control In Gaza" [https://www.youtube.com/watch?v=kqm1Nac6_b0]. The meeting took place on 25 Tammuz 5751 (1991).

CHAPTER 14

1 *Koheles Rabbah* Ch. 7. See also *Sefer Chassidim*, sec. 155.

2 For discussion of many themes in this chapter, see *B'Rega HaEmet*, pp. 349-352.

3 *Karasi V'Ein Oneh*, Vol. 1, pp. 325-326, Motzaei Shabbos Re'eh 5738 (1978).

4 The Rebbe had expressed this opinion in 1978. By 1985, however, he saw the situation as more dire, stating, "The vast majority of Arabs living in Judea and Samaria are themselves terrorists, as they readily admit." See *Sichos Kodesh 5746*, Vol. 2, p. 265, Motzaei Zos Chanukah (1985). This shift in perspective indicates that piecemeal deportation of terrorists alone may not be sufficient; a more comprehensive approach addressing the underlying cultural and ideological factors that fuel anti-Jewish terrorism must be pursued.

5   *Yechidus* with Tzvi Kaspi, printed in Halperin. *Yechiduyos*, Vol. 4. pp. 148-151. See *Karasi V'Ein Oneh*, Vol. 1, p. 2. See also *Daas Torah*, p. 226.

6   From the Popular Front for the Liberation of Palestine — General Command. Not to be confused with the Popular Front for the Liberation of Palestine.

7   Israel in First Prisoner Exchange with Arab Terrorist Organization — Jewish Telegraphic Agency [https://www.jta.org/archive/israel-in-first-prisoner-exchange-with-arab-terrorist-organization].

שביית החייל אברהם עמרם בלבנון – ויקיפדיה [https://he.wikipedia.org/wiki/ שביית_החייל_אברהם _עמרם_בלבנון].

8   The English version of the *sichah* is available at *Motzaei Shabbos Parshas Bamidbar, Shabbos Mevorchim Sivan, 5739 (1979)* — SIE.org; *Sichos Kodesh 5739*, pp. 730-734; *Karasi V'Ein Oneh*, Vol. 1, pp. 435-436, *Bamidbar* 5739 (1979); Audio of the Sichah [https://ashreinu.app/player?parentEvent=2996&event=2999]. See also *Daas Torah*, p. 97.

9   In the Jibril Agreement. For a record of these exchanges, see Before Gilad Shalit, Israel exchanged prisoners for other live soldiers — Jewish Telegraphic Agency [https://www.jta. org/2011/10/11/default/before-gilad-shalit-israel-exchanged-prisoners-for-other-live-soldiers].

10   See Israeli doctors saved the life of Hamas leader, whom they now blame for the October 7 terrorist attacks, when he was in prison, reports say; Compassionate and gracious... — Israel Today [https://www.israeltoday.co.il/read/compassionate-and-gracious/]. For a testimony from Sinwar's prison warden, Betty Lahat, see Sinwar was a fox, Always Kept his Hands Clean. He Cried Bitterly When He found out He Had Cancer [https://news.walla.co.il/item/3508856].

11   *Daas Torah*, p. 97, footnote 5.

12   *Rambam, Hilchos Matnos Aniyim*, 8:12.

13   *Sichos Kodesh 5746*, Vol. 2, p. 264, Motzaei Zos Chanukah (1986).

14   The fall and rise of Marwan Barghouti [https://www.arabbarometer.org/media-news/the-fall-and-rise-of-marwan-barghouti/].

15   'Palestine's Mandela' publishes book detailing his life in an Israeli prison [https://english.alarabiya.net/articles/2011%2F11%2F02%2F175059].

16   *Karasi V'Ein Oneh*, Vol. 2, p. 385, Vayeishev 5748 (1988). See, for example, Operation Brother's Keeper | IDF [https://www.idf.il/en/mini-sites/wars-and-operations/operation-brother-s-keeper/operation-brother-s-keeper/]. The kidnappers who abducted and murdered three Israeli teenagers in 2014 had served time in Israeli prison for prior terrorist attacks.

17   *Sanhedrin* 37a; *Mishneh Torah, Sanhedrin*, 12:3; *Rotzei'ach U'Shmiras HaNefesh*, Ch. 1.

18   Yehoshua Salome [http://en.hebron.org.il/fallen/250].

CHAPTER 15

1   *Likkutei Torah, Toras Shmuel 5637*, Vol. 1, p. 324. See also *Maamarei Admur HaZakein 5572*, pp. 35, 51, 287; *Toras Menachem 5750*, Vol. 4, p. 79 (1990).

2   How Israel's internal divisions helped spark the bloody Hamas massacre — AIJAC [https:// aijac.org.au/op-ed/how-israels-internal-divisions-helped-spark-the-bloody-hamas-massacre/]. For analysis, see Israel's 9/11? How Hamas Terrorist Attacks Will Change the Middle East — War on the Rocks [https://

warontherocks.com/2023/10/israels-9-11-how-hamas-terrorist-attacks-will-change-the-middle-east/]; Judicial Reform Controversy Emboldened Israel's Enemies: Gatestone Institute [https://www.gatestoneinstitute.org/20395/israel-enemies-judicial-reform]; Will Hamas and Hezbollah Try Again to Tear the Israeli Spiderweb? [https://besacenter.org/will-hamas-and-hezbollah-try-again-to-tear-the-israeli-spiderweb/].

3 See *Sichos Kodesh 5730,* Vol. 2, pp. 371-374; *Toras Menachem 5730,* Vol, 3, pp. 27-31; *Karasi V'Ein Oneh,* Vol. 1, p. 37, 12 Tammuz 5730 (1970); Audio of Sichah [https://ashreinu.app/player?parentEvent=1609&event=7631].

4 Leviticus 26:6.

5 Israel's enemies in the Middle East have frequently been embroiled in conflicts with one another, undermining the potential for a united front against Israel. The region has witnessed numerous internecine Arab and Muslim conflicts between 1948 and 2024. Notable examples include Black September in Jordan (1970), the Lebanese Civil War (1975-1990), the Egyptian-Libyan War (1977), the Iran-Iraq War (1980-1988), the Algerian Civil War (1991-2002), the Iraqi Insurgency (2003-present), the Syrian Civil War (2011-present), the Yemeni Civil War (2014-present), and the Second Libyan Civil War (2014-present).

6 See *Sichos Kodesh 5735,* Vol. 1, pp. 146-150; *Karasi V'Ein Oneh,* Vol. 1, pp. 93-96, 20 Cheshvan

5735 (1975); Audio of Sichah [https://ashreinu.app/player?parentEvent=2030&event=2035].

7 See *Sichos Kodesh 5735,* Vol. 1, p. 150 (1975).

8 *Sichos Kodesh 5740,* Vol. 1, pp. 428-429; *Karasi V'Ein Oneh,* Vol. 1, pp. 504-505, Motzaei Shabbos *Chayei Sarah* 5740 (1979); Audio of Sichah [https://ashreinu.app/player?parentEvent=3166&event=3173].

9 *Vayikra Rabbah* 26:2.

10 *Bereishis Rabbah* 38:6; *Toras Chaim* 74d ff.

11 See *Karasi V'Ein Oneh,* Vol. 1, p. 35, 12 Tammuz 5730 (1970); Audio of Sichah [https://ashreinu.app/player?parentEvent=1609&event=7631].

12 See the Responsa of Maharam of Rotenberg #636; *Sefer HaShtaros,* Rabbi Yehuda Bartzeloni, p. 43; *Otzar HaGeonim, Kiddushin* #146-151. Cited in *Karasi V'Ein Oneh,* Vol. 1, pp. 26-27, 6 Tishrei 5730 (1970). See also *Karasi V'Ein Oneh,* Vol. 1, pp. 30-32, Purim 5730 (1970).

13 *Mishneh Torah, Hilchos Shmitah V'Yovel,* 10:8.

14 *Karasi V'Ein Oneh,* Vol. 1, pp. 30-31, Purim 5730 (1970).

15 Leviticus 19:16.

16 See *Karasi V'Ein Oneh,* Vol. 1, p. 139, *Bo* 5736 (1976); pp. 140-142, 10 Shvat 5736 (1976).

17 *Karasi V'Ein Oneh,* Vol. 2, p. 17, 19 Kislev 5740 (1979).

CONCLUSION

1 Isaiah 11:6.

2 *Mishneh Torah, Hilchos Melachim,* 12:5. See *Raavad* there, who notes that on a literal level, predatory animals will also not do harm in the Messianic era. The Rebbe elaborates on this point in *Likkutei Sichos,* Vol. 7, pp. 188ff.; Vol. 27, pp. 191ff.

3 *Mishneh Torah, Hilchos Melachim,* 11:4.

4 See *Likkutei Diburim,* Vol. 3, *Likkut* 23:40, p. 422a-b; in English, Vol. 3, pp. 153-155 (Sichos in

English, 2023).

5 See, for example, *Sichos Kodesh 5752,* Vol. 1, pp. 343-344, 354-355 (1992); Vol. 2, pp. 524-525, *Shmos;* p. 555, *Va'eira; Toras Menachem, Reshimos HaYoman,* pp. 112, 225, 374, 478; *Sichos Kodesh 5725,* Vol. 2 p. 35 (1965); *Toras Menachem, Tiferes Levi Yitzchak,* Vol. 3, p. 53.

6 *Berachos* 12b; *Haggadah, Maggid,* s.v. *Amar Rabbi Elazar Ben* Azarya.

7 Isaiah 2:4.

8 *Mishneh Torah, Hilchos Melachim,* 12:5. See also *Mishneh Torah, Hilchos Teshuvah,* 9:2.

NOTES TO SUPPLEMENTARY MATERIAL

1 Cassius Dio Book LXIX.

2 A joint Sasanian-Jewish army conquered Jerusalem in 614 CE, retaining control until 628 CE.

3 The Fatimids regained control of Jerusalem in 1187 CE and the Crusaders had some presence in Israel until 1291 CE.

4 Among them Rabbi Yehudah HaLevi, Nachmanides, and 300 members of the *Tosafos* school of Talmudic interpretation, in what is known as *Aliyat Baalei Tosfot.*

5 During the Ottoman Empire, the region known historically and biblically as the Land of Israel did not correspond to a specific administrative unit with a single name. Instead, the area was divided into several administrative districts. Broadly, these were the districts of Jerusalem, Syria, Beirut, Nablus, and Acre.

6 "*Aliyah*" literally means "rising up." The term describes Jews "going up" from exile to the Land of Israel.

Originally, the term refers to the Jewish people going from Egypt to Israel, and Israel is north of, and has higher elevation than, Egypt. See, for example, Genesis 13:1, 46:4.

7 See Why are there so many children in Israel? | מרכז טאוב [https://www.taubcenter.org.il/en/research/why-are-there-so-many-children-in-israel/]; Israel's birth rate remains highest in OECD by far, at 2.9 children per woman [https://www.timesofisrael.com/israels-birth-rate-remains-highest-in-oecd-by-far-at-2-9-children-per-woman/]. See also Weinreb, A., Chernichovsky, D., & Brill, A. (2018). *Israel's exceptional fertility.* In State of the Nation Report 2018. Taub Center for Social Policy Studies in Israel. https://www.taubcenter.org.il/wp-content/uploads/2020/12/exceptionalfertilityeng.pdf

8 For reflections on the connection between Islam and anti-Jewish activity, see Ben Ari, M. (2024). *Vision and Dagger: Islam and its War Against Heretics.* Alim Press. See also Arnon-Ohana, Y. (2013). *Line of Furrow and Fire: The Conflict for the Land of Israel 1860-2010.* Achiasaf Ltd.

9 Note that this write up is not meant to implicate Islam as inherently antisemitic. Jews did not fare much better during the Christian conquest of the Land of Israel.

10 The dust of aggression cleared, and the smell of blood remained, intermittent dreams and a continuous catastrophe [https://www.alquds.com/en/posts/71775].

11 This area included two border regions: Naharayim in the north, near the Sea of Galilee, and the Zofar enclave in the southern Arava desert. For reference, this is an area twice the size of Washington D.C., or three times the size of San Francisco.

12 Namely Arab citizens of Israel who enjoy full civil rights.

13 Thanks to Rabbi Elkanah Shmotkin, Rabbi Mendel Misholovin, and Rabbi Shmuly Avtzon for their guidance in preparing this statement of policy.

14 Numerous talks and letters relating to the Rebbe's views on the Land of Israel were not included in *Karasi V'Ein Oneh.* These are scattered throughout the Rebbe's printed works, or as of yet are unpublished. The Sichos in English Institute and Jewish Educational Media (JEM) are in the midst of compiling a more comprehensive catalog of the Rebbe's teachings on the matter.

15 Ethics of the Fathers 3:17.

Dedicated by

Blanca Garazi Schoonover

ברכה בת אסתר

*with the heartfelt prayer that the light
of redemption will illuminate
the souls of the hostages,
bringing them immediate and
complete freedom from captivity.*

With boundless gratitude to the Rebbe — for his ceaseless teachings and the profound inspiration to seek and discover Hashem. May our beloved children, the Rebbe's dedicated Shluchim, be showered with blessings and goodness in all aspects of their lives. May their paths be illuminated by divine light, leading them to continue spreading the Rebbe's passion and devotion, always finding favor in the eyes of Hashem. May we all, together with Klal Yisroel, merit greeting Moshiach immediately!

Ella and Avrohom Licht

────────── ● ──────────

Dedicated in honor of and in great appreciation to the
Shluchim of The Shul Club of Harbor Island
Rabbi Isser Dovid and Rebbetzin Chana Silverman
From
Sylvia and Jimmy Saada and family

────────── ● ──────────

לזכות
הרה"ח מנחם מענדל ופערל גראנער
ובנותם
העניא דבורה, הדסה אסתר וחי' מושקא

────────── ● ──────────

לזכות
חיים מנחם מענדל וזוג' רבקה ומשפחתם סירוטה

────────── ● ──────────

In loving memory of **Naum ben Moshe Sapir**
Dedicated by his grandson **Lev Podelko**

In loving memory of my mother and father,

Susha Liba

and

Menachem Mendel Moishe.

*They should have tremendous nachas
from their daughters and grandchildren.
May their souls be uplifted.
Thank you Hashem for all of my blessings,
especially my children,*

Zusha Moshe

and

Shlomo Zalman.

With love,

Shani Katz